Hinduism & Hierarchy in Bali

World Anthropology

Series Editors Wendy James & N. J. Allen

A Greek Island Cosmos
Roger Just

The Pathan Unarmed
Mukulika Banerjee

Turkish Region
Ildikó Bellér-Hann & Chris Hann

Hinduism & Hierarchy in Bali
Leo Howe

*Imagined Diasporas among
Manchester Muslims**
Pnina Werbner

Modern Indian Kingship*
Marzia Balzani

* forthcoming titles

Hinduism &
Hierarchy in Bali

Leo Howe

Lecturer in Anthropology
University of Cambridge
Dean of Darwin College

James Currey
OXFORD

School of American Research Press
SANTA FE

James Currey
73 Botley Road
Oxford OX2 0BS

School of American Research Press
Post Office Box 2188
Sant Fe, New Mexico 87504-2188

British Library Cataloguing in Publication Data
Howe, Leo
   Hinduism & hierarchy in Bali. – (World anthropology)
   1. Hinduism – Indonesia – Bali Island 2. Ethnicity –
   Indonesia – Bali Island 3. Ethnicity – Religious aspects –
   Hinduism
   I. Title
   305.6′945′05986

ISBN 0-85255-914-3 (James Currey cloth)
ISBN 0-85255-919-4 (James Currey paper)

Library of Congress Cataloging-in-Publication Data
Howe, Leo
   Hinduism & hierarchy in Bali/Leo Howe.
     p. cm. – (World anthropology series)
   Includes bibliographical references.
   ISBN 1-930618-09-3 (cloth: alk. paper) – ISBN 1-930618-10-7 (pbk. : alk. paper)
   1. Hinduism–Social aspects–Indonesia–Bali (Province) 2.Bali (Indonesia:
   Province)–Religious life and customs. 3. Bali (Indonesia: Province)–Religion.
   I. Title: Hinduism and hierarchy in Bali. II. Title. III. World anthropology.

BL1163.5.H69 2001
294.5′09598′6–dc 21   2001047538

Typeset in 10/11 pt Monotype Photina
by Saxon Graphics Ltd, Derby
Printed and bound in Great Britain
by Woolnough, Irthlingborough

For
Elizabeth, Tom,
Jo & Daniel

Contents

Illustrations

MAP

TABLES

FIGURES

Acknowledgements

Fieldwork in Bali was funded at different stages by the Economic and Social Research Council, the Evans Fund of the Faculty of Archaeology and Anthropology of the University of Cambridge, Darwin College and the University of Cambridge Travel Fund. I am very grateful to these bodies for their generous support.

My research in Bali was conducted under the auspices of Lembaga Ilmu Pengetahuan Indonesia, the officers of which were always kind and unfailingly helpful. I wish also to thank my sponsor, Prof. Gusti Ngurah Bagus of Udayana University in Bali, for his warm friendship and advice over the years. Special thanks are also due to Dr Anak Agung Madé Jelantik, particularly for his medical skills when I needed them, and to Dr Gedé Pitana, for his encouragement and assistance. I want also to express my thanks to Prof. James J. Fox for helping to expedite the granting of a research visa in 1993.

Chapter 6 is a much expanded and greatly revised version of an article which appeared in Cambridge University's *Social Anthropology*, 4, 3 (1996) under the title 'Kings and priests in Bali'. Chapter 8 appeared in a modified form in *Review of Malaysian and Indonesian Affairs*, 33, 2 (1999) under the title 'Sai Baba in Bali: identity, social conflict and the politics of religious truth'. Some of the material in Chapter 3 was previously published in 'Status mobility in contemporary Bali: continuities and change', in Occasional Paper no. 27 (1995) of the Centre for South-East Asian Studies, University of Hull. I am grateful to the respective editors of these journals for permission to use this material here.

Several colleagues and friends have read and commented on all or part of this book. I am particularly indebted to Declan Quigley and David Gellner, both of whom subjected the work to a close and critical scrutiny. I have benefited from their advice enormously. Marilyn Strathern, Susan Bayly, James Laidlaw, Stephen Hugh-Jones, Michel Picard and Martin Ramstedt all contributed invaluable and incisive comments on one or another chapter. I am also very grateful to my youngest son, Daniel, who used his computer skills to design most of the book's figures.

My greatest debt, though, is to those Balinese amongst whom I lived and who contributed so much to make life in Bali enjoyable, stimulating and productive. In Pujung I single out Wayan Gina and his family, who have provided us with hospitality and great kindness ever since we first met in 1978. Their many neighbours in Pacung have helped us in ways too numerous to count. I wish also to thank Ketut Mijil, Jero Kubayan (now deceased), Jero Mangku Dalem and Jero Mangku Pandé for patiently explaining so many aspects of Balinese society and culture to me. In Corong I especially wish to thank Anak Agung Oka, Anak Agung Alit, Cokorda Gedé Pemayun, Déwa Gedé Ngurah, Ida Bagus Nyoman Oka, Ida Bagus Loji, Ketut Togog and all my many friends in Banjar Guliang who cheerfully won money off me at '*ceki*'. Researching the Sai Baba and Hare Krishna movements was greatly facilitated by the kind and generous help of Wayan Jendra and other lay officials.

Finally I would like to thank my wife, Elizabeth, for her generous love and for providing me with the space and time to complete this work. This book is dedicated to her and to our children Tom, Jo and Daniel.

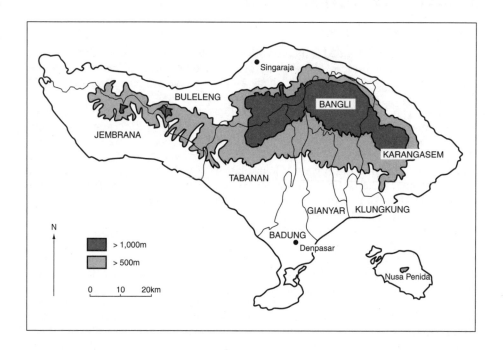

Regional map of Bali

1
Introduction

Three ethnographic themes organize the theoretical arguments of this book. One of these concerns the creation of a new, state-authorized, form of Balinese Hinduism, officially named *agama Hindu*. This new religion is in part a continuation, and in part a reconceptualization, of pre-colonial customary knowledge and ritual practice (*adat*). It was produced, and continues to change, both as a response to events outside Bali and as an outcome of struggles within it. Its emergence was effected through a process in which 'traditional' Balinese religion was reconnected with and realigned to certain strands of contemporary Hinduism in India, on the grounds that in the distant past Indian Hinduism had been one of the principal sources out of which pre-colonial Balinese religion had itself developed. However, as *agama Hindu* took shape in the 1950s and 1960s, in tandem with a rapidly increasing interest in the Hinduism of India, Balinese intellectuals and reformers quickly became aware that this Indian Hinduism was not a unitary religion but contained many diverse traditions. Consequently, from the late 1970s onward, some Balinese grasped the opportunity to introduce other, specifically devotional, forms of Hinduism into Bali. This latter development also occurred alongside the emergence in Bali of a range of indigenously inspired new religious movements.

I wish to make clear at the outset that when I say that *agama Hindu* is a new religion in Bali, or that it has been 'invented', I emphatically do not mean that Balinese religious practices in the past could not be described as being in some sense 'Hindu'. There is abundant evidence that during the first millennium AD Bali (and many other parts of the Indonesian archipelago) was strongly influenced by ideas and practices from India, including Buddhism. Though clearly modified over the intervening period, by the nineteenth century these included institutions of divine kingship, an elevated priesthood using Shivaite liturgy, a framework of categories similar to the Indian *varna* system, a hierarchical social structure resembling the caste systems of India, ranked descent groups practising endogamous or hypergamous marriage, widow immolation amongst the highest ranks, numerous Sanskrit-derived words in the Balinese language, and so forth.[1]

What I do have in mind, in contrast, is that many of the practices and doctrines of *agama Hindu*, as they have been introduced over the last fifty years (and by no means

---

[1] The archaeological, philological and historical literature relating to the Indianization of South-East Asia is very large. For an introduction, see Gonda (1952), van Leur (1955), Bosch (1961), Soedjatmoko et al. (1965), Hall (1981) and Hefner (1985). For discussions on the Indianization of Bali, see Boon (1977), Geertz (1980), Lansing (1983b) and Vickers (1989).

It should also be added that, after about 1000 AD, the links between Bali and India, which had usually been mediated by Java anyway, were broken. As Java became progressively Islamized, Bali remained 'Hindu'. Balinese religion had, of course, an indigenous base, in particular an ancestor cult, and was also mixed with Buddhist and Polynesian elements, so that it developed in its own unique way.

entirely successfully), are new to most ordinary Balinese. They have been explicitly and consciously borrowed from other Hindu traditions by religious officials and intellectuals, and are thought of as re-establishing the connection with Bali's ancient Hindu roots. In this sense, while a form of Hinduism has existed in Bali for many centuries, *agama Hindu* is a new creation. Even if Balinese did not conventionally describe themselves as 'Hindu' in the past, despite the many aspects of their society exhibiting an Indian provenance, they certainly do so now.

When Balinese religion began to be criticized and belittled at the end of the nineteenth century by some Dutch colonial officials and some Muslims as primitive, adhering to animistic spirit worship, being too ritualistic and for not possessing a holy book or a unitary god, it was only natural that the Balinese turned to India and to Hinduism for models of what their religion should be. Moreover, the gradual and on-going reform of pre-colonial Balinese religion into *agama Hindu* has been facilitated by the neo-Hindu revival in nineteenth- and twentieth-century India since it was largely along similar lines that Balinese religion needed to be changed to stand comparison with Islam and Christianity. So, in Bali, attempts have been made to rationalize and ethicize religious practice by simplifying ritual performance and underpinning it with scriptural teachings in a manner that amounts to a state-imposed doctrinal orthodoxy.

The contemporary religious landscape in Bali is thus considerably more complex than it was a century ago. Customary ritual practices (*adat*), though much changed, are still assiduously maintained, *agama Hindu* has been established, devotional movements have been imported from India and new religious movements have sprung up all over Bali. The conflicts which this religious diversity has precipitated are frequently referred to, by Balinese religious officials, Balinese intellectuals and the media, as a 'spiritual crisis'. However, such a description is partly motivated by state religious authorities recognizing that, in a country where the combination of politics and religion can be explosive, uncontrolled religious innovation is a potent source of political instability. In seeking to contain such instability the state attempts to impose forms of religious orthodoxy, closely supervises new religious movements and regularly brands the latter as deviant and harmful. The description of religious diversity as a 'spiritual crisis' thus conceals more than it reveals, and therefore there is a need to look more closely at the wider situation in order to locate the meanings and causes of this complex phenomenon.

One relevant issue, which constitutes the second theme of the book, is the process of Balinese identity formation. Although *agama Hindu* is a new creation which emphasizes doctrine, scripture and theology, it is represented by many Balinese as an age-old tradition. For example, they can draw on written chronicles, many of them dating back no further than the nineteenth century, which purportedly document the origins of Balinese descent groups, and which almost always begin with how Indian gods, sages and gurus were the distant ancestors of the Balinese and the first to bring Hindu teachings to Bali. However, because the links between India and Bali were severed, largely as a result of the Islamization of Java, this tradition is now conceived of as having become gradually distorted by turning into *adat*, which stresses ritual action. In other words, on the basis that there is a venerable Hindu tradition in Bali, the origins of *agama Hindu*, which in fact are recent, have been projected into the past as a lost tradition only recently rediscovered. This 'old' tradition has also now come to be seen as the well-spring of Balinese culture and Balinese art. Moreover, the 'reconstruction' of Balinese Hinduism into *agama Hindu* has formed part of a strategy Balinese used to resist the expanding influence of Islam within Indonesia. Thus, when Balinese religion and culture were challenged in the colonial era, the religious reforms which later eventuated in the institution of *agama Hindu* came also to act as an internal unifying symbol differentiating Balinese as an ethnic group from other Indonesians.

However, this process of ethnogenesis, which has had its strongest impact on urban and educated Balinese, has been interrupted by subsequent events. One of the most important of these is that the Indonesian state forbids the exclusive connection between a religion and an ethnic group. Just as the Balinese began to define themselves explicitly as 'Hindu', through adherence to *agama Hindu*, they found that this new religion had to be universalized throughout Indonesia, with the result that many other Indonesians converted to it. Moreover, as *agama Hindu* was being promoted as the defining marker of Balinese identity, further religious innovation was occurring, and this created opportunities for new forms of identity, not specifically ethnic in nature, to take shape. In other words, one way of reconsidering the 'spiritual crisis' is to see it as a crisis in identity.

Religious diversity and the 'crisis' it has provoked may also be viewed both as an outcome of and as an arena for political and ideological struggle concerning the existence of Bali's hierarchical 'caste' order, which is the book's third theme. In the colonial period, arguments about Bali's traditional religious practices and their links to Hinduism were carried out within the terms of a debate between elites and commoners concerning the place of hierarchy in modernizing Bali. Commoners wanted to detach hierarchy from religion and ultimately to eradicate it, whereas elites wanted to preserve the link so that religion might continue to justify the hierarchical social relations from which they derived various privileges.

When Bali was incorporated into Indonesia in 1950 this conflict was gradually absorbed into a wider struggle, between the army and the communists, landowners and landless and rich and poor, over economic change, land reform and political control of the state. It ended with the massacre of the communists in 1965–6 and the rise to power of General Suharto. The New Order, ushered in by Suharto, was dominated by the military and suppressed virtually all forms of mainstream political activity. Consequently, to maintain their pressure on the hierarchy, Balinese commoners turned to a religious politics. Many Balinese commoners organized themselves into Bali-wide descent group associations and campaigned for equality with the aristocracy; some joined devotional movements which are relatively egalitarian, anti-ritual and anti-priesthood; and others have become members of new indigenous religious movements, which to some extent rework and democratize some of the ideas and practices that informed the pre-colonial connection between hierarchy and traditional religion.

But the situation is rather more complicated than this. The continuing preponderance of high-caste individuals in positions of power and influence in contemporary Balinese society means that hierarchical relations have retained a pervasive significance. Consequently, many Balinese are ambivalent about the hierarchy, in some contexts denouncing it, in others trying to turn it to their advantage. Despite the attacks on the 'caste system', steady economic growth between 1970 and 1998 has led to an intensification of forms of status competition and to Balinese of all ranks attempting to convert new wealth into hierarchical status and ritual prerogatives.

Hinduism, identity and hierarchy are thus intertwined in complex ways. The remainder of this chapter provides a brief synopsis of the book's main arguments.

Hinduism & identity in Bali

In 1906 the Dutch invaded south Bali and extended their control to the whole of the island, north Bali having been brought under colonial rule fifty years earlier.

At that time it would have been very difficult to isolate and identify something called 'Balinese religion', in the sense of a domain of belief and practice bracketed off from other, economic and political, spheres of life, and between which only limited relationships obtained. There was, for example, no Balinese word for 'religion'. If, generally speaking, contemporary western societies circumscribe religion by conceiving of it as a private matter of individual faith, thus marginalizing its influence on 'secular' activities, in Bali 'religious' activity permeated every aspect of communal customary practice, *adat*. Kinship groups were equally temple congregations practising ancestor worship; subsistence production was highly ritualized, with success depending on the blessings of deities and the observance of taboos; relationships between lords and subjects paralleled those between gods and people; states were not political organizations based on a social contract between ruler and ruled, but magico-religious realms underpinned by sacred kingship; and crime was not merely a legal wrong but a polluting event, which had to be rectified by a purification ritual.

By and large, the Balinese lived this reality rather than reflected on it, and thus were not conscious of 'possessing' a 'culture' or 'religion' which they might have to justify or explain to outsiders or to which they might have to adopt a critical attitude. Of course, there were many forms of contact between Balinese and others in the archipelago and beyond, as a result of trade, warfare, marriage or political alliance, but according to Vickers (1987) they did not encounter societies radically different from their own. Distinctions of dress, manners and even religious practice were considered by the Balinese as largely superficial differences covering basic similarities. At that time Islam was not the aggressively proselytizing force it was later to become, and Balinese and Muslims interacted easily. Consequently, Balinese did not conceive of themselves as having an ethnic group identity fundamentally distinct from that of others. The oppositions that existed were between people of Bali (including Muslims and others) and those of other islands; and differences within Bali, such as those between different social strata, were as great as those between people of different islands.

In the course of the twentieth century much of this situation was transformed as Balinese were forced to think about and react to the effects of colonialism, Islamic assertion, war, revolution, incorporation into the Indonesian state, economic and political turmoil, mass tourism and processes of economic and cultural globalization. I am not here arguing that pre-colonial Bali was in any sense static, an exemplar of Marx's notion of the unchanging, Asiatic despotic state, for it clearly was not (Vickers 1989; Schulte Nordholt 1996). But I am suggesting that, since about 1850, Balinese have encountered powerful and radically different social forms and ideas which have had profound and long-lasting effects on their society.

Never passive observers merely trying to cope with change, Balinese have instead responded creatively by exploiting the opportunities which change brings. It is therefore problematic to argue that these large-scale social forces shaped Balinese culture by acting on it from the outside because 'Balinese culture', as a homogeneous entity, did not and does not exist. Change occurred from the inside as Balinese individuals and groups responded to innovation in diverse ways. Changes originating elsewhere were mediated by existing conflicts and differences of interest amongst the

Balinese. Thus, in the third decade of last century, catalysed by the threat of an expansive and aggressive Islam and by western ideas of democracy and the meritocracy brought in by the Dutch and imbibed by Indonesians educated in Dutch schools, reformist-minded commoners and conservative elites heatedly debated the nature of Balinese religion, the links between Balinese 'religion' and Hinduism and the relation between religion and the hierarchical caste order. In subsequent decades these debates widened, changed and ramified throughout Balinese society, informing economic and political struggle in the 1950s and 1960s as Bali became a part of the Indonesian state and was racked by civil and class war. A narrative account of some of these developments is provided in Chapter 2. Here I sketch the outlines of the argument I shall make in Chapters 7, 8 and 9, concerning processes of religious change and their effects on Balinese identity formation.

Chapter 7 focuses on the background to these processes. As a trade-off for rejecting Muslim demands for an Islamic state, the new rulers of Indonesia in 1950 acquiesced to Muslim proposals that only world religions (Islam, Protestantism, Catholicism and Buddhism) be officially sponsored and supported by the state. To be included, a religion (*agama*, the term used in Indonesia to denote official 'religion') minimally had to have a high god and a sacred book. The Balinese version of Hinduism was considered not to meet these criteria and was initially excluded. This was deeply ironic given that *agama* is a Sanskrit term. The Balinese were dismayed at this outcome since, being classified as people 'without a religion' (*belum beragama*, Ind.), they would become the objects of conversion and missionary activity by members of other religions. This dire situation led to a campaign to have Balinese Hinduism included on the list of state religions. By arguing that they did indeed have a high god and that they possessed sacred literature (Indian religious texts, such as the *Bhagavadgita*, were translated into Indonesian in the 1930s) and by promising to rationalize and 'Hinduize' Balinese customary religious practices, Balinese intellectuals and religious officials succeeded in gaining state recognition for their 'religion' in 1958. This religion thus became an *agama* and thereby achieved an elevated status similar to other *agama*. This newly created religion, called *agama Hindu*, emphasized doctrine, belief and theology over ritual, and India rather than Bali as its source. Consequently, while *agama Hindu* overlapped with *adat*, there were many differences between them, and the Balinese population now had to be educated, through the school curriculum, Indonesian-language texts and the admonitions of religious officials, about their new religion.

The invention of *agama Hindu* enabled the Balinese to resist a proselytizing Islam. It also helped to assuage the sense of inferiority that Balinese intellectuals had experienced during the 1930s when they felt incapable of mounting a coherent reply to criticisms from both Dutch and Indonesian, mainly Muslim, scholars that they did not have a religion but practised indiscriminate spirit worship. It was precisely this kind of derogatory remark which galvanized the Balinese into thinking and arguing about their religion: who was their god, what were their religious beliefs, what beliefs ought they to have, what is the point of ritual?

But, once religious innovation had started, it proved very difficult to contain. If *agama Hindu* was now the Balinese version of Indian Hinduism, what was to stop Balinese drawing on other traditions from this very diverse religion, traditions which might serve quite different purposes? If *agama Hindu* was introduced from the top by the state and by the Balinese intelligentsia, there was little to prevent ordinary Balinese from doing something similar. Thus, not content to allow state religious agencies to set the agenda for religious reform, some Balinese have more recently imported other forms of Hinduism into Bali. These are the devotional movements of Sai Baba and Hare Krishna, which are examined in detail in Chapters 8 and 9.

His devotees, whether they live in India, Bali or elsewhere, conceive of Shri Sathya Sai Baba as the incarnation of the universal God. He has a large ashram in the south Indian town of Puttaparthi, which is visited by thousands of devotees from all over the world. They congregate there to receive his blessings, listen to his sermons and witness his miracles. The Hare Krishna movement was founded by the Bengali A.C. Bhaktivedanta Swami Prabhupada in 1965 to continue Caitanya's sixteenth-century tradition of devotion to the supreme manifestation of God, namely, Krishna.

In fact the distinction between top-down and bottom-up processes is not as sharp as I have made it because, once the connections to India were re-established, Balinese intellectuals and religious officials also became interested in the whole spectrum of religious personalities and movements in India. Specific organizational forms are still limited to Sai Baba and Hare Krishna and, while these were introduced into Bali outside official religious channels, the most prominent advocates of the former are well-known intellectuals, some of whom have official positions in state religious agencies. None the less, the fact that these movements were not in any sense state-sponsored partly explains why Hare Krishna is a banned movement, though it is still active, and why Sai Baba, though not banned, has occasionally come under intense official scrutiny. On the other hand, the rapid emergence of many indigenous new religious movements is largely attributable to grass-roots activists who are dissatisfied with aspects of *agama Hindu*.

The creation of *agama Hindu* and the appearance of forms of devotional Hinduism both raise important issues concerning the nature of the relationships of Balinese to their religious life. These new religious forms are not subsumed within *adat*, but instead have distinctive relationships to *adat* and also to each other. In some contexts, these relationships are ones of similarity and overlap, but in others they are contradictory and oppositional. Moreover, as the religious field expanded through the introduction of new religious movements and practices, so too did the semantic field, through the inclusion of new concepts and discourses, and these religious forms now have identifying names (*agama Hindu, adat*, Sai Baba, etc.).

As a result, there is now an increasing separation between religious practice and other aspects of social life. In the nineteenth century, Balinese ritual practices and the social relations of hierarchy mutually reinforced one another in a relatively seamless web of activity, providing a hegemonic conjunction which legitimated inequality between the different strata of Balinese society. Now, however, the relation between religion and hierarchy is extremely problematic and varies greatly depending on which religious form one adheres to. For example, members of devotional Hinduism denounce many of the institutions most closely associated with the 'caste' order, such as the role of high priests and their exclusive guardianship of esoteric religious knowledge. The argument could equally well be made the other way around. It was partly because many Balinese found the hierarchy oppressive that they sought more egalitarian forms of religion through which they could express their criticisms of it. In short, religion in Bali does not constitute a unitary field so much as an arena in which religious and political struggle is played out.

No doubt some Balinese had a critical attitude to various aspects of pre-colonial religion, but there were very limited ways to think about or express this. In the twentieth century the appearance of new religious forms prompted Balinese to compare and contrast these with already existing *adat* religious practice. Thus thrown into relief, *adat* began to assume the status of a distanced and distinctive 'object', and some Balinese began to think through the nature of their relation to it, many coming to the conclusion that it was seriously deficient and acted to disadvantage them in various ways. On the other hand, Balinese have become very proud of certain aspects of this religious culture, especially dance, drama, art and temple festivals, because these are admired by approving tourists who want to see 'authentic' culture. Once Balinese were confronted with options and alternatives, they were able to reflect more critically and comparatively on both the new and the old religious forms. This is an important process because, as the religious forms take on the appearance of 'external' objects of scrutiny, they can also be enlisted as crucial markers of difference and as ideological resources in political struggles.

Religious innovation did not stop with the importation of devotional Hinduism. Since about 1980, many new indigenous religious movements have also emerged in Bali. These are not given the official status of *agama*, but are instead called *aliran kepercayaan* (Ind. 'streams of belief'). They have to be registered with the authorities and conform to the same state ideological principles which underlie *agama Hindu*, and this is how they advertise themselves. In reality, however, and not very surprisingly, they share some features with 'traditional', *adat*, practices, practices which *agama Hindu* increasingly wishes to eradicate. In particular, many *aliran kepercayaan* are movements based on Balinese notions of mystical power, *sakti*, the control, accumulation and use of which was at the heart of pre-colonial Balinese politico-religious organization. *Agama Hindu* only speaks of *sakti* when it wants to brand it as an 'irrational' idea in the context of the modern world. New religious movements based on recycled notions of *sakti* thus create considerable unease and suspicion in many quarters. An especial concern is that some movements unsettle and confuse the Hindu community of worshippers, making it difficult to disseminate the officially sanctioned religious beliefs of *agama Hindu*. Religious authorities and others have thus constructed a discourse of 'crisis', which sees leaders of such movements as motivated by self-interest and engaged in deviant practices that harm their gullible followers.

A similar kind of problem also creates conflict between *aliran kepercayaan* and devotional Hinduism. The latter rejects the pursuit of *sakti* as false and illusory, and emphasizes much more the individual's development of 'spirituality' (*kerohanian*, Ind.). This is a new idea in Bali, and one which is now also espoused by the doctrines of *agama Hindu*. However, this does not bring *agama Hindu* and devotional Hinduism into alliance because, whilst the latter is very critical of many aspects of the former, especially its continuing endorsement of hierarchy, the former considers the doctrines of the latter as subversive.

What thus began as a struggle to promote a specific version of Balinese 'religion', as a way of staving off Muslim conversionary activity, eventuated in tremendous religious diversity. This diversity has fuelled conflict over the nature of religious truth, the role of high priests, the purpose of ritual, the links between religion and the state, the link between religion and hierarchy, and much else. Consequently, the conflicts that have been generated are as much political as religious, and at bottom are about the future shape of Balinese society.

In this sense Balinese 'culture' cannot be construed as the essential attribute of the Balinese people, but rather as the contested outcome of struggles historically constituted (Clifford 1986: 19; Pemberton 1994). Balinese 'culture' and Balinese 'religion' are not simply contexts for social action; they are also the very issues Balinese are fighting over. The issues are about how Balinese should identify themselves, what kind of political organization and what form of religion are best suited to the modern world and what kind of society Bali should become. What we are dealing with here, then, is a cultural politics of religion and the impact this has on identity formation and the critique of Balinese hierarchy. Consequently, this book is informed by a theoretical discourse which views cultural practice as polysemic, relational and historically constituted and as an active production of agents located in structures of opportunity and constraint (Bourdieu 1977; Ortner 1984, 1989).

The production of religious diversity and conflict has had significant repercussions on identity formation. Broadly speaking, the establishment of *agama Hindu* has been used by Balinese intellectuals, religious authorities and promoters of Balinese tourism to define what it means to be Balinese. Although *agama Hindu* is a new creation, it is represented as the recovery of a lost tradition (Hobsbawm and Ranger 1983), and thus as the inspiration for Balinese culture and their famed artistic genius. In one metaphor, religion is the root, *adat* is the trunk and the plastic and performing arts are the leaves and branches. According to Picard (1999: 17), members of the intelligentsia are prone to declare that 'so long as [the Balinese] are aware of the indivisible unity of religion (*agama*), tradition (*adat*) and culture (*budaya*), their identity will remain intact'. The problem, however, apart from the fact that this 'indivisible unity' is itself a very recent construction, is that such a description of the situation has been overtaken by other events. There are now several different forms of Hinduism on the island, and these are being used to construct different and competing identities.

In the past, Balinese identities were for the most part particularistic. They were based on local, highly ritualized traditions of ancestor worship (conducted through houseyard, village and descent-group temples), on attachments to a territory protected by divinized ancestors and other guardian spirits and on long-term, personalized ties to lords and priests. In any one region, these local *adat* traditions were basically similar, but Balinese represented (and still do) custom and belief as varying across Bali. Superficial details of lord–subject relationships, ritual offerings, ritual procedures, village constitutions, foundational myths, agrarian practices, and so forth, differed from one village to another. These differences, denoted by the pithy phrase *desa kala patra*, created and gave substance to villagers' adherence to local traditions, on which identities were founded, identities which thus remained highly localized.

The lords and nobles, especially those of high rank, to some extent transcended this localism. They were involved in inter-regional alliances and widespread networks of kinship and affinity, they had control over subjects dispersed through different villages and of large tracts of land dispersed over a wide area, and they helped manage temple systems whose jurisdictions were far-flung. Although they spoke the same language as their subjects and carried out similar rituals (although on a much grander scale), they shared neither the same interests nor the same parochial world as villagers. As a result, the differences between them precluded the formation of a common identity.

Below these lords, Balinese were divided into numerous descent groups, many with their own specific traditions, titles and ritual prerogatives. These groups jockeyed for status and position in a fluid hierarchical organization. Additionally, in many contexts vertical ties between lords and peasants were more significant than horizontal ones. This too meant that identities remained multiple, distinct and local. Balinese identified themselves as members of a village or descent group, as subjects of a particular lord or as engaged in a particular occupation, but never simply as 'Balinese'.

Collective identities, based on the sharing of similar characteristics and on attachments to unifying symbols, only began to emerge in the twentieth century as Balinese sought to construct themselves as different from other islanders. Again, this was largely a top-down process. As we have seen, Balinese were very concerned about the status of their religious beliefs because of the criticisms being made about them by the Dutch and by Muslims. Balinese intellectuals, such as those discussed by Vickers (1989: 150–55), Bakker (1993) and others, responded by trying to bring their 'religion' into view, by redefining it as a form of Hinduism which could stand comparison with Islam and Christianity. On the one hand, this resulted in conflict between elites and commoners concerning the exact nature of this religion and its relation to the hierarchy. On the other, however, Balinese Hinduism began to be promoted by state authorities, religious officials and tourist entrepreneurs as the source of their cultural and artistic genius, as a symbol of their religious unity, and thus as *the* diacritical marker of Balinese ethnic identity. No wonder that the state is so concerned about the recent and rapid emergence of so many new religious movements which it refuses to describe as *agama*.

The manner in which the Dutch colonial regime, the Indonesian state and the tourist industry have appropriated, commoditized and promoted Balinese culture has made Balinese aware that they 'possess' a culture, in much the same sense that they also 'possess' a religion (Picard 1996). The reification of this culture as an object serving their own and others' interests has encouraged Balinese to be both proud of and anxious about it: others admire it and it brings in large revenues, but concern is expressed over its fragility. However, once this religious culture was externalized and once Balinese developed a relation to it, it could be re-appropriated as the unique feature that defines 'Balineseness' (*kebalian*, Ind.).

However, as this ethnic identity assumed clearer outlines, the varieties of Hinduism on the island began to multiply, rendering the linkage between ethnic identity, Hinduism and culture very contentious. An important sign of this is the significant numbers of Balinese joining the devotional movement of Sai Baba. Sai Baba is very different from the variants of Hinduism already established on the island and owes very little to traditional Balinese religious practices. In fact, its doctrines and its forms of organization and worship are in many respects conspicuously different from *adat* practices. In mounting a stinging critique of other forms of Hinduism in Bali, Sai Baba has helped to foster an identity which is not necessarily 'ethnic' and which thus transcends being 'Balinese'. So, while not seeking to undermine the definition of Balinese religion as Hindu, some Balinese have begun to ask what particular form of Hinduism is best suited to contemporary life in modern Bali. Some Balinese now pose themselves the question as to which is more appropriate: an exclusive Balinese ethnic identity based on a specifically Balinese form of Hinduism, or a more inclusive, modern and global identity centred on the incarnation of the universal God, one which is thus less constrained by the limitations of ethnic group and state boundaries.

Hierarchy in Bali

Dutch colonial rule in south Bali extended from 1906 to the beginning of the Japanese occupation in 1942. During this brief period, the Dutch attempted a reorganization of Balinese hierarchy. Conceiving of Indian caste as an immutable and rigid structure (Lekkerkerker 1926; Liefrinck 1927), the Dutch were confused by the apparent inconsistencies in the Balinese system. They encountered what to them appeared erratic and varying interpretations of the ranking of groups, a pronounced fluidity in the manner in which groups were related to the Balinese version of the *varna* scheme, competing claims concerning the privileges and prerogatives deemed appropriate to these groups, a confusion over which groups could lay authentic claim to status titles, and commoners holding high positions in rulers' courts.

Thinking that the system must have fallen into disarray, the Dutch set about 'correcting' it. They enlisted the help of high priests to provide an 'objective' explanation of the hierarchy to which they then gave a legal backing. The main distinction the Dutch subsequently introduced was between the three highest classes (Brahmana, Satria and Wésia; collectively Triwangsa) and the rest, who were classified as Sudra, the latter amounting to about 90 per cent of the population. While the Sudra were made to perform unpaid service for the colonial state, the Triwangsa were exempted. Far from dampening status conflicts and aspirations, the creation of this rigid hierarchy and the way it determined eligibility for labour service fomented a struggle for position. But now social mobility up the hierarchy could only be accomplished by submitting claims to courts presided over by the priests, and many of these claims were rejected. Such a restructuring also caused a hatred of the elites who had collaborated with the Dutch to protect their positions and interests.

One response by commoners to this newly imposed Dutch system was to question the traditions on which Balinese kings, nobles and high priests based their positions of superiority. Educated commoners in north Bali challenged the ascriptive privileges of the high castes, whom they depicted as bastions of an anachronistic and feudal order standing in the way of modernization and progress. Instead of birth, they advocated the importance of talent, education, wisdom and achievement as criteria for determining prestige and standing.

Religion was a key issue in these debates, both because customary practice revolved around expensive rituals, which many could not afford, and because status and rank were encoded in caste-linked ritual prerogatives. Consequently, while elites pressed for the preservation of the link between religion and hierarchy, commoners sought to break it. The latter denounced the hierarchy as unjust and began to question the purpose of ritual. They argued, for example, that the emphasis on ritual and on getting ritual right had distorted the real meaning of religion, and suggested that the destruction of wealth in ritual, particularly cremation, was a pointless waste of money since it had no effect on the condition of the soul. What was important was how people behaved rather than how much was spent on ritual; it was moral conduct in life, not ritual after death, which determined the fate of the soul.

However, it was not difficult for the Dutch-backed aristocracy to defuse this situation either by exiling the dissidents and troublemakers or by co-opting them into safer and less controversial projects concerning, for instance, the study and recording of popular cultural and religious traditions (Vickers 1989: 152–3). None the less, the die had been cast and, though the context of these arguments has since changed, they remain as vital today as they were in the 1920s. In Chapter 4, for example, I examine contemporary struggles between elites and commoners concerning hierarchy and equality; competing understandings of the role and purpose of the local community association, known as the *banjar*, which is one of the most important institutions in Balinese society; the relevance of commoner origin myths, whose recent politicization contests the aristocracy's superiority, itself based on an origin myth; and competing definitions about the fundamental nature of Balinese social structure. The radical critique of the hierarchy enunciated by the new devotional movements, such as Sai Baba, has recently added new dimensions to these controversies.

Despite these attacks, Balinese social relations of hierarchy have retained immense significance up to the present day. Much village ritual activity, social and linguistic interaction, marriage and, to a lesser extent, the distribution of occupations are still strongly influenced by principles of hierarchical ranking. Ritual paraphernalia and prerogatives, particularly at cremations, are linked to status and jealously guarded. On the whole, relations of superiority and inferiority are maintained through a whole series of asymmetrical exchanges in ritual, language and marriage, forms of bodily posture, and in many other ways. Commoners overwhelmingly marry other commoners, while Triwangsa either marry amongst themselves or take women from inferior groups. Finally, by and large, gentry predominate in the higher echelons of local state administration, the professions and the military, while commoners are over-represented in manual work.

The importance and continuing relevance of hierarchy are probably best seen in forms of status mobility, several examples of which are discussed in Chapter 3. All over south Bali, commoners and Triwangsa alike are engaged in status drives to improve their positions in the hierarchy. These attempts cause considerable resentment, occasional physical confrontation and sometimes a complete breakdown of social relations. Movements of status assertion, often but not always motivated by new wealth, usually involve groups claiming prestigious caste-linked titles on the basis of newly 'discovered' origins more illustrious than those they presently enjoy. Establishing their new position requires them to initiate new exchange relations with others, who, in turn, regularly repudiate such claims if they cannot be authenticated in appropriate ways. What is at issue in these contexts is disagreement over relative ranking rather than the principle of ranking itself. If the titles which attach to ranked descent groups and the ritual and linguistic preroga-tives which are associated with them were unimportant, why would Balinese bother to claim them and why would such claims be so vigorously contested?

In this respect, the book can be seen as an ethnography of how hierarchical social relations work in modern Bali. While there are excellent accounts of the hierarchy for the pre-colonial and colonial periods (Geertz 1980; Wiener 1995; Schulte Nordholt 1996), there is no comparable study for the modern period other than that by Boon (1977). My treatment of the topic is, however, very different from Boon's, since what interests me is the contested nature of hierarchy in the context of develop-ments which were only just beginning at the time he did his research in 1972. While Boon has much to say about the internal dynamics of hierarchy, he rarely mentions the existence of counter-ideologies, commoner denunciations of the hierarchy, the politics of language use, ritual inflation and the consequent intensification of status competition, all of which issues are analysed in Chapters 3, 4 and 5. Moreover, in 1972, the controversies created by increasing religious diversity, mass tourism and identity formation were far less significant than they are today.

In this study I use the term 'hierarchy' in a different sense from that employed by Dumont (1980) in his analysis of Indian caste, where he defines hierarchy as the principle by which the elements of a whole are ranked in relation to the whole. Since Dumont saw Indian hierarchy as an essentially religious institution, the ranking had to be religious in nature. Consequently, 'religion', represented by the Brahmin, was conceptually superior to, and encompassed, 'power', represented by the Ksatriya. The Brahmin and the Ksatriya together constituted a unity in opposition to the Vaishya, whose realm was the economy; and all these three were opposed to the

Sudra who performed services for their superiors. This series of oppositions, the idiom for which is the contrast between the pure and the impure, generates both the *varna* hierarchy and the more complex ranking of castes and subcastes.

This understanding of hierarchy in India led Dumont to claim that the Brahmin fulfilled the religious function, and that the Brahmin priest was the pinnacle of purity, while the king had a purely secular, political function. The disjunction between status and power meant that wealth and political position did not correlate with caste ranking, and therefore Indian hierarchy was a fundamentally different kind of social organization from systems of economic stratification found in the west.

Balinese hierarchy does not fit this Dumontian model very well. Balinese kings always displayed a magico-religious aspect, and priests and kings did not stand in a fixed relation of superiority and inferiority, as required by the Dumontian theory, but vied with each other for pre-eminence in what was a shifting and ambiguous relation. The king was the primary mediating link between the human and divine worlds and, by virtue of that position, he tried to claim the highest status, a status sometimes shared with and sometimes contested by the Brahmana priest whose rituals legitimated the kingship.

In Chapter 6, which is the pivotal chapter of the book because it links the struggles over hierarchy to issues of long-term religious change, I examine the complex and changing relationship between kings and priests in Bali, both in the context of what others have written about Bali and in relation to recent debates concerning caste in India. These latter debates have tended to polarize around two competing theories, one based on a hierarchical model, with the Brahmin at the top, and the other based on a model of centrality, in which the king is the centre of a realm. I draw two conclusions from this analysis. The first is that the precedence often given, in contemporary Bali, to Brahmana priests over descendants of the nineteenth-century rulers is a recent phenomenon, resulting from contingent factors which have their origin in nineteenth- and twentieth-century developments. The second is that the Balinese polity cannot be understood by reference either to a model of hierarchy or to one of centrality, because the evidence suggests that both of these models are simultaneously present. The king and priest each claim superiority by reference to one of these whilst being figured as inferior by reference to the other.

Given the theoretical complications surrounding Dumont's definition of hierarchy, I have instead used the term in a descriptive sense to refer to the linear ranking of groups, since by and large this reflects contemporary Balinese practice. Asked to provide an account of the hierarchy, Balinese almost invariably begin with the *warna* (Balinese version of *varna*) classification, listing in order of precedence: Brahmana, Satria, Wésia and Sudra. As in India, the connection between these broad categories and local descent groups is ambiguous and contested.

To make things more concrete, Table 1.1 gives a version of the ranking of descent groups for the village of Corong in south Bali, where I carried out fieldwork in 1993. This table requires some explication. In contemporary Bali, Balinese make a distinction between the top three categories of the *warna* (or *wangsa*), which are collectively designated as Triwangsa. These are distinguished from the rest of the population, who are designated Sudra. These terms are not in fact much used by the Balinese, who usually refer to this distinction as that between *jero* ('insiders') and *jaba* ('outsiders'). In this book, following Geertz and Geertz (1975), I usually refer to this as a contrast between gentry and commoners.

Members of gentry groups are easily identified by their names. All Brahmana have personal names which include their titles: *ida bagus* (for males) and *ida ayu* (for

Table 1.1 *Ranking of title groups in the village of Corong*

Title	Warna	Term of address
ida bagus (male)	Brahmana	*ratu, surya, 'gus*
ida ayu (female)	Brahmana	*ratu, dayu*
cokorda	Satria Dalem	*ratu, cok*
anak agung	Satria Dalem	*ratu, 'gung*
déwa (male)	Satria	*déwa*
désak (female)	Satria	*désak*
ngakan	Satria	*ngakan* (male)
		sang ayu (female)
sang	Satria	*sang*
gusti	Wésia	*gusti* (male)
		ayu (female)
pandé	Sudra	*pandé*
pasek	Sudra	Birth order terms,
		teknonyms or
		personal names
Others	Sudra	As above

females). Similarly, Balinese in the Satria category have personal names which include their titles. Thus a member of the Anak Agung descent group might have the name Anak Agung Gedé Jaya. Gentry are usually addressed by their titles, but the highest ranks may sometimes be addressed by honorifics, such as *ratu* (king) or *surya* (sun; exclusive to Brahmana men and women). Ideologically these gentry titles mark out their holders as persons of substance, refinement and beauty, and even, in some sense, as closer to the gods than commoners. The term *ida* is an honorific also used to address gods, *bagus* means 'handsome' whilst *ayu* means 'beautiful'. *Anak agung* can be translated as 'big man' or 'great man', whilst *déwa* is a term which also means 'god'. In contrast, among the commoners, only those in Pandé groups (many of whom are metal smiths) are addressed by their title. Other commoners, though the descent groups to which they belong may have titles (such as *pasek*), have simpler names and are never addressed by their title. Instead, birth-order terms, teknonyms or given personal names are used.

The term Satria Dalem (*dalem* also meaning 'inside') denotes a superior category to the unmarked term Satria. There is usually considerable dispute not only about which groups authentically belong to this category and which are merely Satria, but also about relative ranking within the Satria category. As far as the commoner groups are concerned, it is important to note that relative ranking is not usually a particularly pertinent issue amongst themselves, so that when commoners claim a higher rank it almost always entails a claim to a position within the gentry part of the hierarchy. In the following chapters, I examine status drives from both the village of Corong and other villages in south Bali. These involve groups from the whole range of the hierarchy. They include the claims of commoners to be gentry and of Ngakan to be Déwa. I also discuss conflict amongst commoners and between commoners and gentry and the highly contested nature of the relation between the Brahmana and Cokorda groups.

In Dumont's theory of Indian caste, the primary criterion for organizing relative rank is the opposition between the pure and the impure. The pollution idiom is also pervasive in Bali. Balinese men and women become polluted (*sebel*) as a result of contact with death, birth and other transitions in the life cycle. Menstruation is polluting, as is contact with other bodily wastes. Crime pollutes the perpetrator as well as the scene of the crime. Pollution is also an issue in relations between groups of different rank. Eating the leftover food (*paridan*) from the offerings in a ritual dedicated to a member of an inferior group results in pollution for the superior, as does praying to the ancestors of an inferior group. Insulting language to a superior renders him or her polluted.

Yet idioms of purity are rarely used to explain why some groups are superior to others. Occasionally Balinese say that Brahmana groups are at the top of the hierarchy because they are the most pure (*paling suci*), but for other parts of the hierarchy different idioms are usually employed. Balinese talk of superiors as being 'higher' (*duuran, tegehan*) or 'bigger' and 'greater' (*gedénan*) than inferiors, who are spoken of as 'small' people (*anak cenik*). Balinese also use the very important opposition between *alus* and *kasar*, which refers to qualities and attributes in people, language and objects. What is *alus* is smooth, refined, beautiful, controlled, quiet, oblique, etc., while what is *kasar* is rough, coarse, ugly, loud and direct. Yet this too is only infrequently used to describe relative rank in a general way. In short, while idioms of purity and pollution describe inappropriate exchanges between people of different rank, they are rarely used to describe the basic structure of the hierarchy.

Fieldwork

This book is the outcome of several periods of fieldwork in different locations of south Bali, conducted over twenty years between 1978 and 1999.

The first spell of eighteen months, in 1978–9, was spent in and around the village of Pujung (which is its real name) in the northern part of the region of Gianyar (see the map on page xvi for locations). At that time Pujung, with a population of about 1400 inhabitants, was very difficult to reach. The metalled road winding up the valley ridge from the south ended at Tegalallang, leaving a four-mile stretch of dirt road full of potholes and occasionally blocked by fallen trees and landslides.

Pujung was not in any sense isolated economically or politically. While most villagers owned sufficient land to grow a subsistence crop of irrigated rice, many were also engaged in producing goods and services, especially wood-carvings, for the market. Nevertheless, the great majority of villagers spent most of their lives in Pujung (85 per cent of all the marriages were between co-villagers), only leaving occasionally to visit relatives, go to another market, attend religious ceremonies at temples elsewhere, transport carvings to middlemen, and so forth.

Since then Pujung has changed dramatically. The road to Pujung has been completed and now stretches over the mountainous interior of the island to form a main artery between the south and the north. While agriculture has declined in importance, wood-carving has become the backbone of the village's economy. Many villagers have long-term associations with foreign dealers, and products from the village are shipped all over the world in large quantities. Four or five men now own 'factories', employ a large amount of migrant (Balinese) labour and turn out a bewildering array of Balinese 'art'. The dramatic location and beauty of the temple situated in the valley between Pujung and its neighbouring village, Sebatu, has also become a popular tourist attraction. In 1980 we hardly saw a tourist from one month to the next; now perhaps twenty-five coachloads of tourists visit this spot on a daily basis.

My interests in Pujung centred on religion, ritual and kinship and the general collective social life of the village (Howe 1980). I was particularly concerned to document the relationships and parallels in the ritual symbolism connected to the rice cycle and the life cycle. Pujung was a good place to do this because the coordination between the growth of the rice and its attendant ritual had not been disrupted by the change to the new, faster growing, strains of rice which had been introduced in many villages further south. Additionally, since most other anthropologists worked in villages dominated by high-caste Balinese, I decided to locate my research in Pujung in order to examine the nature of social relations in an all-commoner village. My focus was therefore on the contemporary situation in Pujung and some neighbouring villages, and for the most part I ignored the wider religious and political changes that were taking place in Bali.

On returning to Britain I took up a temporary teaching position at the Queen's University of Belfast. When that came to an end I began a three-year project on the sectarian nature of long-term unemployment in Belfast (Howe 1990). Analysing the confusing research data that accrued from this research helped me think through, in a very practical way, the post-structuralist critique in anthropology and sensitized me to the importance of history.

At the same time, in the 1980s, a new generation of anthropologists had begun to shift the direction of research on Bali in two interconnected ways. One of these was a pronounced interest in detailed historical studies of Balinese society, before, during and after the colonial period. The other concerned a new interest in Bali's relationship to the Indonesian state and in issues of modernity in Bali. Here the focus was on political conflict in twentieth-century Bali, on indigenous debates about tourism, 'religion', 'culture' and 'art' and on a critique of anthropologists' and others' representations of Bali.

However, it seemed to me that an important topic was missing from this research agenda, namely, how the hierarchy worked in contemporary Bali. Hierarchical social relations formed the context of much research, but not its primary object, almost as if it could be taken for granted that we fully understood it. Consequently, when I eventually returned to Bali, for six months in 1993 and two months in 1994, it was to look into this central aspect of Balinese society. I did not therefore return to Pujung but instead chose to stay in Corong (a pseudonym). Corong, also situated in the Gianyar region but at a much lower altitude than Pujung, is a much bigger village with a population of about 4,000 people. It was an ideal choice because it boasts large numbers of gentry, amongst whom Brahmana and Cokorda descent groups are very prominent.

In 1993 I lived with an extended family of Anak Agung, whilst the following year I stayed with Cokorda Gedé in his 'palace' (puri) located in the very centre of the village. Even though I never lived in a Brahmana house, on both occasions most of my neighbours were Brahmana, and I became very well acquainted with them, being able to enter their houses whenever I wanted.

In many ways, Corong is a very different village from Pujung. In some respects, it can almost be described as a dormitory village. Many of its inhabitants have jobs in nearby towns and tourist areas, as government officials, medical personnel, building workers, and so forth. When they left Corong in the early morning, the village became very quiet and was only enlivened by a coterie of young, uneducated, high-caste men, who gambled for a living at card games and at the cock-fights, which, at certain times of the year, took place almost every day.

While in Corong I documented many aspects of Balinese hierarchy. I also spent time in other villages because interesting cases of status assertion or 'caste' conflict had been brought to my notice by friends in Corong. Principally these were the villages of Klakah (a pseudonym) near Corong, Genteng (also a pseudonym) in the region of Tabanan and a village on the island of Nusa Penida. I also paid frequent visits to Pujung, both to see old friends and to re-examine aspects of hierarchy amongst commoners in the light of the situation that I found in Corong. Chapters 3 to 6 are largely based on material I collected in these areas.

When I began to write this up in 1995–6, I quickly became dissatisfied with the rather flat and monochrome image of Bali that it seemed to present. From reading new studies of Balinese history that were becoming available and because, while living in Corong, I had come across a number of scandals to do with new religious movements, which were reported in the Balinese press and discussed locally, it was clear that there were many new developments in the field of Balinese religion. I was also conscious of the fact that *agama Hindu*, whilst a reworking of village *adat* traditions, was in other ways a very different kind of 'religion'. However, at that time I was not clear how these changes were related to issues of hierarchy. Moreover, whilst aware that Balinese ethnicity had become a controversial issue within Bali, I did not appreciate the complex links between identity formation, religious change and the Indonesian state's attempts at creating a national culture, an issue I discuss in Chapter 7.

In order to rectify some of the gaps in my understanding of these questions, I began research into new religious movements in the summer of 1997. Having been told by friends of the existence of Sai Baba and Hare Krishna devotional movements in Bali, I decided to concentrate on these, with a view to making contact with other new religious movements (the *aliran kepercayaan*) at a later date. Because these devotional movements have their centres in or near Denpasar, Bali's capital town, I decided to live there in a small family-run hotel, which I had often used before when visiting the city.

In effect, it was this research which opened the way towards a more rounded view of Balinese hierarchy, and which enabled me to see much more clearly how the indigenous critique of hierarchy was inextricably connected to long-term and far-reaching religious change. I was particularly struck by the enormous differences between these devotional forms of Hinduism and *adat* ritual traditions, and the way in which such differences constituted a springboard for a vigorous and explicit ideological challenge to hierarchical institutions.

This is the story which the book tells and, to some extent, the unfolding of its general argument follows my own path of discovery. The first half of the book relates mostly to a description of the hierarchy in action, but always with a view to how it has changed in the context of developments in other areas of Balinese life. The second half examines new religious movements from the perspective of, on the one hand, their intersection with social relations of hierarchy and, on the other, how they produce new conditions for both identity formation and different kinds of religious experience.

A note on foreign terms

I have tried to keep the number of terms in foreign languages to a minimum, but in some cases it is better to use the indigenous words to avoid clumsy translations and inelegant circumlocutions. Words in the Indonesian language are denoted by the abbreviation 'Ind.'. All other words in the text are Balinese, apart from a small number which are either Sanskrit or derive from Arabic, but I have not marked these in any way since the context usually makes it clear that the term is not Balinese.

Terms such as brahmana, déwa, anak agung, and others, might cause confusion because they are used in different ways. These terms can designate groups and titles and they are also often parts of personal names. I have therefore used the following system to distinguish these uses. The capitalized term Anak Agung refers both to the group and when it is part of the name of a member of this group; and the title of individuals in this group is *anak agung*. Thus Anak Agung Madé Jaya is a member of the Anak Agung group, and has the title *anak agung*. I also use the form Brahmana adjectivally, thus a Brahmana priest, a Brahmana woman. This latter capitalized term, along with several others, is also used to refer to categories or classes of Balinese people, thus: Brahmana, Satria, Wesia, Sudra; and also Triwangsa, Satria Dalem.

2
Bali's Recent Political History

Introduction

In nineteenth-century Bali, regional overlords held control over large tracts of land cultivated by their subjects who provided the former with a range of services. These included acting as soldiers in times of war and supplying corvée labour for ritual spectacles and building projects. Kings, their kin, nobles of lesser rank and court priests had prestigious titles; as a category they were 'insiders' (*jero*). The nobles were mythically descended from the rulers of the Javanese empire of Majapahit, who invaded Bali in the fourteenth century, while the high priests (*pedanda*) came from the various Brahmana groups descended from the several wives of Danghyang Nirartha, who is mythically reputed to have founded many of Bali's most famous temples. Collectively, commoner peasants were 'outsiders' (*jaba*); they were subjects and servants (*kaula, panjak*), and many were slaves (*sepangan*). They had to show deference and subservience through forms of bodily posture, linguistic etiquette and in many other ways. This hierarchy inflected most, if not all, social relations. Wives were subordinate to their husbands, children to parents, younger siblings to elder siblings and sisters to brothers.

It was nevertheless a fluid hierarchy. Rulers depended on their noble followers, without whom they were nothing. But equally the latter depended on their overlords, who gave them prestige and titles, delegated control over subjects to them, and provided them with security and booty in times of war. Each noble, while under the nominal authority of a higher ruler, had his own entourage of followers, which gave him a separate and partially autonomous power base. All these relationships were highly personalized and were often characterized by distrust, intrigue and competition. They regularly fragmented and new combinations of alliances emerged. Followers who proved unreliable or unsuccessful faded away and lost titles. Alternatively, commoners of ability, because they were less likely to be involved in palace intrigue, achieved high administrative positions in a ruler's entourage and had titles and other privileges conferred on them, which could then be inherited by their descendants. Subordinate rulers occasionally became more powerful than their overlords and claimed autonomy or incited rebellion. Rulers defeated in war lost land and subjects and were demoted in status or exiled. Men with obscure origins sometimes accumulated followers and resources, converted these into rank and titles and, through war, marriage alliances and other means, established their own little kingdoms in competition with others (Schulte Nordholt 1996: ch. 2).

This brief description of the Balinese pre-colonial polity is usually termed that of a 'contest' state (Adas 1981; Schulte Nordholt 1996) and is rather different from Clifford Geertz's analysis of the nineteenth-century Balinese state, the *negara*, which he glosses as a 'theatre' state. The principal issue which divides Geertz and his critics (notably Tambiah, 1985a, and Schulte Nordholt, 1992, 1993, 1996) revolves around the relationship between lords and peasants, Geertz arguing that peasants privately owned their own land and were thus largely autonomous agents who willingly supported their lords' ritual and other projects, the latter claiming that lords exercised considerable control over the peasants. These different accounts agree that the king was at the apex of the hierarchy and the centre of a realm; he was an 'exemplary centre', who mediated between heaven and earth and gave the state its shape. But, while Geertz implies that this ideology was implemented in practice, his detractors assert that political practice deviated from the ideal (Schulte Nordholt 1996: 6).

Geertz argues that the *negara* cannot be interpreted with the conventional tools of western political science, for it was not an organization of command nor did it have a monopoly over physical violence. Such interpretations also privilege material power over the symbolism that legitimates and disguises it. In contrast, according to Geertz, in the *negara* symbolism was the substance of the state, not simply its trappings.

> Court ceremonialism was the driving force of court politics; and mass ritual was not a device to shore up the state, but rather the state, even in its final gasp, was a device for the enactment of mass ritual. Power served pomp, not pomp power.
>
> (Geertz 1980: 13)

The *negara* was thus a theatre state directed to spectacle, ceremony and ritual. Kings were the impresarios, priests its directors and peasants the supporting cast, stage crew and audience (ibid.).

In this formulation, elites and peasantry appear almost to inhabit two separate worlds, and indeed Geertz claims that the former did not interfere much, if at all, in village life. Government was instead a local-level matter conducted through a set of peasant institutions: village (*désa*), hamlet (*banjar*) and irrigation society (*subak*). Consequently, 'power was not allocated from the top, it cumulated from the bottom' (ibid.: 63), and, while elites busied themselves with theatrical expression and culture, peasants were concerned with instrumental government and politics. The theoretical and ethnographic problems which Geertz never resolves, however, are the relation between these two strata, the apparent willing compliance of supposedly autonomous peasants in the projects of the aristocracy and the violence and wars that were pervasive and endemic throughout the nineteenth century.

Although I shall discuss some of these issues more fully in later chapters, especially Chapter 6, it is worth noting here that, while Geertz depicts kings as silent and sacred icons, they also had to be active, warlike leaders; that warfare, itself described as a form of ritual, was in fact often bloody and violent; that lords controlled peasants through their control of land, trade and large-scale irrigation works; and that peasants were often enslaved through debt and by petty infractions of the numerous rules of etiquette. Leaders *aimed* to become immobile, exemplary centres, but in order to achieve this they had to be able to mobilize vast resources. The iconic sacred king was thus not the start but the end-product of a struggle conducted through political and symbolic means.

None of this is to understate the great significance of mass ritual and spectacle, but, whereas Geertz tends to see these rituals as ends in themselves, others interpret them as political gambits in the fight for power. Large-scale ceremonies were high-risk events and served as a means of prosecuting the contests with other leaders (Vickers 1991; Howe 2000). Successful ceremonies demonstrated a leader's control over human and material resources, showed him to be a powerful man who could provide protection and thus acted as a magnet attracting the followers of other leaders who failed to compete adequately. If war was a form of ritual, then ritual was also a form of war.

Since the beginning of the colonial period, Balinese society has undergone rapid political, economic and religious change. These changes have affected the hierarchy in complex ways as some groups and individuals have sought to eradicate it, others to reform it, yet others to preserve it, and many, of course, to turn it to their advantage. In contemporary Bali, nevertheless, hierarchical social relations remain highly significant, as can be witnessed, for example, by the numerous attempts to enhance a group's position in the hierarchy and by the frequent, protracted and heated discussions in the Balinese newspaper, the *Bali Post*, concerning both the relevance and the desirability of the 'caste system' (*sistim kasta*). Many commoners, urban intellectuals, academics, officials of state bureaucratic agencies and those who, for whatever reason, find themselves disadvantaged by its continued presence, question its continuing existence in a modern world increasingly defined by ideologies of equality, democracy and meritocracy.

Present-day attacks on hierarchy are a continuation of those which began in earnest in the first decades of this century, which were stimulated by changes introduced by the Dutch. Sentiments of nationalism, anti-colonialism and opposition to the old feudal order gathered momentum during the colonial period and the Japanese occupation, and eventually manifested themselves in dramatic fashion at the end of the Second World War, when Bali and other areas of the nascent republic were convulsed by political violence and civil war. The most explosive expression of tension, however, did not occur until 1965–6 when perhaps 80,000 Balinese (and perhaps close to 500,000 people for the whole of Indonesia) were slaughtered in the aftermath of an attempted coup in Jakarta, alleged to have been inspired by the Indonesian Communist Party.

The violence in Bali erupted as a consequence of the growing polarization between antagonistic factions (nationalists and communists; rich and poor; landed and landless; gentry and commoner) over issues of land reform, control of the local state, gentry hegemony and the future direction of Balinese society. By 1967 the Communist Party had been obliterated and Suharto, who had replaced Sukarno as president of the republic, was in control of central state institutions. Sporadic violence continued to occur both in Bali and in other parts of Indonesia, but, as the New Order regime (*Orde Baru*, Ind.) gradually consolidated its hold on the whole country, almost all explicit forms of dissident politics were squeezed out of the system.

Despite these tumultuous events, hierarchical social relations, now rather different from those which existed in the pre-colonial period, continue to be important at all levels of Balinese society. In this book, I examine both the social forces sustaining hierarchy in modern Bali and some of the more significant challenges to it. This chapter provides a brief overview of developments in Balinese society over the preceding century,[1] while in the immediately following chapters I concentrate on issues of status assertion and status rivalry, since these provide the clearest indications of the continuing salience of hierarchy.

---

[1] This brief historical introduction is intended only as a broad context for the material which follows. For a more detailed introduction to the nineteenth-century history of Bali and the colonial period, see Pendit (1954), Hanna (1976), Boon (1977), Geertz (1980), Schulte Nordholt (1986, 1996), Agung (1988), Vickers (1989), Robinson (1995) and Wiener (1995).

Political developments in Bali since 1850: an overview

After three wars and the loss of many Balinese lives, the Dutch gained effective control of northern Bali in the middle of the nineteenth century (Hanna 1976: 41–50). The subjugation of the rest of the island was completed in the first decade of the twentieth century with the invasion of south Bali. At first, this met fierce resistance, but in 1906 and 1908 the kings of two kingdoms in south Bali (Badung and Klungkung), together with their wives, children, servants and followers, committed mass suicide by either killing themselves or walking straight at the Dutch guns, which continued to fire despite the absence of retaliation. These events, known to the Balinese as *puputan* ('the end'), sent shock waves through some of the capitals of Europe and led to vigorous protests.[2] Partly to make amends for these terrible incidents and partly to deflect interest away from them, the Dutch decided to refrain from interfering with the purely religious and cultural institutions of Balinese society, and instead to 'protect' and study them (Vickers 1989: 92). One outcome of this Dutch colonial policy was the beginnings of tourism and the representation of Bali as an exotic cultural paradise. In 1908 the colonial government opened a tourist bureau in Batavia and, while initially it focused on Java, Bali soon came to be described as 'the Gem of the Lesser Sunda Isles' (Picard 1990b: 4).

This colonial policy was also influenced by various images the Dutch held of Bali (Boon 1977; Vickers 1989). With its dramatic scenery, strange customs and beautiful, bare-breasted women, Bali was 'exotic'. But the dams, dykes and irrigation channels of its wet-rice agriculture also made Bali familiar and reminded the Dutch of their homeland. Adding to the charm of Bali was the fact, that while Hindu-Javanese culture had 'degenerated' under the impact of Islam (Raffles 1817, vol. 2: ccxxxvi; Friederich [1849] 1959: 2), Bali remained staunchly 'Hindu'. It therefore came to be represented as a kind of natural museum and repository for customs thought long since defunct in Java, a contemporary version of what Hindu-Javanese society had once been in the past. Consequently, the organizing principles underlying ancient Javanese society could be reconstructed by reference to what was still visible in Bali. Conversely, the descriptions of village social structures in Bali (Korn 1933; Grader 1937a, b) were heavily influenced by Rassers's (1922) conjectural theories of dualism, supposedly typical of ancient Java.

Bali was also 'little India' since, for the Dutch, it had a 'caste system' with despotic rulers, who ruthlessly exploited the rest of Balinese society and whose widows were cremated on their husbands' funeral pyres. In some contexts, the aristocracy was seen as an alien and oppressive imposition on the stout and essentially democratic indigenous folk, who lived in independent 'village republics' (Korn 1933; Covarrubias 1937). As a result, the reform of Balinese social and political organization, through the insertion of 'enlightened' Dutch colonial rule and the demotion of Balinese autocratic rulers, could be represented as releasing the Balinese to follow the customs of their ancient culture. According to the Dutch, interfering with Balinese political institutions was one way to protect and foster authentic Balinese culture.

But on this issue colonial policy was a contradictory mix of idealism and prag-

---

[2] There are many accounts of the period of gradual Dutch encroachment in the affairs of the south Balinese kingdoms, but by far the most detailed is Wiener's (1995) analysis of the colonial encounter between the Dutch and the Klungkung royal dynasty. For a Balinese account written from the perspective of a descendant of the Gianyar royal house, see Agung (1988).

matism. If Dutch sensibilities were offended by the privileges enjoyed by the elites, they nevertheless needed to preserve these to ensure the loyalty of pre-colonial rulers whom they used as the local representatives and agents of colonial domination. Therefore they outlawed the most 'disgusting' practices while providing support for the traditional elites.

Moreover, the Dutch had difficulty in understanding Balinese hierarchy. The existence of a large number of descent groups with their various names and titles, commoners enjoying high positions in the noble courts, and many groups and individuals laying claims to higher rank caused the Dutch to think that the 'original' system had broken down and become confused. Presuming Balinese hierarchy to be very similar to Indian caste and thinking that the latter was an immutable order in which everyone had a fixed position, the Dutch transformed what had been a complex and fluid organization into a more rigid system (Schulte Nordholt 1986; Vickers 1989: 146).

They were especially keen to make a clear distinction between the three highest status categories (collectively Triwangsa, i.e. Brahmana, Satria and Wésia, the Balinese versions of the Indian terms Brahmin, Ksatriya and Vaisya) and the large residual population, who were now all to be classed as Sudra, despite the many differences amongst them (Schulte Nordholt 1986: 31), and thence to prevent movement between these categories. The term Sudra was hardly used by Balinese before this period and indeed is not much used now, the usual designation for 'commoners' being *jaba* ('outsiders').

Using the help and advice of priests (*pedanda*) from Brahmana groups, particularly those in Klungkung (the highest-ranking kingdom in Bali), the titles attaching to descent groups were codified and simplified. The Dutch achieved this partly in accordance with their ideas about Indian caste, but it was also strongly influenced by Brahmana ideology, since it was essentially these priests who worked out the finer details of 'who could use which title, and what the proper moral duties and ceremonial rights were for each caste' (Vickers 1989: 148).

This had precisely the opposite effect of what was intended. As a result of trying to determine once and for all who had rights to which titles, many Balinese moved quickly to establish themselves as high caste (Triwangsa) before the door was permanently shut on them (Schulte Nordholt 1986: 30–31). Instead of reducing 'confusion', the reform created an arena in which claims to higher rank and titles flourished (Vickers 1989: 147).

A prime motive for these status claims was that in the new system those designated Triwangsa were to be exempted from performing unpaid labour (*heerendienst*) for the state, while Sudra, whatever their origins and previous positions, were obliged to contribute labour to state projects. Prior to the colonial period, Balinese of ability from commoner groups were often employed in important administrative positions in the local noble courts and thereby gained privileges (certain exemptions, grants of land, honorifics, and so forth), not just for themselves but also for their kin and descendants. With the imposition of Dutch colonial rule, many of these jobs and positions disappeared, and thus the privileges that went with them. The Dutch allocated the jobs that remained to members of the Triwangsa, considering them to be the 'natural' rulers, an idea inconsistent with the view of the aristocracy as an alien imposition. Such interference resulted in a more marked distinction between gentry and commoner, and the newly instituted barrier between them became harder to cross. But, if it could not be crossed, those commoners who had done well under the old rulers would lose out.

Previously, rulers decided on conflicts over status and titles, but, in the new, Dutch-imposed system, the only route open to aggrieved or opportunistic commoner groups was through newly instituted courts presided over by *pedanda* priests. Many of the cases heard in these courts were brought by commoners attempting to claim gentry titles, and some of these became jokingly known as *gusti ponnis* or 'verdict *gusti*' (Schulte Nordholt 1986: 37) and *satria kertas* or 'paper *satria*' (Robinson 1995: 64), these terms indicating status positions in the gentry part of the hierarchy. Some groups ignored the negative adjudications handed down and refused to undertake corvée labour, as a result of which there were occasional violent clashes with the military (who were mostly Balinese soldiers under the command of Dutch officers), in which several Balinese lost their lives (Vickers 1989: 149).

Since the Dutch had neither the manpower nor the expertise to rule the Balinese on their own, they enlisted the traditional elite to rule as their regents. It was the *raja*'s assistants, the *punggawa, perbekel, sedahan* and other gentry officials of the pre-colonial states, who had to coerce the ordinary Balinese peasant to contribute labour and taxes for the colonial regime. The irony of this was that, although the Dutch initiated and enforced the corvée system, its detailed implementation was in the hands of the Balinese who were its local agents, and who could therefore manage it for their own, often traditional, ambitions. For example, under this system a lord in Mengwi district managed to complete the building of a royal temple, which had previously proved very difficult because of the problem of mobilizing sufficient labour (Schulte Nordholt 1991a: 153).

Moreover, as managers of this new and more exploitative system of enforced labour, it was the Balinese who became the targets of sporadic rural unrest, rather than the distant and invisible Dutch. Protesters were sometimes fired upon by the native police force and they were tried according to Balinese law. Not surprisingly, little anti-Dutch sentiment was expressed, but relations between elites and commoners grew increasingly fractious (Robinson 1995: 69). Such were the contradictions of Dutch colonial rule that they not only escaped denunciation by the majority of Balinese people, but also succeeded in stimulating divisions amongst them.

During Dutch control of Bali, the colonial regime prevented the introduction of plantation systems that had taken such a toll in Java (Geertz 1963a; Breman 1983) and Sumatra (Stoler 1985), but it was still a harsh and unremitting time. Peasants were worse off under the Dutch than they had been under their own lords. They were required to provide a greater number of days of unpaid labour, and taxation on land, trade and the slaughter of animals increased (Robinson 1995: 54–64). Furthermore, because taxes had to be paid in scarce Netherlands Indies cash, many Balinese were unable to meet the increasing demands on their meagre resources. In response they either raised production of cash crops or sold land; sometimes they had to do both. In some areas this resulted in large transfers of land from small farmers to large landholders (Schulte Nordholt 1988: 273). Very probably this increasing inequality was one of the root causes of later conflict over land reform in the 1950s and 1960s.

In 1942 the Japanese landed in Bali and the few hundred Dutch present on the island surrendered, something of a shock to many Balinese, who had become accustomed to thinking of the colonial power as invincible. Whilst initially the Balinese welcomed the 'liberators', the Japanese occupation turned out to be worse than Dutch colonialism. Forced extraction of agricultural and industrial produce reduced many Balinese to a starvation diet, while the ridiculously euphemistic Bali Volunteer Labour Corps forced Balinese to work on construction projects, from which many

never returned. Like the Dutch, the Japanese also used indigenous elites to administer many aspects of these systems of extraction. Some Balinese benefited from this,
further fuelling tensions amongst Balinese that had been ignited by similar Dutch
practices (Robinson 1995: 70–94). These repressive regimes left lasting residues of
hatred for the colonial and occupying forces, but they also exacerbated long-term
and deep divisions within Balinese society.

The period between 1945, when the Japanese occupation ended, and 1950, when
independence was formally ratified and the Republic of Indonesia was established,
conditions in Bali were complex and chaotic. The Dutch tried to reassert their control
in the face of competing Balinese interest groups. These groups were constructed
around newly resurgent political parties, the power bases of the old rulers, the armed
forces of the revolution, youth groups, and so forth, all to one degree or another influenced by the emerging but still weak central state. Although the alliances created
during this period shifted quickly as the course of the civil war in Bali unfolded, they
tended to coalesce around conservative and republican factions. The conflict became
a fight about the direction Balinese society should take, either a reversion to an old
'feudal' order or forward to a more democratic state. According to Robinson (1995:
107–10), at the outset, these divisions did not crystallize entirely around antago-
nisms between gentry and commoner groups, since members of both could be found
in fairly large numbers on each side. However, within a couple of years republican
forces began to focus their criticisms against the traditional elites. Nevertheless, it
was to be another fifteen years before these divisions exploded into brutal violence.

After independence, the new republic had very little control over what was
happening in the provinces, and political violence continued in Bali, and elsewhere
unabated. In Bali, the crucial issues of the time were growing political factionalism,
challenges to the elites and conflict concerning the reform of religion. In this context,
according to Vickers (1989: 164), 'Balinese developed a new awareness of their
origins' and there was a 'great outpouring of commoners' dynastic genealogies'. In
part, these were attempts to establish Bali-wide commoner descent-group organizations to challenge the 'feudal' aristocracy, who were perceived as having formed
alliances with both the Dutch and the Japanese to retain their privileged positions.

This search for origins (ngrereh kawitan) entailed the forging of new relationships
with more inclusive descent groups. Small commoner groups established who they
were, that is, who their founding ancestor was (their origin point, or kawitan),
through the revelations of traditional mediums and then joined larger, better-
organized groups of the 'same' descent line. If these latter were also commoner
groups, there were few significant implications for status, and some groups practised
an open-door policy (Stuart-Fox 1987: 139).

The rekindled interest in origins, however, was also fuelled by more traditional
ambitions. With the Dutch colonial regime overthrown and the 'traditional' rulers
unable fully to reassert their control, frustrated commoners took the opportunity to
activate dormant claims to higher status. If the Dutch reorganized Balinese society
and made the hierarchy more inflexible, events during and after the Second World
War conspired to loosen it up again. The tensions that accumulated in these earlier
periods found an outlet in a resurgence of forms of social mobility because, as
Balinese in Tabanan said, 'now there is no law against it' (Boon 1977: 166).

The first few years in the life of the new republic, based on western models of representative parliamentary democracy, saw the revival of political mobilization and the
re-emergence of mass-based political parties (many of which had been formed during
the colonial period, but had been subsequently banned by the Dutch and their

Plate 2.1   Monument to the revolution, built in 1993 and situated at the southern end of the village of Corong in south Bali

leaders imprisoned and exiled).[3] In Bali the principal parties were the nationalists and the socialists. Muslim parties which were very important in Java, Sumatra and elsewhere in the republic, had very few members in Bali. President Sukarno attempted to remain aloof from the political infighting characteristic of the time by representing himself as a modern version of traditional forms of authority, a political icon of unity transcending the divisions among the parties (Anderson 1972a). But, with political and economic conditions deteriorating throughout the 1950s and concluding that parliamentary democracy was hindering the continuation of the revolution, he suspended the 1950 constitution, restored that of 1945, which gave him a great deal more executive power, and bowed to army demands for martial law. This began the transition to Guided Democracy.[4]

During the years 1959 to 1965 in Indonesia, Sukarno tried to preserve a precarious balance between the four major forces vying for political ascendancy: the army, the nationalists, the rapidly expanding Communist Party (PKI) and the Muslim parties. This proved too difficult and the army and the communists became ever more polarized. Deep social and political fissures opened up as the economy slid from bad to worse. The PKI and its more militant peasant organizations began to agitate in the countryside for land reform and new tenancy arrangements. In both Java and Bali, violent confrontations between rival groups were frequent in both the towns and rural areas. The army and the nationalists grew increasingly alarmed at the penetration of communists into influential positions in both state and provincial agencies and even into sections of the armed forces (Crouch 1988: 82–7).

Economic circumstances deteriorated rapidly in Bali in the five years to 1965. The general malaise of the Indonesian economy was compounded in Bali by poor harvests, rat plagues and insect infestation. In 1962 the eruption of Bali's biggest volcano, Gunung Agung, took 62,000 hectares of land out of production. As a consequence people fled the region around the mountain and flooded into neighbouring areas and into the towns (Robinson 1995: 239), and malnutrition and starvation were common. During these years, despite its reputation as a fertile island of plenty, Bali became excessively dependent on subventions from the centre and, as 'economic dependence increased, the distribution and control of goods became the main political issue in Bali' (ibid.: 244).

To a large extent, the channels of distribution had hitherto been controlled by local state agencies, the island's emerging new capitalist class and the old aristocracy, in all of which the nationalists were very influential (Geertz 1963b). However, Sukarno continued to protect the interests of the PKI, not only because he considered it the main force for sustaining the fervour of the revolution, but also because he needed the communists as a counterweight to the army, which was increasingly dissatisfied with his rule. In 1961 he transferred the highest military authority in Bali to the

[3] There is now a vast literature on the emergence and development of nationalism, democracy and communism in Indonesia. For a general history of Indonesia, see Ricklefs (1981). Early accounts of political developments in Indonesia, such as Kahin (1952), deal with the rise of nationalism, other political movements, the revolution and the general political scene from the beginning of the twentieth century to the end of the war. Anderson (1972b) has produced the most detailed account of the postwar revolution, but concentrates on Java and the role of youth movements. For biographies of some of the leading figures of Indonesian nationalism and the revolution, see Rose (1987) on Mohammed Hatta and Mrazek (1994) on Sutan Sjahrir.

[4] For accounts of the general Indonesian political scene in this period, see Feith (1962) on the decline of parliamentary democracy and Lev (1966) on the transition to Guided Democracy. For Sukarno's own version of his role in the revolution and later as first president, see Sukarno (1965), but for a more objective account see Legge (1972).

island's governor, Anak Agung Bagus Sutéja, who was a communist sympathizer. Thereafter Sutéja could further the interests of the PKI in Bali through state patronage, thus threatening the partial hegemony the nationalists had built up previously.

The desperate economic conditions prevailing in Bali in the early 1960s, which encouraged disadvantaged groups (peasants, labourers, commoners) to join the PKI in large numbers, also coincided with the beginnings of the active phase of land reform. In theory, those owning land above a stipulated acreage (depending on density of population and the quality of the land) had to surrender the excess to the state for redistribution to landless peasants. New legislation concerning forms of tenancy arrangement, which favoured the tenant over the owner, were also enacted. Because many large landowners held powerful positions on the committees insti-tuted to put this legislation into practice, little progress was made. Owners failed to declare accurate figures for the land they owned, transferred land to kin and clients so as to hide and disperse their holdings and lied to the committees about the identity of the tenant (Robinson 1995: 268).

As the PKI grew in strength in Bali, land reform was implemented more vigorously and, where there was resistance to it, peasant organizations affiliated to the PKI began to engage in unilateral seizure of land in what was known as 'one-sided action' (*aksi sepihak*, Ind.). This, of course, provoked violent clashes and contributed to a deepening of tensions.

On 30 September 1965, six army generals stationed in Jakarta were kidnapped and murdered by a group of middle-ranking officers led by Lieutenant Colonel Untung. Within twenty-four hours, General Suharto had crushed the coup and gained control of the most important strategic resources in Jakarta. While Untung may have been a communist, there is still controversy as to whether the PKI authorized or even played a significant role in the coup. But, whatever its precise origin, Suharto used it as a means of branding the PKI as deeply implicated in a treasonous plot against the republic. Because Sukarno was himself so closely associated with the PKI, his tenure of the presidency was effectively at an end. Moreover, with the army in complete command of the situation, the balance of forces in Indonesia decisively changed in its favour, and over the course of the following year hundreds of thousands of 'suspected communists' were slaughtered and herded into camps and prisons.[5]

In the years that followed the inauguration of the New Order regime, Suharto gradually reversed the policies of the Sukarno period and, instead of privileging politics over economics, he emphasized economic development over everything else. He rejected Sukarno's pro-China stance, called on western powers to provide aid and recruited economists trained in America to institute policies designed for rapid economic growth, a process greatly helped by the massive increase in the price of Indonesian oil in the early 1970s. To facilitate his control, he gradually curbed party-political activity by banning the PKI and assembling all the Muslim groups into a single party and all other parties, including the nationalists, into another. By collecting parties with different ideologies and interests into single units, he effec-tively reduced them to a condition of disunity, weakness and internal squabbling.

[5] The literature on the coup, its aftermath, the emergence of Suharto and the role of the army in politics is very large. Perhaps the best guide is still Crouch ([1978] 1988), but see also Suryadinata (1989). Mortimer (1974) has charted the rise and destruction of the Indonesian Communist Party, but Kartodirdjo (1984) is a better guide to the rural unrest in Java during the peak of communist activity. On the political conflict and violence in Bali after the coup, see Hughes (1968), Vickers (1989) and Cribb (1990), though Robinson (1995) is by far the most detailed analysis.

In addition, and in line with the new doctrine of the 'floating mass', it became illegal to engage in party-political activity outside short periods prior to general elections, held every five years. Thus, emasculated political parties were unable to mount any serious challenge to the ruling regime for 30 years.

To guarantee his political ascendancy and his re-election to the presidency, Suharto made very effective use of Golkar (*Golongan Karya*, 'functional groups'). Initially a loose confederation of anti-communist groups (civil servants, professional organizations, worker groups, business associations, religious bodies, women's groups, and so forth), Golkar was transformed into a vote-winning election machine and the semi-official party of the government. Until 1998 virtually all government officials and members of the police and armed forces were members of Golkar. Under the concept of 'monoloyalty', civil servants were strongly discouraged from being affiliated to a political party, and the bureaucracy thus became inextricably associated with the Suharto regime and a major arm of his political power.[6]

During this period state control penetrated to the very heart of Indonesian village life. Local village government was reorganized, village constitutions were standardized and local officials were incorporated into the lower rungs of the state. New Order ideologies of *pancasila*,[7] 'development' (*pembangunan*, Ind.) and 'advancement' (*kemajuan*, Ind.) were disseminated in compulsory indoctrination courses for government employees, community leaders and business and private company employees. The school curriculum was and remains very strictly controlled by the government, and has become an important means of creating a new sense of Indonesian citizenship and identity.[8]

Up to 1998, in terms of the votes cast at general elections, the province of Bali appeared to be a Golkar stronghold, although considerable dissatisfaction with the Suharto regime was voiced privately. There were, of course, positive reasons for Balinese support of the regime, such as its antipathy to the aspirations of Muslim groups for an Islamic state, the island's sustained and rapid economic growth and the fact that village leaders, themselves appointed by the state, were the only channels through which central funds could be directed to village projects (schools, market buildings, sanitation, running water, and so forth). But there were also very limited

---

[6] For a general introduction to various aspects of economic and political developments ushered in by the New Order, see Budiman (1990), Hill (1994b) and Schwarz (1994); for detailed accounts of the rise of big business, capitalism, the influence of Chinese capitalists (the *cukong*) and the modern political economy of Indonesia, see Robison (1986) and Bresnan (1993). Reeve (1985) provides the best analysis of the rise of Golkar. On more social and cultural developments in Indonesia, see, for example, the collections in Anderson (1990c), Budiman (1990), Hooker (1993) and Schiller and Martin-Schiller (1997). An early account of the rise to power of the state bureaucracy can be found in Emmerson (1978). Indonesia now has a vast system of state functionaries, who, since the reforms of local government in 1979, have penetrated to the very heart of village life and enabled the state to tighten its control (Schulte Nordholt 1991b: 22–6; Warren 1993: 238–70).

[7] *Pancasila* is the national ideology first enunciated by Sukarno in 1945. He called for a nation based on five principles (*pancasila*): belief in one god; nationalism; humanitarianism; democracy through deliberation and consensus; and social justice. The New Order government also appealed to *pancasila* as an ideology best suited to its need to integrate the country under its authoritarian control (Morfit 1986). It has become the sole ideological basis for all political parties and all other recognized organizations, including religious ones, as well as the state as a whole. In effect, it proscribes mobilization around local symbols of tradition and any appeals to ethnic, regional or religious sentiments that may be construed as opposed to national unity. See Chapter 7 for details.

[8] On this issue, see Parker (1992a, b). Education has been a primary beneficiary of oil-derived revenues. Today, in Indonesia, free primary schooling is available to children up to twelve years of age, and secondary education is spreading rapidly (Hull and Jones 1994: 161–77). However, secondary school is expensive, and university is financially out of the reach of all but the rich.

ways in which dissent and resistance could be expressed, and opposition to the regime was disorganized and subjected to blatant and sometimes violent intimidation (Schulte Nordholt 1991b: 23; Wenban 1993). However, two years after the fall of Suharto in 1997, the first genuinely free general elections for 45 years were held, and many political parties contested the parliamentary seats. Bali had 2.04 million registered voters, of whom 1.5 million voted for the Democratic Party (Partai Demokrasi Indonesia–Perjuangan) led by Megawati Sukarnoputri (Sukarno's daughter) and only 200,000 for Golkar.[9]

In the mid-1990s, some new forms of resistance had begun to emerge in Bali. Rapid development of tourist facilities sparked debate and protest amongst all ranks of Balinese. The unveiling of government plans to spend 40 million dollars on a statue to rival the Statue of Liberty was greeted by a storm of protest (Picard 1995; Suasta and Connor 1999). The proposed building of a massive new hotel and golf complex next to an important temple in south-west Bali also led to large and persistent demonstrations. The project was suspended for a time, until the army cracked down on the protesters, whereupon building was resumed (Warren 1998; Suasta and Connor 1999). These protests are part of an increasing realization that external capital is exploiting Balinese resources and severely damaging the island's potential for sustainable development. With an influx of foreign workers, increasing pollution, congested roads, a creaking infrastructure and most of the tourist revenues leaving the island, the fall of Suharto allowed Balinese to express their dislike of his policies and their desire to have a much greater say in matters that affect the island's future development.

A note on the Balinese economy

Bali's economy has changed enormously since 1966. The modern economy has created many jobs in infrastructural development, the security services and education; in transport and its supporting networks of garages, petrol stations and dealerships; in big hotels and budget boarding-houses; and in textiles, crafts manufacturing and a host of other small industries. Village economies that were primarily subsistence-orientated, with the sale of surpluses and some cash crops, are now considerably more diversified. While agriculture is still very important, it has declined rapidly as a proportion of Bali's gross domestic product. Quite often today, farming is seen as a much less prestigious occupation than it once was, and people keep land and buy new plots more as an investment opportunity than to farm it themselves.[10]

The expansion of the economy has, however, distributed its benefits very unevenly. Within the up-market sector of the tourist industry, most of the investment comes from Jakarta and foreign sources, whence the profits return, leaving the Balinese to deal with the environmental problems and cultural paradoxes of tourism (Vickers 1989: 184–213; Picard 1990b: 8). On the other hand, many Balinese living on the main tourist routes have enriched themselves by converting

---

[9] On the background to Suharto's fall from power and its immediate aftermath, see Aspinall, et al. (1999), Budiman et al. (1999) and Emmerson (1999).

[10] Surveys of Bali's economy can be found in Daroesman (1973), Bendesa and Sukarsa (1980) and Jayasuriya and Nehen (1989). Geertz (1963b) pioneered the study of economic change in Bali, but anthropologists have since rather neglected this area. However, useful discussions can be found in Poffenberger and Zurbuchen (1980), Connor (1982), Poffenberger (1983), Nakatani (1995) and Robinson (1995). For overviews from different theoretical perspectives of the Indonesian economy, see Robison (1986), Bresnan (1993) and Hill (1994a).

their houses into 'homestays', which cater for the budget traveller. Tourism has also provided many spin-off services, which can only be provided locally by Balinese. Many of the new businesses developed over the last thirty years have greatly benefited their owners, but the wages received by the lowest-paid in 1997 could be as low as Rp1000 per day for unskilled female labour, an amount sufficient to buy about a kilo and a half of rice.[11]

Despite the fact that many commoners, in those parts of Bali where tourists are numerous, have become moderately affluent, and that some have risen to high positions as government civil servants, a process likely to accelerate as the rich become able to educate their children at universities, it remains the case that gentry acquire a disproportionate number of state jobs and, generally speaking, the most influential ones. During the period between 1950 and 1966, the traditional aristocracy had receded into the political background, even if it prospered economically (Geertz 1963b: 82–141). However, when Suharto came to power, a new era of depoliticization and economic development was set in motion, and the gentry reasserted itself. Since then Bali's governors (*Gubernur*) have all been men of very high rank, as have most of Bali's eight regional governors (*bupati*). At the district level of government administration, many district heads (*camat*) are commoners. However, below this, at the village-cluster level, headed by a *perbekel* or *kepala désa*, Balinese from high-caste groups again predominate. In those villages which have large concentrations of gentry, the *perbekel* is very often a direct descendant of the precolonial ruling family and frequently the highest-ranking member of the local palace (*puri*). This pattern is repeated right across south Bali (Parker 1992b: 96; Warren 1993: 273; Nakatani 1995: 78). Sutton (1991: 117) remarks that 45 per cent of the faculty at Udayana University, Bali's foremost university, are gentry.

The predominance of the traditional elite in the modern political administration of Bali's towns and villages, however, does not necessarily mean they behave according to the same norms and values they did a century ago. Whilst there is no reason to doubt that they are often elected by the popular vote of villagers of all ranks, this is not necessarily because the electors were once their clients. Many of those elected are genuinely concerned to improve the quality of life of all Balinese rather than to feather their own nests, though clearly this happens too. Such an orientation to the community is partly based on the pressure emanating from above to carry out a wide variety of development schemes, rather than on any inherent altruism. Palace-backed officials and other gentry have sometimes been in the forefront of locally based self-help initiatives, which have produced widespread benefits, as Parker (1992b: 96–7) and Warren (1993: 189–207) have demonstrated. The economic development of one's own village, at the expense of a competitor village, however, also brings in its train a variety of private benefits, which local leaders may take advantage of.

The fact that so many gentry are in positions of power and influence, at both local and regional level, continues to mark them out as persons still seen by many as peculiarly able to lead. To some extent, this is a continuation of the nineteenth-century ideology that menial labouring jobs were the preserve of commoners and thus beneath the dignity of gentry, whose duty was to rule, arrange and supervise. Of course, ideologies of labour that valorize inactivity as a sign of status and power are also now in conflict with new meritocratic ideas, which place a high value on work and achievement and construct idleness as parasitic. Nevertheless, gentry distaste

---

[11] On the low wages paid to female factory labour in Java, see Wolf (1992) and, for other parts of South-East Asia, see Kung (1978) and Ong (1987).

for labouring jobs is reinforced by the various beliefs which they still hold about themselves and commoners, such that the former are more intelligent, have a propensity for scribal work, are more refined, have a better command of high Balinese, have 'brighter' faces, and so forth. Today in village Bali, there remains a noticeable division between the kinds of work and jobs which gentry and commoners do. Even if there are numerous exceptions, gentry tend to find jobs in government agencies, business and the professions, while commoners predominate in agriculture, skilled and unskilled labour and daily waged work generally.

Professional jobs and appointments in the civil service are eagerly sought after, despite being badly paid. The daily wage of a craftsman may be twice that of a civil servant. But the latter enjoys a number of desirable benefits: job security, monthly rice quotas, undemanding duties, an additional income through bribes, short working day, etc. Civil service jobs are difficult to obtain, since personal connections and the ability to pay a bribe are as important as merit.[12] Since *Triwangsa* already have a disproportionate presence in the bureaucracies and also retain wealth from the past, they are clearly in an advantageous position to maintain their ascendancy.

A note on village organization in Bali

Although Bali is rapidly urbanizing, the great majority of Balinese, commoner and gentry alike, still live in small villages, known as *désa*, whose populations range from about 500 to over 5,000.

Agnatically related extended families occupy large, walled compounds, which comprise sleeping quarters, kitchens, granaries, a family temple, open pavilions, back garden, pigsties and chicken coops, and so forth (see Howe 1983). The term *désa* denotes the consecrated ground (*tanah désa*) on which residential houses, village temples, markets, communal meeting pavilions, and so forth, are built. The authority over this area ultimately lies with the village's ancestral founders, now converted into deities worshipped in the temples. It also denotes an association (*krama désa*) which is composed of the senior married couple from each house built on village territory. In many villages, this association meets regularly and is responsible primarily for the maintenance of village temples and the performance of ceremonies held in them. Villagers are also members of a very important institution known as the *banjar* ('hamlet'). The association of members (*krama banjar*) consists of all the married couples living in the houses belonging to that *banjar*. Like the *désa*, the *banjar* meets regularly and is responsible for a wide range of village activities, particularly the cremation of its members and their dependent kin. Both the *désa* and *banjar* have written constitutions (*awig-awig*), which govern all their activities and which specify fines and punishments for infractions of their rules.

In many cases, a village's population is divided into several *banjar*, and often these may be territorially discrete, which thus makes the *banjar* appear to be a section or part of a *désa*. In other cases, though, the houses attached to different *banjar* are dispersed across the village territory. There are also many villages where there is only a single *banjar*, in which case it is problematic to speak of the *banjar* as a subsidiary section of the *désa*.

[12] Patronage, nepotism and corruption are pervasive in the Indonesian economy and bureaucracy (Bresnan 1993: consult index under corruption, Schwarz 1994: ch. 6) and, since 1997, have figured very prominently in the national and local press. For a cultural account of some of these issues, see the fascinating study by Shiraishi (1997).

Villages often differ in the precise organization which they take. The main complication is that there are two kinds of *désa*, the *désa adat* and the *désa dinas*. The former is the pre-colonial 'customary village', which still exists informally and which maintains its contemporary coherence because many activities, especially religious and ritual ones, are still organized by reference to it. During the colonial period the Dutch began to reform village organization, mainly by amalgamating small *désa adat* into larger administrative villages, which are now called *désa dinas*. In some cases, this also meant transferring small sections of one *désa adat* to another. Further reforms have been carried out by the Indonesian state, and today it is the *désa dinas* which is the formal administrative and political unit.[13]

Notwithstanding these reforms, the traditional *banjar* (hamlet) is a local institution of tremendous significance. But this does not mean that the *banjar* has remained a stable entity. In later chapters I shall argue that the *banjar* has in fact undergone considerable change since pre-colonial times. The *banjar* has such great contemporary significance for organizing many important activities that the populations of even the largest towns are also divided into *banjar*.

Gentry, who constitute about 8 per cent of the total population of Bali, are not evenly distributed. Generally speaking, villages in the interior of the island, and thus at higher altitudes, rarely have resident gentry. Conversely, many large villages in the southern plains have concentrations of gentry, approaching 25 per cent in some cases. High-caste Balinese still often occupy the 'palaces' (*puri*) of their pre-colonial forebears, who dominated the local scene. Invariably these *puri* are situated at the centre of the village, with the houses of other gentry surrounding them and commoners occupying the outer sections of the village (see Chapter 6). *Puri*, to a great extent, are simply much larger versions of ordinary Balinese houses, which are known as *umah* (Geertz and Geertz 1975: 51, 149).

While many Balinese live most of their lives in and around their home village, in no sense are villages economically or socially self-sufficient. Large amounts of manufactured goods and agricultural produce are transported into and out of villages on a daily basis. Every day, thousands of men and woman leave their villages to work in the towns and in the hotels, restaurants and shops of the now numerous tourist centres. Increasing numbers of Balinese are building second homes near their places of work. Many other institutions, such as temple congregations, agricultural water-use associations (*subak*), new religious movements, which draw their members from a wide geographical area, title-group networks, and so forth, cut across village and hamlet groups.

---

[13] For further information on this and related issues, see Korn (1932), Geertz (1959), Guermonprez (1990) and Warren (1993).

3

The Inflation of Titles
& the Search for Origins

Introduction

During the twentieth century, hierarchical social relations in Bali came under incessant attack. Describing the hierarchy as *feodal* (feudal), many Balinese argue that its emphasis on ascriptive privilege is out of touch with the ideologies of democracy, equality and meritocracy increasingly embraced by the wider Indonesian society. Hierarchy, they feel, should be consigned to the dustbin of history so that Bali can enter the modern world. And yet hierarchical social relations continue to be vital and highly relevant in contemporary Balinese social life.

Perhaps the clearest sign of this are the pervasive disputes over relative ranking, which occur at all levels of the hierarchy. Even commoners, who at other times vociferously decry the hierarchy because it disadvantages them, regularly try to improve their status, suggesting that their attitudes to hierarchy are highly ambivalent. Another indication is that, since about 1970, Balinese, like the hierarchical Toraja of Sulawesi (Volkman 1985), have devoted increasing resources to their ritual performances to enhance their own status and prestige by outdoing others. This has happened despite attempts by reformers to rationalize, streamline and economize on ritual activity, partly with a view to dampening such competition. Moreover, while extreme linguistic and other forms of deference have largely disappeared, the remaining hierarchical features of the Balinese language are endorsed and praised almost as much by commoners as by high castes. Hierarchy is changing, but predictions of its imminent demise are exaggerated.

These and various other issues are explored in Chapters 3 to 6. Chapters 3 and 4 address some key points concerning the dynamics of hierarchy in contemporary Bali by reference to several case-studies. Chapter 5 examines changing linguistic practices and ritual inflation, while Chapter 6 looks at the highly ambiguous relationship between the two groups at the apex of the hierarchy.

The cases of status mobility discussed in this and the following chapter explore how social relations of hierarchy are subject to both processes of change and reproduction. The perpetuation, in part, of the nineteenth-century elite as a late twentieth-century elite and the rapid development of the Balinese economy since 1970 have created conditions for status competition to flourish. On the other hand, war, revolution, the incorporation of Bali into the Indonesian state, the growing significance of ideas of democracy and equality and a more equitable distribution of land and other economic resources have led to hierarchy becoming problematized in indigenous discourses. None the less, criticisms of hierarchy and of the privileges enjoyed by high-status groups are not always effective, because the ideologies in which they are embedded are open to varied interpretations and can be used to entrench relations of hierarchy.

In this chapter the three case-studies are all examples of groups raising or trying to raise their own positions in the hierarchy. From one perspective, they indicate a relationship between wealth, prestige and power on the one hand and hierarchical status on the other, but from other perspectives the validity of this relation is denied. In the first two cases, groups attempt to enhance their status because a gap is perceived between their current rank and their material achievements, but their claims are vigorously contested because, despite their new wealth, they cannot be authenticated by the ancestors. In the third, a commoner group, whose claims to higher status are properly validated, is unwilling to enforce its new privileges because it lacks the economic and political resources thought to be commensurate with higher status.

Interestingly, this indigenous argument about the relation between status on the one hand and power and wealth on the other echoes an earlier academic debate about the proper way to interpret the caste systems of India, Dumont (1980) arguing that there was a profound disjunction between power and status, while Bailey (1957) and Marxist writers (Meillassoux 1973; Mencher 1974) claimed the opposite. It is probably more fruitful to view assertions and rejections of such a relationship as strategies in the arena of status competition.

The second example also makes another point. Here it is the status titles in themselves which are the crucial issue. While some Balinese denounce the titles attached to gentry descent groups as outmoded or reinterpret them as nothing more than optional personal names empty of any wider significance, gentry continue to take their titles very seriously. In most respects, many gentry are materially indistinguishable from their commoner neighbours and co-villagers. Precisely because these are often the only remaining signs of a once more encompassing superiority, gentry assign considerable symbolic importance to their titles and defend them zealously.

In discussing these examples, reference is made to counter-ideologies which Balinese draw on to denounce hierarchical relations, although the topic is addressed more fully in Chapter 4. Nevertheless, it is useful to state here what these ideologies are. Mention has already been made of the anti-caste movements, which began in the early years of the twentieth century. These contested the relevance of birth and descent and substituted ideas of education, merit and achievement. Such ideas have developed in various ways, fuelling cases of 'caste' conflict. They have also generated a wide-ranging controversy over competing – hierarchical and egalitarian – interpretations of Balinese social organization. Another significant theme is the recently emerging importance of certain myths which conceive of the origins of commoner groups as further back in time than those of gentry. Since, in Balinese ideas, origins are closely linked to 'truth' and authenticity (Schulte Nordholt 1993: 296), the growing significance of such myths adds a further dimension to the contemporary cultural politics of the island.

Until recently, those Balinese hostile to the hierarchy had few opportunities to escape it, and so have attempted reform from within. Whilst in India untouchables and other low castes have sometimes converted to Islam or Christianity (Lynch 1969), this option has only been taken by very small numbers of Balinese. However, during the last twenty years the establishment of the Hindu devotional groups of Sai Baba and Hare Krishna, newly imported from India, and discussed in Chapters 7 to 9, has provided Balinese with novel opportunities to express critical views of hierarchy and authorized forms of Hinduism in a more cogent, focused and explicit manner. Both Sai Baba and Hare Krishna are relatively egalitarian and espouse a critique of forms of religion based on ritual and the authority of priests.

In later chapters I shall develop arguments about how these devotional movements have had an impact on changing conceptions of identity in Bali. I shall claim
that Balinese who join them are rejecting or downplaying a parochial ethnic identity
as 'Balinese', an identity which is itself relatively new and which has been fostered
elsewhere in Balinese society as a means of distinguishing Balinese from other
Indonesians. The latter is being replaced by a more inclusive, global and modern
identity based on membership in an imagined religious community which, though it
has its centre in India, is widely dispersed throughout the world. These identities are
in the process of being constructed at higher levels of society and consequently have
been adopted by only a small but growing segment of the population, mostly urban-
based and middle-class. As they grow and become more influential, they are
beginning to interact with the highly localized identities of those Balinese who live
most of their lives in village communities. As Geertz (1973b) has explained, these are
for the most part based on status title, public office, temple affiliation, kinship status,
and the like. They serve as schemes of classification which distinguish among
Balinese within one village and between Balinese of different villages.

Before presenting a description of some movements of status assertion, I want to
expand the remark, made above, concerning the ambivalent attitude of many towards
the hierarchy, since this has implications for understanding the forms of resistance to
it. To the Balinese, the hierarchy appears as a finely graded structure in which each
group always has other groups which are status-near. In theory, any particular group
gives deference to superiors and extracts it from inferiors. As a result, those not at the
extreme ends are often ambivalent about their particular position within it, experiencing hierarchy as both oppressive, in relation to superiors, and satisfying, in relation
to inferiors (cf. Fegan 1986). Thus, while hierarchical values are sometimes endorsed
and sometimes contested, it is very often the same individuals and groups who do both.

I have discussed elsewhere some of the problems which this kind of situation raises
for Scott's (1985, 1990) theory of domination and resistance.[1] The point I want to
make here is that his bipolar model of society, consisting of the dominant and the
subordinate, is blind to the ambivalence and contradictory nature of life in societies
like Bali's. Linking domination and subordination to easily identifiable and polarized
groups oversimplifies both the Balinese case (Vickers 1989; Robinson 1995: 252,
263) and many others (for example, White 1986; Humphrey 1994; Gal 1995), in
which forms of domination and subordination are exercised at every level of the hierarchy or where varying and shifting alliances between the state, local elites and the
masses make domination and subordination relative and contextual.

In Bali many groups claim that their real position in the hierarchy should be
higher than the one currently occupied. Competition then arises as groups try to
negotiate a more advantageous balance between deference due to others and that
due to themselves. Most usually this entails attempts to assert an elevated status. In
such conditions it is difficult to withdraw from status competition by affirming
equality with other groups, because superiors interpret this as an unjustified claim to
a rank equivalent to their own and react by insisting on the recognition of their
status prerogatives. On the other hand, objections to another group's attempts to
elevate its status may be expressed in terms of a criticism of the hierarchy itself.

---

[1] In line with Gal (1995), Ortner (1995), Kulick (1996) and many others, I have questioned Scott's
emphasis on resistance at the expense of ideological incorporation, his neglect of the internal politics of
subordinate groups, his problematic distinction between 'public' and 'hidden' transcripts, and various
related issues (see Howe 1991, 1994, 1998).

It is therefore important to distinguish conflict about relative ranking which reproduces, intentionally or otherwise, the saliency of the hierarchy from conflict which
involves an explicit challenge to it. Such a distinction is necessary because, occasionally, these two forms of conflict are conflated, leading to claims that there is more
resistance to the hierarchy than is perhaps justified. The following description of
what is a fairly typical form of status assertion also allows me to examine the
argument that Balinese cremations are events during which resistance is often
expressed to hierarchical values.

Asserting status: the Déwa of Genteng

Although status drives have been regularly reported in the literature (Geertz and
Geertz 1975: 120–22; Boon 1977: 166 and *passim*; Howe 1984; Guermonprez
1987), few such movements have received detailed description. The rest of this
chapter is therefore devoted to a consideration of three such cases.

The first concerns a section of the all-commoner population of the hamlet (*banjar*)
of Genteng in a large village in Tabanan regency in western Bali, who have claimed
the gentry title of *déwa*. Adopting a gentry title also requires other attributes to be
modified: new ritual practices, rededication of family temples to 'real' origins, new
terms of address and reference, and so forth. However, such changes are highly
contentious. They can only be established if the rest of the hamlet is willing to
acknowledge them as appropriate by altering existing forms of interaction. New
attributes, therefore, are validated by new forms of exchange (cf. Parry 1979: 92).

Boon has much to say about the recent proliferation of Déwa groups in the
Tabanan area. In pre-colonial Tabanan only one Déwa line, brought specifically by
the ruler from the eastern part of the island to serve as court medical practitioners,
was officially recognized. Déwa groups had been absent up to that time because the
title was considered superior to that held by the ruler himself, who was a *gusti ngurah*
and who did not want subjects whose titles exceeded his own. According to Boon
(1997: 166), other Déwa groups which migrated to Tabanan were forced to use
inferior titles, which the Dutch law courts classified as Sudra. Possibly because the
ruler's title was changed to the superior *cokorda* in 1938, on the authority of the
colonial government, some groups tried to reactivate 'lost' Déwa origins. Boon notes
further that:

> after the Dutch left and before political activity intensified, many impoverished Satria-Wesia
> lines in Klungkung and Gianyar discreetly sent scouts to other districts to contact status
> seekers. Genealogies were then prepared in the form of sacred *prasasti* manuscripts; the
> palm leaves were stored in a smutty hearth for aging and later sold to the appropriate
> commoners when they journeyed east seeking an elevated source.
>
> (Ibid.: 166–7)

In the Tabanan region, then, status assertion began to manifest itself, after the Dutch
had withdrawn, in the form of commoner groups trying to reactivate dormant claims
to a Déwa origin. Sometimes this was done by purchasing bogus genealogical
charters from Déwa groups in eastern Bali, who were willing to fabricate them for a
price. The following example examines one particular attempt at such a status drive.

During the 1960s in the hamlet of Genteng, a group of about thirty families,
tightly knit and intermarried, began to claim the title *guru*. The rest of the hamlet did
not like this affectation, but it was not taken very seriously. However, around 1978

the group claimed they were of Déwa status, which is a much superior title. Until that point the entire hamlet had been commoners, though gentry reside elsewhere in the village. The hamlet leader (*klian banjar*) was a member of the group and he insisted on their right to the title, arguing that it had been bestowed on them a long time ago by the ruler of Tabanan. He said they were in possession of a genealogical charter (*prasasti*) which verified the claim. The Déwa stopped worshipping at a temple where previously the whole hamlet had prayed collectively, claiming that its gods (deified ancestors) were now inferior. In retaliation the commoner group pointed to the obvious fact that all the tax bills, school registers, identity cards, and so forth, recorded these Déwa as having commoner names. Heated arguments and physical confrontation followed, as the Déwa attempted to extract linguistic deference from the commoners. They insisted, for example, on commoners addressing them with their new title and using other forms of respectful high Balinese. However, the latter refused and continued to use low Balinese towards them, as they always had.

By 1990, the two factions were completely separated. They patronized different coffee stalls, hardly communicated at all except for the barest social niceties and, apart from cremations, were not invited to each other's celebrations. There had been no marriages between the two groups since the conflict began. The Déwa maintained their membership of the *banjar*, perhaps the strongest of Balinese village institutions and the one primarily responsible for carrying out cremation, and so reluctantly took part in the cremations of their adversaries. However, they only did what was absolutely essential to fulfil their obligations. In short, the attributional changes that the Déwa tried to introduce caused almost all ordinary and ritual social relations to break down. Unable to convince the commoners of the authenticity of their case, the Déwa were incapable of validating their new status by instituting appropriate new forms of exchange.

According to the commoners, the Déwa have not cremated any of their own dead in the last twenty years, because they do not know what to do; they have simply left them interred in their graves in the village cemetery.[2] True Déwa in other hamlets of the village, themselves feeling offended, have not volunteered to help. Lacking advice on what offerings to use, what sarcophagus to make or how many roofs to build on the vehicle which takes the deceased's remains to the cemetery, all of which provide an index of a group's status position, they decided not to cremate at all. Some commoners claimed that they were also frightened to proceed for fear of the event being sabotaged.[3]

The situation became intractable and the governor (*bupati*) of Tabanan was asked to adjudicate. To substantiate their claim the Déwa produced a palm-leaf manuscript (*lontar*), supposedly given to their ancestors by the Tabanan ruler in the nineteenth century, and claimed that this was an ancestral genealogy (*prasasti*) proving their right to a *déwa* title. Their opponents have no idea where the document came from.

---

[2] Normally Balinese bury their dead and carry out cremations months and often years later. Depending on the resources available to the deceased's family and the scale of the cremation they wish to undertake, what is disinterred from the grave varies from a small amount of earth to the entire remains of the body.

[3] The reluctance of the Déwa to cremate any of their dead was beginning to cause a scandal. Periodically there is a major purification ceremony at Bali's most prestigious temple, Besakih, situated on the slopes of the volcano Gunung Agung in the regency of Klungkung. Although there is apparently no textual justification for it, religious authorities now demand that all the corpses in Bali be cremated before the ceremony begins. If for some reason this is not possible, the group concerned has to ask for a special type of holy water from a *pedanda* priest to 'fence off' the graves of their deceased members so that they do not pollute the ritual proceedings. This is the course of action that the Déwa have been following, though commoners considered it inappropriate for the circumstances that existed in their village.

The Déwa were instructed to take the manuscript to Klungkung to have it read and authenticated by a *pedanda* priest. When they complied, the document was pronounced not to be a *prasasti* at all but a *pengéling-éling* (from *éling* meaning to remember), and it failed to substantiate the group's claim to Déwa status. The priest verified that the document had been presented by the ruler of Tabanan to people in this hamlet, but it merely acknowledged and commemorated a service faithfully and reliably rendered. The service was that of palanquin bearer; wherever the ruler travelled, his carriers were chosen from this group. In other words, the Déwa were really just servants, and the commoners felt they had been vindicated.

Despite this outcome, the situation in 1993 remained much as it was in 1990. This is not surprising, given the strength of feeling on both sides and the great difficulty that external agencies have in exerting authority over hamlet affairs (Geertz 1983: 178–9; Warren 1993: 43–54). Since to Balinese the origin of something implies its truth, the only way the Déwa can persuade the commoners to modify their behaviour towards them is to anchor their origins more firmly to a high-status past, and up to now they have failed to do this.

What sparked off this status drive was almost certainly a gradually accentuating difference in the wealth and occupations of the two groups. The Déwa group includes many professionals, government employees and businessmen, who have become more affluent and better connected than the rest of the hamlet. They own cars and have invested money in refurbishing their homes and houseyard temples. Consequently, a discrepancy has opened up between their 'pragmatically earned' and their 'divinely endowed' status (Boon 1977: 184), which they have sought to close by elevating their title.

For commoners the problem consists in some villagers arrogantly trying to place themselves above the rest and thereby threatening the relations of collective equality which are today a cornerstone of hamlet (*banjar*) social life. Even though some hamlets accord gentry members certain privileges (for example, they are exempted from carrying the body of a commoner to the graveyard, since this would place them physically under the corpse), all over Bali the *banjar* has become one of the most important egalitarian and democratic institutions in social life. At meetings all members, whatever their status, sit at the same level, they all have the same rights to speak and vote, they speak the same level of the language, and subscriptions, other dues and labour obligations are the same for all.

Similar attempts to improve status in the hierarchy are not at all uncommon in south Bali. They testify to the continuing importance of hierarchical relations by showing how groups try to convert new forms of wealth and prestige into enhanced ritual status. Because relative status ranking becomes explicit at cremations, it is these events which sometimes provoke anger and even violence between the contending parties. While I would assert that such behaviour is rarely an attack on hierarchical relations, and is in fact an implicit endorsement of them, Warren has claimed the opposite, arguing that violence at cremations is a form of resistance to hierarchical values. It is useful to examine her arguments before moving on.

In light of the importance of egalitarian relations in hamlet life, Warren has pointed out that the emphasis placed on hierarchy in much writing about Bali has de-centred these other, equally significant, aspects of Balinese society. While Geertz (1980: 117) sees the (royal) cremation as the key symbol of status inequality and aggressive status assertion, Warren (1993: 82–3) notes that cremation symbolism is also about 'fertility, cyclic renewal, and balance in Balinese cosmology'. If at one level cremation is infused with hierarchical values, at another it is pervaded by values of equality. She argues that the occasional disruptions of death ceremonies, in which the tower taking the corpse to the graveyard is violently jostled and partly or wholly destroyed and which sometimes even extends to maltreatment of the deceased (Connor 1979),[4] are expressions of antipathy to the hierarchical order and that therefore status inequality and corporate egalitarianism are 'competing frames of reference around which Balinese culture revolves' (Warren 1993: 80, 83); it is what Geertz and Geertz (1975: 167) call 'the war' between *Homo hierarchicus* and *Homo aequalis*.

Although she tends to conflate them, I think there are two separate issues in Warren's argument, and I suggest that both are open to other interpretations. The first concerns the extremely boisterous behaviour of participants during a cremation, while the second concerns attacks on the corpse and/or the damage inflicted on the cremation tower and offerings. She suggests that, while both these forms of behaviour may demonstrate resistance to the hierarchy, the second is the more extreme expression of such resistance.

In relation to the first, Warren's argument relies on a rather uncritical acceptance of Bakhtin's (1968) discussion of the European carnival, in which the reversals and play elements are explained as forms of popular culture which contain expressions of resistance to the established hierarchical order. Balinese cremations are indeed full of noise, irreverent behaviour and an energetic activity seemingly bordering on chaos. But there are three reasons why this need not be considered as resistance. One is that all rituals, to be successful and enjoyable, must be *ramé* (crowded, busy, bustling, lively, noisy, etc.). This is a very positive value, and one eagerly sought after. Any event (market, drama performance, temple ceremony, cock-fight, etc.) which is not *ramé* is to some extent a failure and a negative comment on those who organized it. Secondly, a *ramé* atmosphere at cremations is not created merely for enjoyment, but also because it entails the appearance of supernatural forces, which can be enlisted by the men to help them carry the very heavy cremation tower bearing the corpse.[5] Thirdly, following Vickers (1991), I have argued elsewhere (Howe 2000) that collective rituals of this kind are only successful to the extent that the forces purposely unleashed by riotous behaviour are ultimately contained by the ritual's managers, this control demonstrating both the managers' power and the spirits' approval. In all these senses, the production of apparent chaos does not necessarily constitute disruption or resistance, because it is an indispensable part of the intention of the rituals.

Warren's second argument is that attacks on the corpse or on the cremation tower are strikes specifically against hierarchy. Sometimes this may indeed be true,[6] but

---

[4] Connor (1979) describes cases of corpse abuse in the Bangli region more violent than anything I have witnessed in Gianyar. In Bangli it is apparently not uncommon for one group to make off with the corpse and, if they hated the deceased, tear it limb from limb.

[5] Noise is very important at cremations, as it is at many other rituals. Depending on the interpretation, noise can distract spirits from causing mischief or it can help enlist their supernatural power to assist those carrying the very heavy tower. Often men shout: '*Suryiak! Suryiak!*' ('Shout'!) to urge other participants to yell and scream. In previous eras, ceremonies of the elite often ended with gunshots and other types of percussive noise (Needham 1967); and today the end of temple festivals, when the gods are being 'sent home', is accompanied by loud gamelan music, much shouting and boisterous jostling. On the oppositions between noise and silence, and chaos and order, see Vickers (1991).

[6] Vickers (1989: 170) describes the cremation of a very high-status man in Klungkung in 1965, which became the occasion for a clash between the nationalists and the communists. Clearly here the principle of hierarchy was at stake and not merely the particular character of the deceased or his group, but cases like this seem to be quite rare.

Plate 3.1   Scene at the very crowded cockfight arena adjacent to the temple of Samuan Tiga in Gianyar, south Bali. Most temple festivals are accompanied by several days of cockfighting which attract gamblers and spectators from a wide area

there are other reasons for it as well. Most cremations entail some mild playing with the corpse, called *ngarap bangké*, and with the tower, *ngarap wadah*. There is often, for example, a form of tug of war or mock battle when the corpse is transferred to the tower, signifying the ambivalent feelings of the hamlet at having lost a valued member but wishing to speed him on his way to the next world. In some cases, this can look like abuse if the corpse is dropped or roughly handled. In its journey to the cemetery, accompanied by much laughter, water spraying, mud throwing and encouragement to the carriers to be even more daring, the cremation tower may crash into walls, veer alarmingly all over the road and tilt dangerously this way or that. At road junctions, the tower is revolved three times to confuse the departed, so that his spirit cannot come back to haunt the living. In one large cremation I witnessed in 1993, a water tanker was hired which followed the tower and used its high-pressure hose to soak both carriers and spectators. Consequently, damage to the tower is almost inevitable and expected. The fact that such behaviour is appropriate and staged suggests that it cannot be explained as an attack on anything.

If the corpse is badly treated, the tower partially or wholly destroyed and real anger shown, then this is a true 'disruption', which goes beyond what is expected. However, even this cannot necessarily be construed as a challenge to hierarchy, since it is much more likely to be a protest against the family performing the cremation or the person being cremated. Cremation is the occasion *par excellence* for delivering final judgements on the character and behaviour of the deceased and/or his immediate kin group. If the deceased's conduct in life was deplorable, his family is very unpopular or his descent group is making an unjustifiable claim to a status position above that which has general assent, then disruption is likely. It is probably for this reason that the Déwa group of Genteng was unwilling to cremate any of its dead, suspecting, with good reason, that the ceremony would be a fiasco. While an attempted Déwa cremation would probably generate conflict between those wishing to restore the *status quo ante* and those desirous of establishing a hierarchical relation where none previously existed, such a conflict would not be about hierarchy in general, but only about this specific and contested assertion of superior status.[7]

These arguments can be extended further. The first point to note is that cremation constitutes a secondary treatment of the corpse (Hertz 1960). At death the corpse is buried and this ceremony is small-scale, quiet and sombre and involves the ritualized (and real) expression of mourning and weeping, though a great show of emotion is not considered appropriate. The noise, exuberance and unbridled emotions of a cremation can thus be seen as the structural counterpoint to burial (Bloch 1982).

Second, if burial is primarily about the death and loss of a specific individual, cremation is more about the release of the soul and its future reincarnation, and thus about fertility and the reproduction of society. Consequently, it becomes, in part at least, a joyous event to be celebrated.

---

[7] It would also appear that disruptions at some cremations are motivated by reasons which have as much to do with preserving the roles and status of high priesthood. In the village of Tribhuana in Klungkung, several cremations have been disrupted. Most of the villagers are members of the commoner Pasek group. Within this group there are two very different views on whether priests of this Bali-wide group, some of whom have now been officially elevated to a level equivalent to *pedanda* (Brahmana priests), should be allowed to officiate at cremation and other ceremonies instead of the *pedanda*. By far the largest faction in the village wishes to stay with the Brahmana priests, and has terrorized the smaller faction with tactics which include stoning their houses and burning their fields. There were also attempts to attack a cremation tower, but this did not materialize because the police were called in to safeguard the event. The larger faction had even taken to calling itself 'the *pedanda* loving group' ('*kelompok pecinta pedanda*') (Pitana 1997: 305).

Third, if primary burial is to cremation as silence is to noise, this does not finish the matter, for right at the end of cremation when the corpse is burning, silence again prevails, accompanied only by some restrained singing. Moreover, in some cremations I have witnessed, there is a short and very hushed ceremony on the day after cremation, called *ngirim* (to despatch). At dusk a small procession returns to the cemetery. Before it reaches the graveyard, but, when it is in sight, the participants sit down quietly, the priest says a few prayers and, drawing a line across the road with a staff, he marks the final separation between the living and the dead.

Fourth, cremation performances conform well to the normal rules of hierarchy concerning precedence of high castes over low castes, relative head height and proper linguistic usage, suggesting that reversals of status are not very prominent.

Finally, status and wealth provide privileges but they also carry obligations. Those who are rich, powerful and of high status must be socially accessible, distribute their wealth in lavish ceremonies and feasts, treat people with respect and participate enthusiastically in hamlet affairs. Failure to behave appropriately gets one branded as arrogant, aloof and mean and generates strong emotions, which may be violently expressed at cremation. If hierarchy itself were the target of abuse at cremations, disrupted gentry cremations would be the rule, not the exception, and the character of the deceased would be largely irrelevant. I have seen perhaps twenty gentry cremations in various parts of Bali, and only one of these, which is described in the next chapter, could be properly described as disrupted; I also make reference to a disrupted cremation in the next section of this chapter, but I did not see it. Virtually all the examples Warren (1993: 79–84) draws on in her account also refer to the way in which participants felt the deceased had been negligent in his or her obligations to others during life. In fact, then, what is at issue most of the time is the discrepancy between the expectations the hamlet had concerning the dead person or his descent group and the manner in which either has practically behaved. In such circumstances, any expression of criticism might best be seen, not as a challenge to the hierarchy, but rather as an affirmation of it. High-status people who have behaved fittingly during their lives are usually given a resounding send-off.

Inflating titles: the Ngakan & Déwa Gedé of Corong

In the colonial period, the Dutch restructured Balinese hierarchy in the image of what they thought a stable caste system should look like. They ignored the many differences that existed amongst the large number of commoner groups, whom, on the advice of the high priesthood, they lumped together and called Sudra. This became a category sharply distinguished from those of high caste, the Triwangsa. Amongst the former were some individuals and groups that had risen to prominence in the administration of the noble courts and had thus secured valuable privileges. Once reclassified as Sudra, they suffered the double blow of losing their privileges and becoming eligible for corvée labour for the state. Consequently, these and other commoner groups strove to prove that in reality they should be accorded Triwangsa status. In freezing caste, the Dutch unwittingly increased status conflict.

However, explanations for this form of status mobility do not address the issue of those already enjoying a high position striving to raise themselves even higher.[8]

---

[8] I am grateful to Raechelle Rubinstein for pointing this out to me.

In such cases, status aspirations were not pursued to avoid corvée labour, since the groups concerned were already exempt. This suggests that status climbing may also be a function of the prestige and the related forms of identity that attach to titles qua titles. Superior titles secure augmented prestige, 'higher' ritual prerogatives and further forms of deference from inferiors. The forms of identity involved are disjunctive, since they are not about being 'Balinese' but about being very particular kinds of Balinese.

In the following example, concerning two gentry groups in the village of Corong in the Gianyar region, the Déwa and the Ngakan, there is little more at stake than the right to use particular titles and to benefit from the immaterial status prerogatives which accompany them. The absence of other considerations demonstrates just how significant titles in themselves still are.

The Déwa and Ngakan are located at the lower end of the gentry part of the hierarchy, being placed below the Brahmana, Cokorda and Anak Agung groups but above the Gusti. The Déwa are usually accorded superiority over the Ngakan by other villagers.

For a long time, the Ngakan have been claiming Déwa status, while the Déwa have been trying to maintain their distance from them. The full title of the former group is *pungakan*, and its literal meaning is 'chipped' or 'broken', usually of a knife or the piece that has broken off, leaving the knife jagged. It is the name of a status group of the Satria category; Barber (1979: 619) employs the phrase 'a chip off the satriya block' to describe them. Friederich (1959: 110) says that Pungakan are 'Satrias who have much Sudra blood in their veins'. Clearly not a flattering name, it suggests that the group originated in a discreditable manner.

Several stories recount their origin. In one, *ngakan* is the title given to descendants of a ruler's subordinate wife, those from the primary wife having the title *déwa*. In another, it is the inferior title bestowed on the children of a liaison between a ruler and a commoner woman. A third records that the son of a ruler with a *déwa* title is demoted to *ngakan* and then exiled because he slept with one of his father's wives (Sueta 1993: 26). In some of these stories, female Ngakan have the title *sang ayu*.

The thirty houseyards of the Ngakan of Corong are mostly concentrated in one of the village's four hamlets. They do not constitute a cohesive group but are divided into several different descent lines, some with origin temples (*kawitan*) in Corong, some in nearby villages. On the whole, the Ngakan are not very active in formal and public village political affairs, holding just a few minor posts. None of them is a hamlet leader and none has been the village head.

About half of the group owns wet-rice land, but the difference between Ngakan owners (0.5 hectare per capita) and the commoner owners who live in the same hamlet (0.47 hectare per capita) is negligible. A small majority of Ngakan are occupied in farming either their own or other people's land, but many are also engaged in a wide variety of other economic activities of a skilled or unskilled nature. Some also have jobs as schoolteachers and policemen, and some work in the regional and provincial government offices in Gianyar town and in Denpasar, Bali's capital. Many of those in higher-level positions have moved out of Corong and built houses in the towns where they work, and a dozen or so work in the cities of Java and elsewhere in Indonesia. Many of these latter families nevertheless maintain contact with their natal homes, reinvesting in them to repay the debts to their kin whose sacrifices provided the opportunities for their advancement. Those resident in Bali regularly attend major ceremonies at home because failure to do so angers the ancestors. Their continuing influence on village life is still keenly felt and they have had an impact on the status aspirations of some of the Ngakan groups.

These aspirations are manifest in the new titles some have adopted. Older men continue to call themselves and be called by others *ngakan*, and their wives use the title *sang ayu*. However, many younger Ngakan call themselves *déwa ngakan* or simply *déwa*. These address their children as *déwa* and their wives are called *désak*. When I addressed these as *ngakan*, I was sometimes upbraided and told 'I am a Déwa.' On occasions when I asked a Ngakan if his title was *ngakan* or *déwa*, I was told it did not matter because these were the same. Identifying oneself as Déwa had clearly become an important and sensitive issue. While many of those in the superior Brahmana, Cokorda and Anak Agung groups considered such behaviour presumptuous and an affectation, they were largely indifferent to what the Ngakan called themselves, because it could not be construed as a challenge to them. Several said it was none of their business, and in any case little could be done about it.

Those angered by this swollen claim were the village's group of Déwa, all of whom belong to one unified descent group, worshipping at one origin temple, and who are closest in status to the Ngakan. The group consists of fourteen houseyards and their genealogies show a great deal of intermarriage. In contrast to the Ngakan, there are no blemishes attached to the group at all, as is clear from their full title, *déwa pikandel*, the latter term meaning 'trustworthy' and 'reliable' (Warna 1978: 43). According to some, the title was bestowed on them by the local ruler because of the dependable manner in which they carried out their duties in and around the palace. These pre-colonial links have now all disappeared, but many Déwa willingly provide voluntary labour at the palace and give the Cokorda enthusiastic support.

To nullify the threat from the Ngakan, the Déwa too had begun to change their titles. What incensed them was the fact that, once a male child became *déwa ngakan*, he would be addressed simply as *déwa*, the *ngakan* part being dropped. Such titles were thus indistinguishable from those of male children of Déwa parentage, who would also be called *déwa*, thus suggesting that the two groups were of equal status. By such a strategy, the Ngakan obliterated the main distinction between themselves and the Déwa.

While the distinction between these two groups is not confined solely to titles, there are, in fact, few other features that clearly differentiate them. Déwa consider themselves to be direct descendants of the old Klungkung ruling dynasty and thus to be Satria Dalem (*dalem* indicating a greater degree of 'insiderness' than *jero*), and they claim nine roofs for their cremation towers and various other ritual prerogatives. However, those in Anak Agung descent groups repudiate this and maintain that Déwa are entitled to only seven roofs, which is the number usually used by Ngakan. Nevertheless, in the cemetery, Déwa are buried just downstream of Anak Agung and upstream of Ngakan, who are interred a little upstream of Gusti, these placements giving a crude physical representation of status differences (see Figure 6.1). Finding it very difficult to secure their claims to Satria Dalem status because of resistance from above, the Déwa are also concerned that their position should not be further undermined by being eroded from below. But, since little else distinguishes the Déwa from the Ngakan, the titles in themselves have become a crucial criterion of relative ranking. Because of this conflict, there have been few marriages between the two groups in recent years, and they are not invited to each other's rituals.

At this point, it is necessary to supply some background information on marriage patterns, with more details provided in later chapters. In villages such as Corong, marriage is preferentially title-endogamous amongst the gentry, so that, for example, Brahmana marry other Brahmana, Déwa marry other Déwa, and so on. Hypergamous marriages, in which, for example, Brahmana men take women from lower-status groups, are also approved and quite frequent.[9] Hypogamous marriages, men marrying women from higher-status descent lines, are tolerated so long as the gap in status is not large – a female Brahmana marrying an Anak Agung man, for instance. While many commoner women are taken in marriage by gentry men, the reverse is still quite rare. In the past, extreme hypogamous marriages, between Brahmana women and commoner men could be punished by death for both spouses, and even today such marriages are often detested by the parents of the woman, who subsequently gets 'thrown away' (*makutang*), that is, she is no longer recognized as a daughter by her parents. Because relative ranking is not very important amongst commoners, they marry amongst themselves with only limited concern as to their respective titles.

In contemporary Bali, titles are usually inherited through the patriline. In theory all those sharing a title are agnatic kin, but in practice such kinship is restricted to those who also share a founding ancestor marked by an origin temple, a *kawitan*. It may well be that in any particular locale the different *kawitan* of groups who share a title are also related, but usually the links can no longer be specified.

The relevant point to note here, and I shall discuss the issue in detail in Chapter 6, is that marriage between members of different gentry title groups entails the recognition, through certain asymmetrical exchanges, that one group is inferior to the other. This creates severe problems if the two groups dispute relative ranking, and the usual solution, the one adopted by the Déwa of Corong, is for the higher group to avoid marriages between its members and those of the lower group if it cannot guarantee that the latter will acknowledge its inferiority.

Those Ngakan families who have adopted new titles did so individually and at different times, so there is substantial variation among them. The Déwa group, however, collectively decided on a change of title for all their newborn children at a meeting, held around 1965, to discuss the matter. To re-emphasize the difference between Déwa and Ngakan, titles of the former were changed from *déwa* to *déwa gedé* (for males) and from *désak* to *déwa ayu* (for females) (see Table 3.1). The change is clearly marked in their genealogies, an example of which is provided in Figure 3.1 (a *ngakan* genealogy is reproduced for comparison in Figure 3.2).

Table 3.1   Name/title changes effected by Ngakan and Déwa groups

Previously		Today
(Males)	*ngakan*	*déwa ngakan*
(Females)	*sang ayu*	*désak*
(Males)	*déwa*	*déwa gedé*
(Females)	*désak*	*déwa ayu*

[9] I use the term 'take' here because that is how Balinese, men and women, habitually speak: men 'take' (*nyuang*) women in marriage.

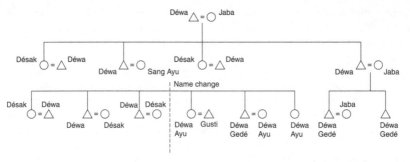

Figure 3.1 Simplified genealogy of Déwa Pikandel family showing the point at which name/title changes were instigated, from *déwa* to *déwa gedé* (males) and *désak* to *déwa ayu* (females)

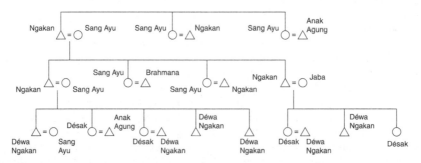

Figure 3.2 Simplified genealogy of Ngakan family showing name/title changes from *ngakan* to *déwa ngakan* (males) and *sang ayu* to *désak* (females)

Even after 30 years, some Déwa individuals are still rather sensitive about the whole business. While collecting genealogies, I enquired into the change of titles and, though some people were prepared to talk about it, others politely deflected the questions. Some Déwa denied there had been a change of title at all. Names and titles were unimportant these days, they said, and you could call yourself whatever you wanted. It was up to oneself if one wanted to be called *déwa* or *déwa gedé*. 'What is *gedé?*' one asked rhetorically. 'It is just a name anyone can use, lots of people are called *gedé*.' Even if there had been a change of title what did it matter to anyone else? Interestingly, Ngakan used very similar arguments to explain the changes they had adopted. Their point is that in the past titles were important, but now they are just parts of personal names. Therefore, such changes should be of no concern to outside parties.[10]

The significant issue in this argument is the conflation of titles with names, and the resulting ambiguity this raises. Gentry names consist of their group title, followed by a birth order term, followed by a given personal name. Thus, in the name Déwa Gedé Madé Suasta, *déwa gedé* is the title, *madé* means 'second-born' and Suasta is the given

---

[10] Of course, in the Indonesian state there is an administrative need for names to remain constant (for tax bills, identity cards, licences, etc.) and it is therefore very difficult to sustain a formal change of name unless it is ratified by the authorities. However, many villagers note that in the local context very little can be done if a family or group decides informally to use a different title. Indeed, I discovered that the titles attached to people's names on land-tax bills were frequently different from those they were now known by in the village.

personal name. The title is used as the form of address and reference. Choice can only be exercised for the given name. The same argument holds, *mutatis mutandis*, for the Ngakan and all other groups whose titles are parts of names. The word *gedé* ('big') is indeed frequently used as a personal name (I Wayan Gedé, a commoner name, for example, in which the first term is a gender marker, the second a birth-order term and Gedé is the given name), but this is quite different from the word being used as part of a title given to every member of the group as a matter of course.

Now, in contemporary Bali, many people condemn the status hierarchy by arguing that personal talent and achievement are more important than who one's parents are and that therefore titles are losing their value. By claiming that the titles are nowadays devoid of wider significance and are really nothing more than names and that names are a matter of individual taste, Balinese who change their 'names' can appear to conform to this increasingly dominant meritocratic ideology at the same time as they engage surreptitiously in enhancing their status. Of course, the claim that titles are now just personal names, and thus unimportant, is undermined by the way they are systematically changed, which indicates that gentry still invest their titles with considerable significance. If titles are inconsequential, why bother to change them?

Answers to this question, when I received one at all, almost always relied on another aspect of this new ideology. Briefly, for I shall address the issue in more detail in the next chapter, many Balinese now make a distinction between *kasta* and *warna*. *Kasta* is the hierarchical division of groups based on descent and origins. So, for example, Cokorda are superior to Anak Agung because they have closer genealogical ties to pre-colonial ruling dynasties; and the children of Cokorda keep the same title as their father irrespective of what they do in life. *Warna*, in contrast, is said to refer to the India-derived, fourfold division of the population in terms of function, and carries no ascriptive hierarchical implications. Society is based on a division of labour, the argument goes, in which everyone performs a function for the good of the whole, and titles (ruler, priest, merchant, servant, etc.) can be attached to these functions. But, if the son of a Brahmana priest becomes a labourer, he should be classed as Sudra and, if the son of a Sudra becomes a governor, in theory he should adopt the title of *cokorda*. *Warna* maintains the titles but puts them to the service of the meritocratic ideology, because the titles are rewards for achievement.

In practice, however, the *warna* theory is used mostly in a partisan way, either to claim a higher title because the one presently enjoyed does not sufficiently reflect the prestige of the job the person holds, or to complain about how others' titles convey a status disproportionate to their occupations. For example, both commoners and gentry frequently use *warna* ideology to deride the status pretensions of Brahmana youth who are uneducated and dissolute; and the Déwa of Genteng, described in the previous section, used their professional jobs to justify their elevated status claims. In Corong, one Déwa answered the question indirectly by describing the example of a family in a neighbouring village which, over three generations, had changed its title from *déwa* to *anak agung* to *cokorda*, because the office of village headman had been held by successive members of his family. Those villagers unhappy about this had been bought off with gifts and bribes.[11]

[11] I was given a slightly different version of this story from a friend who had recently retired from an administrative position in the office of the Public Prosecutor in Gianyar, and who personally knew the case. According to him, the Déwa had begun to use the title *cokorda* before he had been appointed village head. The regional governor (*bupati*), however, told him that he must drop the affectation as a condition of his appointment. He did confirm the fact that the Déwa had used bribes to effect the change of title to *cokorda*.

A further interesting theme emerged from conversations about title changes. As already mentioned, both Ngakan and Déwa claimed that the changing of a title/name should not be a cause of trouble, and other villagers said there was little they could do about it. However, some friends suggested that aggrieved ancestors might bring serious misfortune. Cremation is performed so that the deceased's soul can return to its place of origin and join the descent group's purified ancestors. This is a long and hazardous business, entailing many ceremonies. The dead person's family obtain information from a spirit medium about how the soul is progressing, whether it has reached its destination, whether it is happy and whether they have done all they can to help.

Suppose the dead person is a Déwa but his descent group have been calling themselves *anak agung* (a hypothetical case I was given). The family asks how he is and the soul replies: 'All is not well; you say I am *anak agung* but I have not yet been called. My bones have been dug up, my body has been cremated and the offerings have been made, but no one calls my name.' At cremation the name of the deceased is inscribed on a strip of palm leaf and attached to the corpse or its symbol, and it is through this that the ancestors can recognize one of their own and call the soul to them. Moreover, before cremation begins, the relatives should inform the ancestors that so-and-so is on the way to them, but if they use the wrong name there will be confusion and the soul remains in limbo and may return to haunt the family, causing sickness and misfortune.

Some Brahmana friends used this line of reasoning when discussing the commoner groups with the title *pasek*. In the past, members of Pasek groups had risen to prominence in various courts as administrators. When the Dutch lawcourts refused to recognize their privileges and instead demoted them, some put up resistance, which provoked armed retaliation from the authorities. As the century progressed, these groups often claimed descent from much more illustrious origins, stirring Brahmana to become very critical of their social-climbing pretensions: 'Pasek are *jaba* [outsiders] and will never be anything else' was how one put it. Should they try to elevate themselves, they will anger their ancestors and their souls will be unable to 'go home' and will thus return to cause trouble amongst their living descendants. Such ancestral judgements are clearly very useful for elite legitimation of the hierarchy.

It was just this kind of process that was used to explain why one large, extended family of Ngakan, living in four houseyards, had suffered so much trouble over the last ten years. Several members of this group have been highly educated and have prospered economically, moving to the capital, Denpasar, and to other areas of Indonesia. Many return to Corong at times of important ceremonies, and money is contributed to the upkeep of the houseyard temples. More recently, the group bought some land in their hamlet and built a large and impressive descent temple, in which these families now worship their ancestors. As one friend, an Anak Agung, put it to me, 'They are rich, they have nice homes, many live in Denpasar and own cars, they are educated and have good jobs, and they have an imposing temple; and if they have all this they want to change their title.' This echoes Boon (1977: 167), when he wrote that within 'a set of houseyards the wealthier family heads sometimes spearhead upward mobility, and they oblige their lower, less presumptuous kin to affirm the claims' (see also Barth 1993: 233).

The affluence of this particular group contrasts vividly with their dilapidated and moss-covered origin temple, *kawitan*, which is in a village about five miles from Corong. Those living there are still Ngakan but are mostly poor and uneducated labourers; they are the rustic relatives from which the Corong Ngakan wish to distance themselves. Since the new descent temple has been built, the Corong group has increasingly neglected their obligations to their *kawitan*. Many no longer attend the temple's annual festival (*odalan*), and for less important ceremonies there they do not even send offerings.

While improving themselves, they suffered a series of misfortunes and accidents. A child was born lame and died whilst still young. Quarrels, jealousies and malicious gossip led to an increase in the incidence of *puik*, a state of institutionalized silence between the parties to a row. But it was two further events that encouraged the family to consult a spirit medium about their troubles. The first concerned the events at a cremation in 1987. The group constructed a cremation tower with nine roofs instead of the usual seven and thus confronted the hamlet with a tower inappropriate to the status of the dead man. However, and with ill-concealed glee, friends told me that the Ngakan could not have been too confident about what they were doing since the tower was 'so small that it needed exceptionally good eyesight to count the roofs'. On the day of the burning, when the hamlet men carried the tower to the graveyard they were so excessively boisterous that it almost fell apart, and various offerings were destroyed. Moreover, when the procession passed the section of the village in which most of the Déwa live, some of them eagerly joined the fray to cause further damage. It was impossible to turn back to build a new tower and make new offerings, as it is dangerous to discontinue a ritual project once started, so they went ahead and finished off as best they could.

The other event, which occurred in 1990, was even more disastrous. An elderly Ngakan man was hit by a truck when crossing the main road which runs through the village, and he died two weeks later in hospital. This was a violent, 'bad', death, known as *salah pati*.[12] Such deaths are never 'accidents'; rather, they are sure signs that something is amiss, and to discover what the problem is the family must visit a spirit medium. The revelation disclosed that they had been very negligent towards their *kawitan* and thus to their ancestors, who had therefore become angry. The death was just one of many signs they had sent over the years to get their descendants to mend their ways. The remedy required the group to acknowledge their 'real' *kawitan*, pray there regularly and prepare a major set of offerings to atone for the previous lack of respect. Since this happened there has been a split within the group, some members returning to their *kawitan*, thus implementing the ancestors' instructions, whilst others have continued to stay away.

What is also interesting about this status drive is that it is not a peculiar and merely local affair. Many villages neighbouring Corong have resident Ngakan, and at least some of them have adopted the same kind of name changes. Equally, the Déwa Pikandel group is not confined to Corong, and Déwa in other villages have implemented changes in the names of their children. In travelling to various parts of south Bali, and in discussion with many Balinese, there is frequent mention of Ngakan on the rise. In 1993 the *Bali Post* newspaper (12 April 1993) published a report about a group of Ngakan on Nusa Penida, an island off the south coast of Bali. The article concerned several families of Ngakan in the village of Sompang who had begun using the title *predéwa*. The piece appeared because the regional governor of Klungkung (under whose jurisdiction the island falls) had been called in to ratify the change, but so far had refused to do so. He argued that he had not the power to forbid such a change so long as it was only a change of name and did not include a change of

---

[12] On death, bad deaths and cremation in general, see Warren (1993: Part 1) and Connor (1995, 1996).

descent origins. He went on to say that the Ngakan are indeed descended from Predéwa, but are now Ngakan because in the past they 'slipped caste' (*nyerod*) several times. According to the governor, it is not a light matter to change one's title. It should not be done just on the wishes of the individual or on those of a sectional interest. It requires the whole village to agree to it and for it to be authenticated by the ancestors. Only then can the governor ratify the change. The process of discussion must be carried out very carefully, otherwise there is a good chance conflict will arise within the village.

Lost origins, lost kin

In the previous examples, status elevation was presented as an ambition, and the means used to achieve it as an explicit strategy. What was clear, however, was how difficult it is for a group to improve its position in the hierarchy. Correspondingly, the passionate resistance status climbing often provokes indicates just how important relative status remains. In contrast, in this next example I document a rather unusual case of raising status. It concerns a commoner group on the island of Nusa Penida that was eventually incorporated into the Déwa Pikandel descent group in Corong. This outcome, unforeseen at the outset and therefore not based on any conscious strategy, derived from the fact that the commoners, revealed through a spirit medium to be worshipping at the 'wrong' origin shrines, had their 'true' origins, and therefore their new status, revealed and validated by the unquestionable authority of the ancestors of the Déwa group which was coincidentally searching for a section of its kin 'lost' in the distant past.

In recent times, many commoners have obtained admittance to other, larger and better organized, commoner descent groups, known generally as *warga*, through claiming identical origins. The latter have in turn often eagerly sought and welcomed new recruits because enlarging the group has enabled it to press its interests in a more determined way against other, usually gentry, groups, who also have their own *warga* associations. Potentially the largest of these commoner *warga* is the Maha Gotra Pasek Sanak Sapta Rsi, which is a pan-Bali organization of people with a *pasek* title. It was founded in the early 1950s and has campaigned for equality with Brahmana, especially by seeking to consecrate its own priests and to have them recognized as equivalent in status to Brahmana priests, the *pedanda*. The organization has in fact been successful in getting these priests formally acknowledged by the Parisada Hindu Darma Indonesia (the religious institution which administers the affairs of the Hindu community throughout Indonesia) as similar in status to *pedanda*. However, in practice, even many members of *warga* Pasek refuse to use these priests, preferring to remain with their *pedanda*, since leaving their priest is a sin and may elicit the latter's curse (Pitana 1997, 1999).

These new alignments, however, involve only small changes in status and are thus relatively easy to establish. Some commoner groups practise an 'open-door' policy by accepting at face value a medium's revelation that a petitioner is in fact a 'true' member of the group, relying on future ancestral retribution to correct the situation should a mistake have been made (Stuart-Fox 1987: 138–40).

The case I now describe must be sharply distinguished from these instances, since it entails gaining entrance to a group much higher in the hierarchy, a process which has always proved considerably more difficult and uncertain. A further unusual feature of this example is that, despite the new gentry status of the commoner group being properly ratified, it did not insist on its new prerogatives being observed, both to prevent alienating its commoner neighbours and because it would have established a disjunction between ascribed and achieved status where none had previously existed.

As explained already, the fourteen houseyards of Déwa Pikandel constitute a unified descent group in Corong, where their origin temple (*kawitan*) is situated. One of my friends in this Déwa group introduced me to a youth of about sixteen who was attending the secondary school in Corong and boarding in a Déwa house. He was not originally from Corong but came from Nusa Penida, an island off the south coast of Bali and part of the regency of Klungkung. The youth was addressed as Putu.[13] This is a high-caste birth-order term, different from the one used by commoners, so I asked whether Putu was a Déwa. Well, he was and he wasn't, came the reply. It transpired that Putu was a member of a descent group which had only recently been 'revealed' to be Déwa and admitted to the group of Déwa Pikandel. As they lived in Nusa Penida and were very poor and until recently had been commoners, they were reticent to call themselves *déwa* for fear of being considered arrogant.

How had it come about that a group in Nusa Penida had suddenly discovered themselves to be Déwa, and that their *kawitan* was in Corong? Putu himself offered an explanation. In the distant past, he said, some Déwa were expelled from their village in Bali because one of them regularly insulted (*nyabagin*) higher castes, and they ended up in Nusa Penida. As they settled down, they became *jaba* (commoners) like everyone else there and over the generations forgot they were Déwa. Eventually their true Déwa ancestors grew angry at not receiving due deference and began to blight them, which was revealed to them during a visit to a spirit medium. Later, a palm-leaf manuscript (*lontar*) suddenly appeared in the dead of night, accompanied by a blaze of fire, in the houseyard temple of a member of the group. The *lontar* was taken to the medium, who confirmed that it was a genealogical charter attesting that their real *kawitan* was in the origin temple of the Déwa of Corong. Some members of the group then visited Corong to consult the Déwa. After much discussion, they were accepted officially into the Déwa descent group.

Some aspects of this story seemed authentic. That villagers could be chased away for persistent insulting language is certainly possible. That they would flee to Nusa is also consistent with other aspects of Balinese politics. Nusa was a dumping ground for undesirables, political opposition, defeated enemies and the like (Covarrubias 1937: 47; Holt 1970: 67; Wiener 1995: 45–6), and no doubt this partly explains the island's unenviable reputation as a source of disease and powerful black magic. That misfortune besets those who forget their origins and who worship at the wrong shrines (*salah kawitan*) is also a well-known theme of Balinese culture.

On the other hand, the story also seemed preposterous. That *lontar* (and other magically imbued objects) suddenly appear in this fashion is a quite common mythical theme, but that they become the basis for discussion with distant groups who have to be convinced of their authenticity is far less plausible. Possibly the charter was fabricated. But, if so, why would the Corong Déwa be taken in by it? What had they to gain? But the most telling argument against fabrication is that the Nusa people did not appear to gain anything from this status leap other than an end

---

[13] *Putu* is a gentry birth-order name. All Balinese have one of four birth-order names. For commoners, the series is *wayan*, *nyoman*, *madé* and *ketut* (there are some variations in the second and third terms), with the fifth child again being *wayan*, whereupon the series repeats itself. For gentry the series is *putu*, *nyoman*, *madé* and *ketut*. *Putu* is therefore a clear marker of high status, and is used metonymically to refer to gentry.

to their troubles. These people were clearly not status seekers of the kind Boon has described. It became evident from Putu's description of his life back home that, although they were now Déwa, they did not attempt to draw deference from their commoner friends and neighbours, in particular, by demanding the appropriate forms of high Balinese; and they did not use the *déwa* title, for fear of irritating their co-villagers, with whom they wished to remain on good terms. This is a very different scenario from the Genteng Déwa described earlier. Indeed, the Nusa Déwa appeared to be worse off, at any rate in a material sense, because they were now obliged to celebrate major life-crisis rites with larger and more expensive offerings than had been the case previously, and they had to meet the costs of annual visits to take offerings to their new *kawitan* in Corong. All this might be seen as a burden hardly offset by their meagre status gains. Why would they go to all this trouble and expense for such apparently insubstantial rewards? Later, I visited Nusa with Putu and some Déwa friends, and the following is a combination of material from both Corong and Nusa.

A long time ago, a group of Déwa Pikandel lived in the village of T adjacent to Corong. One family of this group was expelled for persistent insulting language towards gentry. The family wandered for a while before settling down in Nusa in village K. They owned nothing and had to make their living as farmers. As everyone in the vicinity were commoners, they too confessed to this station. Gradually, the family took on a life indistinguishable from their neighbours. Since it was never used, the *déwa* title was forgotten. As the memory of their true origins faded, they came to believe they had always lived on Nusa and had always been commoners. They had built ancestral shrines and worshipped at these as though they were the family's *kawitan*.

Life was tolerable and the group began to expand, but even today they remain essentially poor. Their houses are small, dirty and dilapidated. The earth is very marginal and yields are low. Even at sea level, water is very scarce and salty, but it is virtually non-existent in the foothills and, when the wells run dry, it has to be fetched in jerrycans some two kilometres up a steep hill. In more recent times, villagers have left the island for jobs on the mainland, and others have volunteered for the transmigration schemes and begun new lives on other Indonesian islands.

Around 1972 problems began to occur. There was a series of illnesses in the group which could not be cured. At a cremation, things kept going wrong. Two people were seized by malevolent spirits (*kasusupan kala*) and ran about wildly crashing into offerings and breaking things. People bickered about the correct construction and ingredients of offerings. On the day of the burning, the men were unable to lift the cremation tower, a very good indication that the invisible forces of the Balinese world were not willing to help in the event. On its short journey, it was frequently dropped and it was a wreck by the time it reached the graveyard. People were confused (*pusing*) and could not understand why so much misfortune had befallen them. During this period, a young man, who had been ill for some time and who was thought to be bewitched, had been having a recurring dream in which he saw himself seated in a temple he did not know, but it was very peaceful and it felt good.[14] He told his father but he could not explain it.

Because of these problems, they decided to visit a *balian taksu* in Klungkung. A *balian taksu* specializes in going into trance, during which time spirits speak through the medium in order to impart revelations from the invisible world (*niskala*) (Connor

---

[14] This dream refers to the origin temple at which the group should be praying. In other cases of *salah kawitan*, Balinese say that once they enter their true *kawitan* they find it calm, peaceful and serene; that it is like being at home; that it 'fits' (*cocok*); see Geertz and Geertz (1975: 79) for similar information.

Plate 3.2 Poor and low-caste Balinese on the island of Nusa Penida who have recently become members of the prestigious Déwa Pikandel descent group of Corong

1982). During the seance, they were told they had been worshipping at the wrong *kawitan*, so their true ancestors were angry at being so long neglected and abused. They had sent messages in the form of dreams and illnesses to change their ways. The revelation also included practical information: they were refugees (*palarudan*) and their real origins were in village A in Karangasem, the easternmost regency of Bali.

On a propitious day, some members set out to visit this village, but they were not received kindly and no one took an interest in their story. They went home bitterly disappointed. There then followed a series of further visits to other mediums in different parts of Bali. On some occasions they obtained no revelation, the medium being 'dark' (*peteng*). On two occasions they were merely told that their ancestors were angry and so they should prepare various offerings. They obliged in a half-hearted way, themselves convinced that *salah kawitan* was the source of their troubles. Two other visits had also produced this explanation, and in one an unnamed village, having such and such characteristics and located near the town of Bangli, was mentioned. This time only two men went to find the village. On one occasion they thought they had found the village, only for the residents to be as indifferent to them as when they had visited Karangasem.

At this point they gave up the search, having exhausted what little spare cash they had and too dispirited to carry on; anyway they had their crops to grow. Meanwhile, far away amongst the Déwa of Corong the solution to their problems was beginning to emerge, and without them knowing anything about it.[15]

Around the same time as these events were occurring in Nusa, the Déwa group in Corong held the annual festival (*odalan*)[16] in their *kawitan* temple. Things did not proceed as they should have. Described as chaotic, quarrels broke out, a woman's tall offering fell to the ground, the dogs were restless and barked all the time, and a man was stabbed in the leg by the spur of a fighting cock and almost died of blood-poisoning. As in Nusa, it became clear that something was behind all this. The temple priest and others visited a medium but came away with the revelation that they must consult the ancestors at their own *kawitan*, since that was where the trouble lay.

The god of the temple told them, through the priest acting as medium, that long ago a group of Déwa had fled from village T and gone to live in Nusa Penida, and the ancestors now wanted them to return to the fold. The god also told them to go to the area of village K in Nusa and look for a man called Meriug, who could be identified because he had an eye defect. Three men were dispatched to Nusa to look for Meriug. However, they could not find him, but instead located a man called Kriuk who had a squint! The Corong party asked his family to assemble and told them why they had come. Each group told their respective stories and it was evident they were *saling alih*, 'searching for each other'.

Shortly after this, a group from Nusa went to Corong, where a meeting was held to introduce the newcomers. The whole story was told from both sides. After much heated discussion, it was decided to hold a test. The priest of the temple informed the

[15] In all of this account, there was no further mention of the magical *prasasti*. When we asked about this in Nusa, it turned out that Putu had confused the story of its appearance with the events concerning the search for their origins. Anyway, it transpired that it had not been a *prasasti* at all, but an unspecified palm-leaf manuscript which a very ill old man had obtained subsequent to his repeated all-night vigils in his family temple. Apparently, when the manuscript was soaked in water, the water assumed remarkable curative properties. When he died, the manuscript could no longer be found.

[16] A detailed description of a Balinese temple festival (*odalan*) can be found in Belo (1953). For the political significance of temples see, for example, Bateson (1970), Lansing (1991), Schulte Nordholt (1991a) and Stuart-Fox (1991).

god that the refugees had been found and wanted to enter the temple. If they were really 'lost' Déwa they should be allowed to enter without hindrance. As it turned out, they passed through the gate with ease. The Nusa group were then accepted as true members of this descent group.

On returning to Nusa, ceremonies were held to convert their family temple into a 'way-station' (*panyawangan*), so that they could now pray to their true ancestors while still in Nusa. Moreover, whilst in Corong, the god had advised them not to give themselves airs and graces and not to boast. To this day, they do not insist on high Balinese from their commoner neighbours, do not use the title *déwa* and have not changed their names. However, children born subsequently are now given the gentry birth-order names, such as *putu*, and to this is added the honorific *gedé* ('big'), which is also now part of the title of Corong Déwa.

Representatives from Corong have visited Nusa several times to instruct them on the making of offerings for major life-crisis ceremonies, particularly cremation. They now use a seven-roofed tower, instead of one which is normal for commoners, and the sarcophagus is a bull (*lembu*), rather than the mythical fish (*gajah mina*) which commoners generally use. On the first occasion the Nusa people carried out a cremation and used a seven-roofed tower, other villagers threatened to tear it down. An emissary from Corong was summoned so that the situation could be explained.

Clearly, the most striking fact about this story is the fantastic coincidence it embodies. One group of low-status Balinese has 'lost' its origins, and another, across the sea and some forty miles away, has 'lost' a section of its descent group. Through a curious series of revelations and wanderings, in which the two search for each other, they become united, and the commoners are elevated to a relatively high position. But this is not a straightforward case of status seeking, because the Nusa Déwa are reluctant to set themselves up above their commoner friends and neighbours. They were not the agents primarily responsible for their promotion, for they were (willing?) pawns in a game directed by others, but one in which status elevation was always a distinct possibility.

As mentioned, Nusa Penida was renowned as a place for refugees, criminals and exiles, and the belief exists that those banished there were often decasted. So it is no surprise when groups 'rediscover' lost origins. Moreover, since Nusa is supposedly home to many exiles and refugees, worshipping at the wrong shrines is a likely diagnosis for the kind of relentless misfortune which struck the Nusa group. And, of course, it is a revelation likely to be accepted with some alacrity by the petitioners. No longer are they just commoners of little account: they now have a validated connection to a prestigious high-status group in the heartland of south Bali.

In Corong, a somewhat similar scenario is played out. A series of unusual and troubling events accompanies a major ritual. Such events are always symbolic of something other than their immediate referents. In the normal course of events, women do not drop elaborate offerings, people do not quarrel in a temple and men very rarely get injured at cock-fights. For these things to happen simultaneously indicates a hidden cause. This can only be divined by gaining access to the invisible world (*niskala*), inhabited by ancestors and spirits, which otherwise remains concealed to ordinary mortals inhabiting the visible world (*sekala*). Revelations through spirit possession, dreams, visions, voices from the sky, unusual objects, and so forth, are the recognized channels by which people can obtain 'true' knowledge concerning the hidden connections between apparently unrelated events.

What is now remembered is what for these Balinese constitutes the essential kernel of truth, that there was a lost group and that they were found in Nusa. For them, what the gods say is axiomatically true, even if it is often confusing, oblique and difficult to interpret,[17] and the details are of only passing importance. In Nusa, the sequence of the many trips to mediums was very hazy. Since they were largely false trails, there was no need to remember them. When the people from Nusa tell the story, they begin with the 'fact' that originally they were exiles from village T near Corong. But they did not discover this until the Corong Déwa had contacted them. Up to that point, they had been told they originated either in Bangli or Karangasem. The story is now a reconstructed narrative focusing on origins, one that brings together only what, in the end, turned out to be 'true'. Probably, over time, the story has been moulded to fit the end result. Certain pervasive cultural themes concerning divine revelations, the character of the island of Nusa Penida, the notion of reuniting long-lost kin and the search for origins were acted out in line with and brought to fruition by personal and group interests. The coincidence is not so astonishing if one considers that it could easily never have happened, and that there are probably various groups of people still 'looking for each other'.

Conclusion

Attempts to raise status are pervasive, and the preoccupation with hierarchy is still strong. Claims to higher status enter the public domain in various ways: changes in names/titles, possession of genealogical charters, the building of new 'origin' temples, changes to ritual paraphernalia, divine revelations, and so forth. Such claims succeed only if they are acceptable to other groups, and this depends on allegedly new origins being authenticated as 'true' origins. This can be achieved by deities, speaking through mediums, or by experts in genealogical history validating claims to new ancestry and ratifying incorporation into superior groups. If this happens, new attributes are endorsed through the implementation of new exchange relations. Conversely, claims are regularly contested and repudiated if they cannot be substantiated in acceptable ways.

Commoner groups are as involved in status assertion as are gentry groups. While some criticize hierarchy as anachronistic, others try to elevate themselves to gentry status, and some do both in different contexts. Some commoner families of Genteng proclaim Déwa origins, and across Bali the large commoner groups known as Pandé and Pasek assert that in reality they have very illustrious origins and so campaign for equality with Brahmana (Guermonprez 1987; Pitana 1999). In addition, individual commoner families attempt to disguise their lowly status by using gentry titles as personal names. They give their children grandiose names, such as I Wayan Gedé Agung.

In the three cases discussed in this chapter, material factors play a significant role in status assertion. Wealth, education and prestigious occupations produce a

---

[17] This is also true of spirit mediums who provide revelations. People prefer to visit mediums in other villages because they are less likely to know anything about the problems that beset the petitioners, and therefore they can have more confidence in what is disclosed. However, mediums are notorious for the confusing and sometimes contradictory messages they reveal, thus forcing the petitioners to divulge more details of their plight, which in turn helps the medium to fine-tune the revelation. The spirit speaking through the medium may also question the petitioners, who are obliged to answer, and they can be domineering and quarrelsome, ordering supplicants not to question what they say. If spirits make conflicting statements, that is not something petitioners should question, for what can they know of the *niskala* world?

situation in which a group sees its ritual status as out of step with its material accomplishments. Material affluence and political power combine to generate a gap between a successful, cosmopolitan group and its backward and poor relatives, encouraging the former to disassociate itself from the latter and to close the gap between itself and those above. This may set off a chain reaction, in which superior groups struggle to maintain distinctions of rank they see being whittled away and inferior ones strive to preserve equality as status distinctions are introduced where none previously existed. The example of the commoners from Nusa Penida reinforces this conclusion. It was because they were so poor that they could not insist on their new status prerogatives.

While these examples seem to demonstrate that status, wealth and power are intimately connected in Balinese minds and are not independent systems of prestige, the connection depends on whose perspective is being considered. Groups which become affluent try to convert wealth into status, but those they leave behind reject the association by arguing that the only authentic test for acknowledging a rise in status is ancestral validation of descent from more celebrated origins. Many Balinese bridle at having to show deference to those with a higher title but whose poverty, weakness or disreputable behaviour renders it less noteworthy. Conversely, others maintain they themselves should have a higher title because they possess material wealth, good jobs or powerful political positions. Members of the commoner Pasek group in Corong, for example, denounce gentry pretensions on the grounds that in modern Indonesia 'we are all now the same', but in other contexts proudly proclaim their allegedly high-caste ancestry. In light of this, one can conclude that there is no intrinsic or necessary relation between wealth and power on the one hand and status on the other, but only *claims* that certain relations do or do not exist, claims that are advanced by particular individuals and groups to achieve specific ends.

4
The Politics of 'Caste'
hierarchy & equality in conflict

Introduction

For much of the twentieth century, many Balinese have been engaged in a series of critiques of 'traditional' gentry practices. These have often had very specific and clear aims, such as reforming cremation procedures. Because they were, and remain, a mainstay of elite status assertion, royal cremations developed into spectacular rituals requiring massive expenditure (Geertz 1980). At different times this had inflationary repercussions on all cremations, because those lower down the hierarchy competed to keep up with those above by making their own burnings more elaborate. As a result some Balinese were reduced to penury and many could not afford to cremate at all. Consequently, as part of the more general critique of traditional religion, some Balinese began to raise objections to cremation procedures in the 1920s on both economic and religious grounds, and over the course of that century many reforms making cremation easier and less expensive were implemented (Warren 1993; Connor 1996; I return to this issue in the following chapter).

But, by protesting against the costs of such ceremonies and by arguing that it is a person's actions in life that determine the fate of the departed soul, rather than the status-sensitive paraphernalia of cremation, such a commentary becomes a form of cultural politics directed against those practices which encode status hierarchy. As such it amounts to an egalitarian critique of gentry dominance. While it remains very difficult to dislodge the gentry from their politically and economically powerful positions in Balinese society, attacks targeted at the cultural basis of their domination can be effective.

Other indigenous critiques of Balinese society have similar intentions. In later chapters, I look at a number of issues concerning the cultural politics of religion in Bali, in which new, relatively egalitarian devotional movements are seen as both alternatives to and sources of inspiration for the reform of the hierarchical and ritual-bound traditions of village and court religion.

In short, these critiques tend to have as a constant and underlying theme an egalitarian critique of hierarchy. In this chapter I examine aspects of this critique by looking at some of the processes which, over the course of the twentieth century, have led to changes in the relationship between ideologies of hierarchy and equality.

While some authors have denied the existence of egalitarian relations in pre-colonial Bali (Schulte Nordholt 1986: 31), others have argued that hierarchy and equality are engaged in 'a war without end' (Geertz and Geertz 1975: 167) and yet others claim that relations of equality are of paramount importance in modern Bali

(Warren 1993).[1] I try to make sense of these disparate views by arguing that the relationship between hierarchy and equality is historically contingent rather than stable and that, since 1900, egalitarian relations have gradually, but contentiously, assumed greater significance in Balinese life.

My argument grows out of ethnography from the all-commoner village of Pujung, where I first carried out fieldwork. In the particular context of the cultural politics of identity in Balinese society I note the importance of the recent politicization of a myth that has prominent egalitarian features. This myth is being increasingly used by commoners in the Gianyar area of central Bali to anchor their origins further back in time, and thus more authentically, than those of gentry. As such, this myth provides a sense of identity and pride, which is both independent of and a counterpoint to the previously dominant gentry myth of origins. This latter myth depicts the civilizing of Bali by the refugee rulers of the Hindu-Javanese kingdom of Majapahit, who fled to Bali from central Java in the fourteenth century to escape from encroaching Islam. They established a court in Gélgél, now seen as *the* origin point for Balinese gentry. Through the building of temples and palaces, as subordinate replicas of those in Gélgél, across the landscape of Bali, they expanded their control over the island and converted ordinary Balinese into subjects, dependants or slaves.[2] Through this rule nobles supposedly introduced into Bali the elaborate forms of hierarchy, etiquette and art of Javanese court society. However, this is not a simple matter of opposing one myth against another, because ambitious and powerful commoners are often eager to set themselves up as gentry in villages where 'real' gentry are not present. To distance themselves from other villagers, they adopt gentry strategies in ritual and marriage and try to emphasize those hierarchical themes which are subdominant in the commoner origin myth.

In the subsequent section, I describe a case of violent 'caste' conflict in the village of Klakah. In this long-running dispute, commoners have been trying to coerce a gentry group into giving priority to its obligations to the collective social life of the hamlet (*banjar*) instead of to its more exclusive descent traditions. The conflict is played out primarily in relation to the use of the cemetery and cremation ground. On the surface, it appears to be a struggle between the more egalitarian relations of co-residence and the more hierarchical relations of kinship and descent. However, the case highlights how there are also rival interpretations of what the modern *banjar* stands for and whether it is antagonistic to hierarchy or can accommodate it.

Finally, I examine a contemporary controversy concerning divergent interpretations of the fundamental nature of Balinese social structure. In brief, many Balinese, but especially commoners, public officials and urban intellectuals, expound an

---

[1] There is a further aspect to this issue which should be mentioned, though I do not propose to discuss it here. This is the idea that Balinese residing in the mountainous regions of the island and one or two other areas are the 'original' Balinese, the so-called Bali Aga or Bali Mula, who evince more egalitarian forms of social organization than those living in the rice basins of the coastal plains. Usually such arguments revolve around the difficulties of producing a surplus at altitudes where irrigated rice cannot be grown and where dry-garden production systems dominate. Where wet-rice cultivation generates surpluses, hierarchical relations have emerged. For details, see Liefrinck (1927), Korn (1932), Grader (1937a), Lansing (1983a), Guermonprez (1987, 1990), Howe (1989b), Hobart et al. (1996) and Reuter (1999).

[2] The myth is recorded in the *Babad Dalem*, the chronicle of the kings of Gélgél and Klungkung, though aspects of it form a background and context to a great many other texts. Most temples have shrines dedicated to Majapahit, and the outlines of the myth are well known to most Balinese, though it is primarily gentry who routinely refer to it to explain where they came from, and therefore who they are. The relation of the Majapahit myth to actual historical events and the general sociological significance of the myth have been hotly debated (Hinzler 1976, 1986; Supomo 1979; Schulte Nordholt 1986; Vickers 1989; Creese 1995; Wiener 1995).

ideology which was first developed in the 1920s, though in a rather different form. It states that a social organization based on hierarchical status ascribed by birth and defined by titles, and denoted by the term *kasta*, is a mutation of a prior, more authentic and more meritocratic organization, denoted by the term *warna*, in which titles should only be associated with the functions that people perform in society. These conflicting arguments, which pit a reformist, egalitarian doctrine against the hierarchical ethos of the old aristocracy, provide another context in modern Bali for contesting the future direction of the island's development.

Hierarchy & equality in Pujung

What is fascinating about ideas and practices of hierarchy and equality is that together these antagonistic models of social organization constitute an important aspect of an indigenous cultural politics about the ultimate origins of the Balinese, and therefore about their 'true' nature and identity.

The concept of 'origin' (*kawitan*) is enormously important to contemporary Balinese because it connects Balinese to their ancestors and so to the source of life, prosperity and safety.[3] As we have seen, if Balinese do not know their origin point or have been told they are worshipping at the wrong one, they go to great lengths to find their true origin. Balinese say that ignorance of their *kawitan* causes disorientation and confusion. Moreover, ancestors are jealous and demanding and, if they cannot establish relations with their descendants through the proper channels, the temple shrines, they resort to direct and dangerous methods, such as afflicting them with misfortune and illness.

By anchoring Balinese in the past, the *kawitan* establishes their place in the present and the proper forms of relationship they have with others. However, the last century witnessed a growing struggle over the nature of the relationships that should exist among Balinese, which has in turn problematized the positions which Balinese now occupy in society. Because the present is ineluctably linked to and flows from the past, this struggle often manifests itself in conflict over origins. Questions about who the original Balinese were, what form their institutions took and what was the status of a group's real ancestors are not therefore of merely historical interest, but highly political issues of contemporary significance.

Gentry represent themselves as descendants of Javanese elites who mythically invaded Bali in the fourteenth century and introduced court culture and the 'caste system'. In contrast, many commoners see themselves as ultimately descended from a pre-conquest Javanese/Indian sage, Rsi Markandeya, whose followers founded many villages in south central Bali and imbued them with a markedly egalitarian social organization.

The concept of origin plays a complex role in this conflict. In the Majapahit myth, origin is significant in three connected senses, all of them concerned with hierarchy.

---

[3] Whether the concept of *kawitan* has always had the significance it now possesses is a difficult question. Guermonprez (1987: 54-65) argues that, in the past, while *kawitan* linked Balinese to their ancestors, this was used merely to express differences at a local level which were not hierarchized. As Islam spread through Java during the seventeenth century, Balinese rulers used the myth to integrate local differences into a much wider and totalizing scheme of classification, which attached differential and hierarchical value to *kawitan* in terms of distance from the centre. The Majapahit myth then became a form of ideological resistance to the threat of Islam by constructing Bali as the last bastion of Hinduism in the archipelago (Schulte Nordholt 1986: 11-13).

First, the more illustrious a person's origin point, the higher the rank in the contemporary hierarchy. This is why claims to higher status require validation by reference to more prestigious origins. Secondly, the genealogically closer to the origin, the higher the rank, so a ruler's son is superior to his brother's son. Thirdly, chronological closeness to the source correlates with rank, so that elder siblings are superior to younger ones and later descendants are inferior to earlier ones.

In the Markandeya myth, however, only the last of these has any force, so that Balinese with earlier origins construe themselves as more authentic than those with later ones (cf. Reuter 1999). In Balinese discourses, then, the concept of origin is ambiguous. In one sense it concerns the hierarchical ordering of groups in accordance with the relative ranking of their original ancestors, but in another it concerns an argument about chronology. I shall first examine this issue in relation to ethnography from the village of Pujung in northern Gianyar.

Pujung, with a population of about 1,600 people, is located a few metres below the altitude at which irrigated rice can be grown. It is an all-commoner village, as are nearly all its contiguous villages to the east, west and north.[4] There were undoubtedly connections with the noble court at Gianyar in the nineteenth and part of the twentieth centuries, but these were never very significant. The village's name, deriving from the terms *pa-* (place marker) and *ujung* (tip, edge), indicates that it was on the outer periphery of court influence.

The establishment and growth of Pujung are documented in a series of myths which evince striking egalitarian features. The first one I provide is another example of *saling alih* ('searching for each other'), but this has no overtones of status climbing.[5] In fact, it has the opposite intention, for it provides justification for the egalitarian aspects of the social structure of Pujung.

In the distant past, the great volcano of Gunung Agung in eastern Bali erupted and caused devastation. Many homeless people wandered the countryside before they found a place to settle. One group of five men strayed into the area of Pujung and decided to camp overnight. Each member of the group was carrying a special object (livestock, blowpipe, rice and wine, staff, gold and silver). During the night a second group of five men stumbled into the area. These had no possessions at all. When they saw the first group they became envious and planned to rob them. They waited until all were asleep, quickly snatched the objects and ran off.

The first group tracked their assailants to Pujung and, thinking that the thieves must have come from there, went to find the village headman. He denied responsibility for the crime but offered his help. The real culprits were soon found, and the two groups confronted each other. Before they could fight, the headman stepped between them. He asked each one in turn where he had come from and what he had been carrying.

The result of the questioning was that both groups protested they were the rightful owners of the various objects. Even when those robbed described in great detail their

[4] Most Triwangsa reside in the larger villages of the southern plains, where the major noble courts are situated, and are virtually absent from villages at higher altitudes. This geographical centrality of high-status groups correlates with their central location in the villages where they do live. Royal and noble lineages are thus literally, as well as ideologically, at the centre (see Chapter 6 for further information).

[5] The practice of *saling alih* is evident at more inclusive levels of the state. A prime motive of pre-colonial kings in Bali and Java was to unify the realm. However, because many features of the South-East Asian Indic states created pressures leading to disruption, partition of the state often occurred (Schrieke 1957: 82; Ricklefs 1974). Mythically, one means of trying to ensure future unification was to separate princely children at birth to opposite ends of the kingdom, so that they could later marry and bring the factions together again (Boon 1990: 224).

possessions, the robbers refused to admit their guilt, saying that they themselves had brought these things. The village headman was hopelessly confused and decided to ask advice from the god of the main village temple. The god, speaking through the entranced priest, asked the same questions and received the same replies, but immediately noticed that the members of the two groups were related to each other, and thus had the same origins: the man from Batukaru was really the lost brother of the man from Batukang, the one from Sri Merta was the lost brother of the one from Sri Kentel, and so forth. Once the god had told them this, they began to discuss biographies and soon discovered the truth of what the god had said. Finally, the god announced that, since the objects were not the sole property of either group, those things which could be divided up should be shared, whilst those which could not should be held as heirlooms in the temple, and that they should all reside in Pujung. All concurred with the god's proposals and the rice and wine were passed around to celebrate the agreement.

This is no mere legend; it is actually enacted every year in the dead of night during the temple's annual nine-day festival. Under the eerie light of the full moon, many of the village's young men take part in what is an exciting and dramatic spectacle. The ceremony ends with the making of plain rice pudding, which is distributed just before dawn to all farmers, who take it to their rice fields to give to the rice goddess, Déwi Sri. Since, in the legend and in the ritual, everyone eats and drinks the rice and wine from the same containers, thus connoting similar status, it is one of several features of Pujung life which points to the egalitarian dimension of its social organization.

A second origin myth concerns the legendary trek across Bali of Rsi Markandeya and his followers. Markandeya is recognized as the founder of part of the Besakih temple complex, the foremost temple in Bali. Even though the existence of this myth has rarely been mentioned in the literature, the first published account of it appearing in 1974 (Anandakusuma 1974), I believe it to be quite old. I collected several versions of it in 1979 in and around Pujung, where it was very widely known (Howe 1980). According to MacRae (1998: 119), several new Balinese publications have now recorded the myth in print, and in the Ubud area 'the story [is] trundled out routinely' to explain the foundation of local villages and temples. However old this myth may be, I suggest that its political ramifications have only more recently come to the fore. In line with both a postwar resurgence of commoner aspirations to play a more significant part in deciding Bali's future, which entails a more concerted opposition to continuing gentry dominance, and the growing importance of the 'Hinduizing' of Balinese religion, the Markandeya story has assumed a significant role in Balinese cultural politics, at least in the Gianyar region. Markandeya has become important to the construction of identity among some commoner groups, who now see him as their primordial, and Indian, ancestor.

The most detailed version of the myth I collected narrates that Markandeya was a *yogi*, the grandchild of the Hindu god Pasupati, and that he was the first to bring Hindu teachings to Bali. He left his home in India and first meditated on the top of a mountain in Java, where he received instruction to spread the teachings of Hinduism further east (i.e. in Bali). He gathered his many followers and set off. Eventually they reached a heavily forested area, which they began to cut down. However, this unleashed a plague and many of his followers died. Dispirited he returned to Java. He tried once again and this time, before chopping down the trees, he instructed his priests to carry out various rituals to placate the evil spirits. This proved successful and he and his followers subsequently founded and populated many villages in central Bali. He then travelled eastward until he reached the slopes of the volcano,

Gunung Agung, where he erected a shrine, which became the basis for the Besakih temple.[6] As told in Pujung, twelve families of Markandeya's following settled in a region which they called Telepud (Pujung's name on occasions ritually significant for the whole village).

These events are said to have taken place a long time before the arrival of the Javanese conquerors from Majapahit, to whom gentry look to establish their origins. Since disputes about relative status are commonly phrased in idioms of ultimate origins, if commoner groups cannot enhance their status in terms of the Majapahit model of origins, they now have recourse to an alternative that pictures their origins as even deeper in the past, a model that supports their credentials both as the first and most authentic Balinese and as the proper heirs to an ancient Hindu heritage. Politicizing this myth also reinforces the 'tradition' of corporate equality as historically deep.

It is in the final part of the myth, of which there are several different versions, that an ideology of collective equality emerges. The accounts differ in relation to the composition of the settler families. In one version no names are mentioned, the implication being that they were all of equal status. This is corroborated by a second version, which names the leader as I Nengah Bedil, an obvious commoner name. A third version, in contrast, names the leader as Sri Dalem Jangkus, which incorporates a very high title, while the other families all have commoner names. However, notwithstanding these variations, there is general public assent to what is considered to be the most significant part of the story, which is that, while the settlers may have been of different status, once they arrived in Telepud it was decided that these distinctions should be suppressed. Everyone in the village, rich and poor alike, stress this aspect of the story. They say 'we are all equal' (*onyangan patuh*), 'we are all from a single source' (*tunggal sumbah*), 'of one family' (*manyama*). The Markandeya legend is therefore invested with a strong egalitarian emphasis, enabling commoners to resist the hierarchical implications of the Majapahit model of origins and descent by substituting another and older model.

However, the Markandeya story can be interpreted in radically different ways. In public, members of elite families in Pujung enthusiastically endorse the egalitarian lessons embedded in the Markandeya legend in order to harness village support for development schemes (for example, a new market-place, the renovation of temples to attract tourists, and so forth). These schemes often entail equal contributions from all villagers, irrespective of their ability to pay. This leads to accusations that, because the rich are able to take greater advantage of the rewards the schemes generate, they benefit more than the poor. In other and more private contexts, however, some of the same elites emphasize the version of the myth naming the leader as Sri Dalem Jangkus, presumably to substantiate their claims to superiority over other villagers (*sri dalem* being a title also associated with the first kings of the Gélgél/Majapahit dynasty).

Another part of Pujung's origin myth concerns the villagers' need to obtain the services of a blacksmith (*pandé*). The leader of Pujung prayed to god to send them a blacksmith and one duly arrived. It was explained to him that the division of people into different status groups was not known in the village and therefore it was not necessary to speak high Balinese. The blacksmith agreed, as he did to the condition that the number of roofs on his cremation tower be reduced from seven to five as a

---

[6] For further details of the Markandeya legend and its relation to Besakih and to the temple networks and villages of the Wos valley, see Stuart-Fox (1991), Pitana (1997: 126–8), and MacRae (1998).

sign of his good faith.[7] Today in Pujung this injunction is still observed, but there is an interesting aspect to it. At cremation, Pandé use a five-roofed tower, whereas everyone else uses only one roof, which clearly maintains a dimension of status hierarchy; and Pandé always take precedence over other commoners, though not priests, in formal processions. However, this privilege is tempered by two other practices. Very infrequently, the village carries out a massive post-cremation ritual (*nyekah*). This requires effigies of all those who have been cremated in the period since the previous ceremony to be cremated a second time, but on this occasion all on the same five-roofed tower, irrespective of whether they are Pandé or not. Here, then, all villagers are elevated to the same status position as that of the Pandé, rather than the Pandé being demoted to the lower status of other villagers.

The second point concerns the manner in which the different descent groups in Pujung pray in each other's temples, a clear and unequivocal sign of equality. In 1979 the village was divided into three descent groups (Pandé, Pasek Gélgél and Pasek Batuan), all of commoner status, and a large number of families who would not admit to being a member of any named descent group.[8] The two Pasek groups were both quite small but at the core of them were the richest and most powerful men in the village. They held high positions in village religious administration, several were important priests, and many local government officials were their clients. This tight-knit faction was resented by others, who compared its methods of directing village affairs to the way a farmer leads his cow; the latter called the rest of the village the *banjar belog* (the 'stupid' *banjar*) because of its apathy.

Each of the descent groups possessed a temple where they prayed to their ancestors. Now in most parts of Bali it is unusual for members of one descent group to pray in the temple of another. As often as not, such groups compete with each other (Geertz 1967; Geertz and Geertz 1975: 76–84). However, in Pujung the situation is entirely different and the vast majority of families are members of all three worship

---

[7] The status of Pandé groups is very complex and this is not the place to go into the details. Guermonprez (1987) has written extensively about many groups of Pandé, including those to be found in Pujung. They have a very ambivalent relationship to the gentry, since some claim to be much earlier inhabitants of Bali than the latter, who are mythically descended from the Javanese conquerors of Majapahit and who are thus seen as newcomers. This is one of the reasons why many refuse to use the ritual services of *pedanda* priests but instead use their own priests, and why some Pandé claim to be of equivalent status to Brahmana, also asserting that their progenitor was the god Déwa Brahma (Pitana 1997: 108). Their association with fire and metals marks them out as a magically powerful group and may be one reason for others to accord them the high status that is indicated by their multi-roofed cremation towers.

[8] I emphasize that this was the situation in 1980. When I conducted further fieldwork there in 1993, quite a few of these non-committed villagers now asserted that they were, and always had been, members of the Pasek Gélgél descent group. In one sense, this change seems indicative of the general relevance status and hierarchy still retain for ordinary commoners, since being a member of a Pasek group in Pujung confers local prestige. On the other hand, the change is partly attributable to the growing awareness of villagers about the increasingly influential pan-Bali organization of Pasek groups known as the Maha Gotra Pasek Sanak Sapta Rsi ('The Great Family of Pasek Descendants of the Seven Saints'), founded in the early 1950s, one of whose main objectives is to fight for equality with other groups, especially Brahmana, on the basis that caste is irrelevant and all Balinese are equal.

As far as I am aware, however, the importance of this organization is still not very great in Pujung or in surrounding villages. Despite the fact that all the villagers are of commoner status, and thus there are no gentry to resist them, villagers with *pasek* titles have not yet begun using cremation towers with seven tiers, as is enjoined by their written chronicle, the Babad Pasek. Such seven-roofed cremation towers are now being occasionally used elsewhere in Bali (Pitana 1997: 203). Nor are Pasek villagers obtaining holy water from priests of this organization, known as *sri mpu*, since they still receive it from Brahmana priests. In other parts of Bali, even some committed members of the Pasek Sanak Sapta Rsi refuse holy water from *sri mpu* priests and will not allow them to officiate at their ceremonies (ibid.: 299–307).

congregations, so that the two Pasek groups pray at the Pandé shrines, the Pandé pray in both the Pasek temples and the non-committed pray at all three.[9]

These features of collective equality in Pujung, endorsed by the Markandeya legend and reinforced by the forms of hamlet equality to which attention has already been drawn, are enough to prevent elite groups in the village from being too explicit about their own status ambitions. Nevertheless, there are also aspects of Pujung's social life which clearly reflect hierarchical concerns. Prominent among these are the marriage ideologies and practices of the core members of the Pasek groups, which are similar to the strategies that are used elsewhere by gentry. Most villagers have a preference for village endogamy and for second cousins through males (*mindon uli muani*). Families of the elite Pasek and Pandé groups, however, prefer descent-group endogamy and marriage with first cousins through males (*misan uli muani*).[10] The principal families in the Pasek groups sometimes eschew village endogamy to forge marriage alliances with same-status families in other villages, another typical gentry strategy.

These marriage arrangements do not draw on the Markandeya myth of equality, but on a theme of the Majapahit representation of hierarchy, which coordinates types of marriage to status. It has been reported many times that actual first-cousin marriage is especially approved for gentry (Korn 1932: 472), whilst for commoners second-cousin marriage is appropriate. Boon has argued that such marriage practices reflect the idea that the higher one's status, the genealogically closer should one's marriage partner be. Gods are said to be properly incestuous (they may marry their twins); kings may marry their sisters 'so that the royal blood would pass undiluted to his successor' (ibid.: 471); gentry may marry their first cousins; whilst commoners may marry no one closer than second cousins. First-cousin marriage 'confirms the sanctity of the parties involved and is thought to please the ancestors', but it is also risky and one should be of 'exceptional merit to attempt it' (Boon 1977: 133). Finally, a close marriage, 'if fruitful, concentrates ancestral power (*sakti*) and manpower in the most prestigious genealogical space' (ibid.).

Clearly, marrying close relatives is also a strategy to assert claims to higher status, and in Pujung it is the core members of powerful and prestigious descent groups who do this. However, villagers articulate an ambivalence over first-cousin marriage, because, although it is status-enhancing, it is also dangerous or 'hot' (*panes*). If the parents lack the inherent capacity to sustain such a dangerous match, the marriage may produce conflict, sickly children, infertility, or even early death for the spouses. Most such marriages, and there are not many of them, are arranged. Despite the potential for disaster, some parents say that it is worth 'trying it once', because if it is successful it demonstrates one's superior status and capacity.

A further aspect of the status preoccupations of those in the Pasek groups is highlighted by the way in which core members speak of themselves as 'bigger than' (*gedénan*) and 'higher than' (*duuran*) other villagers, and that 'this house is bigger than that one', where 'bigger' can only be understood in status terms. The man (and his family) located at the very heart of the Pasek Gelgél descent group has gradually improved his personal prestige far above everyone else in the village. Wealthy, very

---

[9] They do not just pray in these temples; they are full members, who are called to meetings, subject to its regulations, pay subscriptions and have a say in all decisions concerning the temple.

[10] There are clearly stated 'rules' about such marriage practices. The Pasek families say: 'Do not marry outside the range of first cousins' (*sing dadi pegat mamisan*), and this is stated more vigorously by the core members; whilst ordinary villagers tend much more to the rule: 'Do not marry outside the range of second cousins' (*sing dadi pegat mamindon*).

talented, a one-time official in Gianyar and a highly respected priest, he has also become something of a recluse, a practice associated with all traditionally powerful people in Bali. Bar his immediate family, almost everyone in the village speaks to him in high Balinese, and his position and reputation in the village and beyond, and even his physical appearance, have come to resemble that of a Brahmana priest; and it was this man who referred to the leader of the village founders as Sri Dalem Jangkus.[11]

More details could be added to document the status divisions between the descent groups in Pujung, such as the more elaborate life-crisis rites, using bigger and more expensive offerings, which members of the Pasek groups mount, but this is sufficient to show that these groups represent themselves as the local equivalents of gentry.

The relationship between equality and hierarchy can be examined further through a discussion of the *désa* and the *banjar*. In the past, these terms have often been loosely translated as 'village' and 'hamlet', respectively, which leads one to expect that a *banjar* is a subsection of the *désa* and that the latter may consist of several *banjar*. However, many villages comprise one *désa* and one *banjar* (Guermonprez 1990), suggesting that the *banjar* cannot be viewed as merely a residential section of the *désa*. In Pujung the *désa* is an association ideally consisting of the senior ranking male (together with his wife) from each of the compounds built on *désa* territory. Mythically this is the territory marked out by the original inhabitants and kept consecrated by periodical rituals at the main village temples. The association is responsible for the moral order within this territory and for the maintenance of temples under its jurisdiction. The *banjar*, on the other hand, is composed of all married men (and their wives) in the village. Since most such villages have expanded beyond the *désa* territory, the *banjar* is several times larger than the *désa*.

Both associations meet regularly once a month, though in accordance with different calendars. The *désa* meets in a temple for a communal meal but no business is transacted; the *banjar*, in contrast, meets in a more secular building, the *wantilan*, outside the temple, and is a formal arena for the discussion of many issues (Hobart 1975). *Désa* officials obtain office by virtue of holding hereditary titles; they are unpaid and serve for an indefinite period, and they must undergo a purification ritual. *Banjar* officials are elected, paid by government and serve for a stipulated period, and they need not undergo any purification ceremony.

In Pujung both associations require priests. Those of the *désa* are temple priests, who are chosen by divine revelation, and they are almost always young, often teenagers, at the start of their careers. They can officiate only at temple ceremonies and at other ceremonies directed to gods, but are specifically excluded from life-cycle rituals and all post-mortem rites up to and including cremation, their presence at which renders them polluted. *Banjar* priests are appointed by the *banjar* after years of exemplary service, and are therefore always old. It is these priests who officiate at life-cycle rites and burial and cremation, but may also assist temple priests during temple festivals. Temple priests wear white, whereas black is more appropriate for *banjar* priests, and in the hierarchy of colours white is always 'above' black. Both types of priest should be spoken to in a more refined language than is used to ordinary villagers, but the rule is more vigorously stated for the former, who also always take

---

[11] Every house in Pujung has its own family temple (*sanggah*) in the north-east corner of the houseyard. The most sacred space of commoner temples is usually occupied by the shrine known as *ibu*, dedicated to Ibu Pretiwi, or 'Mother Earth'. However, in this priest's temple the *ibu* shrine has been displaced to make way for a *padmasana*, a shrine to the sun and to Siva, usually found only in the family temples of gentry groups.

precedence over the latter in processions and undergo a higher level purification ceremony than *banjar* priests.

In Pujung, at least, there is therefore a clear hierarchical relationship between the *désa* and the *banjar* (cf. Guermonprez 1990: 67–71). However, Warren has advanced a different interpretation of these two institutions, which, she seems to suggest, has wide-ranging applicability over both time and space. She argues that the relation between the two is one of 'identity and representation (the *banjar* is or acts for the *désa* in certain contexts) [rather] than one based on an encompassing hierarchy of value of a sacred-secular, superior–subordinate sort', and that therefore 'the *banjar* must be regarded as a practical executor and institutional expression of the *désa adat* itself' (Warren 1993: 21). In other words, the *banjar* and *désa* are not different, the former being understood as a 'manifestation of', or identical with, the latter (ibid.: 22).

Warren is correct in claiming that, where villages are large and consist of several *banjar*, the *désa* can appear to be, or indeed is, less important, while the *banjar* assumes a very central role. In the village of Corong, for instance, the *désa* association virtually never meets, the distinction between *banjar* priests and temple priests does not exist, and all *désa* issues are handled either in private meetings of *désa* and temple officials or by *banjar* associations.

Warren's argument, however, obscures rather than resolves the initial problem, namely, the coexistence of the *banjar* and the *désa*. If the *banjar* is construed as the 'practical executor or institutional expression' of the *désa*, the *désa* none the less remains as either a separate institution or a distinct concept, and therefore the relationship between *désa* and *banjar* still needs to be specified. If the relationship is one of identity, it is difficult to see why both are present. Anyway, despite the ambiguous nature of the relationship between them that Warren says exists for those of her informants residing in large, multi-*banjar* villages, there are a great many villages in Bali, such as Pujung and most of its neighbours, where the *désa* is categorically distinct from the *banjar*, where the two perform different functions and where there is no ambiguity in villagers' minds. Moreover, the view that the banjar is the executive arm of the *désa* clearly implies that the latter delegates its authority to the former, and in Balinese ideas delegation, whether it be gods to kings, kings to officials or immobile centres to active agents, is conceived hierarchically.

Further insight into this issue may be gained by situating it historically. It may be that today in large, multi-*banjar* villages, the powers and authority of the *désa* have over time been absorbed into the *banjar* for administrative ease, and in such cases the *désa* all but disappears, or remains a shadowy kind of institution that is rarely mobilized. This would account for the fact that residents in such places have difficulty in distinguishing between the two. But that should not blind us to the fact that, where the two do still coexist and are both important, there is a particular relationship between them, and my reading of the evidence is that this is hierarchical.

The relationship between *désa* and *banjar*, therefore, is not essential, but rather historically specific and in process of changing, even if this change is proceeding at different rates in different places. In the next section I argue that in the pre-colonial period the *banjar* was almost effaced by the control gentry elites exercised over villagers, but that subsequently the *banjar* grew in significance and influence. This was because the noble courts declined and because the state began to use the *banjar* as the principal channel for explaining and enacting its policies at the village level. As the *banjar* increased in importance, even usurping the authority of the *désa* in some villages and thus pushing it into the background, so too notions of corporate equality have grown in significance.

Such an interpretation suggests that in the past the ideology of corporate equality, as embodied in the *banjar*, was circumscribed by that of hierarchy, which shaped the relation between the *désa* and the *banjar* and which was reinforced by forms of domination and subordination existing between the gentry courts and commoner institutions. In the pre-colonial period, therefore, hierarchy and equality also stood in a particular relationship. Consequent on various exercises in village reorganization which tended to invest the *banjar* with more and more functions, on the decline of the nineteenth-century rulers and on the emergence of the Indonesian state, the *banjar* has achieved greater contemporary significance. Now, hierarchy and equality appear in a new, more balanced but more tense relationship. In short, the *banjar* may now be a manifestation of the *désa* in some villages, only because the relationship between the *désa* and the *banjar* has changed significantly over the last 100 years.

Present-day Bali is characterized by a more vigorously contested cultural politics about the hierarchical or egalitarian nature of Balinese society. In this context, the political advantages to commoner groups of origin myths such as the Markandeya legend have come to be more widely recognized and deployed in their fights with the old aristocracy. Thus, Rsi Markandeya is considered to be the original progenitor of a commoner descent organization called Warga Bhujangga Waisnawa, which has members in many parts of Bali. This organization, which is paralleled by similar commoner associations for Pandé, Pasek and others, attempts to advance the interests of its members, especially in relation to gaining equality with gentry. For example, its leaders encourage members not to use Brahmana priests but instead to use the consecrated priests, called *rsi bhujangga* or *sengguhu*, from their own group. At major ceremonies, such as those at the 'mother' temple Besakih, these priests co-officiate with *pedanda*. In the past, they use to sit at a lower level than the *pedanda* but, since about 1991, following successful protests, they now sit at the same level (Pitana 1997: 133). However, as we have seen, elite commoner families can rework these myths in line with their own status aspirations. This is also true of the *warga* organizations, which, though they are conventionally described as commoner, each try to claim equivalent status with gentry and therefore reproduce the conditions for status competition between different *warga*. Similarly, while commoners in gentry-dominated villages increasingly reject the Majapahit model of origins and replace it with one more in keeping with their egalitarian aspirations, elite families in all-commoner villagers use aspects of the former to press their claims to higher status.

Village conflict: the case of *banjar* Klakah

Balinese friends in Corong often told me that little can be done if a group changes its title, adds two roofs to its cremation towers, uses a different sarcophagus or establishes a new origin temple. But this seeming defeatism or indifference belies the forms of action that are taken to resist inappropriate status claims. The collective wrath of the hamlet association (*banjar*), ancestral displeasure and intervention by regional government officers may all be mobilized to counteract such claims. However, these forces may be ineffective. From an analytical perspective, ancestral sanctions are unpredictable, since evidence of ancestral anger only emerges if the group later suffers serious misfortune. Similarly, intervention by extra-village authorities gives no guarantee of a solution, as others have pointed out (for example, Geertz 1983: 176–9). Depending on the context, even the *banjar* may be only partially successful in restraining recalcitrant groups.

In this section I describe a long-standing conflict between gentry and commoners in the village of Klakah, situated a short distance from Corong. It revolves around issues of descent group and *banjar*, hierarchy and equality, and sectional interest against civic responsibility. While gentry and commoners are separated by a gulf in purely status terms, neither is a unitary faction. But first some background information.

In the pre-colonial period, Triwangsa families were generally not members of the *banjar*. Instead gentry were orientated to their descent group, to their local palace (*puri*) and to regional alliances. However, there is considerable disagreement amongst scholars concerning the nature of relations between the gentry and commoner village institutions at that period. For Geertz (1980), village institutions were quite powerful; they were separate from and conducted their internal business largely independently of palace affairs, which were themselves dependent on the labour services provided by commoners. In contrast, Schulte Nordholt (1986: 18) quotes an informant as saying: 'Ah, you are asking me now about local *adat* (customs, rules). Local *adat*, what did it matter in those days? It was the lord who decided about local *adat*, for he had power.' What is clear is that gentry did not engage in collective labour organized by the *banjar* and did not assist at the cremations of commoners. The former had their own cemeteries and temples. They neither took offerings to nor worshipped at the village temples supported by commoners.[12]

After independence, however, there could be no return to feudal privileges for the Triwangsa. There was pressure from the new state and the strong pro-republican forces in Bali for them to integrate into the *banjar*. Gentry groups joined their local *banjar* in different ways. One popular method was to constitute their own *banjar*, so becoming good Indonesian citizens while maintaining separation from commoners. Hence there are many hamlets called *banjar satria* (Warren 1993: 18; Nakatani 1995: 93).

A second method was for gentry and commoners to form mixed *banjar*. This was achieved either on the basis of all members, irrespective of status, shouldering identical obligations, or by gentry retaining special privileges to protect their status from potentially polluting activities (such as carrying the corpse of a commoner). This last method was adopted in Corong and consequently all the four *banjar* in the village are mixed, though the actual composition of each varies considerably.

The conflict in Klakah demonstrates that these forces of change are still reverberating through Balinese society. Stated briefly, the village is split into two rival factions. On one side is a large group of Anak Agung, who live in two related and neighbouring palaces (north *puri* and south *puri*) at the northern end of the village, and who are supported by a number of client commoner families, who rely on them for work and access to rice-fields. Arrayed against them is the rest of the village population, who are all commoners. The major bone of contention is the use of the village cemetery, situated at the southern end of the village, and the road which leads to it. On several occasions, going back at least fifteen years, there has been violent confrontation between the two groups when the Anak Agung carried out cremations. Because cremation is one of the most important collective responsibilities of the *banjar*, it is membership of this association which is the central issue in the dispute, rather than cremation itself.

[12] For information on these village temples and the different ways in which they have been interpreted, see Geertz (1959, 1967), Goris (1960), Grader (1960) and Stuart-Fox (1987).

The Anak Agung do not constitute a completely cohesive group; there are those who want to form a new *banjar* and those who argue for some sort of compromise. The latter come mostly from south *puri* but the former have the upper hand and they are led by a high-level official who works in Jakarta. An informant from south *puri* told me that those who disagree with him are ignored and pushed to the sidelines.

According to some commoners, the Anak Agung have left the *banjar* and therefore should not be allowed to use the road which leads to the cemetery or the cemetery itself, because both are *banjar* property. As if to confirm this, the Anak Agung recently purchased a plot of land in the middle of the village with the intention of converting this into a graveyard. However, permission to proceed has been withheld because of villagers' complaints that the spirits of the dead would disturb them and make the centre of the village a dangerous area.

The Anak Agung, however, denied they had withdrawn from the *banjar*. Some still attend *banjar* meetings and take part in collective labour projects, though commoners claim that gentry do their share of the work on a separate day. But more significantly, from commoners' perspective, gentry do not take part in the collective labour arrangements for cremation. Because the Anak Agung do not assist in commoner cremations, commoners refuse to have anything to do with gentry cremations, which fact is used in turn by the latter to justify their separation. Many of the problems dividing the two sides replicate this oscillation of claim and counter-claim.

There is no consensus as to when the trouble started, or indeed what it is fundamentally about. The Anak Agung supposedly arrived on this site in the middle of the nineteenth century, when their overlords allowed them to move there because the living quarters in their old village were too crowded. They were promised the use of one hectare of land for each person making the move. They brought with them their own servants and clients (*panjak, kaula*), who built the palace and farmed their land. Gentry say that those already living in this area were all moved to form a new *banjar* in another village. Commoners claim that only some were moved to make way for the incomers.

This is an important difference, because it relates to an argument about who should worship at which temples in the village. Commoners say they are descendants of those living there when the Anak Agung moved in, and that they already had a *pura dalem* ('death temple', the temple most closely associated with death ceremonies), which they have continued to use up to the present. They assert that this temple is older than the temples which the Anak Agung built within the precincts of the palace, and therefore the whole village should use it. According to the Anak Agung, the commoner temple fell into disuse when all the villagers were moved out and it was only reactivated a long time later, which means their own temple is the older, and that is why they insist on using this one and refuse to use the village death temple. Gentry also argue that it is dangerous for them to worship in a commoner temple, as this would offend their ancestors. (In Corong all villagers worship in the same *pura dalem*.)

Commoners are angry that most of the Anak Agung do not support the village death temple, despite the fact that previously the whole village made contributions to the building of a *padmasana* in its precincts in order to facilitate gentry worship. A *padmasana* is the shrine dedicated to *surya*, the sun, and by extension to Siva, and it is considered essential for those of high status (Swellengrebel 1960: 57). Although some Anak Agung do worship in this temple, particularly those from south *puri*, most still refuse to. Such a rejection is also taken as meaning that the gentry cannot be members of the *banjar*.

Some commoners claim the problem has a more recent origin, when the Anak Agung transferred the ownership of the land on which the village stands from themselves to the village and became members of the *banjar* for the first time. They did not particularly want to do this, it is said, but these changes were occurring all over Bali and they had to follow suit. Since then, they have become affluent and powerful and this has induced them to reassert themselves. With relatives in high places in Jakarta, they can arrange for police protection when confrontation arises. The commoner response has been to accuse them of living in the past, when they ruled the village and controlled most of the land. But, they say, commoners are no longer servants or clients, but citizens in a new country. The Anak Agung never really accepted this loss of power and prestige, and so they remain aloof and exclusive.

Another reason given for a more recent origin, or at least aggravation, of the dispute was the part allegedly played by those in the palace in the killing of several 'communists' in 1966. Commoners claimed that the Anak Agung were very antagonistic to the land reform legislation, threatened their tenants with eviction if they supported it and supplied information and assistance to the army about who were members of the Communist Party. A final reason concerns the eviction of a Brahmana priest from the village because the Anak Agung were distressed at how the villagers had transferred their affections from themselves to the priest's household.[13]

In short, the commoners emphasize the arrogance, exclusivity and lack of civic and collective responsibility of the Anak Agung, while the latter stress their descent-group traditions and the supernatural dangers of worshipping in an inappropriate commoner temple.

During 1993 three cremations were carried out in Klakah. The first was that of an old commoner man who had died very recently, and who was cremated ten days before an enormously elaborate cremation of a locally famous Anak Agung man, reputed to have been 120 years old and, in his prime, a feared and respected healer (*balian*).[14]

The first cremation was an entirely commoner affair, which proceeded without incident. Very few of the Anak Agung provided labour assistance and many did not even make the obligatory donations of bamboo, rice and coconuts (*patus*). On the day of the burning, the Anak Agung studiously ignored the procession to the cemetery and carried on with their own preparations. In response, during the actual burning, several men took the opportunity to destroy two wooden structures which the Anak Agung had erected the previous day as preliminaries for their own cremation.

---

[13] This Brahmana family had been originally invited to move to Klakah to act as priests to the Anak Agung. Land was provided for the family to build their house and they were given rice land. However, one of the Brahmana men eloped with a woman from the palace and this infuriated the Anak Agung. Three quite different reasons were given for their anger. One was that those in the palace might have agreed to the marriage had it been properly arranged. A second was that they were against any such marriage, conceiving of it as dangerous (*panes*) and as likely to afflict not just the spouses but the two families. The runaways were told they could not return to the village, and later the house was abandoned and the Brahmana went back to their original village. The ordinary villagers who had become clients (*sisya*) to the priest were distressed at this outcome, and this prompted a third cause to be mooted, namely, that the Anak Agung had become jealous of the priest and used the marriage as a pretext to get rid of him. With the arrival of the priest, villagers had begun seeking advice and assistance from him. Consequently, fewer people went to the palace, and the Anak Agung felt humiliated.

[14] The more respected and supernaturally powerful a person is, the greater is their accredited age on death. Although I give the figure of 120 years, others said he was even older. Such extreme longevity is an expression of the idea that powerful people live to an age normal people cannot achieve.

Plate 4.1 The remains of wooden structures erected as preparations for a high-caste cremation in the village of Klakah, south Bali, and destroyed by their low-caste opponents

Often, commoners cremate in the wake of gentry, so as to lessen the costs and partake of the more intense excitement of the bigger event, ceding the lead position in the procession to the gentry. In this case, however, the commoner cremation was carried out in undue haste, so some people thought, in order to show displeasure with the Anak Agung; and afterwards the graveyard was intentionally left in a mess. Furthermore, according to informants, on two occasions in the past five years, prior to a gentry cremation, villagers sprinkled broken glass on the ground in the upstream part of the cemetery, where such cremations take place. At these events commoners also intimidated the Anak Agung during their processions to the cemetery, by lining up on both sides of the road and waving sharpened bamboo staves at them. The police had to be called in to keep the peace.

The cremation of the Anak Agung, ten days later, also took place without serious incident for several reasons.[15] First, the deceased was widely revered as a *balian* in the village and beyond it, and commoners had no stomach for disrupting the cremation of someone who had been so powerful, partly because he had helped some of them personally and partly because they were frightened of possible future repercussions. Secondly, the cremation was, for this village at least, a very impressive spectacle, which consumed some 15 million rupiah ($7,500), and the event was widely advertised in the tourist village of Ubud, only five miles away. The subsequent attendance of over 200 tourists made violence unthinkable. Finally, a meeting between the two sides had been held three days prior to the burning, at which the district head and representatives of the police had been present. Both groups signed a declaration that they would unite in the *banjar*, although the Anak Agung would continue to use their own death temple. The Anak Agung also agreed to pay the *banjar* Rp125,000 for the use of the road, though in the event they never did. The agreement had come too late to encourage the villagers to help with the preparations, and most of the work was done by people from outside Klakah, though a few commoners did help to carry the tower to the cremation ground.

On the days after the cremation, the atmosphere did not improve, and it became apparent that little had changed. The Anak Agung suggested that the commoners had now come to realize their wrongs; they were now 'aware' of the 'real' situation. The commoners saw it differently: they had not surrendered, they had been duped: 'The Anak Agung simply did what they had done at previous meetings; they used sweet words and smiles to get what they wanted. But they cannot be trusted since they are stubborn and their true feelings are concealed.'

This case illustrates a number of points. Ironically it shows both the strengths and the weaknesses of the *banjar*. Others have pointed out how cohesive the *banjar* is, how it is the rock on which everyday social relations are predicated. The *banjar* regulations generate a moral community which conducts its affairs in such a way as to minimize strife, competition and deviation. Detailed rules regulate the privileges and obligations surrounding the most important *banjar* activities, such as cremation. The *banjar* is thus very strong when it is confronted by recalcitrant individuals and small groups of families. It has a range of sanctions, minor to begin with, but

---

[15] The only interference with the proceedings was that, for a second time, other preparations at the cemetery had been torn down and burned the day before the cremation. Even though the cremation was not disrupted, few commoners praised the size of the spectacle, as would be normal in less strained circumstances. On the contrary, they criticized the *naga banda* (which was constructed in Ubud at a cost of 3 million rupiah, and usually only used for the highest of the high) as too short and badly made. There was also unconcealed glee when the resting place for the body in the cremation tower was found to be too small and frantic last-minute modifications had to be made, all in full view of the assembled crowd.

Plate 4.2 Procession of the cremation tower for an Anak Agung on its way to the burning ground in Klakah

escalating quickly, which enable it to impose pressure in a cumulative fashion. Precipitate action is rarely taken, because the *banjar* prefers its individual members to persuade and cajole delinquents into mending their ways. But it is also strong enough to defeat determined groups which wish to break away. Warren (1993: 48–54) discusses a case in which twelve families resisted a *banjar* decision and tried to secede from it to form a new one. They refused to pay *banjar* subscriptions and levies or to take part in communal work sessions and meetings. The controversy went on for several years before the faction was defeated. The event bringing the conflict to an end was a death in the dissident faction. Having withdrawn from the *banjar*, they could not use the village cemetery. This was too much for them and they surrendered. Intervention on numerous occasions by various external authorities had accomplished nothing. Though they were allowed back into the *banjar*, they had to pay a huge fee for readmission; and to prevent them reconstituting themselves as a faction they were dispersed among several *banjar*.

The strength of the *banjar* consists in its control of the supremely important arrangements for the death of its members, and the great difficulty of making arrangements privately outside the *banjar*. These give it a power which no external agency can match, villagers sometimes being more frightened about the wrath of the spirits of the dead than they are of state officials.

But its autonomy is sometimes its weakness, for, in the face of determined opposition from a large faction with considerable resources, its sanctions are less effective. Because the *banjar* is largely independent of external authority in matters to do with local custom, it is reduced to persuasion and appeals to common sense. In such situations, if there is no recourse to a 'court of appeal', intransigence, obstinacy and attrition become viable strategies. In Klakah, while the police have at least been able to keep the two sides apart most of the time, intervention by regional government officials has had little success.

What does this example tell us about hierarchy and equality? One reading of the situation, a commoner one, is that hierarchy is central to the issue: the gentry are reluctant to participate fully in the *banjar* because it would compromise the separation between themselves and commoners, and thus demean their superior status. This construes the conflict as one about the incompatibility between hierarchy and the egalitarian ideology of the *banjar*. The preference of the gentry for their own death temple then becomes viewed as a pretext.

The gentry version simply bypasses this argument. While in many villages obligations to the *banjar* override those to the descent group, in some others the *banjar* is less important and plays no role in death rituals, which are instead performed by descent groups (see Stuart-Fox 1987: 142–3 and Nakatani 1995: 94 for two such examples). For the Anak Agung of Klakah, this is the central issue in the conflict. They put their descent group first and are willing to be members of the *banjar* only if this does not damage their descent-group activities; commoners insist on the preeminence of the *banjar*.

But commoners disagree among themselves concerning the link between the *banjar* and ideas of hierarchy and equality. To understand this better, further historical details need to be outlined. As we have seen, there is some disagreement concerning the existence of relations of equality in the past. For Schulte Nordholt (1986: 18, 1996), the *banjar* was weak in relation to the power held by the local gentry rulers. Since commoners in one village were often clients of different lords, it was not the *banjar* which protected them, but the lord to which they were tied. It is therefore difficult to see how, in the pre-colonial period, the *banjar* could have played the kind of role that it does today. Schulte Nordholt (1986: 31) goes on to argue that the Dutch created equality by lumping together a diversity of groups into a single category, denominated 'Sudra', which they considered homogeneous.

In contrast, Geertz has consistently portrayed the *banjar* as being strong and to a large degree independent of supra-village gentry society, arguing that: '*Homo hierarchicus* and *Homo aequalis* are engaged in Bali in war without end' (Geertz and Geertz 1975: 167). A major problem with Geertz's (1980) description of the nineteenth-century Balinese state, however, is the lack of any coherent theory as to how state and village interacted. Since Warren (1993) has demonstrated the egalitarian nature of the modern *banjar*, the likely conclusion is that there has been a considerable change in the nature of *banjar* activity over the previous century.

Since the colonial period, village institutions have distanced themselves from the noble courts and taken over some of their functions. Court patronage of the arts and dance began to dissolve and artists turned instead to the *banjar* for support (Vickers 1980: 7); and many courts transferred ownership of costumes and orchestras to the *banjar* (Picard 1990a: 46). The Dutch confiscated land from defeated lords and tried to suppress the ties which bound commoners to the courts (Connor 1982: 82). The reduction in the power and influence of the courts gave commoners the opportunity to invest their own local institutions (hamlet, village, irrigation associations) with more significance. With the local lords gradually disappearing from the scene and changing their relationship to village institutions, the *banjar* moved to fill the vacuum that was left, and it has become more important and more solidary. The fact that after independence gentry felt obliged to become *banjar* members supports this argument. As the traditional political role of the gentry declined and village institutions rose to greater prominence, so the *banjar* became a site of conflict over the appropriate relationship between hierarchy and corporate equality. Moreover, because of local factors, this has not happened in a uniform way, and so different villages have experienced different outcomes.[16] In short, these values have not been engaged in a 'war without end', as the Geertzes argue; rather, historical changes have conspired to bring them into conflict.

In villages such as Klakah, where the gap between gentry and commoners is unmediated by groups of lower gentry, such as Déwa and Ngakan, the reluctance of the Anak Agung to join the *banjar* is easily attributed to gentry preoccupation with hierarchical status. Some commoners therefore accuse them of being anachronistically feudal. They see the dispute as being about the nature of civic life and the declining relevance of ascribed status in modern Bali and thus as a conflict between hierarchy and equality. Their intention is to coerce the gentry into the *banjar*.

Other commoners, however, provide a rather different perspective by arguing that gentry membership of the *banjar* does not entail surrendering their status. Some weeks after the Anak Agung cremation, a third burning was carried out. A woman from south *puri* died suddenly and was cremated immediately. This time the whole village, gentry and commoner alike, took part – the former because she was one of

---

[16] In Corong, both gentry and commoner think their four mixed and integrated *banjar* have worked very well. Partly this is because Corong was a centre of pro-republican activity during the revolution and the Cokorda were at the forefront of the resistance to the Dutch and their Balinese allies; two Cokorda met their deaths during this period, and other villagers, including Brahmana, spent long periods in the Dutch jails in Gianyar before the conflict ended. This set the tone for post-revolution integration, and the incorporation of gentry into the *banjar* caused few problems. I detected little evidence of gentry antipathy to *banjar* membership, and attendance rolls for monthly meetings showed no disproportionate absence of gentry as opposed to commoners.

their own, and the commoners because she had always turned up for work when the *banjar* was called (*turun ka banjar*).

There was no sense of grievance on the part of the commoners that she was given all the status prerogatives her title demanded, the nine-roofed cremation tower for example. Commoners spoke about her in a deferential way but also with great affection, for she had been an uncommonly kind and generous woman. It was pointed out to me that her status was in no way compromised by being a *banjar* member; on the contrary, it was because she was a good *banjar* member that the commoners were happy to celebrate her status by giving her a brilliant cremation. The ceremony was extremely boisterous (*ramé*), but the corpse was treated with respect.

At this point, it is worth reconsidering those arguments which see the *banjar* as pre-eminently egalitarian. While the *banjar* has a democratic structure and its members all sit at the same level, in fact some hierarchical features remain. During communal *banjar* work sessions, for example, the status of gentry is not entirely suspended or irrelevant, since, in informal conversation and interaction, appropriate levels of the language are maintained, and there is a weak association between status and the kind of labour that is performed at these events. Moreover, in mixed *banjar*, gentry are usually allowed special dispensation where communal work conflicts with their status; for example, they are not obliged to carry the bodies of deceased commoners. Even in the formal settings of a *banjar* meeting, hierarchical relation-ships are still present and recognized, since the membership is addressed not as a single collectivity but as a collection of groups possessing different statuses: they are addressed as *ida-dané sareng sami*, the first word, *ida*, referring to those of very high caste and the second, *dané*, to those of lower status (*sareng sami* meaning 'all together').[17] While the *banjar* has a strong egalitarian emphasis, it does not have a fundamental antipathy to hierarchy.

This can be refined further by focusing on the phrase *turun ka banjar* ('to go to work for the *banjar*'). The Balinese words *turun, tedun* and *tuun* all mean 'to go down'. When gods occupy a temple during a ceremony, they *turun kabéh*, 'all come down'. Villagers going to work for the hamlet, or other associations, are said to *tedun* or *turun*. Becoming a member of the hamlet association for the first time is termed *tuun mabanjar*.

Physical location on a vertical axis is crucial to Balinese conceptions of proper interaction. People of different status should ideally arrange themselves so that they sit at levels commensurate with their status, except at *banjar* meetings, where they all sit at the same level. Gods are conceived to be above people and offerings to them are placed on high altars, whilst those for malevolent spirits are placed on the ground. Hierarchy is talked about in terms of being 'bigger' (*gedénan*), 'above' (*duuran*) and 'higher' (*tegehan*).

Going to work for the *banjar* therefore implies a 'going down', which can suggest a temporary flattening of status differences, a lowering of everyone to a similar level. It is this view of the *banjar* which is said to disconcert the Anak Agung most, just as it is this interpretation which encourages some commoners to see gentry membership of the *banjar* as a defeat of their hierarchical pretensions. But other commoners see it differently. Several insisted that *banjar* membership does not entail that those who

---

[17] There are no words in Balinese for collective pronouns such as 'we', 'you' and 'they' if they are to designate an assembly of people of different status; there are only circumlocutions which give each group represented its appropriate linguistic terms.

'go down' give up their status, any more than gods who *turun* to the temple shrines are any less exalted for having made this descent. They pointed out that the *banjar* is not just a location, site of activity or even a communal group, but rather an idea of working together for the good of all. This is achieved, not in spite of status differences between those involved but, on the contrary, because of them, since a communal benefit is derived from the differential contributions of all those who live in the village. Such commoners often compared Klakah to Corong and argued that the latter was prosperous precisely because gentry were enthusiastic members of the *banjar*. According to this view the reluctance to play a full role in the *banjar* is simply foolish because it is detrimental to all and thus self-defeating.

In sum, the conflict is based on a disagreement about the nature of the modern *banjar*. For the Anak Agung the *banjar* is less important than their own descent group, its traditions and therefore the essential link with their ancestors. Being forced to worship in the village death temple would compromise this and render them vulnerable to ancestral wrath. It is less their hierarchical status they are worried about than their ancestry and their spiritual safety. Commoners perceive this as a self-serving argument. While all commoners claim it is gentry arrogance which prevents them from wholeheartedly embracing the *banjar*, some say it is also gentry ignorance because their claims are grounded in a misunderstanding of the 'true' nature of the *banjar*, which does not entail a loss of status. So, while some want to force the gentry into the *banjar* in order to deflate their sense of superiority, others want them to join for more positive reasons.

Status and rank are important values in Balinese social life, but so are ideologies of collective equality, and the relationship between these two sets of values has been changing. Ideas of corporate equality have become more prominent over the last hundred years, and values of individual equality and democracy derived from the west are also gaining ground. In one sense it is evident that equality and hierarchy are competing frames of reference. The Surya Kanta organization of the 1920s (see Chapter 7), the communists before 1965 and some modern-day commoner organizations had, and have, as their aim, to eradicate hierarchy or at least to modify its nature. Equally, many gentry reject these ideas and cannot envisage a world in which status distinctions ascribed by birth are no longer important.

In another sense, though, these two ideologies do not compete but coexist and complement each other. Here equality is restricted to those at the same level of the hierarchy. For many Balinese, commoners and gentry alike, the world is made prosperous by the differential contribution of people of different ranks. The problem for them is not hierarchy *per se*, but that so many people seem to enjoy ranks inappropriate to their contributions, a theme I explore further in the following section.

Warna & *kasta*: competing interpretations of social structure

Whether in the urban centres or in the villages, many Balinese of all ranks increasingly question the relevance and morality of hierarchy. In private, commoners frequently engage in those mild acts of sabotage and resistance described by Scott (1985). They also scorn the gentry, make jokes about them and assert that respect must be reciprocated. Even in public, gentry pretensions are easily pricked. Although it is a fast-declining practice, strangers try to find out each other's status before they begin to converse, using the appropriate levels of the language. The traditional question for discovering this: 'What is your position?' (*nunas antuk linggih?* where the final term means both 'seat' and 'rank'), might today elicit the sardonic reply: 'I'm sitting on my motor bike.'

However, because the pre-colonial elite has reproduced itself as a modern political and economic elite by disproportionately filling high offices of government and administration, by monopolizing village leadership positions and through success in business (Parker 1992b: 96; Warren 1993: 273; Nakatani 1995: 78), commoners are forced into maintaining traditional forms of deference to protect their jobs and livelihoods. Consequently, they frequently adopt obsequious postures, use respectful language or lapse into silence when the latter are present. Of course, the battle lines are not stable but shift according to context. As the cases already described show, conflict is just as likely to arise amongst commoners or amongst gentry, as between commoner and gentry.

Practical forms of resistance are buttressed by ideological forms: 'new' commoner myths, emerging ideologies of equality, commoner organizations campaigning for equality with Brahmana, rival interpretations of status titles, and so forth. In later chapters, I examine conflicts over religious truth and the authenticity of different forms of Hinduism in Bali.

As these ideologies and movements gain momentum, both high and low castes, particularly in urban and educated circles (these views none the less echoing through the villages), find that in public they are increasingly constrained to state that the 'caste system' (*sistim kasta*, Ind.) is unimportant. Such statements, however, cannot always be taken at face value. Higher castes know that in contemporary Bali hierarchy has become problematic, and so, in mixed gatherings, they endorse this to show they are 'modern' (*moderen*, Ind.) and 'progressive' (*maju*, Ind.), and many are indeed sincere about this. But in other situations they attempt to enforce deferential forms of linguistic exchange, preserve their ritual prerogatives and prevent their women from marrying down. Lower castes, in contrast, say caste is unimportant to give the illusion of having won the fight. Asserting that caste is outmoded is part of the strategy to make it so.

A very significant way in which the hierarchy is being questioned was briefly introduced in the previous chapter. It concerns a controversy, widespread in modern Bali, about the essential and ancient nature of Balinese social structure. The controversy is discussed in academic texts by Balinese intellectuals (for example, Santri 1993) and aired in the editorials and letters column of the *Bali Post* newspaper. The central issue revolves around the purpose of titles. In one interpretation, denoted by the term *kasta*,[18] which is clearly derived from 'caste', groups are arranged in a hierarchical order of superiority and inferiority according to how their lines of descent are related to the pre-colonial ruling families. These groups, with their attached titles, are descent groups, and it is birth into the group which matters. This *kasta* theory therefore enunciates the legend of the fourteenth-century Javanese invasion and the establishment of Majapahit court culture in Bali.

The status prerogatives attaching to gentry titles, such as exclusive rights to certain kinds of rituals, items of ritual paraphernalia, receipt of refined language,

[18] The Indonesian language term *kasta* (also now appearing as a Balinese term in Balinese dictionaries) is the neologism used to refer to the hierarchical separation of descent groups, a term which also carries the implication that Balinese hierarchy is similar to caste in India. Its original use probably dates from the 1920s, when commoner intellectuals began to write articles in Indonesian in periodicals which they established to criticize the hierarchical privileges of gentry and to advance ideas of achievement and democracy. The term may have been in circulation before that time, since the Dutch referred to the hierarchy as the *kastenstelsel*.

elevated seating positions and asymmetrical marriage and food exchanges, are all part of the *kasta* ideology. Interestingly, there is no theory concerning the 'quality' of the blood of different status groups, such as there is, for example, amongst the hierarchical Luwu of Sulawesi (Errington 1989). However, there are other cultural representations about the differences between gentry and commoners. Gentry consider themselves light in colour (*putih*), whereas commoners are said to be very black (*selem-selem*). The faces of Triwangsa shine (*caya*) whilst those of *jaba* are dreary and indistinct (*mueg, urem*). *Macaya ménak* means 'to look like a member of the gentry', that is, to have a face that shines. The faces of children born to a gentry man and a commoner woman are sometimes said to be gloomy. Gentry describe themselves as more refined (*alus*) in their features, with narrow eyes, aquiline noses and small bodies, whereas commoners are coarse (*kasar*). Unsurprisingly, commoner men and women rarely mention these ideas.

Warna is the rival interpretation increasingly used to confront *kasta*. This model eschews ideas of hierarchy, and is instead based on individual achievement, people gaining titles in accordance with the functions they perform in society. Titles are attached to occupations rather than to descent groups, and thus they should not be inherited. Titles are not necessarily prestigious in themselves, as they are in the *kasta* theory, but their holders may attract prestige and respect in accordance with how they serve the rest of society by assiduous performance. In its most radical form, *warna* is an essentially egalitarian interpretation which calls for an end to all those gentry privileges which the *kasta* ideology supports.

Both theories interpret Balinese society holistically, in the sense that the prosperity of society depends on the separation and appropriate performance of necessary functional roles, so that individual ends are subordinated to collective ones. Both also establish a role for titles. The essential difference between them is how these titles are conferred. Proponents of the *warna* model claim that in the ancient past only this ideology existed, the four main divisions of the population being known as the *catur warna*. With the introduction of Javanese Majapahit culture, in which people began to inherit the *warna* titles of their father even if they failed to perform the functions appropriate to them, the *catur warna* system began to change into the system of titled descent groups hierarchically arranged. In the colonial period, this gradually came to be called *kasta*, leaving the way open to reformist minded Balinese to argue that *warna* should be re-established by eradicating *kasta*.

From an analytical perspective, what seems to have happened is that the emergence of the term *kasta* in the early part of the twentieth century to denote the hierarchy and its ascriptive inequalities provided an opportunity for reformers to appropriate and redefine *warna* in non-hierarchical terms. This was facilitated, as we shall see in more detail in Chapter 7, by the importation from India of various Hindu reform ideas. These anti-caste ideas were propagated in Bali by Balinese intellectuals, such as Gedé Pudja, who studied Indian philosophy and religion at Banaras Hindu University in Varanasi, and Ibu Gedong Oka, who read Gandhi's autobiography during the Japanese occupation of Indonesia, translated four of his works into Indonesian and established an ashram in Bali. Pudja argued that in the ancient Indian scriptures it is not birth but way of life which determines which *warna* one should belong to, while Oka claimed that it is the privileges which members of the higher orders derive which distort the essential nature of the system. With others, they argued that the *catur warna* system should be retained, because it is a universal pattern of social organization recognized all over the world and is necessary for the proper functioning of society, but that the ascriptive, hereditary and hierarchical aspects of it should be abandoned because in reality the members of the four *warna* are equal (Bakker1993: 124–6, 210–12; Pitana 1997: 169).

In earlier sections of this chapter, I have discussed some of the different ways in which equality is asserted and claimed, but there are other methods as well. Equality is, of course, most usually advanced by commoners, who now increasingly use the phrase *manusa pada* ('all people are equal') to establish the inappropriateness of hierarchy. Educated commoners are also becoming adept at quoting passages of scripture which imply equality from the new Hindu literature. The state constitution provides useful ammunition as well, since the national ideology, *pancasila*, affirms that all the citizens of the republic are equal (Pitana 1997: 101).

Curiously, the controversy in Bali between *kasta* and *warna* echoes an academic debate among historians and anthropologists concerning the meaning of *varna* in India. Dumont (1980) notes that the ancient *varna* scheme classified the population into four categories (Brahman, Ksatriya, Vaisya and Sudra) on the basis of the different parts of the body of the 'lord of beings' from which they emanated (mouth, arms, thighs and feet, respectively), and then went on to claim that these categories are hierarchically ordered into superior and inferior according to relative purity. Others have argued, in contrast, that the classification is one of (ritual) functions, not people, and implies only separation, not hierarchy (Derrett 1976: 602; Quigley 1993: 163). My point is that in contemporary Bali these two contrasting academic interpretations constitute indigenous theories supporting rival political interpretations of the nature of Balinese social structure.

The controversy is frequently encountered all over Bali. In Corong, for example, villagers were mildly disgusted by the dissolute life led by many gentry, both men and women. Many high castes were heavily involved in all forms of gambling. Card-games were particularly worthy of denunciation, since many considered the morals on display as extremely lax: women sat cross-legged, they were the butt of sexual jokes and mild sexual abuse and the language used was coarse. Additionally, many high castes have no regular employment. They avoid unskilled manual labour, as they feel it compromises their dignity. If this avoidance was in part constitutive of high-status persons in the past, today it often provokes accusations from commoners that gentry are idle layabouts and parasites. Despite possessing the title ida bagus (the form of address for a male Brahmana, a translation of which might be 'honourable handsome one'), why should deference be accorded someone who is plainly ignorant of what Brahmana are supposed to be experts in?

As we have seen, theoretically, *warna* is a reformist social criticism of the *kasta* ideology, but, in practice, things are rather different since it appeals most to those who experience relative status deprivation. If 'I' am a high-ranking official, I should be allowed the title of *cokorda*, whereas, if 'he' is unemployed and uneducated, why should he be *brahmana*? In line with progressive thinking, *warna* is fast becoming the official ideology of some state institutions in Bali and of the modern Hindu movement. According to Ramstedt:

> the public figures of the modern Hindu movement, who very often bear *triwangsa* titles, constantly propagate the irrelevance of these titles ... they agree upon the titles being nothing more than parts of a personal name and having nothing to do with the *warna* [function] of a person. An *ida bagus* working as a room boy in a hotel would have to be classified as a *sudra*, whereas a soldier, named I Wayan something [i.e. a commoner], would have to be looked at as *ksatria*.

(Ramstedt 1995: 13)

In Corong, several government officials with gentry titles expressed these ideas during private interviews: *kasta* is outmoded, status should be based on achievement rather than birth and titles should be treated as personal names detached from considerations of status. These sentiments were used to expound a view of Bali as advanced, developed and modern, as a society conforming to democracy, in which Balinese are no longer to be classified by rank, as in the time of the kingdoms, but instead as equal citizens of the state.

To a large extent such statements express a state ideology to which civil servants are increasingly obliged to conform, and do not necessarily bear much relation to what they really think. In the last chapter, we saw that similar arguments were used by Ngakan and Déwa groups to obscure a status jump by construing a change in title as a change in personal name. Moreover, it is widely recognized that civil servants, who disproportionately come from the gentry, use their influence to obtain jobs for their kin and demand large bribes from other job seekers. One reason why young men from high castes remain unemployed for long periods is that they are waiting, often in vain, for a relative to secure them a job in a government bureaucracy.

In theory, then, *warna* ideology is wholly antagonistic to *kasta*, and is indeed sometimes used in this way by genuine social reformers. In practice, however, diluted versions of it are often converted into arguments that obliquely endorse hierarchy. *Warna* ideology can be used to account for one's own apparent low status in the hierarchy, as a basis for asserting that one should enjoy a higher rank, or for questioning the inappropriately high status of others. In these contexts, it is not the hierarchy as such which is at issue, but only the way in which circumstances conspire to allocate people to the wrong positions. When the *warna* ideology is deployed in this fashion, stripped, so to speak, of its egalitarian cutting edge, it unintentionally preserves the hierarchy, rather than subverting it. As with commoner origin myths and ideas about *banjar* equality, *warna* ideology assumes a double function. In its different guises and in different contexts, it acts both to denounce hierarchy and to perpetuate it.

But it would be cynical to leave the discussion at this point, for it really does matter that *warna* has become a public ideology to which Balinese feel increasingly constrained to conform. Many high-caste intellectuals, academics, civil servants, priests and businessmen do more than pay lip-service to it. After all, it is this class of Balinese who make up a significant part of the membership of the relatively egalitarian Sai Baba movement, who staff the modern Hindu movement and who are at the forefront of calls for greater democracy, freedom of speech and liberalization of the economy. They are enthusiastic about democratic politics, advancement through merit and individual rights, even as they are worried about the degenerate morality and materialism that is thought to be linked with western modernity. My point is that, although many Balinese only outwardly conform to ideologies such as *warna*, such conformity demonstrates their increasing significance and diffusion throughout Balinese society. These ideas can no longer be ignored or dismissed and, as they become publicly sanctioned ideologies, they have to be reckoned with.

Conclusion

Between 1966 and 1998, politics in Bali were tightly controlled by the central state institutions of the Suharto regime, which in turn helped, whether intentionally or not, to maintain gentry influence over Balinese affairs. The governors of Bali and the heads of its eight regencies were almost entirely high-caste individuals during these years, a period which has seen the gentry active and successful in local government and in business and commerce. In large part, gentry were the mainstay of resistance to republican forces after the Second World War, and many supported the extermination of the communists in 1965–6. This political dominance was little changed by rapid economic development from 1970, which made Bali one of the most affluent areas of Indonesia. In this climate, gentry managed to preserve a commanding presence in Balinese society, while commoners frequently tried to convert new wealth and prestige into traditional status. As a result, social relations of hierarchy have to some extent come under the protective umbrella of the state.

None the less, principles of equality, democracy, merit and achievement have also been important in the development of Indonesia since the beginning of the twentieth century. There has been insistent, and sometimes strong, pressure to ameliorate the perceived inequities of Bali's hierarchical society. But, when party politics became disruptive, as during the Dutch colonial period or under Suharto, it was quickly emasculated. Prevented from direct political mobilization, those disadvantaged in these regimes turned 'culture' into a political battleground.

The politicization of commoner origin myths has enabled commoners to exploit cultural resources to oppose gentry domination, even as some commoners adopt gentry models to enhance their own status. Although the traditional elite has in part reproduced itself as a modern elite, its power now depends more on support from above than on control of those below. Villagers are no longer tied to gentry lords as tenants, servants or subjects, but instead, theoretically, enjoy equal rights as citizens of a state. Gentry were forced to join *banjar* and village temple congregations, have lost much of their land and have surrendered orchestras, costumes and masks to village organizations.

With greater material and ideological resources at their disposal, commoners have been exercising their political muscle in conflicts amongst themselves and with the gentry. These are phrased in terms of contrasts between hierarchy and equality; sectional interest and exclusiveness against civic responsibility and the collective good; the traditional and the feudal against progress and development; *kasta* against *warna*. Balinese often summarize these oppositions as a contrast between the old-fashioned (*kolot*, Ind.) and the modern (*moderen*, Ind.), Vickers (1996: 17) showing that this conflict often manifested itself as a challenge to caste.

But what is also clear is that tradition and modernity cannot so easily be disentangled, the modern assuming traditional forms and the traditional being recently invented. Emerging forms of egalitarianism are interpreted both as new, as a result of western influence, and also as the recovery of traditions submerged under the more recent importation of forms of hierarchy. The recent politicization of the Rsi Markandeya myth portrays equality as historically very deep and more authentic than ideas of hierarchy based on the Majapahit myth. The theory of *warna* develops this theme further. Although apparently confined to rather arcane ideas concerning the 'true' and fundamental nature of Balinese society, *warna* resonates with the aspirations of Balinese who want change by interpreting new ideas of achievement and merit as ancient values, all the while establishing these ideas within a holistic and collective moral framework. In consequence, Balinese move into the future by returning to their past, and embrace modernity by reacquainting themselves with old traditions.

5
Language, Ritual & Hierarchy

In the two previous chapters, frequent reference was made to the importance of language and ritual in movements of status assertion. To improve hierarchical status, it is imperative to establish new forms of linguistic exchange and new ritual practices. In this chapter, I examine some related issues which have to do with ritual competition and language change.

The Balinese language is a prime site for the enactment of hierarchy because many of its terms are themselves hierarchically coded, so that speaking Balinese inevitably involves reference to relative rank. The issue I address in the first section of this chapter, then, concerns the resilience of this facet of the language despite major changes in the organization of the social hierarchy. The second section explores a series of issues connected with the way in which status competition is conducted through forms of ritual performance. I am especially interested in forms of ritual inflation, which have been fuelled by expanding economic resources, but also in the processes that limit such inflation so that it does not run out of control.

Speaking of hierarchy

The question I want to address here is this: given that the social relations of hierarchy have become increasingly problematic, how is this reflected in changes to the status dimensions of the Balinese language? I shall argue that while there have been various changes in how Balinese is used, broadly corresponding to changes in the power structure of Balinese society, there are nevertheless many reasons why the status levels of Balinese are being preserved.[1]

The Balinese language is fundamentally hierarchical, and speaking it unavoidably entails making statements about social relationships. Language is therefore one of the most important arenas in which status claims are either accepted or repudiated. Claims to higher status necessarily involve attempts to modify linguistic exchange. One of the most important ways in which a commoner group validates itself as gentry is by establishing asymmetrical linguistic exchange with its previous equals, which entails the latter adopting a more deferential vocabulary when speaking to or about the former. It also requires the former to establish broadly symmetrical linguistic relations with groups which were superior but which are now deemed to be

---

[1] It is not necessary to embark on a detailed discussion of all aspects of Balinese speech, as this would take me far beyond the themes I am interested in. Further information on the language can be found in Kersten (1984: 16–29), Zurbuchen (1987), Hunter (1988) and Eiseman (1990: 130–46). I am also not concerned here with the complex relations between Indonesian and provincial languages, such as Balinese and Javanese. For an introduction to these topics, see Anderson (1990a, b) and Errington (1998).

much closer in status. As shown earlier, it is very difficult to persuade the relevant groups to comply.

The most basic distinction in speech is that between *alus* (refined, smooth) and *kasar* (rough, coarse). At its simplest, more refined words have to be used to or about people of higher status, who in turn use less refined words to or about those of lower status. The majority of Balinese words have only one form, may be used in any context and are thus status-neutral. However, those sensitive to status are the most important everyday words. They pertain principally to the body; actions and movements; ideas, thoughts and feelings; common nouns, adverbs and adjectives; many kin terms; pronouns, relatives, conjunctions and negators; and so forth. Some of these have only two levels, such as *adep* and *adol* (sell). Others have three, such as *yéh*, *toya* and *tirtha* (water). A number of very important words have many levels: 'to eat', for example, can be translated by more than ten different Balinese words, ranging from those applicable to insects and animals (the most *kasar*), those pertaining to people of low status, polite words used to strangers and those words that must be used to rulers, *pedanda* and deities (the most *alus*). Additionally, some words are far more significant for status than others. These include pronouns and words referring to the body and its actions, thoughts and feelings.

Alus and *kasar* are a continuum rather than a dichotomy, speech being more or less *alus* or *kasar* according to circumstances. It is not just title status that is relevant, moreover, since age, occupation, gender and behaviour all influence linguistic choice. This is perhaps more the case today than in the past. Similarly, different speech registers are accompanied by paralinguistic features, such as speech rhythms, bodily postures, head and arm gestures, eye movements, and so forth. Cutting across the continuum of *alus* and *kasar* are important rules denoted by the term *sor-singgih*. These enjoin one to elevate (*nyinggihang*) one's interlocutor and humble (*ngesor*) oneself.

The most significant feature of the language, for my purposes, is the impossibility of speaking without also conveying further messages about the relationship between the speaker, the audience and third parties. Hierarchy is enacted through asymmetrical linguistic exchange. But the language also encodes equality. Status equals eat the food from each other's ritual leftovers, worship each other's dead, marry each other and exchange language at the same level. Those who dispute relative status tend to stop speaking to each other or switch into Indonesian, which is the lingua franca of the Republic of Indonesia and status-neutral. Words can be combined very flexibly and subtly, so speech can express resistance, disrespect and insolence. The use of very obsequious language, excessive humility and flattery, what Appadurai (1990: 97) calls 'coercive deference', can be used as a tactic of social control to force superiors to accede to requests from inferiors or risk losing face.

Clearly the Balinese language is an instrument of domination. But the extent to which it is so has changed considerably. In the past, power and status differentials were marked by extreme forms of deference, linguistic and otherwise, which had to be offered on pain of severe sanctions. In addressing a ruler, high priest or noble, subjects lowered their bodies, averted their gaze and used the thumb for pointing. Failure to observe such rules symbolically reduced the superior to the level of the inferior, causing the former to become polluted. These rules were very rigorously applied in earlier periods (Swellengrebel 1960). Even the most minor transgressions were met with physical punishment, banishment or a hefty fine, non-payment of which often resulted in debt slavery. The wide range of seemingly trivial infringements enabled rulers to enslave significant numbers of Balinese who could then be sold to acquire the cash which provided the aristocracy with weaponry, opium and luxuries (Schulte Nordholt 1996: 43).

The power structure is now very different. The power, wealth and influence of the nineteenth-century elite have declined, Bali has been incorporated into the Indonesian state, and new state-wide legal codes have been established. Consequently, sanctions enforcing the rules of deference can no longer be applied, and this has resulted in a partial liberalization of language use. Movements of protest against gentry have always included resistance to the hierarchical dimensions of the language, and today those strongly opposed to hierarchical separation frequently assert they will use Balinese to others only if the same level of language is reciprocated. In north Bali, where the social organization is more fluid and the hierarchy correspondingly less important than in south Bali, the 'appropriate levels of the language have fallen into disuse' (Barth 1993: 233).

The most significant change is the contemporary avoidance of the extremes of the language, something which is also happening in Java (Errington 1998: 43–4). The most *kasar* terms are still used in some commoner households, but are rarely used outside the family by superiors to inferiors, as they once were in the pre-colonial period. (Ancestral spirits and deities, speaking through mediums and priests, may so address their clients and congregations.) Conversely, commoners are today freer to use less servile forms than once was necessary. A related change concerns the increasing significance of what is called *basa madiya* or *basa pasar* ('middle' language or 'market' language). These are polite forms, neither very *kasar* nor very *alus*, which can be used to strangers (for example, those one deals with in a market, office or shop) and people of moderately higher status. Pure *alus* is generally reserved for speaking to *pedanda* and others of very high status, and during marriage negotiations, village meetings and other formal occasions.

As a matter of fact, some sanctions against improper language use have survived, but they have little bite. It is open to someone who has been publicly insulted to complain to the hamlet association, which can impose a fine on the offender. However, unless the violation is great, the insult gratuitous or the insulted party a person of some standing, such complaints are discouraged. The only case which came to the hamlet in Corong in recent years involved a spat between two women, a commoner trader in the market and another commoner, who, having married a member of the gentry, had appropriated the honorific *jero* and thus became entitled to receive more refined Balinese. The former abused (*nyabag*) the latter, rendering her 'dirty' (*leteh*). A complaint was made, but the hamlet association imposed only a derisory fine on the perpetrator and ordered her to pay for a small purification ceremony.

The liberalization of language is none the less contentious. While many Balinese still offer deferential language to status superiors, others use forms deemed unsuitable by the latter. Modified bodily forms of subordination are also still in evidence in relation to high priests and some descendants of former rulers, and Balinese still often arrange themselves to coordinate relative head height with status when, for example, Balinese of different rank sit together on the steep steps leading up to a house. But this is a far cry from the grovelling postures subjects adopted in the past.

Some gentry appear unaffected by the unseemly language and lack of deference shown by inferiors, but others complain that it makes one 'confused' (*pusing*), causes an unpleasant sensation in the pit of one's stomach or gives one a headache; and it provokes a combination of both anger (*pedih*) and shame (*lek*). As far as the superior is concerned, the inferior acts boorishly because he 'does not know shame' (*sing nawang lek*), but the former also feels shame because doubt arises concerning his ability to extract deference from others, this being a negative comment on his status (Keeler 1983). In such situations, as also when stubborn wives do not submit to their husbands, Balinese sometimes note, with dismay, that the inferior 'will not give in' (*sing nyak kalah*), implying that superiors attempt to inculcate submission as a virtue among inferiors and the weak (Hatley 1997: 91).

Obtaining redress is problematic. Often the disparity between expected and actual speech is not great; formal complaints might sour friendships or other important relationships, and it is difficult to determine if intent is involved. To complain publicly also demonstrates one's lack of power to elicit proper deference, and may thus make one look ridiculous. In the event, schooling oneself to remain calm and silent and to let karmic retribution take its course is a common response. The possibilities for provocation and abuse stemming from the ambiguity and fluidity of contemporary interaction are sometimes keenly exploited by some commoners. A Brahmana friend came home from his menial government job almost everyday complaining of headaches caused by his commoner boss using what to him were insulting words. In such situations, it is very difficult to tell whether we are dealing with cases of commoner resistance to gentry hegemony or gentry resistance to the establishment of new norms of language exchange; what was perhaps once relatively clear is now blurred.

Despite these changes, the language still encapsulates hierarchy in a remarkably comprehensive way. Many commoner Balinese still use deferential forms to those of higher rank and are enthusiastic to retain the use of high Balinese. It is obvious why gentry are keen to maintain the appropriate use of language levels, but it is not at all clear what motivates commoners to cooperate. Why have the levels of the language not disappeared along with the sanctions?

Some help in clarifying this issue is provided by Geertz's account of similar Javanese practices. Much as in Bali, status in Java is partly founded on the ideology that the higher the rank, the greater the requirement for a still, calm, inner life. Amongst themselves, low-status Javanese use coarse, direct and blunt speech, but should use refined speech to their superiors. Those of high status adopt dignified, oblique and circumspect language amongst themselves, but are direct to their inferiors (Geertz 1960: 254–60; Keeler 1987, 1990). Geertz thus interprets all forms of etiquette as an offering that shields superiors from disturbance. Since Javanese can only partly protect their own sensibilities, it is up to others to do it for them. 'Etiquette is a wall built around one's inner feelings, but it is, paradoxically, always a wall someone else builds, at least in part' (Geertz 1960: 255). This is easy to accept for equals because the act of protecting the other with refined speech is reciprocated, and hence both benefit. But it is harder to see why, without sanctions, inferiors continue to protect superiors. Geertz implies that deference is readily given because it is a cultural requirement.

Siegel challenges this explanation because:

> the undiminished hierarchical quality of Javanese poses a problem. The burden of High Javanese is put on those who speak up, who show deference through speaking High Javanese. Given the opportunity to avoid the implication of social inferiority by substituting Indonesian for Javanese, why should Javanese have kept its vitality?
>
> (Siegel 1986: 22)

Siegel's own argument is obtuse, but he seems to say that low-status Javanese continue to use high-Javanese language and to show deference to others, because by doing so they obtain recognition and respect for themselves. They derive enjoyment from the use of high Javanese for it confirms their ability not merely in the Javanese language, but in the 'language' of Javanese culture.

Although this conclusion holds for Bali, it is inadequate. Many Balinese confer respect on superiors because, as Siegel argues, they expect to receive it back; and some Balinese appear willing to use high Balinese to superiors, as Geertz (1960: 255) says, 'in deference to the other's greater spiritual refinement'. But neither of these explanations is fully satisfactory, since many other reasons account for the persistence of the levels.

To take the argument further requires some description of the everyday use of Balinese. Although today there is a lack of consistency in the use of the *alus–kasar* levels, there are nevertheless some anchor points. First, all public and formal occasions on which Balinese is employed require the use of *alus*. Second, speech behaviour in more relaxed and informal contexts is less restrictive. Third, refined Balinese should be used to priests, puppeteers, healers and so forth, irrespective of their title-group status. Fourth, in general, the use of 'levels' is concordant with the social hierarchy, so that those in lower positions by and large speak a more refined version of Balinese to those in higher positions and in return receive a somewhat less refined version. The actual difference between what is given and what is received depends on other factors. Age in and of itself demands respect; there is slightly less pressure to speak high Balinese to women than to men of the same title; it is always good practice to be respectful to those who are wealthy and in powerful and influential positions, whatever their status title; and some people are far more fastidious about language than are others. I now provide some simple examples.

1. I was drinking coffee at a stall with Wayan, a well-respected commoner, several of whose children have been to secondary school. An older Brahmana joined us. Wayan immediately said we should speak *alus* to him. When Wayan actually spoke, however, his speech simply included the use of certain key words, and was very different from the Balinese used on formal occasions. He generally used the appropriate *alus* terms for anything connected directly with the Brahmana: his food, sleep, opinions, etc. The latter replied in a lower form of Balinese but every now and then inserted a more refined term. While deferential in his choice of language, Wayan was not deferential in any other way, and was not averse to disputing some point or other with him.

This sort of exchange is typical in Corong. Commoners regularly told me that they did not find it demeaning to speak to gentry in a higher version of Balinese than they received back, though this was often tempered with a statement about the necessity for respect to be mutual, and that one need not be too fussy with lower gentry. Equally, many high castes, while speaking 'down' to persons of lower standing, occasionally used relatively *alus* words.

2. I visited a Brahmana house with a young, unemployed Déwa friend who only knew this family by repute. He was clearly ill at ease, and in introducing himself he went to great lengths to explain his inadequacy in *alus* Balinese and asked them to forgive his mistakes. On another occasion, we visited a commoner household, where he again was not well known, but this time he spoke very ordinary Balinese, whilst even the older men, in work and in their own house, spoke 'up' to him.

3. One of the Anak Agung with whom I lived insisted on several occasions that I should always use the very high pronoun *titiang* when speaking to him, and that I

needed to be very respectful towards his mother. He always spoke to me in relatively high Balinese and frequently corrected me if I fell from the high standards he expected when I was talking to somebody else. He has three uncles in the house, all of whom were generally unconcerned about what level I used so long as it was not too low, but we were never consistent. Sometimes they spoke a relatively refined Balinese, sometimes they switched to distinctly lower levels. It was as though they could not make up their minds how I fitted in, and therefore could not decide on the most appropriate level. Nakatani (1995: 33) has described very similar experiences and puts it down to being an outsider, who cannot easily be situated in the hierarchy. However, I think it is a more general condition, because I noticed frequent shifts of level amongst Balinese.

I had very different linguistic exchanges with the wives of these uncles. One was excessively formal and used pure *alus* every time I spoke to her, while another was almost the opposite. I once told the latter that when I stay in Pujung I am called *nanang*, a relatively low form of the Balinese for 'father' and a kinship term used for the vast majority of married men in that village. She and her husband thought this was very funny, but a nephew thought it vile and contemptuously spat out '*kasar!*' ('how coarse!').

4. One of the Brahmana houses in the village is used as a venue for gambling at various card games. The players come from all status groups. Several gentry women were regular players, and the dealers (who receive a small payment for each deal) were always women. The language here was often quite basic, and the behaviour of some players, especially towards the women, was frequently vulgar. It was in such situations that the levels used sometimes changed frequently, when commoners sometimes spoke to gentry as if the latter were commoners, and when men (commoner and gentry alike) made playful sexual attacks on high caste women.[2] In private, gentry complained frequently about this moral and linguistic laxity, but seemed powerless to do anything about it.

5. Young men congregate at village coffee-stalls (*warung*) every evening for several hours. Some older men are usually present, but it is the youngsters who dominate the conversation. The clientele come from all status groups and the talk is relatively free. People tell stories, the events at recent cock-fights are mulled over, the talk often turns to witchcraft or happenings of a strange nature, and some play practical jokes. Those who are good friends and neighbours swap a relatively low Balinese, even if they are quite different in status. It is not at all unusual to hear commoners speaking almost exactly the same level to their age-peer Brahmana friends as to other

---

[2] Balinese society segregates the sexes in public life. Often husbands and wives do not acknowledge each other as they pass in the street, and it is rare for them to go anywhere in each other's company. Men and women do not sit at coffee-stalls together and rarely converse with each other in public. At ceremonies, men and women congregate separately and not as families.

At the card-games, however, women take their place next to men and often wear dresses or culottes, so that they can sit cross-legged (unheard of for women in any other context). During the games, men often caress the thighs of women, pinch them, make clumsy lunges at their crotch and mime sexual intercourse with their hands, fingers or any object that can possibly be regarded as a penis substitute, all punctuated by a lot of talk about sex and genitalia. To a large extent, the women take this without complaint, and with a nervous laugh they push hands away and pull down their dresses. Older women are relatively immune, but the four or five (all gentry) who are aged between thirty and forty-five, have to withstand and tolerate this treatment on a daily basis. It is these women who organize the games, provide the cards, often act as dealers and get the games going in the morning by encouraging the men to come in and play. For them it is a way of making a living. Many men enjoy their company, since it lends an added excitement to the games. But the situation is morally highly ambiguous: the same men who take advantage of the women and enjoy their company also describe them in very derogatory terms.

commoners, with only the occasional *alus* word inserted to preserve a facade of status separation. It is again the perceived lack of respect in these situations which Brahmana and other gentry privately complain about.

6. One of the most surprising aspects of language use in Corong was that commoners corrected my Balinese (that is, told me to use a higher form than the one I had used) more often than gentry did. If they heard me use high Balinese or if I used it to them, I was sometimes praised with a 'thumbs-up' gesture, or a phrase such as: 'Ah, you can speak *basa alus*, that's good.' Similarly, on first acquaintance, many commoners spontaneously told me to use *alus* to gentry – I did not have to coax it out of them. On one occasion, I was quite bluntly reprimanded by a male commoner friend after he heard me speak to a Cokorda youth in what he thought was a disrespectful manner.

7. During an informal gathering someone asked me, from some yards away, where my friend Anak Agung Alit was. I replied that he was at home asleep, and unthinkingly used the word *pules*. Words for sleeping are almost as sensitive to status as words for eating, and *pules* is relatively *kasar*. My remark was immediately greeted by hoots of laughter and mild rebuke. For several days after, friends (gentry and commoner alike) kept the joke going by repeatedly asking me the same question and then mimicking my answer. One even had the temerity to address Alit as Wayan, as though he had been reduced to commoner status.

8. The final example concerns a conversation, not untypical by any means, between a Ngakan schoolteacher of about 50 years of age and a much younger Brahmana who works in a hotel. The latter began speaking to the teacher at a relatively low level and the teacher responded in Indonesian. Within a few minutes, the Brahmana had shifted up and the teacher began to use an equivalent version of Balinese. They maintained this for a while and then gradually moved down. All the while, there was no hint that either was annoyed or offended, and the whole thing, apparently, went off very smoothly; it was not at all clear to me that they were conscious of the several shifts that occurred in a matter of minutes.

These simple vignettes demonstrate that, while the extremes of the language are rarely used, the hierarchical levels, despite evident variation, still command wide approbation. Even if the gap between what gentry receive and what they give back is no longer as wide as it once was, and not as wide as some would like it to be, none the less a gap still exists. What, then, accounts for the persistence of these levels?

One reason is that most Balinese children, including those in commoner households, are taught them from a very early age, and it is this which explains a feature of language use which at first puzzled me. Despite encouragement to friends to speak to me as they would to their own close friends, many found this difficult and kept reverting to higher forms. This is probably because the stratification of the language is internalized during childhood, not only cognitively but also emotionally. After all, inappropriate language is not merely insulting, it makes one feel ill. Balinese can become anxious and shamed (*lek*), even almost paralysed, if they cannot speak well enough in front of high-status persons, and the use of unsuitable words sometimes provokes strong reactions in those present (laughter, anger, embarrassment). As one learns the language, those Balinese terms which are very status-sensitive take on colours and associations which render them peculiarly appropriate in certain contexts, and it requires an effort of will to think of them as mere words. Consequently, the levels become natural, deeply ingrained and compulsive. This explains why some gentry experience unsuitable words so keenly and within their body, and why some commoner Balinese feel impelled to offer the required deferential terms.

If we add to this that a lack of fluency in high Balinese inhibits interaction and thus keeps one silent, that its flowery formality is often as important as its content, that it can be ambiguous because its few terms have to carry a broad range of meaning, and that its use is still demanded by those in powerful positions either because of their hierarchical status or because they are employers or patrons, then the levels of Balinese appear very constraining; they may seem like a linguistic prison. These are, of course, the reasons why it has been, and in part still is, a tool of domination.

But this is only one side of the story. The pressure exerted on me by commoners to use high Balinese and the pleasure which many evidently obtain from using it suggest that high Balinese is not simply constraining but also enabling. It is the diverse ways in which high Balinese is empowering which give it its resilience and vitality.

First, the existence of 'levels' allows almost everybody to reap some rewards from using them. While there are always people one has to speak 'up' to, there are usually also people one can speak 'down' to. Just as the graded structure of the social hierarchy provides incentives, however equivocal, to maintain it, so too does the correspondingly structured language.

Second, many commoners only use high Balinese to gentry so long as it is understood that they are to be respected in return. A phrase people, including gentry, often use, is *saling menghormati*, which means 'to respect each other'. That this is an Indonesian phrase, there being no real Balinese equivalent, suggests that the idea is a recent innovation. Gentry cannot address commoners with undiluted *kasar* language and expect to be treated with respect. Even direct descendants of pre-colonial ruling families need to be circumspect about how they speak to commoners, since they rely on their votes, their paid labour and their voluntary work during ceremonies. Gentry therefore often insert refined words when they speak to commoners to ease the gap in language levels, and levels can be constantly adjusted to keep the flow of conversation smooth and free of tension. Commoners continue to use the levels because they can extract some respect from others in a way they formerly could not. The disappearance of negative sanctions and the attenuation of the levels have, perhaps paradoxically, generated positive inducements for commoners to use the language levels. One might also say that informal sanctions now operate which encourage gentry to conform to more equal linguistic exchanges.

Third, high Balinese is deemed good in and of itself. Commoners and gentry alike extol the virtues and beauty of high Balinese, and some speak reverently about it. It is, after all, the language offered to high priests, ancestors and minor deities. A refined term for 'tell' and 'say' is *atur*, which, in the form *aturan*, also means 'offerings'; one does not therefore merely 'speak' to a god, one presents an offering. Many friends told me that it is always good to speak *alus* even if one is being talked 'down' to. This shows both that you value yourself and cannot be intimidated and that you have control of yourself, and such control connotes refinement. If you carry on speaking *alus*, the other is shamed and moves up. Ideally, people should speak *alus* not simply to pay respect to others, but because it bespeaks a good and generous (*polos*) character. Moreover, competence in high Balinese, as in high Javanese (Errington 1998: 42) is an index of social worth and marks a refined inner nature. Commoners who can speak it well thus make a claim to augmented prestige, if not caste status. On the other hand, commoner fluency is also threatening to elites, as it suggests that their exclusivity is artificial.

Fourth, the ability to speak 'pure' *alus* brings recognition from others as an achievement of some distinction. From time to time, Balinese have to visit a *pedanda*, a high official or a healer/spirit medium. On such occasions, people express concern that their lack of fluency may offend and be punished by a curse or sorcery or that they will become tongue-tied and embarrassed. The dilemma can be circumvented by asking a friend or relative, known for his abilities, to speak on your behalf. Furthermore, some Balinese men join groups, known as *seka pepaosan*, to read and sing Balinese poetic literature (for example, the *Ramayana*). The group is led by someone proficient in the language of these texts (Old Javanese, or Kawi). After a line is sung, it is translated into high Balinese, and there may be discussion of the meanings and etymologies of words. Those deemed capable are expected to sing at temple festivals and other ceremonial events. Balinese well known for their linguistic skills lead the negotiations in arranged marriages. In these and many other ways Balinese gain reputations for their abilities in high Balinese and Kawi. A good command of language in all its varieties is a valuable resource, partly because these social skills can be construed as status attributes.

Fifthly, the Balinese language, like almost every other aspect of Balinese life, is an arena for competition. Despite their feigned modesty in being able to speak it, Balinese actively compete to outdo others (see Tisna 1935 for a fictional account of a linguistic battle between men at a *pepaosan* reading). After formal visits of the groom's party to his intended bride's house, during which conversation is incredibly polite, there is usually a discussion about which side got the better of the talk. There is another aspect to this as well. The use of formal high Balinese at such events is appropriate because it gives gravity to the ceremony and a 'set-apart' quality.

A sixth factor concerns the myriad uses of the language for 'religious' purposes. All prayers and incantations directed to deities and spirits are in high Balinese or Kawi (Kawi being considered 'above' *alus*), and all Balinese have to be proficient in these to one degree or another. Many commoners are temple priests (*pemangku*) and have to learn a large number of mantra, dedications and litanies (Hooykaas 1977). Even ordinary farmers need to know some simple prayers so that they can make their offerings to the goddess of rice, Déwi Sri. Maintaining correct linguistic usage in relation to deities and ancestors is vital to safety and prosperity, since inappropriate words can bring misfortune. Maintaining contact between mortal and ancestral worlds through the proper use of hierarchical speech registers makes the speech levels appear divinely ordained.[3]

Last, most Balinese performing arts require a knowledge of a number of levels of the language, including Kawi. The prototype is the shadow theatre (*wayang kulit*), which portrays the conflict between two related families, the Pandawas and the Korawas, as recounted in the ancient Indian epic poem the *Mahabharata*. The principal protagonists are kings, princes, gods and priests, who all speak Kawi. Translations into Balinese are provided by the servant-clowns (Hobart 1987, Zurbuchen 1987), who also furnish light entertainment in the form of slapstick, wordplay and jokes. However, maintaining the linguistic levels in the shadow theatre and other performing arts is not anachronistic, because Kawi is relatively insensitive to status differences. It is only when Kawi is translated into appropriate Balinese that the status differences are made explicit. Thus, while the characters

---

[3] In one sense at least, language is thought of as a gift of the gods. Saraswati, the Balinese (Hindu) goddess of learning and writing, resides in the tip of the tongue, from where speech is thought to emanate (Rubinstein 1987: 65). Balinese letters (*aksara*) are conceptualized as having divine origin, being imperishable and having supernatural power (ibid.: 75), all of which ideas are entirely Indian. (For further details, see note 24, Chapter 6.)

'*speak* in Kawi', via the interventions of the servants 'they *mean* in Balinese', and are thus in a Balinese social and cultural world (Zurbuchen 1987: 193, her emphasis).

On the one hand, then, the language remains a symbolic system encoding relationships of superiority and inferiority, domination and subordination. Though more tenuously than in the past, these still link commoners to gentry, clients to their priests and all these to gods and ancestors. Today, in addition, they also link employers to employees, office superiors to their subordinates and politicians to their supporters. Because the coercive nature of the language is partly disguised by being learned and inculcated before it can be questioned, hierarchy continues to receive a modicum of legitimation. On the other hand, modern Balinese society supplies many people with a wide range of positive incentives for maintaining high Balinese, and therefore its continued use transcends issues of domination.

Finally, what explains the variation evident in the way Balinese speak to each other? The institution of *basa pasar*, or 'market language', furnishes an obvious clue. The prices of market goods are arrived at through bargaining. Language exchange can also be thought about in these terms. There are many situations today in which gentry find themselves in a weak position in relation to commoners: commoner university graduates and unemployed Brahmana; dissolute gentry and respectable commoners; commoner employers and gentry employees. There are no clear rules to handle the language problems these situations produce. Apart from cases in which the dominant person unilaterally enforces a demeaning linguistic exchange with a subordinate, what appears to happen is that both engage in a bargaining process until an acceptable compromise is reached, though this is always provisional and may change. I have heard Balinese refer to this as *tawar-menawar* (Ind.), the same term that denotes market bargaining.

Because of new prestige systems, the dilution of 'traditional' political relationships and modern ideologies of equality, people bargain linguistic terms all the time. This explains the suppression of the extremes and the burgeoning of the middle respect levels. In the past, linguistic exchange between Balinese was largely determined by the relative status of the groups they were members of and according to rules backed by sanctions. In modern Bali, this exchange has begun to depend more on the choices exercised within individual dyadic encounters, a process that generates wide variation.

The limits of ritual inflation

Whenever Balinese is spoken, messages are conveyed about relative status differentials. This may not be intentional, but it is inevitable. This also holds good for much ritual activity. If the explicit motive of many rituals is to confer well-being on the person who is its subject, the manner of its performance is interpreted by both the holders and others as a measure of the former's worth. Consequently, Balinese are constrained to participate in competitive display or risk compromising their reputation. Since 1970 growing affluence has provided many Balinese with opportunities to devote increasing material resources to ritual in an effort to enhance their own prestige by outsmarting rivals. What, then, constrains such ritual inflation from running out of control?

In the pre-colonial period, status competition through ritual was limited by the sanctions rulers could apply to overambitious subordinates and by the difficulty of mobilizing sufficient labour to carry out large projects. In assuming power, the Dutch colonial administration changed both. In the first case, Balinese rulers gradually lost their power to apply sanctions, enabling subordinates to act more independently. In the second case, because it was Balinese officials who controlled many aspects of the day-to-day management of the colonial regime's new and more onerous corvée system, in which the number of days of unpaid labour due to the colonial state was greater than had been due to the pre-colonial rulers, they were sometimes able to recruit more labour than previously and divert it to their own, traditional, purposes (Schulte Nordholt 1991a: 153).

However, because of the severe economic and political conditions resulting from Dutch rule, the Japanese occupation and postwar political conflicts, a period the Balinese sometimes describe as *dugas guminé uug* ('when the world was destroyed'), ritual inflation did not occur (Connor 1996: 189). Indeed, it was more a matter of ritual deflation: the dead were left uncremated, gamelans were sold or melted down, costumes rotted away and temples and palaces became dilapidated.

On the other hand, the period after 1970 has been experienced by most Balinese as relatively safer and more prosperous, despite the oppressive Suharto regime suffo-cating any kind of political dissent and opposition. As the economy improved and the tourist boom began, raised aspirations, based on rapidly increasing disposable incomes, were expressed in a variety of ways. A great deal of new money was invested in commercial ventures of many kinds, in a wide range of consumer durables and in the improvement of homes.

Balinese have also channelled sizeable resources into ritual and religious activity. Houseyard temples have been renovated, beautified and enlarged; new and expensive ceremonial clothes have proliferated; new and costly items appear in offerings; temple ceremonies increasingly include costly entertainments during the week of the festivities; more animals of all kinds are slaughtered; and, occasionally, rituals are introduced that have never previously been performed. While such activity boosts local economies, it also encourages competitive ceremonial display and the kinds of status drive described in earlier chapters.[4]

In Pujung in 1980, not one of the 225 families in the village owned a gold-ornamented wooden offerings platform (used to take offerings to temples), but by 1993 every household had purchased one at a unit cost of Rp200,000 (US$100). In Corong, long, single-file processions (*mapeed*) are a feature of some temple festivals. Each day a different hamlet takes centre stage, while the rest of the village watches and passes judgement on the beauty of the women, their clothes and the offerings they carry. Each member of the procession must purchase the same set of clothes, or risk shaming the hamlet. In the past no specific form of dress was required for atten-dance at cremations, temple festivals and other ritual events, save for some essential but inexpensive items. Today, however, there is tremendous social pressure to buy more and more elaborate and expensive ceremonial clothes and to own different sets of clothing for different kinds of ritual events (for example, black for cremations and white for temple ceremonies).

It is the very mundaneness of these examples which indicates the extent to which ritual inflation has permeated every aspect of ceremonial activity. More hard

---

[4] Bali is, of course, not the only society in Indonesia to experience ritual inflation. Volkman describes similar ritual escalation and its relation to status ranking amongst the Toraja in Sulawesi. Unlike in Bali, where it has been fuelled by tourist revenues and the expansion of the local economy, ritual inflation in Toraja has been driven by new wealth brought home by returning migrant labour (Volkman 1984, 1985).

evidence is supplied by Poffenberger and Zurbuchen (1980: 120, 129), who worked in the Gianyar region, and Nakatani (1995: 141–2), who worked in Karangasem. Using quantitative data, they argue that, after accounting for price inflation, there has been a rise in the costs of ceremonies at all levels of society. Stuart-Fox (1987: 270) also reports that the main annual ritual at the Besakih temple has increased in cost greatly over the last fifty years, mainly on account of many additional rituals. In short, despite repeated predictions by Balinese and others that the enormous costs of royal cremations mean they will soon disappear for good, ritual inflation below this level is common.

In theory such activity has the potential to become unlimited. If family A spends a specific sum in performing a ceremony, then family B, of roughly equivalent rank in the hierarchy, must spend more on the same ritual to outshine A. This practice, rather more like the North American Indian potlatch than New Guinea 'big man' rivalry, permanently raises the stakes, since the only way A can stay in contention is to spend the same or even more on the next occasion. Pressed ruthlessly, this could lead to unending ritual inflation. In practice, however, this does not happen. But, before considering the constraints on ritual inflation, I provide some anecdotal information on Bali's new prosperity and then on the nature of ritual competition.

Over the last thirty years, a significant number of Balinese of all ranks have become fabulously wealthy in comparison with the recent past. This wealth has been built on the sale of land to developers, success in a wide range of new commercial and industrial ventures, new export industries, restaurants and hotels in the lucrative tourist sector, the sale of indigenous arts and crafts, and so forth. Even in villages such as Pujung, which even twenty years ago hardly saw a tourist from one month to the next, some villagers have become very rich. In 1980 Madé Arta, for example, was a young man making a precarious living carving chess sets, which he sold to a tourist shop. Today he has a four-storey 'factory', which provides work for many employees (migrating to south Bali from poorer regions to the north and east) and exports crafts all over the world. He has numerous clients from western countries who visit his workshops on an almost daily basis. In 1995 he bought a new BMW car to go along with the Toyota he already owned. There are at least four other dealers in Pujung similar in stature to Arta, and nearby villages can boast of similar success stories.

In contrast, some of Madé Arta's neighbours still practise a mixture of subsistence farming and part-time carving. While these too are now considerably more affluent, the economic gap between them and men such as Madé Arta is more extreme than it once was. The contrast is even more stark in villages such as Celuk, Mas and Ubud, all on the main tourist routes, where some Balinese have become dollar millionaires, whilst others eke out a precarious living. Yet they may well be members of the same *banjar*. Some of these 'businessmen' take their *banjar* obligations very seriously. They contribute large sums to village schemes (a list of donors and the size of their donations is posted for everyone to see), participate in cremations, attend *banjar* meetings and maintain a characteristic modesty about their wealth. Others, especially those who have moved out of the village, are often much less fastidious and try to detach themselves from such responsibilities.

Such large differences in wealth are also present within extended families living in the same houseyard. The following example, though dramatic, is not wholly untypical. It concerns a Brahmana residence in Corong. One of the men in the house has two co-resident wives. He has four children from the first marriage, two

Plate 5.1 Wooden carvings and wood supplies on the third floor of a Balinese house/factory in the village of Pujung

of whom live elsewhere. The other two have become very successful businessmen, possess lavish rooms, own trucks and jeeps and many consumer durables (television, radio, video, camera, etc.) and employ several full-time workers. The man also has three children from his second marriage. The eldest daughter married a Brahmana from another village, who, because he was poor, moved into his father-in-law's house. Unable to find work, he spent his time around the house and used whatever money he had to gamble at cock-fights. The couple had so little income that he was reduced to borrowing used razor-blades from friends so he could shave. Thoroughly fed up with her situation and very jealous of her half-brothers, who, she complained, repeatedly taunted her, she began to sell snacks at the card-games in another house in the same street. However, there she was humiliated by the endless teasing, coarse language and sexual advances of the gamblers, and she often sat away from others, staring into space or quietly crying. One evening she violently attacked her husband, who, under the barrage of fists and insults, fell into a groaning semi-consciousness and was taken back to his natal home, where he stayed for a week. During this time there were several family conferences and it was eventually agreed that he could become a driver for one of his brothers-in-law, which meant their current driver had to be sacked. This arrangement seemed to work until the husband's driving licence expired. It only needed a relatively small sum of money to renew it, but he did not have this and his father- and brothers-in-law would not lend it to him. By the time I left the field, the couple were back to square one.

The ceremonies most sensitive to status and prestige, in relation both to individual families and to title groups, are rites of passage.[5] In fact, however, most of these are performed on a relatively simple scale with only close kin attending, and with a range of offerings, which can be produced without the help of others. They are thus largely free of competitive overtones. The rituals of birth and naming, those held at forty-two days, 105 days and one year, and those on subsequent 'birthdays', are most usually in-house affairs and pass largely unnoticed by other villagers. Nevertheless, important and powerful families may opt to perform even these ceremonies in a more elaborate way. They may increase the range of offerings, seclude the subject of the rite for one or three days, arrange evening entertainment and invite guests, who must then be fed. Performing the ceremony at this level increases costs and requires considerable assistance from kin, neighbours, friends and clients. These provide materials, erect temporary shelters, make offerings, slaughter animals, prepare food, clean up, and so forth. This unpaid labour must also be fed and kept plied with coffee, snacks and cigarettes.

When it comes to the major rites of puberty (for girls only), tooth-filing, marriage and cremation, however, the situation is reversed, and even poor and weak families

---

[5] All Balinese have to undergo a series of rites of passage, moving them from birth to death and beyond. The responsibility for carrying these out passes from one group of people to another as the series progresses. The rites from birth up to and including tooth-filing are indispensable for the child's health and longevity, and are the responsibility of parents. The burial, cremation and post-cremation rites for parents are likewise essential for safely ushering the soul into heaven, after which it may reincarnate, and these are the responsibility of children. Weddings straddle this division and the bridal couple are expected to make a contribution to the costs, particularly if they are older and have been working. These reciprocal obligations between parents and children over a lifetime are the most serious and onerous duties a Balinese has. Children accumulate a debt to their parents, which they subsequently repay by the performance of death ceremonies. An emotive expression of the debt children owe their parents is encapsulated in what mothers proverbially say to children who vex them: '*Cang nglekadang cai, magantung aji bok akatih*' ('I gave birth to you, and my life hung by a hair').

Plate 5.2   Village men preparing meals and ritual meat offerings preparatory to a tooth filing ceremony in a Brahmana house in Corong. In other parts of the compound men are slaughtering pigs, ducks and chickens, and preparing other dishes and offerings. Women are steaming rice, boiling vegetables, also making offerings, and serving coffee and cigarettes to the men

experience shame if they cannot perform at a level equal to or greater than their close status rivals. The competitive aspects of spectacular royal rituals, as described by Geertz (1980), therefore have their analogues in the far less extravagant ceremonies of ordinary Balinese of all ranks. By inviting many guests and adopting practices usually reserved for gentry, such as a period of seclusion, affluent and ambitious commoners in Pujung stage ceremonies hardly different from those held by families of Triwangsa in Corong. This process is replicated by lower gentry appropriating some of the ritual prerogatives of higher gentry to press their claims to superior rank. At a more mundane level families of all ranks try to distinguish themselves by slaughtering more animals than their rivals, and more than they did themselves on previous occasions, by purchasing more exotic and expensive food and fruit to adorn their offerings, and by introducing offerings not previously used.

This competition leads to an almost obsessional concern with how others perform their rituals. Almost every time I participated in a major life-crisis ceremony in Corong, I was cross-examined by the holders concerning the merits of their own performance relative to those held recently by neighbours: was the food better, were the offerings more elaborate, was the assembly larger, were the guests more influential, were the gifts of better quality and more expensive, and so forth? On several occasions I was asked to take photographs, not just of the ceremonial activity, but of the rows of cars impressively parked outside the house. Defeat in this competition or an inability at least to maintain parity with status peers and neighbours induces a feeling of shame, denoted by the term *majengah*. This is a potent combination of envy, anger and embarrassment, which spurs people on to greater efforts next time. In 1994 the Anak Agung family I lived with in Corong were planning a massive tooth-filing ceremony, which would not only outdo anything they themselves had previously done but, more importantly, put to shame their Brahmana neighbours, who had recently spent 5 million rupiah (US$2,500) on a similar ceremony. They were already saving hard, had arranged a bank loan and were calling in the debts owed to them by those whom they had assisted in the past.

What, then, are the factors limiting ritual inflation? Broadly speaking, there are three. The first set of reasons concerns the efforts made by intellectuals, reformers and religious authorities to reduce the costs of ceremonies, especially cremations (Connor 1996). Combining a care for the plight of the poor with an agenda for egalitarian reforms of hierarchy, privilege and power, these reformers championed rationalized and less expensive ceremonies.[6] Reforms, eventually legitimated by *pedanda* priests and state religious authorities, include the introduction of streamlined cremations, called *ngabén ngalanus*, which compress the different phases into a twenty-four-hour period instead of twelve days; requiring less preparation, they are thus less costly. Another innovation is the introduction of collective cremations, *ngabén ngiring*, in which a group of families coordinate their activities and share the services of a priest and a number of important offerings.[7] This not only decreases the

---

[6] Connor (1996) has also argued that the increasing number of Balinese in urban, waged occupations makes short, simple, cheap ceremonies an attractive proposition. I have heard this expressed in Corong, but equally many Balinese take advantage of the opportunities which growing affluence creates to display wealth and status in the ritual sphere.

[7] Other ceremonies may also be performed collectively within one or a group of families. Parents may wait until their youngest child is old enough to undergo tooth-filing and then perform the ceremony for all their children at the same time; tooth-filing may be jointly performed with a marriage, or even with a cremation; a poor family may wait until rich relatives are ready to mount a ceremony and join with them to take advantage of the savings this can produce; and there are other possibilities.

Plate 5.3 Priest filing down the upper six centre teeth of a brother and sister until they are uniformly straight. Relatives gather round to provide support and protection. Six other children, still in seclusion, are waiting their turn

Plate 5.4 *Pula gembal*. One of many highly decorative and complex offerings required at life crisis rites such as tooth filing. This one is said to symbolize the 'whole world and all its contents' (*guminé tekén isinné*)

financial outlay for each family, but it also dilutes competition, since rivalry partly depends on families preparing different offerings. Many of these reforms are now common practice throughout Bali.

Other reforms have not fared so well, however. To a large extent these concern attempts to impose new interpretations of ritual activity, especially cremation. In one, reformers have asserted that the efficacy of a rite remains constant irrespective of the material level at which it is performed. Consequently, only a certain minimum of offerings is necessary to perform the ceremony properly, and so the destruction of the offerings and paraphernalia used in more lavish ceremonies is condemned as an irrational waste of money, which disproportionately penalizes the poor. In another, which invokes local versions of Indian karmic theory and western ideas about merit, the fate of the soul is said to depend on the quality of the person's actions during life and thus cannot be affected by ceremonial activity, however much money is spent (Connor 1996: 186–7).

While some Balinese agree that the material extravagance of rituals is not essential to the fate of the soul after death or to its well-being whilst on earth, and can even be counter-productive (see below), the vast majority of Balinese I know continue to believe that offerings are not an optional extra but rather an absolute requirement for the success of a rite, each offering having a specific and necessary purpose. In rites of passage, offerings are provided for deities and ancestors, for the person undergoing the rite and for various 'low' spirits. In all of these food is a major component. The ancestors and spirits consume the 'essence' (*sari*) of the offerings presented to them, and thus are placated and encouraged to reciprocate by protecting the subject of the rite. Likewise, the soul of the initiand is nourished by wafting the essence of offerings towards his or her body. These offerings demonstrate the intensity and centrality of the association between the living and ancestors and spirits. Without them, the latter become angry and take supernatural revenge, and the life-force of the subject of the rite gradually diminishes, leaving him/her to fall ill and die.[8]

Attempts to restrain ritual consumption through encouraging simplified, collective and cheap ceremonial performance is problematic in other ways. For a start, if offerings are essential to well-being, cutting down on them leads to accusations of an uncaring attitude to one's ancestors and children. In the ceremonial sphere, social approbation depends on visible demonstration of substantial ritual activity, and so the substitution of an ethical orientation to religion in place of a ritual one poses severe problems of impression management. Secondly, simple ceremonies may give rise to difficult social relationships. Since the reciprocal exchange of unpaid labour constitutes a cornerstone of harmonious community relations, the pressure both to provide labour for others and to ask it for oneself is very great. Consequently, the performance of ceremonies that require no or little outside help looks suspiciously like an attempt to extricate oneself from such obligations. Villagers who rarely

---

[8] Reformist doctrines concerning the purpose of offerings have a counterpart in a traditional ideology. This is expressed in the Balinese phrase: *suci baan banten, suci baan kenehé*, which translates as 'pure through offerings, pure through thoughts'. Balinese friends gave me two different accounts of this. One was that the use of offerings confers an automatic and direct benefit on the person undergoing the rite and is thus an alternative method to an ethical orientation concerning the purity of one's thoughts and intentions. Others interpreted it as meaning that offerings are an outward sign of inner sincerity, and therefore not really essential. This ambiguity is compounded because, according to Balinese, offerings are directly efficacious only if they are constructed from materials unsoiled by prior usage or theft, made whilst one's thoughts are pure and calm, and ungrudgingly given.

participate in the daily affairs of the hamlet and the rituals of its members become a focus for gossip and anger, and may eventually have their own cremations disrupted. Thirdly, because large-scale ceremonies are redistributive feasts, the holding of simple ceremonies leads to accusations of being mean (*momo*) and raises doubts about the real motives for spending less. Finally, most Balinese thoroughly enjoy these ceremonies. The slaughtering of the animals and the preparation of the food and offerings on the day of the ceremony create a crowded, lively and bustling atmosphere (*ramé*), which Balinese find very pleasurable. Ceremonies that are poorly attended are usually morose affairs which people complain about. All these factors generate tremendous social pressure to continue performing elaborate rituals.

These reforms also sometimes produce effects at variance with those intended. In the past, the high costs of cremation prevented many people from undertaking them. Now that cheaper alternatives are available, everyone feels obliged to conduct them. Moreover, for reasons having to do with creating a pure environment, new regulations have been introduced which stipulate that the huge and increasingly expensive and complex ceremonies at the Besakih temple cannot begin until all the corpses in Bali have been disinterred and cremated. These ceremonies are now held more regularly than in the past, leaving families with less time to accumulate the wherewithal to cremate their dead. Finally, collective cremations can create insuperable problems if the families involved are of different status, particularly if relative ranking is disputed. In such cases, it may be impossible to reach agreement on the offerings to be used, on the priest who is to officiate and on how the corpses are arranged in the tower that carries them to the burning ground. Such cooperation would involve 'the crystallization of claims to status preeminence ... that is at odds with the fluid nature of status competition in everyday life' (Connor 1996: 199). Higher-ranking families baulk at having to share offerings and priestly services with those of lower rank, which may render the former polluted and thus may have an adverse affect on the fate of the departed soul (Warren 1993: 158). Precisely because collective cremations give the appearance of flattening status differentials, those who can afford to cremate individually often opt to take this course of action. The introduction of collective ceremonies ironically provides new opportunities to express differences.

A second set of reasons limiting ritual inflation concerns the relationship between ritual performance and status. While the cultural disapproval of arrogance and boasting and the concomitant injunctions to be humble, modest and moderate are well-developed cultural themes, families are nevertheless expected to perform ceremonies at a level commensurate with their caste status. Those of high status are therefore both privileged and obliged to conduct ceremonies in a more elaborate manner than those of low status. This may dampen rivalry between families of the same hierarchical rank because ideally they can only go so far before they run up against the ceiling imposed by the practices of those of yet higher rank.

Reformers have had something to say about this issue too. They suggested that the level at which rituals are performed should be related less to caste status and more to differences in wealth (Connor 1996: 187). But, again, it is precisely these kinds of reforms which encourage *nouveaux riches* commoners to convert wealth into status by staging expensive and elaborate rituals.

Other forms of social disapproval also have an effect on ritual inflation. The discrepancy between what a family does in the ritual sphere and what is expected of it is closely monitored, and complaints may be made to hamlet leaders (Poffenberger and Zurbuchen 1980: 125). For example, villagers can remonstrate with officials if a family oversteps conventional practice in the amounts and quality of the comestibles (coffee, cigarettes and food) that are served to villagers who help with the preparations. Some hamlet associations have even instituted regulations stipulating what and how much it is permissible to serve on such occasions, and there may be village guidelines for the appropriate number of guests to be entertained at a ceremony (Warren 1993: 157). This is important, because it is these items which account for a sizeable share of the overall costs. The very fact that these injunctions are often a heated topic of discussion demonstrates that ritual inflation is a pressing concern, particularly for poorer members of a hamlet.

Such restraints on spending are seen as harsh by affluent villagers who want to be generous to those who assist at their ceremonies. If they are prevented from being so by strict village codes, paradoxically they can be on the receiving end of others' accusations of being tight-fisted. In addition, some families may have to invite guests from other villages where no such restrictions are in operation, and therefore are forced to default on their reciprocal obligations. Sometimes, of course, accusations of meanness are merited: *yén suba sugih sing nyak maliat tuun* ('now they are rich they ignore the poor') is a stinging rebuke to those who fail to redistribute their wealth either in lavish feasts or in other ways. In any case democratic injunctions which invoke the same limits for everyone in a *banjar* contradict others which specify a link between scale of ceremony and either wealth or status (Warren 1993: 157–8).

Decisions on exactly how to mount a major ceremony are therefore fraught with risk and anxiety (Howe 2000). A lavish ritual may enhance a family's prestige, and it may please the ancestors. But, if the mark is overstepped, villagers may become offended and disrupt the proceedings, though they do this also when the host family is perceived to be too stingy. Overly extravagant ritual activity can also have unforeseen and adverse consequences. In relation to this, Poffenberger and Zurbuchen (1980: 123–5) recount an instructive story from a village in Karangasem, which demonstrates the deleterious effects of carrying out a cremation at a level exceeding what is deemed acceptable in an attempt to enhance status. On the night after the burning, so the story goes, family members were woken by strange sounds, and when they investigated they saw the 'departed relative, his mouth stuffed with the elaborate offerings, moaning that he was too heavy ... to enter heaven'. It is, therefore, extremely difficult to balance judiciously the desire to assert status, the necessity to please ancestors and descent-group deities, the requirement to fulfil reciprocal labour obligations and the need to maintain harmony with other villagers.

The final factor limiting ritual inflation revolves around problems of recruiting the unpaid labour of others, without which such ceremonies could not be performed at all. This is a significant issue, because, while in a pragmatic sense a large ritual obviously requires a large number of workers, in a cultural sense the perceived social success of the performance depends on those who come as helpers and guests, because the size and quality of the turnout provide a measure of the family's worth and substance.

First, the more pragmatic issues. As already mentioned, unpaid ritual labour has to be reciprocated, and it is accurately calculated and closely monitored. Consequently, in order to recruit a large amount of labour for any undertaking, a household must shoulder onerous labour obligations to others. Close kin, neighbours and members of one's descent group are the usual people involved in these arrangements. There is, however, an asymmetry, because those of higher status cannot provide labour for those of lower status without compromising their position.[9] The usual arrangement in Corong is for high castes to make cash donations or send very junior kin to their commoner neighbours. Since the size and complexity of ceremonies often correlate with rank in the hierarchy, those of higher status spend more money to pay for all the materials, but are able to call on a larger number of helpers to meet the increased labour demands required for their bigger ceremonies.

Moreover, clients (tenants, employees, those whom a healer has cured, etc.) should provide labour for their patrons, as should disciples (*sisya*) for their *pedanda* priest and villagers for their Cokorda, as a return for the access to land, jobs, security and spiritual well-being provided by the latter. This again means that affluent and powerful households have access to greater amounts of labour than others.

Balinese rituals depend on a combination of what Strathern (1969), writing about the Melpa of Papua New Guinea, has called production strategies and finance strategies. In relation to the materials needed for a ceremony, Balinese households can often rely predominantly on a production strategy. They can produce most of the foodstuffs (rice, coconuts, eggs, vegetables, fruit, spices, etc.), the materials to make offerings (various leaves, bamboo, flowers, Chinese coins, etc.) and some of the animals (pigs, chickens, ducks) from their own resources, and other materials can be bought. If there are deficiencies, they can adopt a limited finance strategy by calling in debts from those families to which the household contributed materials in the past, and by asking for assistance from others, to whom they then become debtors. In relation to labour, the situation is completely reversed. A household can only provide a small proportion of the labour required, and so must rely predominantly on a finance strategy to obtain the rest. A wealthy gentry household consisting of ten people may need up to an extra hundred workers to carry out a lavish wedding.

The production strategy has the advantage that all the decisions are taken by the household, but the disadvantage that home production may not be able to cope. The finance strategy has the advantage that it can procure labour and materials from much further afield, but the disadvantage that the household is dependent on decisions taken by many other people (Strathern 1969: 43; Gregory 1982: 60).

Because the uncertainty of the availability of labour is greater than that of the availability of material produce, it is often labour which is the more significant factor in deciding the level at which to perform a ceremony. The way that a family manages its finance strategy therefore becomes critical. While rich and powerful households, as explained above, can call on significantly more labour than poorer households, nevertheless a family cannot endlessly increase the labour input to its ceremonies without incurring for itself punitive labour obligations to others. Production problems, however, are never eclipsed by those associated with finance strategies, since, as the number of workers and guests increases, so too do the costs of feeding and entertaining them.

Another brake on the availability of labour revolves around the fact that there is a finite pool of it and there may be conflict over who has prior claims on it. For example, rival households sometimes refuse to exchange labour because such exchange entails that they become pawns in each other's status projects; consequently the

---

[9] The Balinese verbs denoting this labour are *ngayah* for those who provide assistance for those of higher status, and *nguop* for those who provide it for equals. There is no term to describe labour provided by superiors for inferiors.

amount of labour each can call on is reduced. In Corong, the Déwa and Ngakan families in the same hamlet are virtually never invited to assist at each other's ceremonies. Also, since ceremonies must be performed on auspicious days, which appear infrequently, certain days see a village explode into ritual activity. Rival households then find themselves performing ceremonies on the same day and thus competing for the same pool of labour. Conversely, households of roughly equivalent status and wealth can agree to exchange labour and, because of that, also agree to keep rivalry within limits. A group of Déwa households in Corong participate in each other's rites of passage and conduct them at roughly the same level in order to keep competition to a minimum. In all these senses, one can detect inbuilt structural control mechanisms that inhibit households from recruiting ever more labour, and which therefore act to prevent ritual inflation from continually escalating.

Moreover, if increased economic activity has provided households with the income to invest in ritual, it has also put a strain on the availability of unpaid ritual labour. Between 1975 and 1998, the huge building boom in Bali created work for Balinese manual workers and sucked in migrant labour from other Indonesian islands. Alongside those who have jobs in offices, shops, hotels, schools and hospitals, manual workers stream out of Corong between 5.30 and 6.30 in the morning on their way to the main towns and tourist centres. Consequently, many people now have to decide between a day's wages and an unpaid labour obligation. Nowadays, this decision is sometimes made for them by bosses, who are increasingly irritated by their workers' frequent requests for time off to attend a customary ritual event and who, it is said, increasingly prefer to employ migrant workers rather than Balinese.

It is not simply these control mechanisms which limit available labour, since many other problems can arise, and in general the number of helpers anticipated is usually more than in fact turn up. If a household is mean in supplying labour to others, it will have great difficulty in recruiting labour for itself. If hosts make overambitious status claims or do not treat their helpers generously, the latter become alienated and may even sabotage the event, as has already been described in earlier chapters. There are also a variety of singular events which can compromise a household's attempt to perform a ceremony in accordance with its wishes. I provide three examples to illustrate this.

First, when a middle-aged man in Corong suddenly died, his family decided to show how successful and wealthy they had become by cremating him immediately without prior burial. The members of the *banjar* were called to make their contributions and to assist with the preparations. However, for some reason (some thought it a deliberate slight, the family claimed it was a misunderstanding), the *banjar* was dismissed prematurely, and the deceased's extended family carried out the killing of the pig and preparation of food and meat offerings on their own. When the members of the *banjar* were summoned again to carry the tower to the burning ground, many failed to turn up, and those who did were very angry. The corpse was maltreated when it was transferred to the cremation tower and, because the tower was too heavy for those present to lift easily, it suffered great damage during its journey to the cemetery. Second, what another family hoped and expected to be a very large and prestigious marriage ceremony for their son turned out a flop when many villagers failed to arrive on the morning of the wedding day to help with the myriad preparations. They stayed away in retaliation against the groom, who, having got into a quarrel with a neighbour whose house was a regular gambling venue, asked the police to raid it and thus became an object of hate. Third, when a commoner temple priest died some years ago, his family wanted to cremate him immediately, since burial is polluting for priests. However, because the priest was an inveterate gambler and a drunkard, he had reduced his family to penury and severely tested the patience of his ill-served temple congregation. Being too poor to proceed on their own, they petitioned the *banjar* for extra help. The *banjar* flatly refused to give the family any resources beyond what was strictly obligatory. The priest was therefore buried and has remained underground to this day. Such events turn ritual activity into social failure, giving rise to ignominy and shame for the hosts.

While these restraints on ritual inflation are acknowledged by Balinese, there is also a further set of reasons which needs to be examined. This relates to an indigenous theory, used more by elites than others. It claims that followers and material benefits accrue to those with *sakti*, supernatural potency. *Sakti* is an ability to influence what goes on in the 'visible' world (*sekala*) by effecting changes in the more fundamental causes of things in the 'invisible' world (*niskala*). While those with little *sakti* have to use brute physical activity to accomplish tasks, people with a large stock of *sakti* do not have to act in any obvious way at all, because people and things automatically do what is required of them (Cole 1983: 260). Consequently, a *sakti* person does not need to coerce or importune villagers to provide voluntary labour: they supply it voluntarily and willingly. This is one reason why such labour must be unpaid. If assistance needs to be bought, it is an unequivocal sign that one lacks the potency to attract willing followers and that therefore one cannot merit the status aspired to.

This potency is acquired in many different ways. The higher one's ritual status, the greater the amount one is born with. Nineteenth-century kings and high priests were thus the most *sakti*, and their mere words were immediately efficacious. Today, the direct descendants of former rulers still enjoy a residue of their ancestors' potency, and *pedanda* priests are often credited with *sakti*. But it may also be acquired as a gift from God, by becoming a spirit medium or by performing diabolical rituals. Strength and invulnerability may also be acquired by purchasing amulets and medicines from specialists. Since *sakti* can theoretically be acquired by anyone, concentrations of power can emerge outside the normal channels legitimated by the hierarchy. A contemporary example of this is the suspicion that those who succeed to high-level state jobs from unpromising beginnings may have employed such means to increase their stock of potency (Connor 1982: 156). It is also very common for Balinese to allege that others undertake ascetic regimes, learn black magic and purchase potions and talismans, which can be used to ensnare a loved one, pass exams, ruin a business competitor, gain promotion, and so on.

Sakti is a theory of personal power which explains why someone has a large number of supporters and followers. Correspondingly, if many people turn up to one's projects, it is a manifest sign of possession of *sakti*. But, once acquired, it is not stable and may flow away to someone else. It must therefore be continually cultivated and demonstrated in visible ways. This is why followers are so crucial to political relations.

The importance of followers for the prestige of leaders is found throughout Indonesia, and nowhere more so than in Bali.[10] While Balinese need to attach themselves to powerful figures for security and access to jobs and land, leaders must also compete for followers. Followers are not a passive audience, but active participants in the competition between leaders. Audiences validate and make manifest their power

[10] For Indonesia, see Keeler (1987), Atkinson (1989), Errington (1989: 101–8) and Tsing (1990). For Bali, see Geertz (1980: 24), Vickers (1991: 107–9), H. Geertz (1995b) and Schulte Nordholt (1996).

(Errington 1990: 44). The ritual performances of Balinese are, therefore, demonstrations of their capacity to control others, and this again makes them replicas, on a smaller stage, of the extravaganzas of pre-colonial kings.

Any major ceremony takes several days of hectic preparations. Helpers arrive at prescribed times and are given specific duties by the holders. But the actual day of the ritual is the most anxious time. Several large pigs and many ducks and chickens have to be slaughtered, the meat from which feeds both helpers and guests and forms a necessary component of many important offerings. In addition, rice and vegetables have to be cooked and many specialist dishes prepared. Much depends on who and how many turn up. Many helpers are constrained to come because, as clients, it is dangerous not to. Others come to repay labour debts, and yet others are establishing new labour exchanges.

Guests are a different matter. The less influential ones come to avoid giving offence. The real worry is whether superiors (in a wide sense) turn up. If they do, this redounds to the credit of the host, who is seen as substantial enough to attract powerful people. But it puts the guests in the invidious position of appearing to be their inferior's followers. In an effort to counteract this inference, high-ranking guests tend to come late, eat little and leave early. Such forms of behaviour are mild snubs, implying that the guests have more important things to do. Consequently, the host tries to keep them there as long as possible. If such guests do not arrive at all, it can be a public relations disaster.[11] A friend who works in the accounts section of a hospital remonstrated bitterly for several days when his boss failed to turn up at his wedding, and complained that he could not sleep because he was *pusing* ('confused'). Conversely, at a girl's puberty rite in a Brahmana household, the host was delighted when more helpers than expected turned up. Though he had to buy another pig and further provisions to feed them all, the commotion and excitement (*ramé*) caused by the extra activity enhanced both the occasion and his reputation, even as it miffed his neighbours.

In general, these ideas have little importance for labour-exchange relations between households that are separated by a wide gap, because in these situations competition is not an issue. But when rivals are close in status the implications for the recruitment of labour may become significant. By not participating in each other's ceremonies, which thus reduces the labour available to each household, they can remain independent of each other and nullify any implications of dependency that might result if they did. Cultural considerations concerning leadership and followship therefore reinforce the reticence, mentioned earlier, of Balinese to be actors in their rivals' status projects. None the less, situations arise in which rivals, because they may be kin or affines or members of the same descent group, are constrained to participate in their opponents' ceremonies. However, private criticisms of incompetent management, tasteless food, inadequate seating arrangements, small offerings and unimpressive guests, alongside assertions about how much better one's own family does these things, speak of a resistance to others' attempts to construct themselves as leaders.

---

[11] Keeler (1987: 141–64) provides a wonderfully vivid example of this from central Java. Which guests turn up, what time they arrive, how long they stay, what they do while present, and so forth, all become crucial factors in determining relative prestige.

6

Kings & Priests in Bali
hierarchy, centrality & change

Introduction

In many South and South-East Asian polities, the relationship between king and priest, and the larger categories for which they stand as exemplars, has often been taken as the principal defining feature of societies in this vast region. However, until recently, this relationship was construed, broadly speaking, in two very different ways. Either the king is secular and therefore the priest is superior, thus producing the hierarchical caste systems of India (Dumont 1980). Or the king is 'sacred' and therefore the priest, a kind of ritual technician, is inferior, thus producing the divine-kingship societies of Thailand (Tambiah 1976) and other areas of South-East Asia. In these theories, the core relationship is taken to be structurally stable and two essentially different polities emerge, depending on how the relationship is constructed.

More recently, however, historians and anthropologists have questioned whether the Indian king was indeed a secular figure. If the Indian king is conceived of as 'sacred' or as having a magico-religious aspect, then the primacy of the Brahmin priest in Indian caste systems is questionable. This new perspective has generated a controversy which, in its starkest form, is about whether Hindu societies conform to a model of hierarchy or to a model of centrality.

For twenty years Dumont's theory of caste hierarchy in India dominated the field. It was based on the 'religious' distinction between the pure and the impure and the disjunction between status and power. According to Dumont, the Brahmin are at the top of the status hierarchy, and the Brahmin priest is conceived as the pinnacle of purity. The king, as the political master on earth, was the secular power (Dumont 1962), and thus took second place. Subsequent research, however, has found much to criticize. Non-priestly Brahmin regularly claim to rank higher than those Brahmin who are priests. Indeed, the priest is sometimes and in some contexts a 'vessel' which absorbs impurity by the act of receiving religious gifts and by performing services for others, sometimes to such an extent that he is considered untouchable (Parry 1980; Fuller 1984; Raheja 1988a). Moreover, rather than the king having become secular at a very early period, as in Dumont's theory, others contend that he retained (or re-appropriated) his magico-religious function (Hocart 1950; Dirks 1987; Galey 1989; Quigley 1993). In an important version of this latter theory, the king is not at the top of a hierarchy; rather, he is at the centre of a political realm, with the other castes distributed around him and in a series of mutual relationships with him (Raheja 1988a, 1989). From this position he organized and supervised the rituals which established order, prosperity and fertility. At the village level, according to Raheja (1989: 82–3), prosperity is produced by the dominant caste (the local analogue of the king) ridding the village of inauspiciousness by making unreciprocated religious gifts to all the other castes, including the Brahmin. These gifts embody the evil which 'comes out' of the donor and is picked up by the recipients. The only way to eliminate their negative effects is to break them up and pass them on to others even further out, or to perform ascetic exercises or ritual actions to neutralize them. Often, however, economic constraints force Brahmin priests to retain the gifts, and they often do not know the rituals which counteract the pollution. Consequently, they become progressively inauspicious and impure (Parry 1980).

This rival theory claims that neither hierarchy nor the opposition of the pure and the impure on which it is based is particularly important in the organization of village social relationships in north India (Raheja 1988b: 519), and that the king was not inferior to the Brahmin in the 'little kingdoms' of south India (Dirks 1987: 4). According to Fuller (1992: 255), however, this is a 'revisionist thesis' which is not well supported by the evidence on the pervasive hierarchical relations of popular Hinduism. While the thesis has provided a valuable corrective to Dumont's theory, the relegation of hierarchy and of notions of purity and pollution to insignificance is less than useful.

One consequence of this debate is that the two competing theories have become rather polarized. Either caste is hierarchical or it is based on a model of centrality; either the Brahmin priest is at the top or the king is; either caste is based on idioms of purity and pollution or it is based on idioms of royal authority, honour and order. While Dumontian theory stresses that caste is a religious institution and therefore the priest must come at the top, Dirks (1987: 5) argues that caste 'was shaped by political struggles and processes' and that 'caste structure, ritual form and political process were all dependent on relations of power'. The problem is that it is relatively easy to find evidence that supports the one and undermines the other.

One way to move beyond this disagreement is to note that a stronger criticism can be lodged against both Dumont's theory and those of his more extreme critics. My point is that both approaches presume the relationship between king and priest to be essentially stable. This is clearly the case with Dumont's ahistorical analysis, but even Dirks's ethno-historical approach stresses that, in practice, the king was not inferior to the Brahmin. To my mind, it is precisely this unwarranted assumption of stability which creates a great deal of explanatory confusion, and much can be gained by discarding it. If the relationship between king and priest is intrinsically ambiguous and contextual, rather than fixed and stable, then it makes little sense to claim that one of these theories is right and the other wrong.

I try to demonstrate the merits of this perspective by drawing on Balinese ethnography. This shows very graphically that models of hierarchy and centrality are both simultaneously present, that idioms of purity jostle with those of royal authority and cosmic order, and that in the pre-colonial period 'religion' and 'politics' constituted a unified domain of practice and knowledge. The consequence of this for Bali is less a stable relationship between king and priest, hierarchically organized or otherwise, but rather an endlessly contested one. Each attempts to claim superiority by reference to one of these cultural models, whilst being figured as inferior by reference to the other. A different way of putting this is to say that kings and priests cannot be put into a fixed relationship because their practices are informed by incommensurate ideologies.[1]

---

[1] This too is Burghart's (1978) point in his essay on the rival claims of Brahmin, king and renouncer to the highest position in Hindu society. He argued that Hinduism was not a unified system but was atomized into three differentially coded hierarchies embedded in three dissimilar modes of action, each epitomized by one of the contenders.

A perspective that finds space for the main elements of both the conflicting theories about Indian caste thus begins to provide a model which is more complex and nuanced and does justice to the dynamism and multifaceted nature of the historical process. According to Trautmann (1981: 285), the fact that in some Indian texts the king is said to be superior to the Brahmin whilst in others the Brahmin is said to be superior to the king amounts to 'the central conundrum of Indian social ideology'. However, if these conflicting statements are seen simply as *claims* concerning the superiority of one over the other made by interested parties in a situation of endemic competition, the conundrum is no longer so mystifying.

A contribution to this debate, based on ethnography from Bali, of course, raises the question as to whether Balinese hierarchy is an appropriate example with which to examine these issues. Lacking untouchability, ascetic renouncers, the link between occupations and castes and ideas of *samsara* and *moksa,* some scholars would deny that Bali is either Hindu or a 'caste' society at all. Because some of these institutions are absent, I have previously called Bali an 'attenuated' caste society (Howe 1987: 145). Yet the fact is that the importance, even existence, of these institutions and ideas is very unevenly distributed in India. Moreover, the Indian *varna* scheme is widely used as a conceptual framework to organize Balinese hierarchy, hierarchical relations are partly founded on idioms of purity and pollution, membership of ranked descent groups is determined by birth, and marriage is preferentially endogamous within these groups, or is hypergamous. Anyway, Dirks (1989: 67) has already effectively made my case for me, since he has argued that the little kingdoms of nineteenth-century Bali had much in common with those in south India.

Moreover, perhaps rather more important than the question as to whether Bali is or is not a caste society is the need for a comparative perspective (Hocart 1950; Quigley 1993). For far too long the debates on Indian caste and political organization, however fascinating they are, have been somewhat parochial. Because caste has often been conceived as founded on Hindu culture and therefore as 'unexportable', the analytical frameworks employed to understand it have often avoided reference to comparative material. My argument is not that Bali can be compared to India because they are similar, but that because there are sufficient similarities an analysis of the relationship between kings and priests in the one can illuminate the relationship in the other.

Because the relationship between king and priest is crucial to the organization of the Balinese polity, my argument also has a bearing on how the Balinese 'state', the *negara,* has been characterized. The form of pre-colonial rule by Satria noble families has been described as: a 'theatre state' (Geertz 1980); a 'galactic polity' (Tambiah 1985a, b); and a dual sovereignty of king and priest (Guermonprez 1989). But, in describing the *negara* as a 'contest state', Schulte Nordholt (1993: 293, 1996; following Adas 1981) has probably provided the most convincing analysis of the Balinese polity. The argument I present in this chapter reinforces and consolidates this approach. The most important contests were those the king had with others (other kings, rivals in his own kin network, subordinates, etc.). One very significant contest though, the principal theme of this chapter, is that between king and priest.

I am not just interested in kings and priests, but the wider relationship between Satria Dalem and Brahmana, the two categories at the apex of Balinese society. It is from these categories that rulers and high priests came. In all cases, *pedanda* priests (including sometimes their wives) are consecrated Brahmana. Families of Brahmana tend to be locally concentrated, and because they constitute a very small fraction of the total population, they are absent from many villages in the southern lowlands. Inhabitants of these villages become clients of *pedanda* living in nearby villages. Moreover, not all villages which have resident Brahmana also have *pedanda* priests.[2]

Those who rule modern Bali are, of course, officials of the Indonesian state, members of the regional and provincial parliaments, and the armed forces. However, a disproportionate number of these, at every level from province to village, are the high-caste descendants of those who ruled Bali in pre-colonial times, and who continued to govern, as regents, under the Dutch. While many commoners have been successful in both economic and political spheres, the nineteenth-century elite has in part reproduced itself as a late twentieth-century elite.

In the nineteenth-century, the king of Klungkung, the Déwa Agung, was recognized as the highest king in Bali, and the organization of his rule was replicated at all the less elevated noble courts throughout Bali. In the village of Corong, the nineteenth-century rulers were those Cokorda (by legend directly descended from the Klungkung royal line) who lived in the local 'palace' (*puri*). Just as the Déwa Agung had his resident high priest, so also did the Cokorda in Corong. To this day, the Cokorda group has maintained a central position in Corong village life, and most of the key local government officials come from this group. The subject-matter of this chapter, then, is not just the relationship between king and high priest, but also its village analogue of Cokorda and *pedanda* and, more generally, the relationship between Satria Dalem and Brahmana.

There is little consensus in the literature on Bali concerning the relative ranking of kings and priests. This is due partly to the different contexts in which the issue has been examined, partly to the competing theories that have been applied to the ethnographic data and partly to endemic competition between the two groups. In the following section, I critically examine this literature. One feature of the available material is that much of it derives from the analysis of Balinese texts. In the third section, therefore, I present some contemporary ethnography from Corong village. This suggests that the ranking of rulers and priests cannot be unambiguously determined because of the coexistence of two rival models, which figure their relationship in competing ways. The final section looks at changes in the fortunes of kings and priests from the pre-colonial period to the present day.

In closing this introduction, I want to make a further comparative point. Dumont's (1962, 1980) argument that the Indian king lost his magico-religious aspect in ancient times and its somewhat uncritical acceptance by those working outside India have led to some confusion concerning the similarities and differences between historical polities in India and in both mainland and insular South-East Asia. Tambiah (1976: 99), for example, analyses the Thai state by stressing the king's divinity and his superiority over the Brahmin, and concludes that this is a transformation of the Indian case (see also Tambiah 1985b). Seneviratne (1987) argues instead, and convincingly in my view, that, since Dumont was wrong about the secularization of the Indian king, the kingdoms of India and Thailand were not nearly so different as Tambiah thinks (see also Gellner 1983; Quigley 1993: 157). If my argument for Bali is valid, it is suggestive for many of the polities in the whole

---

[2] The relationship of Brahmana priests to the rest of Balinese society is in certain contexts ambivalent. While many revere, and even fear, them, others despise them. Some groups of metal smiths (Pandé), some members of commoner groups, known as Pasek, and some villagers in the mountains and elsewhere never use *pedanda* priests, perferring their own priests. Though most Balinese use the services of *pedanda*, criticisms are regularly expressed about their supposed greed and venality.

of this region. At a very general level, they were all 'contest' states, they all appear to have been based on competing schemas of hierarchy and centrality, and the relationship between king and priest was ambiguous.

Kings & priests in Bali: the present state of the question

Early Dutch writers tended to represent Bali as a caste society in which Brahmana were superior to Satria (Boon 1977: 41–5). This dogma, however, concealed a more complicated situation, since rivalry between the two groups was often mentioned.[3] Covarrubias (1937: 54–5), for example, noted a great undercurrent of disagreement and animosity between them. While more recent research has enriched our understanding of the issue, the controversy about the relative ranking of kings and priests remains.

In his discussion of the nineteenth-century Balinese state, the *negara*, Geertz (1980) stresses both the competition between kings and the problematic nature of the relationship between king and priest. He places the king, not the priest, at the centre of Balinese society. The king was divine (Geertz 1980: 124), and the complementary pairing of king and priest was 'at once the most characteristically Indian of Balinese political institutions' and 'the most conspicuous example of the sea change such institutions suffered in their passage south and east' (ibid.: 125).[4] Drawing on Worsley's (1972) translation of a dynastic chronicle, the *Babad Buléléng*, Geertz argues that the king was 'the numinous centre of the world, and priests were the emblems, ingredients, and effectors of his sanctity'. They were 'part of the king's regalia' and 'an embodiment of part of [his] authority, and extension of [his] official person' (Geertz 1980: 126). Additionally, the relation between priest and king was 'less one of pure and impure... as of excellent and superexcellent' (ibid.: 127). While this clearly places the king above the priest, nevertheless the two together formed an alliance.

But other evidence points in a different direction. Geertz remarks that 'on religious grounds the Brahmanas felt superior to the lords', while 'on political grounds the lords felt superior to the Brahmanas'. Moreover, 'each distrusted the other, yet each needed the other'; and ruler and priest were to one another as a ship to its helmsman (ibid.: 37). This represents the priest as equal or even superior to the king, and hints that their relationship did not always reflect the ideal, but was sometimes strained. What is clear, however, according to Geertz, is that the king cannot be glossed as a merely secular ruler. The king, depicted as a silent, exemplary centre, as an icon, was the closest connection to divinity. He was surrounded by magical objects, such as daggers (*kris*), which were endowed with *sakti* (potency) and which wreaked havoc amongst the king's enemies when they were brought out in battle. The king was supernaturally powerful, spatially central and ideologically pivotal.

[3] See, for example, Korn's (1932: 140) amusing summary of the kind of confusion which some Dutch colonial officials created as they tried to iron out the relative ranking of various groups.
[4] This notion of a 'sea change' is a reference to Dumont's (1962) argument that in India, in ancient times, the magico-religious function was stripped from kingship, after which the king was purely secular. However, there is a good deal of evidence (for example, Dirks 1987; Raheja 1988a; Quigley 1993) suggesting that Dumont was wrong on this point, and so there is no necessity to argue that a 'sea change' took place when this institution was transported to Indonesia.

Worsley makes similar points in his analysis of the *Babad Buléléng*. This text does not make a distinction between the religious and the secular,[5] so that the king was instructed in esoteric mysteries and the priest was a military strategist and an expert in the manufacture of weapons (see also Rubinstein 1987: 115–16). Moreover, the two were like 'brothers' who looked after each other in the good times as well as the bad (Worsley 1972: 155; 1979: 111–12).

Three qualifications should be inserted here. First, although this text depicts king and priest as 'brothers', alluding to a kinship link and equality, there is no such thing as equality among brothers. Siblings are ranked, with older brothers superior to younger brothers, and sometimes it is said that the priest is to the king as older to younger brother (Guermonprez 1989: 193). Secondly, in practice, relations between co-resident, married brothers are usually marked by competition and conflict (Howe 1989a), so that the text is portraying the ideal and not the reality. Thirdly, whilst Geertz's intention is to provide a general model of the Balinese polity, Worsley aims to examine the arguments which the text's author used to legitimate the position of the kings of Buléléng, north Bali, at a critical historical juncture when their realm was under attack from different directions and finally succumbed to Dutch colonial rule. It therefore tends to construe the relationship between king and priest as an alliance.[6]

A prevalent theme in the competition and status conflict between Brahmana and Satria Dalem is that the higher (ritual) status of Brahmana is compromised by their material dependency on kings (Schulte Nordholt 1991a: 143; and, for India, see Fuller 1984: 105). In return for gifts of house and rice land and other special privileges, they officiate at the latter's ceremonies, prepare holy water and provide him with advice and counsel. Being thus locked together, a rivalry emerged which the Balinese are clearly aware of, for 'in the many stories about priests and kings the two groups were shown in a kind of uneasy partnership. Sometimes they were rivals for power, sometimes allies. Still today each group claims to be the highest caste' (Vickers 1989: 50).

The shifting and contextual nature of their relationship is also stressed by Rubinstein. In her excellent account of texts written by Brahmana about themselves, she first states that, while Brahmana descent groups were sometimes in bitter conflict with traditional rulers from Satria and Wésia descent groups, none the less high priests 'occupy the highest position in the religious hierarchy' (Rubinstein 1991: 44). The reason for this, she claims, is that Brahmana men may marry women from inferior groups (including Satria), while Brahmana women cannot marry men from inferior groups (I return to this issue in the next section). Despite preserving the dogma of the priest's superiority, Rubinstein nevertheless shows how complex their relation really is. Thus, on the positive side, Satria are ultimately descended from a Brahmana priest, and so the two are related (*sameton* – emerging from the same source or origin). The texts provide examples of unconsecrated Brahmana who emulated rulers and of Brahmana who were appointed as rulers by adoring kings, though in fact this was very rare. Court priests acted as statesmen, ambassadors and judges. The priest at the king's court was 'inseparable from the king' (ibid.: 64), and

[5] In the very different context of Balinese representations of tourism, Picard (1990a: 62–3) discusses the verbal contortions Balinese intellectuals have gone through trying to categorize dance and drama performances as either sacred or profane, so that decisions could be made as to which performances could be held for tourist entertainment and which could not. Neither Balinese nor Indonesian possesses equivalent terms, and the conceptual distinction is quite alien to Balinese culture.
[6] The chronicle does not specify the relationship as older to younger brother, but simply as brothers, which could be a way of sidestepping the thorny issue of ranking.

they behaved as though they were brothers (ibid.: 65). The texts liken the ruler to the captain of a ship, symbolizing the realm, and his priest to the rudder, thus demonstrating the latter's role as counsellor and tactician (ibid.: 65); this is a rather different metaphor from that provided by Geertz.

On the darker side, however, a king could dismiss his *pedanda*, and the *pedanda* had to ask permission from the king to establish his household (*gria*) in the king's realm (ibid.: 66). The texts also relate that priests were sometimes accused by their sponsoring nobles of alienating the affections of the peasantry from the latter to the former (see Chapter 4 note 13, for a description of such a case). This highlights the jealousy of kings towards their priests and shows that the relationship between the two was often one of intrigue, conspiracy and distrust. Sometimes this erupted into violence, as when the *pedanda* of Manuaba was attacked by the local ruler and fierce hand-to-hand fighting ensued, in which another *pedanda* was hacked to pieces.

More recently, Rubinstein has examined the *Geguritan Perang Banjar* (the poem of the Banjar war), Banjar being a town in the region of Buléléng in north Bali. The leader of the Banjar side in its war against the Dutch was Ida Madé Rahi, a Brahmana. But this was not a novel situation, since he was the hereditary ruler, the descendant of Brahmana priests who were priests and rulers at the same time; they were *rajaresi* ('king-holy' man; Rubinstein 1996: 55), and controlled a political realm, a *negara*. A corollary of this is that the terminology used to describe the relationship between a king and his subjects and that between a priest and his followers is identical, and this terminology is martial rather than clerical: priests 'reign' (*andiri*) and their followers are 'subjects' (*wadwa*) or 'troops' (*bala*) (Rubinstein 1991: 69–70).[7]

While king and priest performed complementary and interdependent roles, it is also clear that frequently their roles overlapped and conflicted, resulting in competition for control over subjects and occasionally in violence. This overlap in status and role is also reported by Connor for the region of Bangli. She says that the descendants of the last king describe themselves as Ksatriya-Brahmana and that, in discussing the hierarchy with commoners, 'nearly every title in the spectrum was proffered as the highest', although the one most frequently given was that of *anak agung*, which was the title of the king (Connor 1982: 328).

Up to this point, the literature reveals both alliance and common interest between king and priest, but also competition and struggle. What is also notable is the way in which anthropologists have usually figured the relationship in purely hierarchical terms. Ideas of centrality are clearly present but they have been credited with little significance. Ironically, the clearest view of the importance of centrality appears in the work of Guermonprez (1985, 1989), who has consistently argued the case for the hierarchical superiority of the priest over the king.

Reflecting Dumont's analysis of kingship in India, Guermonprez argues that Balinese kings after the fourteenth century were not divine. In the nineteenth century, the king was just the supreme householder. King and priest together ranked above all others, but, following Dumont's model of hierarchical encompassment, the priest ranked higher than the king. Guermonprez calls this structure a dual sovereignty of priest and king, in which the priest was at the apex of the hierarchy.

Guermonprez derives the evidence for the superiority of the priest and the secularized nature of Balinese kings partly from the consecration ceremony of the king of Gianyar in 1903 (described in Swellengrebel 1947). Carried out in the king's palace,

[7] The *Babad Buléléng* uses this terminology as well (Worsley 1972: 155).

the two *pedanda* priests sat in front of and to the east of the king, led the whole performance and made the indispensable holy water. According to Guermonprez, this spatial layout demonstrates conformity to the most important axis encoding hierarchy in Bali. This is the high–low, mountainward–seaward axis (*kaja–kelod*). It is complemented by a 'secondary east/west opposition in which east is "higher" than west' (Guermonpregz 1989: 192). In this scheme, the 'highest value is not attached to the centre but to the upper part of the relevant totality... In this system, the head, and not the centre, embodies the unity of the whole' (ibid.: 191). The priest is therefore higher than the king, who is in the centre.

However, the opposite case can also be argued. In other cosmological schemes, the centre is the superior point which unifies the whole. For example, the *nawa sanga* (both words mean 'nine') is the form used to set out offerings in a great many rituals. The layout, representing the world and its entire contents, consists of the eight compass points around the centre or 'navel' (*puseh*). Each peripheral point is associated with a god, colour, number, metal, tree, body organ, etc., but it is the centre which constitutes the totality. The centre is white (in the ranking of colours, white is at the top) or multi-coloured and is reserved for Siva, the highest god. Equally pertinent is the Javano-Balinese concept of the king as centre of his palace, which is the centre of the capital which is in turn the centre of the realm. What happens to the king happens to the whole realm, and the behaviour of the king determines the condition of the whole realm (Schrieke 1957: 76–9; Pigeaud 1960–63, vol. III: 110–11).

In an important sense, both of these centre–periphery schemas may be seen as derived from the idea that *kaja* denotes the central, mountainous zone of the island, where the gods reside. *Kaja* is the direction indicator 'towards the mountains', but on the mountain tops *kaja* becomes the centre and *kelod* ('towards the sea') becomes the periphery. Away from the centre, *kaja* assumes a hierarchical relationship to *kelod*, as above to below. Thus centrality and hierarchy are competing transformations of each other.

Let us return to the ritual. The king is in the centre facing east where the priests sit, also facing east. In the last phase of the ritual, however, the king turns around to face his family, lesser lords and subjects, who are all to the west of him. They join their hands over their heads and make the gesture of obeisance (*sumbah*) to the king which signifies inferiority (Guermonprez 1989: 192–3). According to Guermonprez, the priests are superior, first, because they do not make the *sumbah* gesture to the king and, secondly, because priests, king and lords are positioned along an east–west line, with the priests at the 'highest' end.

But this conclusion is derived wholly from the perspective of hierarchy. From the king's point of view, he is in the centre and the others are around him. Moreover, if the priests do not subordinate themselves to the king, the latter does not make the *sumbah* gesture to the former either. The perspective from the centre thus enables the king to reject the priests' claims of superiority. My point is not that the king is unequivocally superior or inferior to the high priest, such a relationship being fixed by reference to a single model, but rather that competing schemas generate rival claims and hence the relationship is intrinsically ambiguous.

As to the secular nature of the king, we have already seen that kings organized, controlled and ordered ceremonies to take place, and thus had a ritual and religious aspect. But were they 'divine'? According to Wiener, the king of Klungkung was ideally a 'semi-divine figure, a *Betara Sekala*, a "visible deity"'. Other kings of Klungkung were widely held to have 'literally embodied the divinity of Mount

Agung', that is, the god of the temple of Besakih (Wiener n.d.: 6,8). On the other hand, Stuart-Fox (1991: 24) argues, from his work on the Besakih temple, that 'kingship is divine, not the king' (cf. Evans-Pritchard 1962: 75–6). The king needs to be pure and sanctified in order to ascend the throne (cf. Mayer 1985). In contradistinction to Wiener, Stuart-Fox (1987: 322–5) states that the king was never identified, even fleetingly, with the god of the mountain on which Besakih stands, and in no ritual was the king transformed into a divinity. Rather, the king had a mystical relationship with the god, and so his presence at ceremonies, while not indispensable, was highly desirable and beneficial. To ensure the prosperity of the realm, the ruler had to support temples, organize ceremonies and be in attendance.

Whether or not the king was 'divine', the point I want to emphasize is that the king and priest had different functions in the ritual, not that one had a divine aspect and the other did not.[8] The primary function of the Balinese king was to create order (Geertz 1995a: 95), to protect the realm against both human and demonic forces and to make the realm prosperous and fertile. Ideally, this was accomplished through ceremonies and periodical purification rituals (Wiener 1995: 56) and by behaving in a righteous manner. In these senses, Balinese kings were similar to their Indian counterparts, who commanded 'the rituals which ensure both cosmic and social stability. This is no more a secular function than the priest's actual performance of the ritual' (Quigley 1993: 150).

The ideology that the major function of Balinese kingship was to create stability and prosperity went largely unrecognized by the Dutch, whose colonial policy often represented them as burdens which the ordinary population was forced to endure. Korn (1932: 306), however, as one of the few Dutchmen to dissent from this view of Balinese kings as despotic rulers, argued instead that the ruler was the head of the religion and had to maintain peace and order so that people could serve the gods. It was his duty to encourage the religion, maintain the temples and ensure that a person's soul reached its destiny via cremation. If descendants were missing, he had to take on the job of cremating the deceased himself. A large part of the taxes he levied was consumed by his obligations to organize purification ceremonies, in which he, his officials and his priests took part. While in practice the king often was a burden, his subjects also conceived of him as an exceptionally potent (*sakti*) personage whose death entailed a magical imbalance through the whole realm.

This perspective reveals two weaknesses in Geertz's (1980) description of the Balinese polity as a 'theatre state'. One is the conceptual separation of ritual and power (reminiscent of Dumont) and the other is his overemphasis on the king as the silent, exemplary centre. On the one hand, Geertz divinizes the Balinese king, and so undermines the disjunction between status and power (priest and king) which Dumont emphasized as a defining feature of Indian caste. But, on the other, he also endorses the distinction by characterizing the state as an elite device for enacting ritual and status competition, while politics and power were vested in village commoner institutions (Geertz 1980: 13, 62–3). Geertz thus combines the sacred

---

[8] In areas such as India, Nepal, Thailand and Indonesia, there is no clear break between the divine and the non-divine. Many categories of people (kings, priests, shamans, renouncers, etc.) participate in divinity, and there are degrees of closeness to the gods. In Bali, for example, newborn children of whatever status are frequently said to be '*nu déwa*' (still gods), because they have been reincarnated from their deified ancestors. As they grow older, they lose this lingering divinity; in marriage they are farthest away from the gods, but old age draws them closer to divinity once again. The degree of participation in divinity thus correlates to position in the life cycle. While pre-eminent kings might have been considered semi-divine, their descendants who did not rule were not thought of as divine in any way.

with the secular in the figure of the king, but separates them to describe the relations between elites and commoners.[9]

The separation of politics from ritual and status is achieved by underplaying the material basis of pre-colonial Balinese kingdoms, Geertz arguing, for example, that the aristocracy owned little land (ibid.: 66). However, right up to 1950, many Balinese lords possessed or controlled massive holdings of land (Connor 1982: 312; Robinson 1992: 79–80; Macrae 1999: 152, n. 25). In the pre-colonial period, they also organized and controlled many aspects of irrigation (Schulte Nordholt 1996); collected taxes on land and opium, on the use of water and on trade (Hanna 1976: 98); and possessed and traded in slaves (de Kat Angelino 1920; van der Kraan 1983; Schulte Nordholt 1996: 41–4). Status and power were thus conjoined in the central figure of the king, and within this framework commoner institutions were subordinate.

Kings used these resources to build palaces and temples, fight wars and mount ritual extravaganzas. These rituals were more than mere rehearsals of the king's status. Rather, they were dangerous events which released magical forces having the potential to threaten the king's capacity to control and coerce his subjects (Vickers 1991; Howe 2000). In performing the ritual the king put himself and his realm on trial and threw down a challenge to other kings.

A more balanced view of the doctrine of the exemplary centre is that the Balinese king has two modalities. He 'turns a terrifying aspect towards his and his subjects' enemies, within and without the realm, and his gentle aspect he turns towards the loyal and virtuous' (Worsley 1979: 112). In other words, the doctrine of the 'exemplary centre' is only part of a wider conception of kingship whose other dimension is the king as charismatic leader and warrior (cf. de Heusch 1997: 228).

Kings throughout Indic South-East Asia strove to consolidate their positions as rulers, but their states were fragile. Suffering from weak administrative organization and poor communications, they were often in conflict with other rulers, plagued by intrigue and potential rebellion amongst their own supporters and prone to their peasants deserting to another lord (Schrieke 1957; Moertono 1968; Ricklefs 1974; Adas 1981). In addition to being a 'sign in a system of signs' (Geertz 1980: 131), the Balinese king, according both to texts (Worsley 1979) and to historical events (Schulte Nordholt 1993, 1996), had also periodically to defeat rebellions, embark on conquest, seize land and slaves and attach the peasantry to him by generosity. Warring king and silent centre are therefore not contradictory modalities, but rather two aspects of a single, but unstable, process.[10]

---

[9] In contrast, Boon (1977: 148) argued that the distinction between status and power was crucial to Balinese social organisation. However, as Connor (1982: 324–6) points out, Boon actually provided a lot of evidence to show that power and status were much more closely tied together in practice than his more theoretical pronouncements allowed for, and was thus forced into arguing that a 'more pragmatic theory of power and rank' somehow both competes with and complements the ideal version of hierarchy in which power and status are separated (Boon 1977: 156).

[10] In some parts of Bali, a ruler was, at different times, both silent centre and warring king (Schulte Nordholt 1993), but elsewhere the double function of the kingship as violent and pacific (de Heusch 1997: 227) was divided amongst two or more people. In Klungkung, in east Bali, ideally, the responsibility of the king was to think and decide, but it was his agents and kinsmen who carried out his wishes. One of these, his nearest male kinsman, was a kind of 'secondary king', who acted as the 'mobile counterpart to the interior king' (Wiener 1995: 157). The organization of internal and external figures is found elsewhere in Indonesia. One example is the dual sovereignty of the Atoni of east Timor. In this the inner sacral lord, conceived as 'female', was responsible for prayer and sacrifice to ensure success in war and agriculture and for mediation between mortal and divine worlds, while the outer secular lords, conceived as 'male', carried out actual administration (Cunningham 1965).

Competition and struggle between rival kings pervaded the little kingdoms of pre-colonial Bali, but this rivalry was also reflected in the relationship between kings and priests. Each could claim superiority or deny inferiority by reference to different and competing ideologies and practices of hierarchy and centrality. The roles of king and priest overlapped, creating tension and ambiguity in the relationship between them. They could be allies, but equally they could be enemies, sometimes in violent conflict with each other.

In the next section I examine the ambiguity these models give rise to in the context of the competition between two groups in Corong, but such ambiguity also has other sources.

Brahmana & Cokorda in a Balinese village

In Corong's population of some 4,000 people, there are large numbers of both Brahmana and Satria Dalem. The highest-ranking group of the latter category possesses the title *cokorda*. Most of them comprise a single descent group, headed by the leading Cokorda, Cokorda Gedé, who is also the village head (*perbekel*).[11] The 'leading Cokorda' occupies the most central and senior genealogical space in the descent group. Cokorda Gedé is the eldest son of eldest sons of the core line, which, it is asserted, has its origin in the first kings of Klungkung, themselves descended from the Hindu-Javanese kingdom of Majapahit. Cokorda Gedé's position makes him responsible for the upkeep of the palace's family temple (*mrajan*), all the heirloom objects associated with it, all the ceremonies conducted in it and the cultivation of all the land attached to it.

In the nineteenth century, the Cokorda constituted a minor noble house owing allegiance at different times to other more powerful groups in the vicinity. Today they claim very high descent status, as witnessed by the eleven-roofed shrine in their temple and their eleven-roofed cremation towers, but they possess little regional political significance. In the village, however, they are very powerful, since core-line members hold many customary and government offices (*perbekel, bendésa,* chairman of LKMD, etc.).[12] They are by far the largest landowners, some hold high offices in the regional bureaucracy or have been successful in business and commerce, and they are respected for their part in the resistance to the Dutch between 1945 and 1949. Those at the very centre, Cokorda Gedé and his uncle, the *bendésa,* are intimately involved, along with the village's high priests, in all the major village and temple ceremonies. Whilst the priest carries these out, Cokorda Gedé is directly involved in organizing them and is always present during their performance.

Only three of the twenty-one Brahmana houseyards have *pedanda* priests, who are all female.[13] Some Brahmana are fairly large landowners, some are wealthy

[11] The *perbekel* is the head of a village and is the lowest rung of government administration. In Gianyar and elsewhere, villages which have sizeable gentry populations normally also have a *perbekel* who is high-caste. Despite being badly paid, the holder has a powerful position in village life. Since the *perbekel* is entitled to a half percentage share of land sales, if he holds office in a village where land is very expensive and sales are frequent, the position can also be very lucrative.

[12] The *bendésa* is a non-government position concerned with village religious institutions. The LKMD (Lembaga Ketahanan Masyarakat Désa, or Organization for Village Defence) is probably the most powerful body in contemporary Balinese villages, and has a large number of subsidiary committees, which, in Corong, are mostly chaired by gentry.

[13] The fact that the three *pedanda* in this village are women is very unusual. I was told that male *pedanda* do not *cocok* ('fit') with the village and therefore tend to die young leaving their (consecrated) wives to carry on after them.

businessmen and many have government jobs or are employed in the tourist sector. Many, however, are unemployed, spending much of their time around the house or gambling at cards and cock-fights. While it is completely acceptable for Brahmana to work their own rice-fields, unless it becomes economically essential few engage in waged manual labour, because it demeans their status (Nakatani 1995: 54).

The remainder of this section examines the relative ranking of these two groups. In general, commoners and lower gentry perceive both as vastly superior to themselves and, broadly speaking, they rank Brahmana above Cokorda. Amongst themselves, however, considerable disagreement exists. Some Cokorda asserted superiority over Brahmana, a few acknowledged inferiority, and some said they were equal; and Brahmana made very similar claims. Older Brahmana were more circumspect than their younger kin and tended to claim equality with, rather than superiority over, the Cokorda. 'We are the same' (*pateh*) and 'we are related' (*sameton*) were two simple ways in which this was asserted. That the two were 'brothers' was mentioned several times, but only once was it said that Brahmana was 'older brother' to Cokorda. Assertions of equality were also framed by ideas concerning the palace–temple axis, Cokorda Gedé ruling from his palace (*puri*) and the *pedanda* conducting ceremonies in the temple (*pura*). Others supported claims to equality in terms of linguistic exchange: 'If he speaks to me in high Balinese, I will speak to him in the same way; if he uses low Balinese, I will do the same' (cf. Connor 1982: 329). Amongst themselves, then, relative ranking appears to be contested rather than fixed.

The absence of a fixed and stable ranking of Brahmana and Cokorda derives partly from the way their claims to high status refer to competing cultural schemas of hierarchy and centrality, and partly for other reasons. I shall consider the former first, and begin with some general information about these schemas.

The vertical axis of the body and relative head height encode relations of hierarchy to a remarkable extent. In most situations, bodily postures and seating positions should be adjusted to coincide with status. In the past subjects bowed before the ruler, averted their gaze and drooped their heads. Kings were referred to as 'Sang Prabu, the "Head"; their lords and retainers, as their *kaki tangan* (Indonesian), "feet and hands"... Rulers or priests could also be referred to as *sesuunan*, "borne on the head", like the seats of deities when carried in processions' (Wiener 1995: 154). Ritual offerings to purified spirits are placed above those dedicated to malevolent spirits. Purified ancestors are *leluur*, from *duur*, 'above', or *lelangitan*, from *langit*, 'sky'. The gods live on the tops of mountains and impurity is washed away downstream. The most dramatic form of subordination is to juxtapose one's feet with another's head. This occurs in many different contexts: for example, in the ritual of *napakin*, when a *pedanda* touches the head of his pupil with his foot during the latter's consecration; in the gesture of *masulub*, when inferiors walk under the raised corpse of their deceased relative; and in the action of *ngenjekin*, when a person treads on the head of another prostrated on the floor to enforce subordination (usually only between kin).

The relative purity and sanctity of the different parts of houseyards and temples conform to the *kaja–kelod* axis and the east–west (*kangin–kauh*) axis. The courtyards housing the shrines are built at a higher level than more secular courtyards, and the most important shrines are in the north-east section, *kaja-kangin*, the closest to the mountains. In villages, temples to ancestors are very frequently at the *kaja* end and upstream (*luan*), whilst the graveyard is *kelod* and downstream (*tebén*).

Centrality is equally important. The gods live in the centre of the island, so that what is highest is also most central. Ritual offerings can be orientated above and below, but when on the horizontal plane they are spaced according to the compass points, with the centre symbolizing unity and totality. The king's palace is ideally at the centre of the capital town, itself at the centre of the realm, and the actions of the former determine the condition of the latter, symbolizing an identity between ruler and realm.

Centrality is also configured in terms of inside and outside, with the former superior to the latter. Many Balinese terms

> presume a perspective of 'coming out' from some implied inside: thus a doorway is a *pemedalan*, a place to come out, rather than as it is in English an 'entranceway', and a clan is a *semetonan*, 'people of one emergence', those who have emanated from a single ancestral source.

> (Wiener 1995: 153–4).

The architectural design of temples and houses evinces distinctions of inside and outside. The innermost courtyard of a temple, raised above the others, is the *jeroan* (the 'inside'). The middle courtyard is the *jaba tengah* (the 'middle outside'), and the outer courtyard, if there is one, is simply the *jaban* ('outside'). Palaces are similar: the innermost area is again the *jeroan* and it is the most secluded and intimate region, where the king slept and ate. The king of Klungkung, the highest-ranking king in Bali, was the *Dalem* ('inside'), the 'ultimate insider' (ibid.: 153). The term *jero* designates particular groups of people, as well as interior space. *Jero* are 'insiders'; they are the gentry, who live in houses called *jeroan*. Those who are not gentry are *jaba* ('outsiders'), who live in *umah* ('homes'). Commoner women taken in marriage by gentry men and those who become priests, puppeteers or palace officials also become entitled to the honorific *jero*, signifying that they have been elevated to the 'inside'.

In the spatial lay-out of the houses in the village of Corong, which is fairly typical of south Bali, Cokorda Gedé's palace is centrally located to the north-east of the crossroads, with the market to the south. The palace (*puri*) is a very large compound, surrounded by a wall almost three metres high. It is, in fact, internally divided into five separate houses, the resident families of which are all interrelated. Cokorda Gedé's is at the very centre and has the highest status. Most gentry houses are adjacent to the palace, whilst the whole of the village periphery is commoner territory (see Figure 6.1).

With one or two exceptions, families in Corong are allocated to its four hamlets (*banjar*) according to the location of their houseyards. Even though the Cokorda are physically located in only two of these hamlets, they are nevertheless distributed evenly, so that they are represented in all four of them. While the vast majority of Brahmana houses are also sited in only two hamlets, it has never been thought necessary to redistribute them in the same way. With its central and commanding position, its high walls and its majestic houseyard temple, the *puri* dominates the village.

If this village spatial organization articulates cosmological schemes of centre and periphery and ideological schemes of superiority and inferiority, other material representations of status display considerable ambiguity. One of these is the location of graves in the cemetery (see Figure 6.2).

The higher the status of the deceased, the further upstream (*luan*) the body is buried, turning the spatial organization of the graves into a graphic representation of hierarchy. However, the eight graves in the most upstream section, laid out in a line east to west in accordance with when they were interred, consist of both Brahmana and Cokorda, indicating equivalent status. The graves of other Satria Dalem (Anak Agung and Déwa) are all significantly further downstream (*tebén*). A gap of about

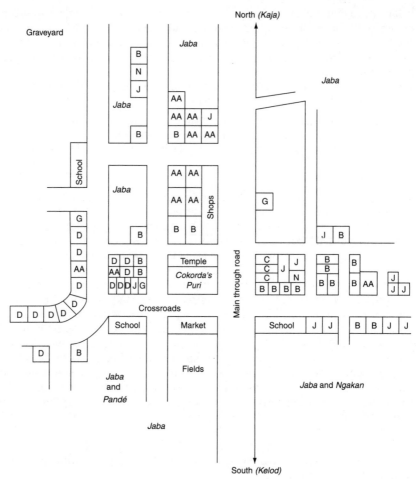

Figure 6.1   The layout of houses in Corong. (Showing most of the Triwangsa compounds, the Cokorda's palace (*puri*) and his family temple, and the general location of commoner houses. Temples, government buildings, meeting pavilions, eating stalls, small paths and streams are not included.
B = Brahmana, C = Cokorda, AA = Anak Agung, D = Déwa, N = Ngakan, G = Gusti, J = Jaba.)

fifteen metres separates these from the section where Ngakan and Gusti are buried. There is then a further substantial gap before the graves of commoners appear in the most downstream section.

Another significant context is cremation and its accompanying paraphernalia. The burial-ground is also the cremation ground. Cremations are carried out in much the same place as the graves were sited, so that gentry are burned upstream of commoners. However, there are some exceptions. While Brahmana are cremated at the most upstream end, Cokorda are burned in the centre of the graveyard on a mound (*pamuun*) about two metres high. This makes relative rank ambiguous, because the site of the cremation is determined by different scales. Brahmana are cremated upstream and more to *kaja* than are Cokorda, but Cokorda are cremated centrally and on a raised mound, which thus places Brahmana on the periphery and

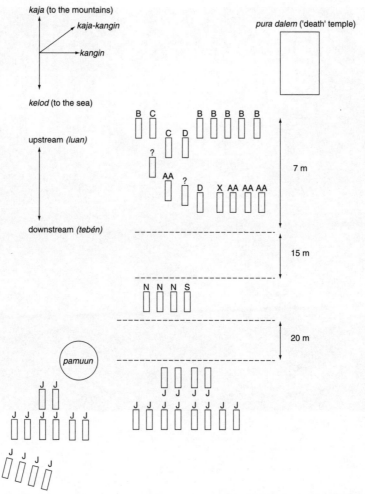

Figure 6.2   The graveyard in Corong, showing the location of all graves as of April 1993. (B = Brahmana, C = Cokorda, AA = Anak Agung, D = Déwa, S = Sang,N = Ngakan, J = Jaba. X marks the grave of a commoner wife of an Anak Agung man and therefore raised to gentry status. All the dead are buried with the head pointing north (*kaja*). *Pamuun* is the raised mound on which core line Cokorda are cremated. Distances not to scale.)

physically lower. There is a further complication to this, because *pedanda* priests should not in fact be cremated in the cemetery at all. Indeed, along with all Balinese rendered pure through special rituals, *pedanda* must not be buried because interment under the ground is very polluting. Ideally, at death *pedanda* should be immediately burned in their own rice-fields.

If they do not possess any, a section of the graveyard may be fenced off and purified and then they can be burned there. Moreover, in the last century, Cokorda were buried and cremated in their own private graveyard in the southern part of the palace, and not in the village cemetery at all. Even today, villagers give the former area a wide berth at night, because of the 'disturbances' which sometimes occur

Plate 6.1 The graveyard/burning ground in Corong. The high mound (*pamuun*) in the centre is where high-ranking Cokorda are cremated

there. Finally, I was repeatedly told that core-line Cokorda, like *pedanda*, are never buried but are cremated immediately.

The incommensurate nature of status scales is also evident in relation to the cremation towers (*badé*) in which the deceased are carried to the graveyard. All Balinese, with the exception of Brahmana, use a vehicle with a variable, but odd, number of roofs. Commoners typically have one, lower ranks of the gentry typically have five or seven, whilst the very highest groups have nine or eleven. In Corong, the Cokorda use an eleven-roofed tower. Since all these vehicles are broadly similar in form, even if they diverge widely in size and elaboration, they may be compared with each other, and thus they provide a clear indication of relative status. As we have seen, adding two roofs to a tower is an unequivocal claim to higher standing. Unconsecrated Brahmana, however, use a *joli*, whilst *pedanda* use a *padmasana*. Both are very different in appearance from the towers employed for other groups, and in particular they do not have roofs. Again, it is impossible to compare Brahmana with Cokorda. It is as though all the groups in the hierarchy up to and including the Cokorda are ranked according to the same scales; consequently they may be compared and competition between them is explicit. At the highest level, however, the practices of Cokorda and Brahmana diverge and become incommensurate, and hence their relative ranking is ambiguous.

If a fixed ranking cannot be determined because each lays claim to superiority by reference to different sets of cultural practices, does this become possible if their exchanges are considered? For example, in linguistic exchange, do Cokorda defer to Brahmana or vice versa? My strong impression is that neither happens. In general, unconsecrated Brahmana use the same terms to Cokorda men and women as they receive. Moreover, while the former speak 'up' to Cokorda Gedé, the latter speaks 'up' to a *pedanda*, and so the ambiguity remains.

In addition to language, marriage and ritual performances are perhaps the most important exchange contexts for determining rank. Commoners generally held the view that marriage between Brahmana women and Cokorda men was hypogamous. Similarly, villagers said that, while it is appropriate for Cokorda to accept *paridan* (leftover food from an offering used in a life-cycle ritual) from Brahmana, the reverse is not. This is in line with their view that Brahmana are superior to Cokorda. Generally speaking, however, Cokorda are able to resist these claims, because the concrete situations which would test them never actually arise. In Corong, at least, Cokorda and Brahmana do not intermarry, and neither offers *paridan* to the other.

There is an almost complete absence of marriages between Cokorda and Brahmana in Corong. I recorded brief details of hundreds of marriages going back three generations. These data show that, while to a large extent gentry marry gentry and commoners marry commoners, both Brahmana and Cokorda intermarry with every other group in the village, including commoners.[14] However, I encountered only one marriage between a Brahmana man and a Cokorda woman; both spouses

[14] Take, for example, two large, extended, neighbouring houseyards, one Anak Agung and the other commoner. Of thirty-six marriages over the previous three generations which the Anak Agung contracted, thirty were with members of the gentry and only six with commoners, all from other *banjar* of the village. Of the fifteen marriages the smaller commoner family contracted, all were with other commoners, save one woman, who married a Ngakan from another hamlet. Of the eighteen marriages contracted in the past fifty years by another commoner family, which has both Brahmana and Cokorda neighbours, only two married lower-ranking gentry, neither of them neighbours. These figures are typical for the whole village.

were of marginal status in their own groups, and husband and wife had not lived together for many years.

Given the large numbers of both Cokorda and Brahmana in the village and their proximity to each other, this is a very surprising finding. Some members of these groups proffered the explanation that it was difficult to find a suitable partner. Remembering that the absence of exchange usually indicates a dispute in status, and noting that marriage is the institution amongst gentry which is the most fraught with status implications, then a better explanation is that the resistance to intermarriage is a strategy either to assert superiority or to deny inferiority. In other words, there is a kind of truce, in which neither group is willing to compromise itself by entering into the marriage game, since to do so would explicitly put to the test what now remains contested. It is not even the case that members of the Cokorda group fail to marry Brahmana because they are busy looking for Satria spouses in royal houses in other villages – a typical royal practice – since many Cokorda take wives from other descent groups in Corong.

It is not clear how widespread this pattern is. In another very large village in Gianyar in which there are large numbers of both Cokorda and Brahmana the same situation prevails. In a long conversation with a Cokorda from this village, he told me that he knew of no marriages between Cokorda and Brahmana. His parents adjudged marriages between them to be *panes* (hot, dangerous), likely to be afflicted with many problems and thus to be avoided. He said it was like marrying your sister, since Cokorda and Brahmana were *kakak beradik* ('older and younger sibling', Ind.).

Wiener also reports that in Klungkung Satria Dalem and Brahmana did not marry one another in the recent past (she does not mention whether they do now). However, she interprets this as a downplaying of their 'kinship' links, rather than as a status gambit. In other contexts, she says, Brahmana and Satria Dalem acknowledged their common descent; for example, unconsecrated Brahmana used to eat the leftovers of offerings (*paridan*) that marked the ruler's life and death, and they still address each other using kin terms, though she does not say which ones (Wiener 1995: 107). I have only rarely heard Brahmana and Cokorda in Corong use kin terms to each other; most often they use each other's titles. There is substantial evidence, then, that in some areas of Bali Brahmana and Satria Dalem do not marry each other.

However, in other areas they do intermarry. In the town of Bangli, 'in each generation there are several marriages between Brahmana women and Anak Agung men' (Connor 1982: 328). Connor does not say whether these unions were thought of as hypergamous or hypogamous,[15] but remarks that Brahmana and Anak Agung continually dispute their relative rank, the latter actually referring to themselves as 'Ksatriya-Brahmana'. However, because there is widespread agreement that wife taking is a superior practice to wife giving, the systematic nature of this pattern of marriage exchange suggests that it is a strategy used by the Anak Agung to assert superiority over the Brahmana; by taking the women of the latter group, they proclaim them to be inferior.

[15] In hierarchical, caste societies, hypergamous unions are those which go 'with the grain'. They denote acceptable forms of marriage, in which men of superior groups marry women from inferior groups. Hypogamous marriages are 'against the grain' and denote culturally inappropriate unions, in which women marry men of lower status than themselves. In Bali, gentry women who marry commoners 'slip caste' (*nyerod*) to the level of their husband, and even today they may be 'thrown away' (*kutang*) by their family. Hobart (1978: 21) remarks that such unions are disapproved of because, since water cannot go uphill, semen should not go 'up caste'.

In contrast, in her discussion of the *Babad Brahmana* Rubinstein (1991: 65) notes that the text 'mentions many examples of *pedanda* and unordained [Brahmana] men who married women from Satria ruling houses'. The reason for this, she argues, is that, since women can only marry equals or superiors, there would have been a shortage of marriageable men in ruling houses, the princes having married lower-ranking women so as to attach important families to their court. Consequently, the excess Satria women were married off to Brahmana men, which also had the result of cementing alliances between these two groups.

This is not a very convincing explanation, however, because it leaves an excess of unmarried females in the Brahmana group who have no superiors whom they can marry. As far as I know, female infanticide (one solution to this problem for very high castes in north India (Parry 1979: 214)) has never been put into operation in Bali, nor, I believe, are Brahmana women ever cloistered for the whole of their lives. It is possible, therefore, that the text is not recording facts about existing practices, but rather staking a claim to superior status by asserting the right of Brahmana men to marry Satria women. It may also be concealing the possibility that Brahmana women marry men in Satria ruling houses.

So far, then, in Corong and one other village Brahmana and Cokorda do not inter-marry, and this was also the case in Klungkung in the past and possibly still is. In Bangli, on the other hand, there is systematic intermarriage between Satria Dalem men and Brahmana women. Finally, texts written by Brahmana claim that their men regularly marry Satria women. Clearly, practice does not conform to a fixed and stable ranking of these two groups.

The material from Klungkung concerning the eating of ritual leftovers (*paridan*) is also very interesting, since it inverts the usual assertion, which is that Satria eat the leavings of Brahmana (Guermonprez 1989: 194–5). The eating of another group's *paridan*, like marriage, is a practice with dramatic and definite implications for ranking. Eating the *paridan* of a group which does not reciprocate creates a lasting asymmetry, whilst refusing it indicates an assertion of superiority or equality. In theory, there are three possible exchanges: Satria accept the paridan of Brahmana, Brahmana accept that of Satria, and each refuses to eat that of the other. As with marriage exchange, we have seen that, in one context or another, all of these occur or are claimed to occur.

It is probably no coincidence that it was in Klungkung where Brahmana were prepared to accept the *paridan* of the king, since that king, with the title *déwa agung*, was the foremost ruler in Bali and thus was powerful enough to exert his superiority over his *pedanda*. The members of the Corong ruling house are also purportedly descended from the same ancestor as the Déwa Agung, as are the Cokorda in the other Gianyar village (see above) where they do not marry Brahmana.

My argument thus consists of three main points. The first is that the ranking of Brahmana and Cokorda is essentially ambiguous and contested, because each group validates its competing claims to relative superiority according to different and incommensurate criteria of ranking. The second point is that the two groups can refuse to exchange, in which case they coexist in an uneasy stalemate. The third point concerns what happens when the two groups engage in exchange. The evidence suggests that exchange does not enact a pre-existing hierarchical order. Rather, it is the exchange itself which generates an asymmetry between the parties to the exchange. It is only when one group consumes the *paridan* of another, which in turn does not reciprocate, that the inferiority of the former is established. Similarly, because the practice of wife giving is inferior to that of wife taking, it is only when marriage occurs that relations of inferiority and superiority are generated. How competing groups actually negotiate these exchanges depends on historically variable factors such as the effective power of the descent groups, their material wealth, their relative size and the importance of other kinds of relationships between them. At any point in time, the hierarchy may evince a semblance of fixity, but over the longer term its shifting, contextual and fluid character becomes clear.

Change & continuity

The situation described in the previous sections provokes the question as to why, today, many Balinese throughout the island place Brahmana above Cokorda? Given the competition for superiority between these two groups, why does the ranking seem relatively unambiguous to others? The answer that I sketch in this section can be stated very succinctly. In the present century, the traditional ruling elite has lost much of its wealth, power and influence, whilst in some respects the position of the Brahmana groups has been consolidated and even enhanced, thus tipping the balance of status and prestige more in the latter's favour.

There are several interconnected reasons why Brahmana are today often given priority, apart from the obvious fact that the *warna* scheme always lists Brahmana in first place. One of the most important reasons for their priority concerns a long-term process of religious change in Bali. As this is a complicated issue, which is pursued in more detail in the following chapters, here I provide only enough information to make the argument intelligible. The process of religious change began in the early part of the century, when educated commoners, especially in north Bali, and their Brahmana adversaries published rival periodicals (*Surya Kanta* and *Bali Adnjana*, respectively), in which many aspects of Balinese religion were problematized. The former argued for a less ritualized and more rational, egalitarian and philosophical 'religion' detached from caste. They were stoutly resisted by the latter, who wanted to retain their caste privileges by continuing to define religion as intrinsically connected to hierarchical customary practices.[16]

This struggle became more general and pressing after independence in 1950. The constitution of the Republic of Indonesia insisted, and still insists, that every citizen acknowledges one of the following monotheistic religions: Islam, Protestantism, Catholicism and Buddhism. During the first few years of the existence of the Republic of Indonesia, Balinese Hinduism was excluded from this list of officially sanctioned religions because it lacked a holy book and was considered polytheistic. Balinese were thus defined as people who 'do not yet have religion' (*belum beragama*, Ind.). Such a situation exposed them to the threat of Christian and Muslim proselytising. However, for some time a rather shadowy supreme deity, Sanghyang Widhi, had been gaining significance amongst high priests and intellectuals, and eventually President Sukarno was persuaded that the religion was monotheistic. Promises were also made to produce a holy book and to rationalize ceremonial practice, in particular by emphasizing the theological dimension of religion at the expense of its ritual side. Consequently, in 1958 the Balinese version of Hinduism, named *agama Hindu*, was elevated to the status of other religions recognized and supported by the state.

---

[16] For details, see Bagus (1969, 1975, n.d.), Geertz (1973a), Forge (1980), Vickers (1989: 150–55), Bakker (1993), Picard (1999); for an east Javanese example, see Hefner (1985: 254–8).

The organization given the task of supervising these developments in Balinese religion was the Parisada Hindu Dharma Bali, whose supreme council was staffed almost entirely by *pedanda* priests.[17] The Parisada carried out its task largely by importing some of the more philosophical and rational doctrines of Indian Hinduism, now seen by many Balinese intellectuals as the source and inspiration for Balinese religion, and by underplaying the ritual and material side of Balinese village religious practices. Some of the central scriptures of Hinduism, the *Bhagavadgita* for example, were translated into Indonesian,[18] students were sent to study in India and Indian scholars were invited to Indonesia (Bakker 1993: 2–3, 299; Picard 1995).

Since the 1920s, then, the Indonesian state and Balinese intellectuals and reformers have sought to 'Hinduize' Balinese religion. By this I mean that the existing similarities between Hinduism in India and Balinese religion became more explicit, self-conscious and valorized, and that in addition new ideas from India were introduced to consolidate this process. For its inspiration, this philosophical Hinduism (*agama Hindu*) drew mostly on the ideas of the Indian neo-Hindu revival of the late nineteenth century, which emerged under colonialism. This revival emphasized reform, social work, spirituality, personal salvation and rationalism and opposed ritual, hierarchy and magic. It also saw Indian intellectuals promote the *Bhagavadgita* as a key religious text, which could stand alongside the Bible.[19]

This new religion is now described and explained in numerous books and pamphlets locally available in the bookshops and markets of the main towns.[20] These books contain discussions, generally quite new to the mass of ordinary Balinese, of the religious principles underlying reform Hinduism: ideas about morality, duty, the soul, the afterlife, reincarnation, the doctrines of *karma*, *samsara* (the cycle of rebirth) and *moksa* (liberation) and the meaning of symbols and rituals (for example, Punyatmadja 1976a, b). In some of this literature, simplistic renditions of the Hindu *varna* scheme and its relation to the Balinese version are also provided (for example, Upadeca, 1968 : 54–5), indicating that the Brahmana point of view is well represented.

While village Balinese do not read these books very much, a surprisingly large

---

[17] Much has changed since the inception of the Parisada in 1958. The congregation it represents has broadened considerably and now its membership outside Bali is as large as its membership on the island. Many other Indonesians have converted to 'Hinduism' to avoid becoming either Christian or Muslim (see next chapter for details). To take account of this, its name has been changed to Parisada Hindu Dharma Indonesia and its headquarters are now in Jakarta. It is still Balinese who dominate the decision-making process in the organization and its supreme council is staffed mostly by Balinese priests, but their preeminent place, once very secure, is now being challenged (for more details, see Bakker 1993; Picard 1995; Ramstedt 1995; Pitana 1999).

[18] The Muslim poet Amir Hamzah was the first to translate the *Bhagavadgita* into Indonesian in 1933. Another translation was made by the Balinese Gedé Pudja in the latter part of the decade 1950–59. Gedé Pudja studied in India for several years in the 1950s and later became Director of the Department for Hinduism and Buddhism (Bakker 1993: 2, 42).

[19] I am much indebted to David Gellner for explaining this to me.

[20] At first most of these books were written by officials of, and published by, the Parisada. Since then, however, there has been an explosion of literature. While much of it is still published under the auspices of the Parisada, many other academics and intellectuals, especially in Bali, have published books on a great many aspects of Indian and Balinese Hinduism, and on the religious teachings of Indian holy men, such as Swami Sivananda, Swami Vivekananda, Sai Baba and many others (for example, Jendra 1996; Wiana 1992, 1995; Titib 1994). Bakker (1993) provides an excellent description of the contributions made to the debates on religion in the twentieth century by the Parisada and four Balinese religious intellectuals.

number of houses have a small collection of them (Geertz 1973a). More importantly, some of these texts constitute the material for religious education. All Balinese children go to school for a minimum of six years, and religious education is compulsory (Parker 1992a). In conversations with late teenagers about the hierarchy, I have been told, often dogmatically, that Brahmana are in top place. This is where the *warna* scheme places Brahmana, and it is a ranking reinforced by the school texts they have to learn, but it does not accord well with the complexities of the situation according to older members of Brahmana and Cokorda groups. Some young people are also quite adept at fashioning explanations for Balinese ritual practices and symbols in which recently introduced, Hinduistic, philosophy is very prominent.

Agama Hindu is thus a text-based doctrinal and ethical religion which, because it is a recognized state religion, acts as a bulwark against Islam. While the tenets of this systematized religion remain only tenuously connected to the highly ritualized practices of village and court religion (Forge 1980: 222; Picard 1999), some Balinese are now able to discuss their customary rituals and ceremonies as if they are merely the outward expression of the underlying theology of *agama Hindu*, something which could not have been done in the past. Becoming more an orthodoxy than an orthopraxy, the links between this new religion and the old ruling aristocracy, who organized the most important rituals and ceremonies constituting customary 'religion', have begun to diminish (Geertz 1973a: 186).

This process of religious rationalzation can in part be interpreted as a successful continuation of earlier commoner attempts to reduce the significance of caste-related ritual practices in Balinese religion, and thus as something of a defeat for Brahmana and Satria elites. However, because Brahmana priests have been heavily involved in supervising this transformation, they have found opportunities to maintain and even consolidate their position in Balinese society.

The most important way in which Brahmana have been able to exert control over processes of religious change is through their domination of the supreme council of the Parisada. A majority of the organization's lay officers are also high-caste and provide support to the priests. Even if the priests also work alongside some commoner academic intellectuals, with whom they often disagree, it is the priests on the supreme council who make the final decisions on matters of doctrine. Because they are 'experts' in religion, Brahmana priests have 'naturally' been expected to play an influential part in defining the new doctrines of Hinduism, just as, under the Dutch, they played a key role in redefining the hierarchy. These positions help to validate their superior status in society.

Nevertheless, in accordance with the increasing democratic and egalitarian tendencies in Indonesian society, the claim to pre-eminence by *pedanda* has also been challenged by temple priests from commoner groups, who argue that their views should also be taken into consideration. In particular, they provide interpretations of religious symbolism at odds with those offered by *pedanda* (Pitana 1999). Not surprisingly, the claim of these commoner priests to equality of religious status with the *pedanda* has caused much controversy within the Parisada.

The process of religious change has also been facilitated by other developments in Balinese society this century, particularly Dutch colonialism and tourism. As explained in Chapter 2, the Dutch attempted to codify and simplify the Balinese 'caste system', whose flexibility they misconstrued as confusion. Partly this was done to administer Bali more effectively and, like the British in India, they were concerned not to interfere overmuch with religious activities, so that they could

Plate 6.2 Some of the many shrines in the extensive houseyard temple (*mrajan*) of Cokorda Gedé's palace in Corong

Plate 6.3 Brahman priest (*pedanda*) carrying out a ritual preparatory to the cremation of a high-caste man in the village of Klakah

preserve Bali's 'exotic' culture.[21] In a phrase, the Dutch took over the control of 'political' affairs but ceded 'religious' matters to the Balinese (Vickers 1989), thus dividing what had been a more unified set of institutions. The emergence of a religious sphere ideologically independent of politics was thus initiated by the Dutch, developed by the anti-hierarchical movements of the 1920s and given further momentum by the state and the Parisada.

There were other effects of the colonial period which have had an impact on the issues under discussion. As a result of Dutch political control and later developments in the political organization of Bali, the power and wealth of the pre-colonial ruling elite are no longer available to their descendants. They have lost the power to tax, much land has been alienated, their magical weapons have lost their effectiveness, their harems and slave-servants are a thing of the past, and they have largely given up their patronage of music and the arts by handing over their orchestras and costumes to village associations (Picard 1990a: 46).

Moreover, the traditional elites are now detached from their former peasant clients, whom they can no longer coerce as previously. Those who work the land that remains are also in a position to negotiate much better rates of crop division than was once the case.[22] Today commoners cannot be forced to provide unpaid labour for the palace's projects, but must be invited and treated with respect. Traditional elites still retain some control but this is now based largely on their positions in the new bureaucracies and on the provision of waged jobs. But equally many commoners are now completely independent of these ex-rulers. They do not need gentry protection or patronage, because there are jobs in the expanding economy and the state supplies civil security. Despite retaining charisma, many gentry are only a shadow of what they were in the nineteenth century.

Although the wealth and power structure of Balinese society has changed, there are also continuities with the past. While the descendants of many nineteenth-century ruling households are now far less wealthy, nevertheless they are sometimes able to wield resources far in excess of what most other Balinese command. For example, it is said of the palace of Corong: *suba gerang buin gorok*, and *berag-beragan gajahé masih ada muluka*. These are proverbs which allude to the fact that, whilst most of the palace's resources ('blood' and 'fat') have been used up, there is still plenty left.[23] The palace's temple, for example, still has twelve hectares of rice-land (an average holding for those who own land in Corong is 0.5 hectare, and perhaps half the villagers own no land at all), and the total landholding of the small Cokorda group in Corong is 28 per cent of the village total. However, until quite recently the palace was in an advanced state of decay. Its decline has only been halted recently by the marriage of Cokorda Gedé's younger brother to a Japanese woman with very wealthy connections. Through her, they have been able to establish profitable hotel and car-hire businesses and now the palace is gradually regaining some of its past glory.

The apex of the 'traditional' politico-religious system was the king–priest axis, but, if the rulers and their descendants have suffered an irreversible decline, the profile of the priest has, if anything, been consolidated. In contemporary Bali, it is true, there is

---

[21] The underlying reasons for this were described in Chapter 2.

[22] In previous times, tenants often only retained one-third of the land, or even one-quarter; these days one-half of the crop is much more common.

[23] It is difficult to translate these literally. The first refers to the fact that Balinese animals are slaughtered by slitting the throat (*ngorok*) and draining the blood, which is a delicacy. Although the *puri* has little left (*gerang*, 'dry'), it can still be 'drained again' (*buin ngorok*). The second is more straightforward: 'The elephant [i.e. the palace] gets thinner and thinner, but there is still fat on it.'

a strong undercurrent of criticism against the Brahmana which in some circumstances becomes quite explicit. Some *pedanda* are considered greedy, and their houses are likened to shops which sell overpriced offerings (Rubinstein 1995). Others are accused of truncating their rituals so that they can 'take their money and run'. Many unemployed Brahmana youth are professional gamblers, and some have a reputation for licentiousness, arrogance and drunkenness.

Nevertheless, in contemporary Bali the high priest's position, while not unassailable, is still very powerful. The Dutch not only refrained from interfering in religious matters, thereby insulating the *pedanda* from the fate befalling the rulers, but it was to the priests that they went in search of authoritative statements about the nature of Balinese society, whereupon they were able to advance their own versions (Vickers 1989: 147). The Dutch also used them in the lawcourts to adjudicate on a wide variety of matters of local importance. Korn (1932: 415) reports that, of the twenty-three judges appointed to the *Raad Kerta* (Balinese courts), seventeen were Brahmana and only one was a Sudra. While the old rulers became Dutch puppets, the priests were able to maintain their hold on important judicial and religious posts during and after the colonial period, for example in the Parisada. Additionally, they continue to officiate at all major regional and state rituals; during the huge rituals at the Besakih temple, the kings have been replaced by the island's governor, but the *pedanda* still preside as in the past.

High priests may no longer be king's councillors, but this has not significantly affected their position in village life. While Cokorda and other gentry no longer have traditional clients, the hold of the *pedanda* on his or her clients has remained intact. They have retained their strong links with the bulk of the peasantry, who still require all the services of the priest that they did a century ago (for example, to obtain holy water, officiate at ceremonies and provide advice on offerings, buildings and the complex ritual calendar). Anyway, extricating oneself from being the client of a *pedanda* can be very dangerous, as one might become the victim of his curse, leading to illness now or torments in hell after death.[24]

[24] While villagers in Corong agreed that extreme deference was required towards both the *pedanda* and Cokorda Gedé, they seemed generally more timid and anxious in the company of the former. A possible reason for this is that *pedanda*, like other 'religious' specialists, are considered dangerous. While Cokorda Gedé may have magically powerful heirloom weapons (the palace has five *kris*, daggers, for example), the priests are dangerous in themselves. This is not a stable distinction, though, but more probably a reflection of the present era. In the past, the highest kings were thought to be exceptionally *sakti*. Nowadays, however, only a vestige of this supernatural power remains, there are few, if any, opportunities for displaying the power of sacred objects and, in many cases, such objects have been lost or destroyed or their power has diminished.

The fear of *pedanda*, and to a lesser degree other religious specialists, is also due to their command of texts. Balinese letters (*aksara*), said to be 'located' in different parts of the body, have divine origins and are imbued with *sakti*. Sanskrit texts are reputed to have been composed by celestial priests and deities. Studying such texts under the appropriate conditions transfers this power to the aspirant priest. The texts must be treated with great deference, for they are dangerous to the uninitiated; untutored reading of them can lead to madness. To consult them with safety, one must undertake the ceremonies which purify and strengthen the mind. One element of these rituals is the inscription of magical symbols (*ngrajah*) on the tongue of the initiate, which then makes their mantra directly effective. When recited or inscribed, letters and mantra transfer their power to the receiving objects or people. One way of causing illness is to utter magical syllables which manipulate the 'letters' in people's bodies. Because many religious specialists are credited with considerable magical prowess and the ability to curse, they have to be treated with great circumspection to avoid offending them. Balinese are thus profoundly ambivalent about all religious specialists. 'Because the mystical power that priests and healers employ is the same as that of sorcerers, and is [thus] morally neutral, it is difficult to tell whether someone is using his powers for good or evil' (Geertz 1995a: 23; see also Ruddick 1986). While leading Cokorda have lost most of the sources of their magical effectiveness, *pedanda* have not and so are thought to be comparatively more dangerous (Rubinstein 1987: ch. 3).

Brahmana have thus been active participants, rather than passive observers of all these changes. *Pedanda* have become more active in village life. It is noticeable that in recent times they have begun to officiate much more directly than before. Previously, for many ceremonies, *pedanda* simply prepared the holy water in their own houses and then handed it to low-caste priests, who conducted the ritual. Now they are regularly present themselves, even if they maintain an inscrutable aloofness in relation to the activity around them (Geertz 1973a: 184). In contemporary Bali, not to have a *pedanda* to 'finish' (*puput*) one's ceremonies is almost shameful.

Moreover, despite several forms of division and rivalry between groups of Brahmana, they often form tightly knit communities. These are based on a variety of relationships: of kinship and affinity amongst Brahmana within one region and between those in different regions; between a *pedanda* and his/her clients (*sisya*); between a *pedanda* and the priests he/she consecrates; and amongst the *pedanda* who control the religious agenda in the Parisada (Rubinstein 1995). According to Rubinstein, such overlapping networks 'play an important part in unifying the Brahmana. [They] also underpin influential alliances that have elevated Brahmana to prominent civil positions' thereby protecting and boosting the group's interests and 'maintaining *pedanda* at the forefront of the religious hierarchy' (Rubinstein 1995: 14).[25]

All of these various factors have conspired to depress the visibility and influence of the descendants of nineteenth-century rulers, at the same time as they have been instrumental in instituting a new religious orthodoxy, in which the Brahmana in general and the *pedanda* in particular have played a prime role. The status of the *pedanda* has also been enhanced by the massive tourist expansion since 1970. Many tourists come to Bali for a cultural experience. High on the list of events tourists clamour to view are the ritual spectacles, especially the cremations, and during these the *pedanda* is at times the centre of attraction, often surrounded by tourists taking photographs.

Tourism has also played a part in helping to produce a separate realm of the 'sacred' so that it can be presented to tourists as a specific cultural attraction (Picard 1996). In this sense, 'religion', as a newly created, autonomous mode of activity, has increased in importance. This helps to consolidate the role of the Brahmana priest as paramount religious functionary. Balinese are often unaware of the historicity of these long-run trends and tend to consider as 'traditional' what are relatively new developments or to see them as a 'renaissance' of the past (Picard 1990a: 65, 74).

In sum, while the fortunes of the traditional ruling elite have conspicuously declined, those of the *pedanda*, and of the Brahmana generally have remained stable or even improved. In this reordered relationship, the nineteenth-century competition between kings and priests is still present, but many aspects of contemporary Balinese society conspire to give the latter a pre-eminence they rarely had in the past.

---

[25] There is a danger here of exaggerating the conservative and reactionary nature of Brahmana and the *pedanda* priests. In the period preceding the slaughter of the communists in 1965–6, some joined the Communist Party and others sympathized with its aims of greater social equality (Vickers 1989: 169). Amongst the thousands murdered in Bali were many high castes and some *pedanda* priests. In Corong a slaughtered ox was dumped in the courtyard of a *pedanda*'s house, hence causing great pollution, because of his close association with communists. Today, individual *pedanda* promote more egalitarian forms of religion, and at least one has given a sermon at the Sai Baba temple in Denpasar.

Conclusion

Three conclusions can be drawn from the preceding discussion. The first is that, both in the pre-colonial period and subsequently, the relative ranking of king and priest was not stable but inherently contested. The endemic nature of this competition in the political organization of the pre-colonial Balinese state suggests that the polarized debate concerning the caste systems of India should be conceptualized in a different way. Rather than privileging hierarchy, religion, priesthood and purity, on the one hand, or centrality, politics, kingship and honour, on the other, it would appear both more fruitful and ethnographically more consistent to examine how these various ideas and idioms were put into play by kings, priests and others to claim positions of superiority, power and authority. In Bali, it is the simultaneous existence of cultural models of both hierarchy and centrality that makes most sense of the data and provides an explanation for the dynamic competition between kings and priests.

Second, despite this competition, it is also possible to trace a change in the overall relation of king and priest. The fortunes of descendants of former rulers have declined, whereas those of the latter have not. Dutch control over economic and political affairs curtailed the power base of the kings and their descendants and, even if this has not accelerated since independence, it has also not been reversed. Balinese gentry may have secured a disproportionate number of influential state jobs, but what ultimately underpins these today is state authority emanating from above and not, as in the past, control over the local population. In a very real sense, the relation between king and priest no longer exists at all, because there are no kings and, even if their descendants strive to maintain some semblance of a royal lifestyle, they no longer have the authority over *pedanda* they once had. The ties which connect the Brahmana and their priests to the Satria elite are fewer and less binding, so that the relation between them has become more tenuous and variable, as each is more at liberty to act independently of the other. A scriptural religion and a bureaucratized state no longer entail that priests have to be closely attached to local power sources. So, while status rivalry still exists between them, the patterning of this relationship is changing. If kings often had the upper hand in the pre-colonial period, the effects of colonialism, independence, tourism and other forces have conspired to bring the priest into contemporary prominence. (It is of course possible that the pre-eminence of the Brahmana might be temporary, since the democratization of Indonesia is likely to undermine it in the longer term.)

Nevertheless, I would still argue that the continuing viability of the groups at the apex of the hierarchy, despite the criticisms increasingly levelled against them, is a powerful factor in maintaining the contemporary relevance of hierarchical social relationships and in providing the main impetus for status drives. The twin pillars of the hierarchy, Satria Dalem and Brahmana, now somewhat differently organized and related, are still entrenched in the political, economic and cultural life of the island. However, at the same time as they jointly provide a point of reference which gives coherence to the whole hierarchy, they also present a highly visible object on which to concentrate dissent.

Third, as a result of processes of religious change (the uses made of *pedanda* by the Dutch, the emergence of an autonomous domain of religious practice and knowledge, the place of the priest in the Parisada and in tourism, the continuing importance of the priest's position in village life, etc.), the *pedanda*'s priestly role has been increasingly emphasized, while his wider sphere of action, as occasional ruler, tactician and weapons manufacturer, has been circumscribed. In the past, priest and ruler shared certain attributes and their roles partially overlapped. Since then the progressive separation of 'politics' from 'religion' has been paralleled by a widening disjunction between Satria and Brahmana, and the *pedanda* is much more explicitly a priest (in the western sense of the word) than he was in the past.

7

Religion, Culture & Identity in the Indonesian State

Introduction

If the main topic of previous chapters has been Balinese hierarchy, the changes it has undergone and some indigenous critiques of it, the subject of this and the following chapters is Balinese religion. But in my treatment of Balinese religion I am less interested in the symbolic interpretation of ritual, the conceptualization of divinity or other similarly traditional topics in the anthropology of religion. Rather, what concerns me is the argument Balinese are themselves engaged in about religion. In pursuing policies aimed at national integration, the state has limited the officially acceptable forms religion can take in Indonesia and has tried to decouple religions and cultures from their ethnic-group frameworks. As Balinese creatively respond to central state directives, this social engineering has unwittingly created a situation of religious diversity and conflict in Bali and, because religion and forms of identity are closely linked, it has also sparked new processes of identity formation.[1]

Vickers (1989, 1996) has pointed out that how the Balinese define themselves, or how they conceptualize their identity, has not been stable, nor, at any point in time, has it been something which all Balinese have agreed on. At different historical periods, Balinese individuals and groups have been pressed to supply to others (other islanders, Dutch traders, Dutch colonial officers, the Indonesian state, tourists, etc.) descriptions and explanations of their 'culture', and thus of themselves, lest others do it for them. They have done this in a variety of ways, sometimes in tune with outsiders' representations of Bali and sometimes in defiance of them.

During the twentieth century, urban-based, middle-class intellectuals took on the task of explaining and presenting Bali and Balinese culture both to the outside world and to the rest of Balinese society. In differentiating themselves from other peoples of the archipelago, particularly Muslims and Christians, they have increasingly come to see themselves, their *ethnic* identity, as defined in terms of a Balinese version of Hinduism. This form of Hinduism, which has come to be conceived of as the inspiration of their famed culture, has continuities with nineteenth-century religious practice, but has also been shaped by new imported doctrines and ideas from India and thus become much more explicitly and self-consciously 'Hindu'.

The Dutch colonial regime, the Indonesian state and the tourist industry have all, in different ways, appropriated, commoditized and promoted Balinese culture and, in doing so, changed it and changed the way Balinese think about it. The terms they use

---

[1] Processes of identity formation in the context of the forging of an Indonesian national culture have been examined by a number of anthropologists, for example, the Javanese (Pemberton 1994), the Dayak (Schiller 1997) and the Minangkabau (Kahn 1993) and Karo Batak (Kipp 1993) of Sumatra.

to talk about 'culture' (*cultuur, peradaban*), 'religion' (*agama*), 'tradition' (*adat*) and 'art' (*budaya, seni*) are all foreign (Dutch, Sanskrit, Arabic, Malay). By attaching specific new terms to particular aspects of Balinese social life, which in the nineteenth century were less differentiated, identifiable bounded domains have been produced. As a result, a new consciousness that they 'possess' a 'culture' and a 'religion' has been created amongst Balinese. Rather than 'culture' being something they take relatively for granted, they now have a specific relation to it. The reification of this culture as an object serving their own and others' interests has encouraged Balinese to be both proud of and anxious about it: others admire it and it brings in large tourist revenues, but concern is expressed over its fragility. However, as this religious culture became externalized, as Balinese developed a relation to it and as they became self-conscious about it, it could be re-appropriated as the unique feature which defines their 'Balineseness' (*kebalian*, Ind.) (Picard 1996, 1999).

In recent years, however, as this ethnic identity assumed clearer outlines, the varieties of Hinduism on the island began to multiply. While Balinese religion is a form of Hinduism, in contemporary Bali there are now several competing varieties of Hinduism, and it is this competition which will be the focus of my discussion. Broadly speaking, there are three varieties of Hinduism, which I call *adat*, *agama Hindu* and devotional Hinduism. For the most part, these Hinduisms do not have well-defined boundaries or exclusive memberships, and in terms of doctrinal content, while there are important differences between them, there is also significant overlap. *Adat* can be glossed as the customary practice which encompasses the Hindu-influenced, ritual-based religion of both pre- and post-colonial Bali. It centres on the relation between Balinese and their divinized ancestors as enacted through temple ceremonies, life-crisis rites and collective community rituals, such as cremation. *Agama Hindu*, in contrast, is the official version of Hinduism in Indonesia, recognized and supported by the state. Largely a text-based and doctrinal religion, it is a recent creation born out of Balinese responses to the Indonesian state's injunctions concerning the nature of acceptable religions. Finally, devotional Hinduism, newly imported into Bali from about 1980 and independently of the state, takes two forms: devotion to Shri Sathya Sai Baba, and the Krishna Consciousness movement, the latter also known as the Hare Krishnas. To avoid confusion, I adopt the convention of using 'Sai Baba' to refer to the movement and 'Baba' to refer to its founder.

Shri Sathya Sai Baba is an Indian 'god-man'. He was born in 1926 in the village of Puttaparthi in the state of Andhra Pradesh. His early life was not particularly distinguished but he liked to sing devotional songs (*bhajan*) and he 'materialized' sweets and other items for his friends. When he was older, he proclaimed himself the reincarnation of the nineteenth-century saint Shirdi Sai Baba, who lived in Shirdi in Maharashtra, thus linking himself to a famous holy lineage. After this, his miracles became more dramatic and increased in frequency, and he began to attract a large following of devotees. In 1950 he built his ashram in Puttaparthi, which has since grown to include a hospital, conference rooms and extensive accommodation for devotees, who visit the ashram from all over the world. In 1963 after an illness, supposedly self-induced and self-cured, he declared himself to be Shiva and Shakti in embodied form. He is said to be all the gods and goddesses of the Hindu pantheon and to be the deity of all religions. His devotees call him *Bhagavan*, that is, God.[2] Baba's highly charismatic appeal rests largely on the notion that he is a manifestation of the universal God and has the power to work miracles and cure illnesses.

[2] For further details on the life history of Sai Baba, see Kasturi (1975) and Babb (1986).

The Hare Krishnas or ISKCON (International Society for the Study of Krishna Consciousness) was established in New York City in 1965 on the inspiration of A.C. Bhaktivedanta Swami Prabhupada when he travelled to America from his home in India. The movement quickly spread from America to Europe and other parts of the world and now has small branches in both Java and Bali. As a young man, Prabhupada had a university education in Calcutta and in 1922 he became a disciple of Bhaktisiddhanta Sarasvati. The latter continued a Vaisnava tradition that went back to Caitanya's teaching based on the worship of and devotion to Krishna in sixteenth-century Bengal. Krishna is not one form of God, but the supreme manifestation of God. Caitanya also preached that all people, regardless of their caste, could reach perfection through devotion to Krishna. It thus became popular among Bengal's low caste population. Caitanya also developed the practice of singing and dancing in the streets (*sankirtana*) as a way to praise Krishna.

Many aspects of Krishna doctrine derive from two texts, the *Bhagavata Purana* and the *Bhagavadgita*. The first, historically more important for the development of Krishna *bhakti*, recounts Krishna's childhood and youth. Portrayed as sweet and erotic, he plays mischievous games with the cow girls, who cannot resist him or his flute-playing. The second narrates the dialogue between Krishna and Arjuna on the eve of the great war in which Arjuna will kill his cousins, Krishna arguing against Arjuna's objections that, in order to fulfil his *kshatriya* duty, he must take this course of action. The *Bhagavadgita* assumed much more importance in India in the nineteenth century, when the Hindu reform movement need a relatively self-contained religious text on the model of the Christian Bible. This is surely one of the main reasons why the Hindu movement in Bali has also appropriated this as a central text.[3]

According to Krishna doctrine, very briefly, the spiritual self is independent but is trapped in a material body, and it transmigrates from one body to another according to the karmic consequences produced by the way the self handles its relations with this succession of bodies. Spiritual advancement is secured by denying the pleasures the body demands and thus by not identifying with the body. This eventually enables the self to overcome the laws of karma, to fully realize itself and to unite with Krishna.

Although Sai Baba and Hare Krishna are, so far as I am aware, the only institutionalized devotional movements in Bali, various other ideas connected to the neo-Hindu revival movement in India have existed in Bali for some years. Consequently, Sai Baba must be seen as simply one current in a much broader river of Hindu 'revivalism'. For example, Rabindranath Tagore visited Bali for a short time in 1927. His endorsement of an open and tolerant Hinduism and his opposition to untouchability and the caste system influenced Ida Bagus Mantra (a future governor of Bali), who had studied at the Visvabharati University in Santiniketan, founded by Tagore, and where other Balinese subsequently studied. The so-called Ida Bagus Mantra group has been very influential in developing the official Hindu discourse in Bali. However, this group's reform credentials have been questioned by others because of its support of *adat* institutions, such as the *catur warna* (caste) system. The group has been criticized by commoner organizations (for example, the Pasek Sapta Sanak Rsi) fighting for the equal status of its 'commoner' priests with high-caste Brahmana priests (Pitana 1999), by the Gandhi group of Ibu Gedong Oka and by the Forum Cendekiawan Hindu Indonesia (Forum of Indonesian Hindu Intellectuals). In addition there are also Hindu youth organizations in various universities across

[3] For further background details, see Rochford (1985), Hopkins (1989) and Deadwyler (1989).

Indonesia, formed in response to a resurgence in Islamic activities (Ramstedt 2001).

This widespread interest of the Balinese intelligentsia in Hindu theology and reformist movements has led to an explosion of religious literature (see Chapter 6, note 20; see also Ramstedt 1995). The publications of the Parisada are mainly concerned with extending the influence of *agama Hindu*, while other academics and intellectuals tend to concentrate on reform Hinduism and on the religious teachings of Indian holy men, such as Swami Sivananda, Swami Vivekananda, Gandhi, and Sathya Sai Baba (for example, Wiana 1992, 1995; Titib 1994; Jendra 1996), thus, in effect, undermining the state's efforts to impose religious orthodoxy.

In this and subsequent chapters, I shall argue that this religious diversity has generated conflict over the nature and locus of religious truth and over forms of religious practice and conviction and has rendered the linkage between identity, religion and culture very contentious. Perhaps the main issue for many Balinese is what particular form of Hinduism is best suited to contemporary life in Bali. While this is debated predominantly amongst the urban-based middle class, academics and intellectuals, it is none the less gradually filtering down into ordinary Balinese society. An important indication of this is that many adherents of devotional Hinduism, and other new religious movements for that matter, who voice criticisms of 'traditional' forms of religion and of the new *agama Hindu*, come from all sections of the population.

The problem I am interested in is this: if the creation of a Balinese ethnic identity, based on a specifically Balinese form of Hinduism, has been taking shape in recent years, what are the implications for identity construction when new and different forms of Hinduism, which owe little to 'traditional' Balinese religious practices, begin to emerge? This issue is reflected in the kinds of questions which Balinese now increasingly ask themselves. In what does religious truth reside? Which form of Hinduism best reveals such truth? Which is more appropriate: an exclusive Balinese ethnic identity based on a specifically Balinese form of Hinduism, or a more inclusive and universal identity founded on an Indian form of Hinduism which is thus less constrained by the limitations of ethnic group and state boundaries?

One way to understand these issues is to examine the different ways in which Balinese conceive of the relationship between these newly emerging forms of religion and 'traditional' Balinese institutions, and here there are two principal alternatives. Should Hinduism retain a specifically Balinese orientation by preserving some connection to the hierarchy, high priests and ritual, that is, in general, to local traditions? Or should it stand alone as a universally valid form for worshipping God, in which case it is partly detached from existing local institutions and instead linked to religious movements well beyond both Bali and Indonesia?

I argue that these two options make for very different perspectives on the hierarchy and different pathways to identity formation. *Adat* and *agama Hindu* are forms of Hinduism which provide a route to the first option, whereas devotional Hinduism supplies a route to the second. *Adat* and *agama Hindu* encourage some kind of commitment to village traditions, which, even if this is equivocal at times, also includes a commitment to hierarchical social relations. Because of the continuing linkage to customary religious practices, they also foster an identity which is specifically Balinese. The second option has become, intentionally or not, another indigenous critique both of traditional forms of religion and of the hierarchy. In relation to *adat* and *agama Hindu*, the Sai Baba and Hare Krishna devotional movements are understood to be comparatively egalitarian in spirit, to be avowedly anti-ritual (though this will need to be qualified later) and to have no role for priests. To their opponents these movements are subversive and dangerous, while to their adherents they are liberating, radical alternatives to other forms of Hinduism. They are a challenge to the hierarchy and to the religious pre-eminence of Brahmana priests, especially in their role as guardians of religious truth, and are seen as more in keeping with the propagation of an image of Bali as modern and democratic. Just as important is the fact that they provide the conditions for a new form of religious experience.

Such devotional Hinduism links Balinese to other believers all over the world, whether through actual contact or through membership in an 'imagined community' (Anderson 1983). As a result, it provides a rather different basis on which to construct an identity. This is still a religious identity with its roots in Hinduism, but it transcends parochial attachments to Bali by connecting Balinese devotees to universal movements centred in India. It is not therefore their 'Balineseness', their ethnic identity, which is any longer so important, but rather their religious convictions and their intense emotional devotion either to Krishna or to the person of Baba.

I should make clear that these two orientations are ideal types and that, in practice, the situation is more complicated. It is perfectly possible, for example, for Balinese to construct an inclusive identity as members of a worldwide movement focused on Baba in India, whilst also conceiving of themselves as Balinese through their participation in all the rituals in their home village. However, if adherents of Sai Baba tend to conceive of these contexts as complementary, their opponents frequently see them as contradictory. This flexibility is far less evident for members of the Krishna Consciousness movement, as will become clear in Chapter 9.

These processes of religious change in Bali have not occurred in a political vacuum. The creation of *agama Hindu* was a result of both external and internal pressures. Balinese leaders, high priests and intellectuals responded to state definitions about the nature of acceptable religions by rationalizing and Hinduizing *adat* to produce an *agama* ('religion') which was more closely linked to what they conceived to be Indian Hinduism. What these Balinese intellectuals took to be 'authentic' Indian Hinduism was, by and large, the range of doctrines, ideas and practices of the neo-Hindu revival of the nineteenth century. However, other and more radical movements erupted into the space created by the separation of *adat* from *agama Hindu*. When, in the 1950s, Balinese began in earnest to import Hindu doctrines from India as part of the campaign to obtain state recognition for Balinese Hinduism, they also inadvertently stimulated interest in other varieties of Hinduism flourishing in the subcontinent. There is no mystery, then, concerning the introduction of devotional forms of Hinduism into Indonesia and Bali. By conceptualizing religion in terms of *agama*, the state forced Balinese to align *adat* religion with more 'authentic' forms of Indian Hinduism. Once this contemporary dialogue with India opened up, however, it became obvious that Indian Hinduism was not a unitary religion. Those Balinese who were not content to let the Parisada and the priests dictate the manner in which religious reform proceeded exploited the opportunities that then became available and began to select forms of Hinduism more appropriate to their particular sentiments and interests. As *agama Hindu* and devotional Hinduism took root alongside *adat*, debates about religious truth emerged and arguments about the structure of Balinese society intensified.

It was not only devotional Hinduism which found a niche in this newly created and much expanded religious landscape, for many new indigenous religious movements have also sprung up. These are almost always denied the status of religion (*agama*) by the authorities and are instead called 'streams of belief' (*aliran kepercayaan*). I have not done any research on these Balinese movements, nor has much been written about them. However, since they play a significant role in my general argument I shall say something about them later in this chapter.

Another aspect of my argument in this and subsequent chapters concerns state–local relations. For much of the period since independence in 1950, the Indonesian state has sought to forge a national unity out of the disparate cultures, religions and ethnic groups within the archipelago. A central feature of this has been the varying ways the state has manipulated local cultures to adapt them to the requirements of nation-building and the construction of a national culture (Yampolsky 1995). Whilst some anthropologists have noted the destructive and violent nature of this process (Acciaioli 1985) and the confusion and resentment of groups ideologically and physically distant from the authorizing centre (Hutajulu 1995), others have pointed to how the latter find ways to express their interests and identity through elaborating new religious, economic and cultural forms within the spaces opened up by state interference (Atkinson 1987). Sai Baba is just such a new religious form, but, while it appears novel, it is represented as a return to a tradition which has become distorted. In charting a path to the future, Sai Baba also plots a route back into the past.

Sai Baba's relation to the state is ambivalent. On the one hand, its sheer presence and the religious (and political) messages it articulates subvert state efforts to produce a religious orthodoxy by containing both religious pluralism and political democratization. In this sense, Sai Baba represents an unexpected, powerful and imaginative local challenge to the state's authoritarian directives concerning what is to count as acceptable religion. On the other hand, Sai Baba's spiritual orientation espouses self-improvement, discipline, hard work, achievement and social justice, values that are more and more underpinning the aspirations of Indonesia's burgeoning middle class and, indeed, state rhetoric (if not state practice). If, in some cases, the central state bends local cultural and religious institutions to its own interests by transforming them into aesthetically pleasing and depoliticized objects for both local and touristic consumption, in other cases, such as Sai Baba, local interests are channelled into new forms which energize religious and political change in ways that slip through state control.

Why has the state, ever since its inception, been so concerned with religion, and monotheistic religion at that? Part of the answer to this lies in the contradictory pulls of Muslim demands for an Islamic state, on the one hand, and the centrifugal forces of ethnic and cultural diversity, on the other. The artificial boundaries of the Indonesian state are those bequeathed to it by the Dutch colonial regime. While Islam is Indonesia's predominant religion, the national territory also encompasses hundreds of different ethnic groups, religions and cultures. Islam could not be Indonesia's unifying force because an Islamic state would have alienated members of other religions. The state was thus presented with a major problem. After the war and in preparation for independence in 1950, the largely Javanese authors of the constitution needed to produce some sort of national unity to counteract local ethnic loyalties. At the same time, they had to find a way of accommodating Islam while preventing the formation of an Islamic state. If Islam was not to be the state's sole official religion, the only way of even partially placating the Muslims was to make 'belief in one god' the first principle of the new state's constitution, and then confine the religions acceptable to the state to those which were monotheistic and thus shared a similar status with Islam. Because this compromise solution of toleration to limited religious plurality has never been endorsed by all Muslim groups, religion has remained a politically troublesome issue.

Another part of the answer is that belief in a single, relatively undefined god suggests a consensus around a divine authority which transcends differences based on parochial local beliefs. In this way, ethnic loyalties legitimated by endlessly variable local and customary forms of religious and ritual practice can be subsumed under an encompassing totality closely associated with the state. Moreover, this connection between a monotheistic religion and the central state is itself symbolically important, since it reproduces the close relationship between political authority and religion (Islam and Christianity, respectively) in some of the pre-colonial states of Java and in the Dutch colonial state (Atkinson 1987; Hollan 1988).

Some progress towards national unity was made before independence by adopting the Malay language, now called Bahasa Indonesia, as the national language of administration, commerce, education and the media. After independence, President Sukarno used a variety of strategies to build nationalism and reduce the centrifugal tendencies of ethnic loyalties: military might to crush regional rebellions and secessionist movements; confrontations with neighbouring powers to generate national solidarity; the rapid extension of a school system with a centrally controlled curriculum and the same structure, language of tuition, and uniform all over Indonesia; the construction of monuments to engender feelings of pride in national endeavours; the invocation of new ideologies (such as *pancasila*) and an emphasis on pan-Indonesian values to instil a sense of common purpose and unity beneath surface differences; and the gradual substitution of ethnic-based political parties by functional groups.[4] As far as the state's interests were concerned, while some permanent gains were made in the period between 1950 and 1965 and Islam became a relatively dormant political force, the attempt at national unity ultimately foundered on the impossibility of maintaining a political balance between the army and the communists, the rivalry between whom eventuated in the massacres of 1965–6.

When General Suharto assumed the presidency in 1967, he too was faced with threats to national unity. Communism had been obliterated, but the political aspirations of Islam resurfaced as the main danger. Many Muslim groups had cooperated with the army in the killings and imprisonment of suspected communists and now expected to be rewarded with a much greater say in the political and religious affairs of the state (Boland 1982: 135–56). However, since Suharto and many of his supporters were exponents of Javanese mystical practices (*kebatinan*), which were anathema to many Muslims, he had no intention of allowing Islam a greater role in state politics. In this new context, Indonesian cultural diversity, up to that time seen as a problem for national integration, now began to appear as a useful counterweight to renewed demands for an Islamic state (Schefold 1998: 273). However, this increased openness also raised the spectre of resurgent ethnic-group activity and the possibility of political mobilization around religious and cultural symbols, thus posing a different threat to

---

[4] On internal rebellions, see Kahin (1952: 290–300); on the confrontation with Malaysia, see Crouch (1988: 55–62); on the extension of the school system, see Leigh (1991) and Parker (1992a, b); on ideological thought in the Sukarno period, see Feith (1963), Anderson (1972a) and Legge (1972). The functional groups are *golongan karya*, abbreviated to *Golkar*, which up to 1998 effectively constituted Suharto's election-winning party machine; on *Golkar's* genesis and role, see Reeve (1985) and Suryadinata (1989). On the centre's construction of uniquely 'Indonesian' values based on a supposedly specific 'Indonesian' personality and approach to authority and decision-making, see Bowen (1986), Acciaioli (1997) and Bourchier (1997).

national integration. To avoid this, the Suharto New Order regime pursued a policy of promoting cultural diversity, but only so long as this was not connected to any kind of economic and political interests. Unfortunately, once the pressure was taken off, with the removal of Suharto from the presidency and the ushering in of democratic institutions in 1998 and 1999, ethnic and religious conflict in areas such as Ambon, Aceh, Lombok and elsewhere emerged in murderous forms.[5]

The following three sections discuss some of these developments in more detail as a prelude to examining the role of Sai Baba and Hare Krishna in the cultural politics of identity formation in contemporary Balinese society.

Adat, agama Hindu & devotional Hinduism

These three varieties of Hinduism have taken shape and been brought into juxtaposition and opposition through a complex political process of religious change, which has been going on in Bali for over a century. Here I briefly review these transformations by developing in more detail some of the points raised previously.

Adat is an Arabic term initially used by Muslim groups in Indonesia to denote indigenous 'customary law', as opposed to imported 'religious law' (Picard 1999: 30), but it rapidly came to be employed by the Dutch to designate the 'traditional' social order of Indonesian societies. The term was introduced into Bali by the Dutch, where it quickly replaced a range of Balinese concepts that denoted a 'field of meanings covering ritual obligation, social institution, legal regulation and ancestral evocation' (Warren 1993: 4), which together provided a sense of communal solidarity in village life. Such conceptions emphasized that 'religion' was not a set of ideas and practices separated from other aspects of social life, but was embedded in thoroughly ritualized social, political and economic institutions of diverse kinds. Balinese religion in the form of *adat* is thus:

> highly localised; it consists of rites relating specific groups of people to one another, to their ancestors, and to their territory. Moreover, religion is a customary obligation for the Balinese: participation in its rites is a consequence of membership of a local community as well as membership of a descent group.
>
> (Picard 1999: 31)

It is probably not very productive to ask whether or not *adat* religion was or is a form of Hinduism in some essential sense. In the first millennium of the Christian era, many regions of what is today Indonesia, and particularly Java and Bali, were deeply and pervasively influenced by social and political ideas and institutions from different parts of India. These cultural flows moved along the developed trade routes between India and China, which weaved their way though the islands of the archipelago. Indic models of kingship, Brahmana priests using Sanskrit texts and Shivaite liturgy, a status hierarchy legitimated in terms of the Indian *varna* scheme, many terms in

---

[5] The New Order government pursued its policies of national integration in a variety of other ways. One of the most significant of these was the promotion, through a host of new organizations penetrating to the heart of village life, of new gender ideologies, through what Blackwood (1995) has called a 'discourse of the domestic'. There is a large literature on the contradictions and ambiguities surrounding the New Order's efforts to domesticate women, that is, to represent them as moral guardians, reproducers and domestic managers, during a period when their numbers in the labour force have grown continually and in the face of a long tradition of very active involvement by women in many sectors of the economy (see, for example, Stivens 1991; Wolf 1992; Hanan 1993; Sen 1993, 1998; Hatley 1997; Brenner 1998).

Javanese and Balinese deriving from various Indian languages, and much more, testify to this lasting influence. That there is much in *adat* religion that some Hindus from some parts of India would find strange, such as the Balinese ancestor cult, is not particularly relevant, since these differences are perhaps no greater than the differences which exist between regions within India. I am thus not interested in questioning whether or not the Balinese were 'Hindus' in the past; rather, my aim is to delineate the processes by which Balinese have come to express themselves more and more as 'Hindu' through the progressive shaping of *adat* to conform more to what Balinese conceptualize as Indian Hinduism.

According to Vickers (1987: 35), this *adat* religion probably did not act as a marker of Balinese ethnicity in the pre-colonial period, and it is doubtful whether the Balinese saw themselves as an ethnic group at all. While they recognized observable differences between themselves and people of other islands (dress, food, ritual practices, etc.), they seemed to have construed these as varied manifestations of a common underlying civilization. In not conceiving of these other groups as having a fundamentally divergent form of social system, the Balinese possessed 'no absolute category of the "alien"' against which they could define themselves as different. Vickers's point is not that there were no differences between Hindus (Balinese) and Muslims (others), but that there were multiple Balinese views of and multiple forms of interaction with Muslims (ibid.: 37). Therefore the orientalist vision of Bali as a monolithic Hindu entity, surrounded and threatened by an encroaching and hostile Islam, ignored the way in which Bali was very much incorporated in a wider regional civilization (ibid.: 57–8), a civilization in which religious distinctions were far less significant and central to identity than they have since become. It was only during the first decades of the twentieth century, with the emergence of the Islamic reform movement, the Communist Party, proto-nationalist movements and unrest and rebellion in rural and urban areas of Java and Sumatra, that religious identities began to assume very politicized and oppositional forms (Ricklefs 1981).

In the ferment of this period, with the formation of numerous associations all across Indonesia (political parties, trade unions, cultural movements and religious organizations), some Balinese intellectuals began to think hard about their own religion and to construct it in a new way. They engaged in this partly to make sense of their own situation in a rapidly changing world; partly because others (the Dutch and Muslims) were asking questions about the content and status of Balinese religion; and partly to counteract the growing threat posed by Muslim and Christian proselytising, given that the Dutch constituted Bali as Hindu in opposition to Islam (Bagus n.d.; Picard 1999). The attempt involved a reworking of their 'religion' into something resembling a free-standing system of doctrine and practice which could be explained to others (both insiders and outsiders). The Sanskrit word *agama* was adopted by Balinese leaders in an effort to elevate this modified religion to an equal status with Islam and Christianity, which were already referred to using this term (for example, *agama Islam*, the religion of Islam).

This project of reinterpretation, however, was also carried out as part of an indigenous debate between low-caste commoner intellectuals (mostly teachers and civil servants) and high-caste gentry in the north Balinese town of Singaraja, which was the headquarters of the colonial administration. Inspired in part by western ideologies of equality and democracy, these commoners challenged gentry hegemony by arguing that status should be based on education and merit rather than on birth and ascription.

In the debate between these groups, carried out in their periodicals *Surya Kanta* and *Bali Adnjana*, two rather different versions of Balinese religion emerged (Bagus 1975; Picard 1999). Gentry argued that the traditional social order (*adat*) was inextricably linked to religion (*agama*) and thus could not be separated. Commoners, in contrast, wanted to strengthen *agama* by expunging from *adat* what was both unfair and an obstacle to progress, which in practice meant the 'caste system'. Consequently, gentry promoted a form of Hindu religion seen as specifically Balinese, tied to the hierarchical social order and with its origins in the Javanese empire of Majapahit, portrayed as the source of aristocratic court culture. Commoners insisted that their religion was properly Hindu and should be separated from caste and that it originated in India (Picard 1999).

In the 1930s, as Picard (ibid.) shows, Balinese leaders developed a low opinion of their own rituals, because they found it difficult to respond to criticisms of their religion from colonial officers and from other Indonesians. In comparison with Islam and Christianity, Balinese 'religion' was derided, since it possessed neither a holy book nor an identifiable (monotheistic) God. Moreover, because it was directed instead to a vast array of spirits, which were considered to be in the realm of *adat* rather than *agama* and thus only had local significance, it was branded as backward and primitive. One of the effects of such criticisms was the adoption by reformers of an anti-ritualism and anti-clericalism (in part derived from Protestant trends in western European thought), which could then be used against the nobility and the high priests.

In one attempt to remedy this situation, a council of high priests was given the task of compiling a holy book. This enterprise failed, however, because the priests argued that *agama* could not be separated from *adat*; since *adat* varied widely over Bali, it was impossible to agree on a doctrine and set of practices that were acceptable to all Balinese. In that period, an *agama* could not be universalized even within Bali.

After independence in 1950, these problems became very urgent. The constitution of the republic was, and still is, based on the *pancasila* or 'five principles'. The first of these is 'belief in one god'. The state is neither secular nor Islamic but is based on broad religious values. The Ministry of Religion, staffed mostly by Muslims, insisted that only religions (*agama*) which were monotheistic, possessed a holy book and a prophet and were not restricted to a single ethnic group were eligible for state support and protection. Initially, this limited the field to Islam, Catholicism, Protestantism and Buddhism and left out Balinese religion, which was classified as 'tribal' and thus not an *agama* (the Balinese were said to be *belum beragama*, that is, 'not yet to have a religion'). This was disastrous for the Balinese, for they would now face the distinct possibility of active proselytization from Muslims and Christians (Swellengrebel 1960: 72; Picard 1999).

During this period, reformist organizations argued that Balinese religion was a variant of Indian Hinduism, Balinese intellectuals went to study in India and Indian scholars were invited to Bali (Bakker 1993: 2–3). Promises were made to rationalize Balinese religion by simplifying rituals, stressing doctrine and theology and translating Indian religious texts into Indonesian. In the face of insistent pressure from Balinese intellectuals and religious officials, President Sukarno accepted that, despite its seeming polytheism, Balinese religion was, in reality, monotheistic and that, in the *Bhagavadgita* and other Indian texts, it possessed a sacred literature. As a result, this religion, named *agama Hindu Bali*, gained official recognition in 1958. The Parisada Hindu Dharma Bali was instituted to supervise these developments. A few years later, in 1964, under pressure from the Ministry of Religion to universalize the appeal of this religion, its name was changed to *agama Hindu*, the word 'Bali' also being dropped from the name of the Parisada. In little more than thirty years, Balinese religion was transformed, at least theoretically, from locally variable ritual practices within Bali to an *agama* with transnational potential.

The Parisada published books in which the more philosophical doctrines of Hinduism were described. They contained justification from Sanskrit sources that Balinese religion was monotheistic, but nevertheless found it necessary to explain who Bali's high God was and what He symbolized (Upadeca 1968: 15).[6] These publications divide *agama Hindu* into philosophy (*tatwa*), ethics (*susila*) and ritual (*upacara*). The sections on philosophy deal with the law of karma, the cycle of rebirth (*samsara*), liberation from rebirth (*moksa*), renunciation, and much more. The principal ethical doctrine is that all creatures participate in each other's lives, so that to help another is to help oneself and to hurt another is to hurt oneself. Consequently, the fourfold division of the population, known as the *catur warna* (the 'four *warna*', i.e. Brahmana, Satria, Wésia and Sudra), is not described as a hierarchical caste system, but as a set of functionally differentiated and interdependent groups. By performing their appropriate tasks, out of communal rather than self-interest, these groups cooperate and help each other to develop the common good. Under ritual (*upacara*), the basic idea is that the paraphernalia, offerings and symbols of ritual are the means to purify one's soul. Offerings are the outward and material signs of inner feelings and convictions. In ritual, one can reflect on God with the aid of visible representations, which allow one's thoughts to unite with God. The thrust of these new ideas is the rationalization of Balinese religion from ritual to scripture, magic to ethics, action to experience and collective to individual.

While some of these teachings (*ajaran-ajaran agama Hindu*, Ind.) can be found in Balinese palm-leaf texts owned by priests and others, most of them were largely unknown to ordinary Balinese, or known in a very different way.[7] These new texts and the doctrines they describe now form the curriculum of compulsory classes in religious education in Balinese schools, and so many younger people have now become conversant with some of them (Geertz 1973a; Parker 1992a).

While the creation of *agama Hindu* is an attempt to add theological substance to and provide philosophical justification for traditional Balinese ritual practices by giving them a rational foundation, these additions also form a reasonably coherent system of doctrine, which, to some extent, stands apart from the ritual practices of village Balinese.[8] Thus, in aligning Balinese religion, with the ethical and theological

---

[6] Writing in 1957, Swellengrebel argued that this high God was receiving more attention from the Balinese than in the past. He quotes from an official report to the effect that all Balinese are believers in a supreme being they call Widi, but goes on to note that this is more a statement of intent and has little factual basis. There were no shrines to Widi in Balinese temples, and He was rarely if ever referred to by ordinary Balinese, whose religion was based on gods and ancestors linked to specific groups, communities and territories (Swellengrebel 1960: 71).

[7] Indian concepts of *moksa* and *samsara* are quite alien to traditional Balinese beliefs. While forms of asceticism (fasting, night-time temple vigils, and the like) are practised by many people for a variety of both religious and secular purposes, wandering renouncers are completely unknown, though it should be added that they are also unknown in large parts of India. Reincarnation is, however, a widespread belief, but it is limited to the idea that one is reborn into the same descent group, ideally into the body of one's great-grandchild, and never as an inferior form of life. *Karma* as an explanation for misfortune is becoming popular now that the doctrine is part of *agama Hindu* and taught in schools, but the more usual and traditional explanations for misfortune are witchcraft, sorcery, attacks by offended ancestors, and the like.

[8] Parker (1992b: 111) notes that in the Balinese school curriculum religion is taught in a very intellectualized manner. 'In real life the main "religious" activity undertaken by girls is the making and presentation of offerings; yet these are barely mentioned in textbooks. Much of the material presented is in the form of codifications and lists', for example of the 'five gods', types of sacred places, the 'five techniques of self-control' and the 'seven darknesses or evils'. Most of these ideas have, as yet, no place in village religious practice.

tenets of Indian Hinduism, officials of the Parisada and other leading intellectuals created a new form of Balinese religion, with its own distinctive mode of knowledge and doctrine. This *agama* has similarities to and differences from customary *adat* religion, but, while *adat* is more an orthopraxy, *agama Hindu* is more an orthodoxy (Geertz 1973a: 186). The latter is not necessarily opposed to the former, since it is designed to underpin it, but when the two come into conflict it is usually *adat* that has to give way (Bakker 1993: 290).[9]

In order to impress state officials and Muslims that Balinese religion was securely anchored in Hinduism, *agama Hindu* had to be represented as a religious tradition (Hobsbawm and Ranger 1983) going back hundreds of years, a tradition that had been brought to Bali from Java and, indirectly, from India, by holy sages. This also meant that the books which the Parisada published, containing the doctrines of Hinduism, the manner in which the sages established religious order (*dharma*) and the temple system in Bali, and the meanings and purposes of all their festivals and offerings, had to be made widely available to the local population so that they could 'reacquaint' themselves with their ancient religion. One consequence of this was that, in contrast to the gentry arguments in the 1920s, the Parisada now had to put new emphasis on the Indian, rather than the Majapahit, origins of this religion. Another result is an unresolved tension between *adat* and *agama Hindu*.

This tension stems from differences of interest both within state agencies and amongst Balinese reformers. On the one hand, religious authorities sometimes express concern that the population is not learning the new doctrines quickly enough, most ordinary Balinese continuing to perform their rituals without much recourse to them. On the other hand, concern is also voiced that the disjunction between religion (*agama*) and customary practice (*adat*) might go too far and irretrievably break the connection between *agama Hindu* and Balinese culture.

For example, in reforming Balinese Hinduism, officials of the Parisada became increasingly concerned to retain its specific Indonesian/Balinese nature, even as they were being pressed by central state bodies to sever the linkage between *agama Hindu* and its Balinese origins. Moreover, while the former stressed the unique nature of Balinese Hinduism and argued for the preservation of the *catur warna* (Upadeca 1968: 54–5), commoner activists continued to advocate the abolition of caste, much as they did in the 1920s. In justifying to ordinary Balinese the retention of this doctrine, the Parisada tried to interpret the four *warna*, not in terms of hierarchical *kasta*, but as complementary and interdependent functions, having the single aim of improving the prosperity of all. However, the manner in which the doctrine was explained betrays the hierarchical thought at the back of it. The members of each *warna* are said to have specific qualities and talents, with which they are born. Thus Brahmana and Satria have the capacities to lead society spiritually and politically

---

[9] Some examples were provided in Chapter 5 to do with communal and streamlined cremations. The Parisada has published booklets on the form of offerings to be used at specific ceremonies, and those villages which deviate are expected to come into line. Reuter has noted the way religious officials have tried to force Balinese living in the central mountainous areas to modify their temple architecture, because many temples lack certain shrines (the *padmasana*, for example) now considered essential for a monotheistic religion. He has also described how the Parisada insisted on a *pedanda* officiating at a temple ceremony, against the wishes of the local population who afterwards held a purification ritual to remove the stain (Reuter 1999: 172–3). Moreover, the Parisada's injunction that *adat* traditions should give way to the written teachings of *agama Hindu* has also been adopted by other Balinese organizations. The organization of Pasek groups, the Pasek Sanak Sapta Rsi, with a huge membership, also strives to disseminate Hindu teachings based on written sources (*sastra agama*) and contends that these must take precedence over 'mere' traditions (Pitana 1997: 178).

('for the good of all'). Sudra, in contrast, are said to have the characteristics of bodily strength and loyalty and to be the agents of prosperity, but only under the instructions and guidance of the other groups (ibid.: 55). According to Bakker (1993: 267, 269,303), personal and political motives were involved in the attempt to maintain the *catur warna*, because most of these intellectuals came from the higher castes. This tension also helps explain why Sai Baba and Hare Krishna, at first viewed in a positive light because they were authentically Indian, were later criticized for being too different from, and thus antithetical to, Balinese traditions. The latter was even accused of harbouring communist sympathies (Bakker 1993: 268) and has now been banned as an illegal organization.[10]

Changing their religion has made some Balinese self-conscious about 'possessing' a religion. This has had at least two profound effects. First, because the creation of *agama Hindu* provides a yardstick against which *adat* religion may be assessed, they have developed a critical and questioning stance to religious practices and beliefs in general. This has been intensified by the appearance of devotional forms of Hinduism, with which agama Hindu can now be compared. Consequently, Balinese can no longer take their beliefs and practices as axiomatic. The co-presence of relatively distinct forms of Hinduism creates both a distance and a relationship between believer and belief. These variants of Hinduism now appear as options, though not necessarily exclusive, which Balinese can choose between. In turn, this engenders an analytical orientation to religion, so that Balinese now require reasons and justifications for making their choice. The second effect of this self-awareness about possessing a religion, a religion which is very different from the Islam and Christianity professed by the groups which surround them, is that Hinduism has been promoted by Balinese leaders as a prime marker of Balinese ethnic identity. In recent years 'Balineseness' (*kebalian*) has been defined by reference to Hinduism. However, the process of ethnic identity formation has been complicated by two factors: in Indonesia, Hinduism is no longer exclusive to Bali; and competing varieties of Hinduism produce different forms of identity.

Because the Indonesian state forbids the exclusive association between an ethnic group and a religion, fearing that such a combination is fertile ground for political mobilization, it has promoted the universalization of *agama Hindu* throughout Indonesia. Turning Hinduism into an ethicized theology, in part detached from local Balinese ritual practices, has enabled people in Java (Lyon 1980; Hefner 1985; Beatty 1999), Kalimantan (Schiller 1997) and other islands (Persoon 1998: 293) to convert to Hinduism, rather than to Islam or Christianity. Consequently, there are now more members of *agama Hindu* outside Bali than inside (Ramstedt 1995: 6), a fact recognized by renaming the Parisada yet again as the Parisada Hindu Dharma Indonesia. One reason for the spread of Hinduism outside Bali is that Balinese transmigrants to other Indonesian islands and civil servants who have been posted to other provinces have introduced their religion into the areas where they now live.

---

[10] In the late 1990s, the situation changed again, so that, while the ban on Hare Krishna remains and is unlikely to be lifted, Sai Baba now appears to be more acceptable and is certainly gaining in popularity. For example, during the months of October, November and December 1999, the *Bali Post* newspaper ran numerous stories relating the miracles (*kemukjizatan*, Ind.) that have been experienced by his devotees, in both India and Bali. One probable reason for this more favourable situation is that the movement now has some powerful supporters. At least two of the principal lay leaders of the movement still are, or have been until recently, prominent officials in the Parisada, one influential *pedanda* is a devotee and the membership includes several university academics; and many other leading intellectuals are sympathetic to the movement.

Another is that some societies within Indonesia, such as the Toraja of south Sulawesi, conceive of themselves as close to the Hindu movement because of the nature of their pre-colonial 'Indic' state systems. If in Indonesia being Balinese is virtually synonymous with being a Hindu, being a Hindu, in Indonesia, is no longer synonymous with being Balinese.

The irony of this situation, recognized more in the circles of urban, cosmopolitan Balinese than among ordinary Balinese, is that, as Balinese intellectuals began to conceive of their ethnic identity as based on *agama Hindu*, they discovered that this religion 'owes its recognition precisely to the condition that it not be restricted to the Balinese alone' (Picard 1995: 17).

In connection with this, I wish to make two important points. The first is that much of the writing on the recent formation of new identities in Bali is based on the rather rarefied debates of academics and intellectuals, with little attention focused on what is happening in the wider population. The second point is that too great an emphasis has been given to the formation of ethnic identities and insufficient attention paid to other forms of identity that are now emerging in Bali.

There can be little doubt that processes of religious and cultural change, in the context of Bali's incorporation into the Indonesian state and the tourist boom, have produced conditions in which ethnic identity formation has occurred, an identity largely constructed in and promulgated from the higher echelons of Balinese society. However, at the same time, the religious scene in Bali has been changing and growing in complexity, with the recent rise of new forms of Hinduism and other, indigenous, religious movements. In many cases, these new movements, driven from below by ordinary Balinese critical of established and authorized forms of religion, foster quite different kinds of identity.

Some Balinese do not aspire to an exclusive ethnic identity based on a unique form of Balinese Hinduism, because both *adat* religion and *agama Hindu* are increasingly considered deficient. Nor do these Balinese necessarily see their interests as best served by such an identity. In accusing these Hinduisms of professing outworn and untrue religious doctrines, restricting religious knowledge to elites and propping up the caste system, they are turning away from them, joining the new variants of Hinduism now available and, through these, seeking other identities. In some contexts, adherents of devotional Hinduism value their Balinese identity, but they are also keen to partic-ipate in a more inclusive, universal and modern faith. While this is grounded in a form of Hinduism, it is rather different from both village ritual practice (*adat*) and official state religion (*agama Hindu*). Many devotees are fairly affluent, middle-class and urban, precisely the group Picard is writing about, but a large number are commoners and many are poor. Devotees see themselves situated in a global movement, which includes members of diverse nationalities. Some Balinese, rather than opting for a 'Balinese' ethnic identity based on a specifically Balinese form of Hinduism, which is anyway now slipping out of their control, join Sai Baba in part to get away from attachments to parochial religious and cultural institutions.

Movements such as Sai Baba, then, are very significant for several reasons. First, they provide a valuable insight into changes going on in the wider society, changes which are partly independent of Balinese religious leaders and state religious institu-tions. Secondly, they provide a vantage point from which a more balanced and nuanced account of change can be obtained. Thirdly, they enable us to examine the interaction between identities created at different levels of society. And, fourthly, a focus on such movements provides information on forms of resistance to and crit-icism of state religious orthodoxy.

In summary, I use the term *agama Hindu* to denote the rationalized and more theological form of Hinduism which has been created by the reform of *adat* religion. Devotional forms of Hinduism in Indonesia are, in practice, anti-hierarchical and largely empty of ritual, deny any role to priests and espouse free and universal dissemination of religious knowledge. While these are critical of *adat* and *agama Hindu*, Sai Baba is more concerned to repair, improve and even incorporate them. Hare Krishna, in contrast, is much more radical and tends to preach rejection of them.

From this discussion, I want to emphasize the spectrum of religious options available to contemporary Balinese; that this has been made possible by a creative and energetic response to state policies of a kind the state could not have envisaged; that the various forms of Hinduism are in competition and conflict; that this conflict is as much about what constitutes religious truth and religious experience as it is about the hierarchical social order, the role of Brahmana priests and the nature of modern Balinese society; and that different varieties of Hinduism provide different kinds of identity. These points will be explored further in the following chapters in relation to ethnography on Sai Baba and Hare Krishna.

The production of national culture in Indonesia

Religious diversity was not the only obstacle to forging national unity, since cultural diversity was equally problematic.[11] Even before the state was established, leading intellectuals and political activists in the revolutionary movement for independence gathered in Jakarta to discuss the future character of the state. One of the issues which exercised them was the shape that Indonesia's national culture should take in the future. The main difficulty was how to produce a national culture, given the tremendous variety of ethnic and local cultures. These ranged from small-scale, preliterate societies in remoter regions of the outer islands all the way through to the great civilizations of Java and Bali.

What sort of relationship should exist between national culture and these local cultures? One possibility was to build a national culture out of contributions from the latter. This was rejected on the grounds that it would generate conflicts over who contributed and who did not, leaving the losers to feel that their cultures had been devalued. Anyway, it was difficult to see how one ethnic group could feel a strong allegiance to a contribution made by another. In short, how could such a culture be truly national? Another possibility entertained was to construct a national culture independently of regional cultures. But, in this case, what was to be its content and what was to be the residual status of the local cultures? What emerged from these deliberations was confusion and contradiction (Yampolsky 1995). In the end, the wording which finally entered the constitution, and which was presumably intended to cover over fundamental disagreements, was: 'The government shall advance the national culture of Indonesia'! Because this was so elliptic an official clarification was needed, but this was itself 'remarkably obscure' (Yampolsky 1995: 703). In succeeding years, while this particular debate was not forgotten, the state bypassed it by taking an increasingly authoritarian and centralist view of its role in the creation of a national culture.

---

[11] There is now an extensive comparative literature on the politics of cultural and national construction. A number of authors have studied this issue in the Pacific (Keesing and Tonkinson 1982; Hirsch 1990; Linnekin and Poyer 1990) and in India (van der Veer 1994).

Despite severe economic and political problems in the new state, Sukarno devoted considerable effort to establishing a framework for national unity, as explained in the introduction to this chapter, but little was achieved by way of providing this with a distinctive cultural and artistic content. On the other hand, Sukarno began the process of incorporating the multitude of 'tribal' groups into the national fold. These groups are known as *suku-suku terasing* (Ind., literally 'foreign' or 'stranger' groups). The phrase denotes forest dwellers, nomadic hunter-gatherers and other small-scale societies living in remote or mountainous regions, and who are not adherents of one of the five state religions. The term also carries connotations of social isolation and distance from mainstream Indonesian culture. Depicting them as backward, primitive and uncivilized, the government conceived its duty in terms of bringing them into the modern world and the national fold. Integration was forced by attempts to extinguish ethnic loyalties through a process of cultural homogenization. 'Pagan' religions were prohibited and people were coerced into converting to one of the religions recognized by the state; local forms of dress, bodily decoration and dietary habits were denigrated; groups following nomadic and dispersed patterns of residence were, and still are, herded into neat and tidy nucleated villages and provided with houses of a uniform type; and they have been incorporated into the structures of provincial administration.[12] At the beginning of the New Order regime in 1966–7, Suharto maintained Sukarno's policy by resourcing the 'development' and 'advancement' of tribal groups in order to standardize national culture.

Up to this point, then, national culture was being created at the centre, with tribal societies being pressurized into relinquishing those aspects of their social organization and culture which did not meet the centre's approval and its definitions of a modern, economically productive and respectable lifestyle.

However, by about 1973, this orientation to local cultures began to change, as Islam emerged once again as the principal threat to national unity. This new policy did not merely tolerate cultural diversity; it actively sought to promote it, for two main reasons. First, it could be used as a strategy to counter a resurgent Islam based on the role some Muslim groups played in eliminating the communists. Secondly, the tremendous diversity of 'authentic' and indigenous cultural arts, styles of architecture, rituals and dramatic performances was what attracted tourists to many different parts of the archipelago (Picard 1990a, 1997; Volkman 1990; Adams 1997).

But such a policy also had a significant disadvantage, since a more positive attitude to local cultures and tribal groups was likely to invigorate local ethnic loyalties and weaken attachments to the new state. As state policy-makers conceived it, the problem was how to celebrate cultural diversity at the same time as preventing political mobilization around symbols of ethnic identity. The ingenious solution was to create and promote *regional* cultural and artistic forms at the expense of *ethnic* ones (Sellato 1995; Picard 1997).

Territorially, Indonesia is divided into twenty-six provinces, only one or two of which, Bali for example, encloses a single ethnic group; most regions (*daerah*, Ind.) include numerous ethnic groups. The policy of the New Order state in regard to the promotion of cultural diversity was 'to control the political content of performances, to control their moral content, and to upgrade their artistic quality' (Yampolsky 1995: 710). Customary dances, songs, rituals, myths and the plastic arts were changed and

---

[12] For examples of the coercive nature of these changes, see Tsing (1993: 92–3), Persoon (1998) and Schefold (1998).

modified by the state's local representatives. Performances have been abbreviated; raised wooden stages have replaced the earthen floor; rough, crude and licentious elements (sexual play, alcoholic drink, rowdiness, rude jokes, etc.) have been reduced or removed altogether; new elements have been added to provide entertaining distractions; elements from one culture have been introduced to pep up the rituals of another; and everything is cleaned up to be more respectable, civilized and in keeping with modern times.[13] In addition, the state has initiated a programme of provincial festivals, in which these and wholly new performances are put on; it has established centres and schools for the performing arts, where students learn their own 'cultural traditions' and experiment with them; and it has enthusiastically promoted various kinds of regional artistic competitions.

The state then presents these new and composite forms as authentic Indonesian cultural expressions representative of an entire region (*daerah*). Consequently, these regional 'cultures' are inventions, which, because they are often stripped of much that made them locally meaningful, have been turned into anodyne forms of aesthetic display. In other words, while the state appears to be celebrating the authentic cultural richness of Indonesia, it is in fact creating a homogeneous national culture through standardizing the cultural diversity of the regions.[14] The various cultural performances of the regions are presented as so many surface manifestations of an underlying Indonesian culture and personality. Through such an enterprise, the state at one blow depoliticizes ritual and artistic performance, creates 'attractive' and 'exotic' cultural objects for tourist consumption, dampens ethnic resistance to the state by dissolving local diversity into regional homogeneity, and yet can still claim to be promoting and safeguarding Indonesia's rich cultural tapestry.

The literature which examines these processes from the local point of view is not without its problems, however. Local forms of knowledge, culture and religion are often described as being devalued, scorned and even destroyed by the symbolic violence (Acciaioli 1985: 158) of state officialdom in its lamentable efforts to manufacture standardized and cleaned-up 'cultures', which can be used to celebrate both regional diversity and national cultural unity. I do not doubt that this is frequently the case, but this is not the only way things need turn out.

Tsing (1987), for example, has noted how the Meratus of Kalimantan have in some contexts been able to turn their designation as *suku terasing* to their advantage. They have received government grants to build new ritual halls and to send shamans to conferences at the Ministry of Religion. Moreover, in responding to state interference, Meratus have made innovations of their own and through these have forged a new sense of their own ethnic distinctiveness and new forms of legitimation for their own religious beliefs.

Similarly, Atkinson (1987) has demonstrated how the Wana of Sulawesi have responded to assertions that they do not have a religion by contending that indeed they do. Wana have conformed to the principle of monotheism by giving a more central role, as the Balinese have done, to their God Pué, which has enabled them to

[13] For some recent examples, see Acciaioli (1985), Taylor (1994), Hutajulu (1995), Sutton (1995) and Yampolsky (1995: 713).
[14] An interesting analysis of one facet of the state's policy in this regard is Pemberton's (1994) examination of the cultural theme park called Taman Mini ('Beautiful Indonesia-in-Miniature' Park), which was built by Mrs Suharto after she had visited Disneyland (probably the Epcot Centre) in America. The main exhibit is twenty-six display houses representing the supposedly authentic customary architectural style of each of Indonesia's provinces.

reinforce their own sense of ethnic identity. By also asserting the ideologically correct formula that all religions have the same God and that therefore such a God unites them with the rest of humankind, they have turned the tables on their Muslim and Christian neighbours, who now find it difficult to reject the idea that the Wana God is the same as theirs. Moreover, Wana relate Islam and Christianity to their own religion through a sibling metaphor which neatly inverts the usual evolutionary thinking about religion in Indonesian state ideology. In line with Weber's theories of the evolution of rationalized forms of western religion and economic organization, in this Indonesian ideology monotheism is a higher and more recent stage than animism and polytheism, which are primitive and old. But, for Wana, priority and seniority confer authority and privilege. By accepting the premise that theirs is an ancient religion, Christianity and Islam can be represented as the 'younger siblings' of Wana religion. This also gives Wana religion a dignity which others have sought to deny it. Of course, these responses result in new cultural and religious forms, but these are not necessarily debased and devoid of positive and locally important meanings.

A second problem relates to the fact that the local population is usually said to respond in one of two ways to these processes of cultural dislocation: either with confusion and resentment (Hutajulu 1995: 648) or by some form of resistance (Foulcher 1990), as though local groups are homogeneous units without an internal politics of their own (Ortner 1995). But frequently local residents, differently situated in their own societies, react in quite different ways. Sutton (1995), for example, has argued that pressure to conform to national aesthetic norms in the region of South Sulawesi is experienced very unevenly, most by the educated urban elite and far less by villagers, which is also true of Bali. Local experts in drama, dance and ritual have not remained passive, but have taken the initiative in reshaping and creating new genres out of existing ones. It is by no means only the state's representatives who are responsible for change, and anyway these officials are often from the local area, have strong local loyalties and can modify and subvert state policy to suit their own ends. Sutton (1995: 697) notes that province-wide festivals, competitions and other inno- vations have provided a dynamic arena in which are produced not only some sense of a provincial, regional, identity, but also a renewed legitimacy for and sense of power in local cultural traditions.

The relevance of these arguments for Bali is simply to stress the point that, like Indonesians on other islands, the Balinese have reacted in a variety of different ways to state interference in the fields of social organization, religion and culture. Warren has provided detailed accounts of the negotiation between Balinese local knowledge and power and that of the state in a wide range of economic, cultural and communal issues. She concludes that this process, with its contradictions, ambiguities and accommodations, is neither predetermined nor unidirectional (Warren 1990, 1993: 299). More specifically, she has pointed to how Balinese villages appropriate aspects of the state ideology of *pancasila*, particularly those concepts which prescribe that decisions should be arrived at through democratic and consensual discussion, and by such means are able to call officials to account and promote their own interests (Warren 1989).

Picard (1996) has produced an equally elegant analysis of tourism in Bali. The island that one sees today is not the pre-colonial Bali preserved or restored, but a new one, which has been forged through Balinese responses to Dutch colonialization, incorporation into the Indonesian state and modern tourism. Various images of Bali, as the last paradise, the land of a thousand temples and the place of artistic genius, all of which were promulgated by others, came to be accepted as authentic representations by the Balinese themselves. As cultural tourism grew, Balinese became self-conscious about their culture, in the same way as they have become self-conscious about their religion. Consequently, the former is increasingly conceived as an object which can be displayed and marketed, even if, at the same time, they are concerned that it may be damaged and polluted. In this process, which Picard (1996: 179) has called the 'touristification of culture', the Balinese were forced to think about their culture through foreign languages (Dutch, Indonesian and English) and in foreign categories ('culture', 'art', 'religion' and 'politics'). Now that Balinese culture is divided into separate and identifiable domains, its artistic productions can be used to promote internal and international tourism, help build the national culture and constitute another important marker of identity. If others began the process of informing the Balinese about who they were and what their culture was all about, then today it is the Balinese themselves who are partly responsible for the continuing '"Balinization" of Bali' (Picard 1996: 200).

The policies of the Indonesian state concerning religious, cultural and ethnic diversity are, of course, not as consistent, unambiguous and machiavellian as perhaps I have made them out to be in what is, after all, an abbreviated account of a very complex set of issues. Precisely because of this fact, we should remember that these policies have been applied unevenly and in contradictory ways and have met with resistance, accommodation and creative energy by the local peoples who have been their object. The varied responses of the Balinese to reforms initiated by outsiders have been as important a factor as any other in determining the direction of change in their culture and religion.

In the next section, I briefly discuss other developments in Balinese religion by describing some of the new religious movements that have sprung up in Bali over the last twenty-five years.

New religious movements in Bali

Sai Baba and Hare Krishna are not the only new religious movements that have emerged in recent years in Bali. Since about 1975, small but significant numbers of Balinese have been joining new, indigenous, religious movements. Although I use the term 'religious', none of these movements are officially defined as 'religion' (*agama*) by the Indonesian Ministry of Religion. Instead, they are known as 'streams of belief' (*aliran kepercayaan*, Ind.; hereafter abbreviated to AK). While I have not conducted any research on specific movements, I have talked to a range of people who know something about them, read some of the magazines published by certain movements and collected newspaper clippings in which AK figure prominently.

Today there are probably between fifteen and twenty such movements which are registered with the authorities, and several more which are not. This means that the former enjoy a legal status and supposedly conform to the state ideology of *pancasila*, which, in turn, implies that theoretically they do not deviate from the teachings of *agama Hindu*. In this sense, they appear to be acceptable organizations. However, it is difficult to define the precise status these movements have in Bali, either as regards the state or as regards the mass of ordinary Balinese who are not members. Both religious officials and ordinary Balinese are often suspicious of their aims, but they are so for quite different reasons. In brief, religious authorities are suspicious because, although AK claim to conform to *agama Hindu*, in fact they often do not. Villagers, on the other hand, are suspicious, because the ritual and other activities of AK often deviate from *adat* practices.

In order to establish itself as an organization and carry out its activities, an AK must apply for a licence and affirm that its basic doctrine conforms to the *pancasila*. Some AK have been active for several years, have large memberships all over Bali and are tolerated by the general population. Other AK, however, have caused considerable disturbance and their practices have been widely reported in the local press. It is these disturbances which have fuelled hostility and led to concern over their existence. Some AK, for example, have emerged rapidly and created tension and antagonism amongst the local population, with the result that police teams have been called in to investigate them. Still others have occasioned violent incidents (arson, physical assault and even murder) between adherents and those who oppose them, and they have subsequently been banned.

AK are also distrusted because non-members often believe that the leaders and adherents of such organizations form exclusive groups, conduct bizarre and dangerous magical rituals and are only interested in augmenting their own stores of power (*sakti*) for selfish motives. Balinese sometimes say that leaders dupe the unwary into becoming members and then exploit them to prosecute their own personal vendettas against other villagers.

The activities of AK are frequently reported by the local Balinese media, but usually only when a scandal erupts. In such reports, academics and religious officials are often asked to debate the merits or otherwise of AK. Officials from the Parisada, priests and other religious leaders express great concern over their proliferation, arguing that AK confuse and unsettle the population and undermine their commitment to orthodox religion, that is, *agama Hindu*. Academics, some of whom are adherents of devotional Hinduism or are interested in other Indian *guru*, often champion AK by arguing that they are authentic religious movements, which others reject out of ignorance and fear. They also often claim that, though their ritual activities may deviate from traditional (*adat*) village practices, they do in fact conform to the tenets of *agama Hindu*. AK, therefore, excite very different reactions among Balinese, ranging from outright hostility to enthusiasm. It should also be noted that these attitudes vary, depending on which AK is being discussed. What many people appear to agree on, none the less, is that the existence of these movements indicates that some kind of 'spiritual crisis' (*krisis spirituil*, Ind.) is occurring in contemporary Bali (*Bali Post*, 26 April 1994, for example).

The difference between *agama* and AK is a subject of heated controversy. In official circles, such as the Parisada, the difference is that an *agama* has a holy book, a prophet and a holy place (church, temple, mosque, etc.), whereas AK have none of these. Moreover, an *agama* is defined as possessing a specific set of universal teachings (*ajaran*, Ind.) which have been directly revealed by God to His appointed prophet, whereas AK are based on merely local original beliefs (*kepercayaan*, Ind.) of the ancestors in a powerful mystical force, which anteceded such revealed teachings (Supartha 1994: vi). In Balinese this force is known as *sakti*, and in Indonesian it is *kekuatan gaib*. Because these indigenous beliefs vary across the different cultures of Indonesia, the state demands that they come under the jurisdiction and supervision of the Department of Education and Culture, and not the Ministry of Religion. Perhaps the main reason that state religious authorities distrust AK is because AK continue to rely on ideas of *sakti*, which are being progressively displaced from *agama Hindu*. From this point of view, AK have difficulty in conforming to *agama Hindu*, despite their claims to the contrary.

Contesting this, members of AK and their supporters insist that these movements are based on the Hindu religion and they should therefore be allowed to define themselves as branches of *agama Hindu*. Consequently, they resist the label *kepercayaan*, which they see as derogatory. In their magazines, members say that AK are similar to *agama* or spring from the same source as *agama*, or that they are founded on teachings derived from an individual's authentic religious experience. Academic commentators on the issue often point out that members of AK remain steadfast in their adherence to official religion, so that *agama* and AK are not mutually exclusive choices. It is often claimed, in addition, that, because members are sincere in their beliefs, they become more diligent in the performance of their religious duties. Though not religious officials, such commentators are often in the vanguard of the modern Hindu movement. They support AK because they want to see further religious change, but are frustrated by the conservatism of the Parisada and its control of religious orthodoxy. To some extent, they ignore the problem of *sakti* and instead emphasize the progressive ideas in AK, such as the reform of ritual practices, vegetarianism and meditation, which are said to conform to the spirit of *agama Hindu*. On the other hand, it is precisely these sorts of activities which are said to disturb villagers, because they deviate from *adat* practices.

The controversy can be summarized as follows. There is a real difference between *agama Hindu* and AK, despite attempts by the latter to claim conformity with the former. AK continue to espouse notions of *sakti*, but *agama Hindu* increasingly conceives of *sakti* as 'irrational' and is in process of replacing *sakti* with ideas of 'spirituality' (*kerohanian*, Ind.).[15] On the other hand, as we have seen in earlier chapters, notions of *sakti* are central to Balinese *adat* traditions, which means that AK are continuations of *adat*. But AK are also different from *adat*, because of the new ritual activities they introduce, activities which are more in tune with the teachings of *agama Hindu*. These facts underscore my earlier point that, though *agama Hindu* is supposed to underpin *adat*, there is a tension between them. In short, AK are both similar to and different from both *adat* traditions and the new orthodoxy of *agama Hindu*. It is this mismatch which is responsible for the ambivalent orientations to AK from various sectors of Balinese society. Moreover, it could well be that AK are proliferating and expanding in size precisely because they represent a blending of some of the new doctrines of *agama Hindu* with older *adat* traditions of *sakti*.

It will be useful here to provide some brief descriptions of AK. One of the largest is Bambu Kuning ('Yellow Bamboo'), which began life in 1989. It is registered with the authorities and has about 17,000 members. Its newsletter, *Wahyu*, repeatedly confirms that its teachings do not oppose those of any *agama*, and these teachings are full of the kind of 'Sanskritic' phrases and quotations that typically abound in the publications of the Parisada concerning *agama Hindu*. Its ostensible aim is to help its members attain purity (*kesucian*, Ind.) and truth (*kebenaran*, Ind.). This is achieved by regular prayer to Sang Hyang Widhi (the name of Bali's high God), through rituals, the use of holy water, prohibitions on the consumption of certain foods and through ascetic exercise. Carried out assiduously, these methods increase one's inner potency (*sakti*, or in Indonesian, *kekuatan gaib*), allowing one to achieve understanding. Consequently, the group's motto is 'Purity is mystery, truth is victory' (*kesucian adalah kegaiban, kebenaran adalah kemenangan*, Ind.).

---

[15] I shall have a lot to say about 'spirituality' in the following chapters, and so shall leave discussion of this important new idea in Balinese religion until then.

Given that Bambu Kuning claims not to oppose *agama Hindu*, what is the point of joining it? Its leaders try to recruit members by telling them that the organization teaches the sciences (*ilmu*, Ind.) of self-defence (*bela diri*, Ind.) and inner potency (*tenaga dalam*, Ind.).[16] Everyone has 'mystical strength', the magazine says, but it requires expert tuition to cultivate it, and Bambu Kuning claims that it can increase one's inner power quickly. In this sense, it presents itself as a superior method of reaching religious truths. One of the interesting aspects of the movement, however, is the way it glosses over the difference between potency and spirituality. While it claims to enhance the former, one leader has referred to the movement as a kind of 'spiritual garage' (*bengkel rohani*, Ind.) in the sense that becoming a member allows one to 'repair' and improve one's spirituality (Supartha 1994: 124).

The martial arts (*silat*) have become very popular in Bali, and most villages have associations which meet once or twice a week to practise. AK such as Bambu Kuning and others, for example Satria Nusantara, have built on this popularity by advancing ideas that inner power (*tenaga dalam*) can be greatly improved through techniques of self-defence (*bela diri*), which then leads to enlightenment. Such groups practise quite openly, but, while their forms of exercise are probably modelled on Japanese martial arts movements, there also appear to be some notable differences. While the movements I have so far mentioned have caused few difficulties, others have been much more problematic.

The movement Tuntunan Suci ('Pure Guidance'; such names are difficult to translate) was investigated by the police in August 1997. The movement began slowly in 1988, when its leader had a dream in which a strange figure appeared to him and gave him a religious message. Subsequently he began to cure people of various illnesses and his followers grew in number to over 1,000. In 1993 he success-fully registered Tuntunan Suci with the authorities. The movement attracted attention four years later in 1997, when the Office of the Public Prosecutor received complaints about it from local villagers. Villagers reportedly complained that the members of the organization carried out ceremonies which deviated from the teachings of *agama Hindu*, in that it forbade both the slaughter of animals and the use of eggs to make offerings. This supposedly worried and disturbed the other villagers and so they lodged a protest. However, during the investigation, it transpired that the leader may well have been using his curing powers to indulge in illicit sex with a female patient. In the event, the movement itself was cleared of charges, but its leader was required to undergo an oath-taking ceremony to prove he had done nothing improper. But before this happened he disappeared. Quite often one finds that complaints about a movement turn out to be complaints about the way a leader or member has used the movement as a cover for nefarious purposes.

This is a good example of the kind of confusion that now exists between *agama Hindu*, *adat* traditions and AK. Though the villagers were reported as complaining that the activities of Tuntunan Suci deviated from *agama Hindu*, in fact it is *adat* religion which insists on the use of animal flesh and eggs in offerings, conceiving of these as essential to feed and placate spirits. *Agama Hindu*, in contrast, does not endorse this view and instead argues that sacrificing animals is unnecessary and

---

[16] To avoid confusion I should point out that there are several forms of terminology that refer to the notion of internal power or potency. In Balinese the only term I use is *sakti* or *kesaktian*. In Indonesian, it may be referred to as *kekuatan* ('strength') or *kekuatan gaib* (*gaib* meaning 'invisible' and 'mysterious') or *tenaga dalam* ('inner power'). Another form is *ilmu*. This word can be used to translate 'knowledge' and to talk of the 'sciences' (*ilmu alam* is 'physics', for example). But among ordinary Indonesians *ilmu* is more often used to speak about esoteric knowledge and magic (*ilmu gaib*).

wrong. It claims that offerings are only the outward signs of inner feelings and convictions, and therefore people should use vegetable substitutes shaped into the form of animals. In other words, as far as *agama Hindu* was concerned, the movement had done nothing wrong, and presumably this is why it was exonerated.

A third example concerns an unauthorized movement, known as Budi Dharma, which sparked violence in the village of Kemenuh, near the town of Gianyar. As reported in the local press (*Bali Post*, 10 March 1993, and subsequent days), its two leaders, together with some followers, kidnapped a priest and two other villagers and subjected them to an ordeal by fire in the precincts of a local temple. Fortunately, the incident was witnessed, the police were called and the culprits were arrested. The three victims were badly burned and had to be hospitalized. One account of the reasons for this violence was given to me by a local resident. According to her, there were two movements in the village, the other being Sri Murni (which did have authorization), and they vied with each other as to which had the greater power (*kekuatan*, Ind.). They did this in various ways, through specific teachings, practising martial arts and carrying out magical rituals. It got out of hand when Budi Dharma became too public and aggressive, and boasted that its members were so strong they were invulnerable (*kebal*, Ind.) to attack. The leaders apparently selected certain victims who had in one way or another antagonized them. Carrying out the torture on a priest in the priest's own temple was supposed to 'prove' that the Balinese gods invested them with the power to do this.

Perhaps the most sensational outbreak of violence occurred in the village of Samplangan in south Bali. According to extensive press reports, a commoner of obscure origins began to call himself by the exceedingly majestic name, Agung Dalem Batara Kalki, thus proclaiming himself to be the final incarnation of Vishnu, who will save everyone at the end of this world age. He gathered around himself a group of young men from other villages, most of whom were unemployed commoners. A great deal of suspicion and distrust grew up between Kalki and other villagers, who thought it reprehensible that he considered himself a god. Such a claim violated the teachings of *agama Hindu*, it was asserted, and thus constituted an illegal and deviant (*sesat*, Ind.) movement. There were several minor skirmishes between the two groups until, on the night of 16 April 1994, Kalki and up to fifty followers crept into the village, burned down several houses and other buildings and wounded a number of villagers, one of whom later died. The police managed to apprehend Kalki and most of his followers in the subsequent days and weeks, and many are now in prison.

I want to stress four points concerning this brief survey of AK. The first is that they provide convincing confirmation of the energy and vitality of the religious innovation that has been sweeping through Bali during the last twenty years. They are responses not only to official forms of religion but also to the feelings of ambivalence and distrust directed at a growing western consumerist lifestyle. On the one hand, these movements re-emphasize religious values, so as to combat materialism and the illusions of the everyday world, but, on the other, many join them to augment their inner power so that they can the better succeed in acquiring the benefits of such a world. I would suggest that it is partly this ambiguity between the ostensible aims of the organization and those of its individual members which generates suspicion among non-members and the authorities.

Secondly, almost all of these movements, while appearing to endorse *agama Hindu*, are in fact an implied criticism of it. They have to work within the guidelines laid down by the state, but in order to recruit members they must provide a religious service which goes beyond that supplied by official religions. They advertise themselves as providing surer and superior ways to religious fulfilment, which thus carries negative implications for the work done by priests and the Parisada in advancing *agama Hindu*. If the latter is perceived as inadequate for the needs of the Hindu religious community (*umat Hindu*, Ind.), then some of them will seek other answers to their immediate problems.

Thirdly, many AK have as their core idea the cultivation and release of individuals' inner power (*sakti*). This aligns such movements with Balinese *adat* traditions, in the sense that pre-colonial Balinese politico-religious organization was also based on the control, accumulation and use of *sakti*. The contemporary conceptualization of *sakti* among the mass of ordinary Balinese is much the same as it was in the past; it is understood as a pervasive force that animates the world and as a morally neutral power that can be used for good or evil. Just as villagers are frightened of the potency of priests and healers, whose intentions cannot easily be read, so the authorities and others distrust the motives of those who seek *sakti* through joining AK, and who therefore may become centres of power outside the legitimate framework of state religious authority. But the movements are also different from *adat* traditions, because AK usually maintain that everyone has a more or less equal capacity to develop their inherent power, whereas in the past such power correlated with status position. One of the reasons people join AK is because the doctrines of *agama Hindu* have no place for ideas of *sakti*, a concept they increasingly refer to as 'irrational' and one which is being replaced with ideas of 'spirituality'.

The final point concerns the ambiguity surrounding the relations between *adat* religion, *agama Hindu* and AK. In theory, *agama Hindu* is supposed to be a set of religious teachings which underpin *adat* ritual practices, in which case there should be little conflict between them. In practice, however, these religious teachings have moved away from traditional *adat* notions, especially as these concern ideas about potency. In doing so, they have created a space for the emergence of new religious movements, which, to varying degrees, continue to base themselves on *sakti*. But, in order to obtain legal authorization, AK have to affirm that their teachings conform to those of *agama Hindu*. Similarly, AK practise ritual activities which, though they often conform to the teachings of *agama Hindu*, actually diverge from *adat* traditions, thus arousing apprehension among Balinese villagers.

Conclusion

The creation of *agama Hindu*, as a Balinese response to the Indonesian state's efforts to produce religious orthodoxy and curtail religious diversity, paradoxically generated conditions in which religious innovation has been able to flourish. While *agama Hindu* is supposed to be the theological and rational justification for *adat*, in fact there are significant differences between them. The importation of Indian religious doctrines to serve as the basis for *agama Hindu* drove a wedge between this new religion and *adat*. Once India came to be seen as the source and inspiration for Balinese religion, the space created by the separation of *agama Hindu* and *adat* provided Balinese intellectuals with the opportunity to introduce yet other forms of Hinduism into Bali.

So far, the new forms of Hinduism imported into Bali have been the politically controversial devotional movements of Sai Baba and Hare Krishna, which have acted as platforms for further attacks on Balinese hierarchy, but it is likely that further variants will appear in the near future if the explosion of religious literature on Indian religion and Indian holy men is anything to go by. In addition, a bewildering variety of indigenous religious movements (*aliran kepercayaan*) have emerged, which have established themselves by exploiting the ambiguity inherent in the relationship between *adat* religion and *agama Hindu*.

This vastly expanded and increasingly complex religious field has wide-ranging implications for the construction of Balinese identities. Until recently, it seemed as if *agama Hindu* would provide the basis for the creation of a new ethnic identity to differentiate Balinese from the Muslims and Christians of other parts of Indonesia. However, two very important changes have made the success of this project increasingly doubtful. First, the universalization of *agama Hindu* across Indonesia means that this religion can no longer be an effective marker for a specifically Balinese ethnic identity. Secondly, the emergence of new forms of Hinduism in Bali is promoting new kinds of identity. Moreover, if the creation of an ethnic identity was largely taking place among the urban-based intelligentsia and the middle class, as they grappled with the problems of trying to present Bali to an outside world, these new identities are being forged in concrete social and religious practices at grassroots level. It is to an examination of how this is occurring in the Sai Baba movement that I now turn.

8

Sai Baba in Bali
identity & the politics of religious truth

Introduction

The religious movement I focus on here, Yayasan Shri Sathya Sai Baba (the Sathya Sai Baba Centre for the study of the Weda), is rather different from most of the new religious movements indigenous to Bali (*aliran kepercayaan*), which were briefly discussed in the previous chapter, because the source of its inspiration, the living 'god-man' Sathya Sai Baba, resides not in Bali but in south India.[1] This devotional movement is essentially Hindu in spirit and preaches an inclusive and universal message of love, peace and individual spiritual development, which, for many Balinese at least, also has egalitarian implications. As such, it stands somewhat apart from the ideas and practices of local Balinese traditions of Hinduism. The movement holds out the promise of salvation through devotion and service, and denigrates scriptural knowledge and ritual activity. For those Balinese who find the archaic ritualism of *adat* embarrassing and the doctrines of *agama Hindu* abstruse, Sai Baba offers a way to re-enchant the world by embedding many modern values in a genuine Hindu tradition, based on devotion and emotional commitment to a living god.

The Sai Baba movement in Bali is fascinating from several points of view. First, its intention is not to supplant other forms of Hinduism but to reform and incorporate them. Secondly, Sai Baba attracts devotees because it provides an identity for many urban, middle-class Balinese, and others too, who are increasingly alienated from more orthodox and local forms of Balinese Hinduism and are instead attempting to situate themselves in a more global and modern context. Thirdly, the focus on the development of spirituality (*kerohanian*, Ind.) and its rejection of inner potency (*sakti*) are quite new to Bali. Fourthly, Sai Baba is based on a personal relationship to a highly charismatic figure, who performs miracles, which is very different from the scribal, priestly and ritual-bound traditions of Bali. Finally, in comparison with these latter traditions, which are thoroughly rooted in a caste order, the Sai Baba movement in Bali is relatively egalitarian and thus provides a new and additional challenge to the hierarchy.

I want to ask, therefore, why many Balinese join this movement, why it is thought dangerous by others and how its presence contributes to broader debates concerning

---

[1] Research on Sai Baba in India is sparse but of high quality. For information on Sai Baba's life story and on the teachings, practices and general Indian context of Sai Baba, see White (1972), Swallow (1982) and Babb (1986). There is also a large literature written by Baba's devotees, which is mostly of a hagiographical kind, references to which can be found in Babb's bibliography. There are also some studies of Indian devotees of Sathya Sai Baba outside India. Klass (1991) has examined the place of the movement among the Indian population in Trinidad, while Lee (1982), Ackerman and Lee (1990) and Kent (1999, 2000) have carried out research in Malaysia. As far as I know, there is no extant study of non-Indian followers of Sai Baba, apart from the small Chinese component of the predominantly Indian membership of Sai Baba in Malaysia.

the future direction of modern Balinese religion and culture. In essence, then, this chapter (and the next) examines how diverse religious ideologies define patterns of social conflict. My concern, therefore, is with the production and shaping of religious practice within certain historical and political conditions. At the same time, however, I recognize that people take sides in political conflicts as a result of being socialized into new religious movements, which in fact they joined for quite different kinds of reasons. In other words, it is not always easy to determine whether religious convictions are a reflection of political ones or whether the reverse is the case, particularly in those societies, such as Bali, in which 'religion' is such a 'political' issue.

The accounts of Sai Baba in India provided by Swallow (1982) and Babb (1986), which focus on the movement's Shivaite symbolism and the meanings of Baba's miracle working, respectively, are only partly applicable to this Balinese case, because such symbolism is largely unknown in Bali, and because most Balinese devotees have never seen Baba. Consequently, I focus instead on the differences and relationship between Sai Baba, on the one hand, and *adat* religion and *agama Hindu*, on the other, and therefore on what Sai Baba means to Balinese, given the conflict now endemic in the wider religious landscape. While Sai Baba worship does not entail conversion, since devotees maintain their adherence to these other forms of Hinduism, there are none the less striking differences in form, content and organization between them.

When the first Sai Baba centre opened in Jakarta, it aroused both admiration and hostility. Some approved of it because they considered it authentically Hindu. Others, however, found the idea of a living god[2] difficult to accept and condemned its teachings as subversive and dangerously close to communism. Since then, it has had an uneasy relationship with the Indonesian Ministry of Religion. As more centres opened and the number of devotees increased, so did concern about its activities. Complaints about the movement prompted an investigation in 1993, which concluded that its activities contravened the proper arrangements for religious life in Indonesia and thus generated unrest among the surrounding local people and disturbed the harmony of the religious community (Supartha 1994: 153). Consequently, early in 1994, a letter was sent to the lay leaders of the Sai Baba centre in Jakarta, informing them that the movement was no longer to be registered with the Ministry of Religion. The press interpreted this as a ban, but this was hotly disputed by Sai Baba leaders and later also denied by the Ministry of Religion, on the grounds that it does not possess such powers. The letter was seen by followers as an attempt to demote Sai Baba from a 'religion' (*agama*) to a 'stream of belief' (*aliran kepercayaan*). However, this was not entirely successful because some officials in other state religious institutions, for example the Parisada Hindu Dharma Indonesia, the body which oversees the affairs of the Hindu community throughout Indonesia, are now themselves devotees of Sai Baba, and they stepped in quickly to argue that the movement was neither a 'stream of belief' nor a sect, but rather a spiritual study group based on the *weda*.[3] In the event, the Sai Baba movement was taken under the umbrella of the Parisada, and thus remains a legal organization. Nevertheless, the

---

[2] In 1963, in front of a large crowd, Sai Baba declared that he was Shiva and Shakti (Shiva's consort) in embodied form. Baba not only loudly and repeatedly claims that He encompasses all the gods of the Hindu pantheon. He also claims to be the deity of all religions, and is thus God (Babb 1986: 166).
[3] The Balinese word *weda* is very difficult to translate. It is clearly a version of the Sanskrit term *veda*, but the *vedas* are unknown in Bali. *Weda* is a term that is found in numerous titles of Balinese 'religious' texts and, in that sense, it probably means little more than 'holy formula' or 'holy scripture' (Bakker 1993: 14). When it is used by members of Sai Baba, however, it tends to refer to sacred Indian texts, in particular, the *Bhagavadgita*.

episode still rankles with devotees, because, while they insist it is an *agama*, their opponents claim it is a harmful *aliran kepercayaan*.

The Sai Baba group is one of the largest of the new religious movements in Bali. It has numerous centres all over Indonesia, boasting over forty in Bali alone. By far the biggest centre in Bali is situated on the outskirts of Bali's capital town, Denpasar. There is no register of adherents, but leaders claim that between 5,000 and 6,000 regularly attend meetings at its various centres on the island (though in many cases a 'centre' is simply someone's home). They also contend that there are a large number of followers who support the teachings of Sai Baba but who do not attend the centres' meetings.[4]

Some explication of the egalitarian aspect of Sai Baba in Bali is required before continuing. According to Babb (1986: 172–3), Sai Baba holds very conservative views concerning India's social and economic institutions. While others should be treated with decency and charity, Baba does not advocate reform of existing hierarchies. In Bali, it is true, no explicit doctrine of equality is propounded, and a significant number of devotees are from the gentry. However, the organization of Sai Baba, the format of its meetings and its universal and fundamentalist message all contribute to a markedly egalitarian orientation when compared with *adat* religion. In other words, it is egalitarian not so much in its conception but in its effects and in its relationships to other forms of Hinduism in Bali.

Sai Baba devotionalism & Balinese religion

Sai Baba worship began in Java when the first centre was opened in Jakarta in 1981. The patron of the centre was a Balinese, Gusti Agung Gedé Putra, who later became the director-general of the Department of Hinduism and Buddhism in the Ministry of Religion. Putra had made several visits to India and had been overcome with emotion whenever he heard Baba speak (Bakker 1993: 155–7).

Activities began in Bali soon after, when worship of Baba was introduced by another Balinese, now deceased, who had been a member of the centre in Jakarta. Initially, meetings were held in members' houses in Denpasar, but in 1984 a permanent site was obtained, on which has now been built a large temple. The most important building is a very large pavilion, whose construction is typically Balinese. At the front are portraits of Baba and a richly upholstered empty chair.

Although apparently empty, the chair is conceived to be actually occupied by Baba. Baba's portraits are surrounded by pictures of other Hindu deities and garlands of flowers. During the singing of *bhajan* (devotional songs), musicians and lay leaders sit at the front, while the mass of devotees sit cross-legged behind them, men on the right and women and children on the left. Another small pavilion contains a room housing recording equipment, and stores of books, cassette tapes and pamphlets for sale. There is also a small shrine for the worship of Balinese gods, located just to the side of the main pavilion, and ceremonies are held there every new and full moon.

Sai Baba worship is organized very differently from local traditions of Balinese

---

[4] Some of these passive followers are reluctant to publicize their association by open attendance on the grounds that they might jeopardize their career prospects in government jobs. Others are strongly attracted to the religious message and speak of themselves as devotees, but find the regular sessions of *bhajan* singing somewhat wearisome and unnecessary. There is also a category of supporters who must find it difficult to attend regularly if they live at a distance from their nearest centre.

Plate 8.1 The recently completed worship hall in the Sathya Sai Baba temple located on the outskirts of Denpasar, the capital town of Bali

Plate 8.2 A portrait of Sathya Sai Baba situated at the front of the new hall

Hinduism. Most Balinese are members of several temple congregations. Their names are listed on a register, they all make equal contributions to the upkeep of the temple and its ceremonies and fines are levied for infraction of the numerous rules. It is a highly structured organization, often with a written constitution detailing the obligations and privileges of members. If special expenses are incurred, people may make voluntary contributions, and these are often publicized so that everyone can see what others have given. Sai Baba centres are completely different. There is no register of members, devotees attend or not as they see fit, expenses are met entirely by voluntary and often anonymous donations, and rich members often pay large bills out of their own pockets. No record of contributions is kept, so that the treasurer is on trust to disburse collected monies in a proper way.

While a Balinese temple congregation has no extracurricular activities, existing only to support the gods of that temple, Sai Baba centres, both in India and Bali, have three broad programmes of activity: the development of devotees' spirituality (*bidang spirituil*, Ind.); religious education (*bidang pendidikan*, Ind.); and service to the community (*bidang pelayanan*, Ind.). For example, Sai Baba centres put on free classes in religious education open to the public (not just devotees), in which more expert members explain and clarify the teachings of Sai Baba in a very accessible manner, and religious literature, including Indonesian translations of the *Bhagavadgita*, is sold at low prices, so that members can study privately. In addition there is a free kindergarten class and also free courses in the English language. Charity work is also a major activity of the centres. Members make charitable donations (money, materials, labour) to help others, whether they are followers of Sai Baba or not. They contribute donations to good causes and for the relief of poverty and help to clean and renovate hospitals, schools, Balinese temples and other communal facilities. Members also help in the preparations for major temple festivals, such as those conducted at Besakih. Sai Baba is therefore a much more open form of organization, with significant social outreach functions, something which facilitates its integration into mainstream society.

Sai Baba services are also strikingly different from Balinese temple ceremonies. They begin promptly at 7 p.m. every Tuesday, Thursday and Sunday. As devotees arrive, they meditate and pray for a few moments. Socializing is frowned upon but takes place in a subdued manner. The special *adat* dress, which is compulsory for Balinese temples, is virtually never worn, devotees wearing a white shirt and trousers. Apart from some flowers and incense, there are no offerings at a service. Priests do not officiate, because Baba is the only *guru*, and all devotees approach Baba directly.

The *bhajan* are in Hindi, Tamil or Sanskrit, but books of translations are readily available. Usually eight *bhajan* are sung at a meeting and, as each finishes, an obeisance is made to Baba as God, with clasped hands raised above the head. While singing is obligatory at most *adat* temple ceremonies, it is performed by small groups of experts. As such, in experiential terms, it is not central to what others are doing. At Sai Baba services, *bhajan* singing is the centrepiece of the meeting, and allows members to surrender themselves to God by expressing their devotion, love and subordination. While many emphasize its calming and soothing qualities, others stress the intense emotional experience it engenders, one long-time devotee comparing *bhajan* to a current of electricity going through him. A lay official, a lecturer at one of Bali's universities, told me that *bhajan* are not just songs, but are 'like a bundle of precious gems', or 'like a road carrying you to God'. He went on to say that singing *bhajan* is a method of freeing oneself from sin and a way of achieving liberation (*bébas*, Ind.). When singing, many devotees appear utterly absorbed in what they are doing, with their eyes closed and in a semi-trance. The pounding rhythms, simple and hypnotic melodies and communal nature of the singing facilitate a subordination of the individual to God through a merging of the self into the group.

After the singing, a member gives a talk lasting about thirty minutes, which is always in Indonesian, never in Balinese, although sometimes the speaker lapses into Balinese for a few moments. The subject-matter may be an account of the speaker's visit to Puttaparthi in south India, Baba's birthplace and, since 1950, the site of his ashram; a sermon on the merits of discipline, vegetarianism and self-sacrifice; an exegesis of Baba's words; or a personal account of what led someone to become a devotee. The group's lay leaders then make announcements about forthcoming events. The final act is the distribution of sacred ash and holy water to the congregation. The ash (*wibuti*), which is brought back to Bali by those members who have travelled to India, is miraculously produced in large quantities from Baba's hand. Balinese devotees told me that the ash was made in a 'magical' way (*dengan cara gaib*, Ind.) and there was a never-ending supply.[5] The holy water is distributed exactly as it would be in Balinese ceremonies.[6]

Balinese temple festivals, in contrast, are replete with elaborate offerings. Priests recite prayers and litanies (some in Sanskrit) largely unintelligible to the congregation and often to themselves as well, and they perform complicated ritual actions unheeded by others. Meanwhile, the congregation passes the time chatting. Apart from the extensive preparations, lay members really only take part in the ceremony at its climax, when they perform acts of obeisance to the assembled temple gods and receive holy water.

It is vital to recognize the tremendous emotional devotion to the person of Baba, evident not simply during the *bhajan* singing, but in devotees' everyday lives. Devotees pray to Baba several times a day to ask for advice and peace of mind, and to surrender themselves to Him. Their homes are full of His pictures and many devotees carry portraits of Baba on their person, in their cars or on their motor bikes. If Baba's miracles are important in initially attracting new members and convincing them that Baba is a living god, it is this intense personal relationship that becomes crucial (Babb 1986). To those who have had a sight of Baba in India, and especially those who have touched Him or been spoken to by Him, it is the experience of ineffable joy that is really impressive. Even those – the majority – who have not seen Him in the flesh frequently dream of Baba and express a great longing to see and touch Him.[7] In speaking about these experiences, either in private or in the public talks at meetings, devotees are often on the verge of tears.

This intimate and emotional experience is unlike anything expressed by Balinese towards the gods of their *adat* religion. Balinese gods are ancestors, who, through the cumulative processes of cremation and post-cremation rites of purification, gradually become divinized. During this process, they progressively lose their individual characteristics and become remote, anonymous, impersonal and conventionalized.

[5] Materializing ash, rings and various other objects, which Baba is famous for, is one of the simpler tricks of Indian magicians (Siegel 1991).
[6] Given the sequence of silent meditation, obeisance to God, both silent prayer and collective public prayer, songs of praise to God, a sermon and the distribution of a holy substance, the organization of a Sai Baba meeting seems much closer to a Christian service than to a Balinese temple ceremony.
[7] Many devotees have related dreams of Baba to me. Often He appears very large and beatific and devotees feel a great wave of love and affection emanating from Him. Others mentioned that they dreamt of such a person before they even knew who He was, particularly when they were ill or in a very difficult situation. Only later when they became devotees did they realize that He was calling them to Him and protecting them. In other dreams devotees find themselves in the same room as Baba, who is bathed in an aura of light, but they cannot quite touch Him and thus feel an intense anguish.

For example, the god of the Balé Bang temple (situated in the village of Pujung) is known as Ida Batara *ring pura* Balé Bang, which simply means 'Most respectful God of the Balé Bang temple'. There is rarely a name or a set of features that serve to distinguish the god of one temple from that of another. During ceremonies, prayers to the gods are formulaic, communal and public; they are directed by the temple priest, who provides instructions through a megaphone, now to pray to this god, now to that one. Outside these communal events, Balinese rarely pray to their gods.[8]

On the other hand, Balinese ceremonies are not without their own emotional effects. The gods descend to the temple; they are 'embodied' in material objects and carried on the heads of worshippers in processions; they are bathed, fed and entertained; and people can make vows to them. The relationship between gods and congregation is thus not entirely formal, but also substantive and occasionally intimate. After the ceremony, Balinese describe themselves as refreshed, calm and happy. None the less, this is a much less intense experience than the passionate devotion to Baba.

A profile of Sai Baba devotees

The active membership of Sai Baba is perhaps some 5,000 people. However, as these are scattered all over the island, and as there is no register of members, it is not possible to provide a full description of their socio-demographic characteristics. What follows is based on information received from 53 devotees at the main centre in Denpasar and from general observations and conversations during visits to the centre and to devotees' homes.

In terms of caste status, the proportions are about the same as one would find in the general population, which is to say that over 90 per cent of members are commoners. The gender ratio is about two to one in favour of men and, in addition, there are very few unmarried female devotees. There is a preponderance of young men between the ages of twenty and thirty-five, but older men are well represented, and it may be that the latter face greater difficulties in attending than the former, an argument that probably also applies to unmarried women.

The most important feature of the membership is their high level of education.[9] Many have, or are in the process of gaining, a university education, most of the

[8] If Balinese display little emotional investment in their gods during a collective temple ceremony, they are increasingly doing so in the confines of their own homes. In recent years Balinese have more and more taken to private prayer in their houseyard temples, where, according to several friends, they address God in a more intimate manner by recounting their woes, asking for help and requesting peace of mind. More recently, the Parisada has encouraged new religious practices in line with reformist Hinduism, such as meditation, private prayer, collective recitation of mantra, priestly sermons and pilgrimages, all of which create overlaps between *adat, agama Hindu* and devotional Hinduism (Ramstedt 2001).
[9] The profile of Sai Baba devotees in India is more narrowly urban and well educated. Babb (1986), for example, notes that most Indian devotees of Baba come from the affluent, urban middle class. He argues that many are culturally rootless and 'distanced from their tradition by background and education', and that Baba provides an identity which links their nostalgia for that lost tradition with their place in the modern world (Babb 1986: 191).

Klass makes similar points for Indo-Trinidadian followers of Baba. They want to be good Hindus but are frustrated and embarrassed by the authoritarian and hierarchical dominance of Brahmin priests, who are adjudged ignorant and illiterate. They turn to Baba because, while it takes them back to an authentic form of Hinduism and to childhood practices of singing and music, it is neither a doctrinaire nor a primitive religion. It best fits the values of the modern world to which its devotees are mostly committed. By being a global movement which transcends local issues, it constitutes 'an egalitarian, universalistic, Western-accepted but *India-derived* belief system' (Klass 1993: 163, original emphasis).

prominent lay leaders of the movement are academics at Bali's several universities and the majority of members have finished secondary school. Such educational qualifications provide entry into good jobs. Twenty-eight of the fifty-three describe themselves as civil servants, professionals, private officials or entrepreneurs, with six more being students. The others are artisans, white-collar workers, ordinary employees, labourers and a few unemployed.

Given this profile, it would be easy to characterize the movement as a religious vehicle for well-educated, urban-based commoners and intellectuals to pursue political change, in particular the eradication of hierarchy and its associated institutions. But there is more to it than this. For a start, a significant number of devotees are poor, have little education and are either unemployed or in unskilled jobs, and appear to be members for a variety of other reasons, described in the following section. Moreover, while one would expect commoners to inveigh against expensive ritual, domination by high priests and the structural inequalities of Balinese society, what is just as significant are the criticisms of religious intolerance, the autocratic control of Hindu religious orthodoxy by the Parisada and the frequently voiced desire of all devotees to be better people and to establish in society a higher moral code of behaviour. As will become clear, the movement is indeed a reflection of wider social and political conflicts, but for many devotees the most important thing about membership is their relationship with Baba and their own spiritual development and happiness. In short, while devotees' desire for political reform in Bali, and Indonesia generally, is strong, they tend to see political change not as an end in itself, but as a means to securing and extending the influence of the religious truths revealed by Baba (cf. Anderson 1977: 21; Hefner 1997: 111–12).

Becoming a member of Sai Baba

Balinese join Sai Baba for many reasons. In the simplest case, people are introduced to the movement by existing members because they have shown some interest, often through reading borrowed books about Baba. Several members told me they were initially sceptical but were highly impressed with the organization of the meetings and the evident sincerity of the followers. For some Balinese, it was the sheer difference from anything they had known before which attracted them. In some cases, new recruits felt nothing during the first one or two *bhajan* sessions, but on the third or fourth occasion were unexpectedly overcome by emotion and spontaneously started crying. For yet others, it was Baba's portraits which attracted them. On seeing pictures of Baba for the first time, one or two said His gaze seemed to penetrate their inner being and they felt they were in the presence of God. Perhaps we should also be cautious of focusing too explicitly on the agency of members. It may look as if devotees make the decision to join the movement for themselves, but many say that, without their knowing it, Baba entered their lives and led them to it. It was His agency, not theirs, which engineered their membership.

Another reason for joining concerns Baba's renowned ability to work miracles and effect astonishing cures, even bringing the dead back to life. Devotees are deeply impressed by the miracles others tell them about or those they have themselves experienced, and they figure very prominently in the talks given at meetings. Devotees implicitly accept the genuineness of Baba's miracles and frequently interpret mundane aspects of their own lives and what others would call trivial coincidences as miraculous outcomes of Baba's intervention.

Compared with the impressive miracles Baba performs for his Indian devotees, which Babb (1986) describes, many of those I heard about from Balinese friends seemed rather tame: the inexplicable and timely appearance of valuables thought lost; the amazing ease with which complex travel arrangements to India have been finalized; the avoidance of apparently certain traffic accidents as a result of Baba's intervention; and so forth.

Some, however, were rather more dramatic. For example, the elder sister of a thirty-year-old commoner devotee, who works as a hotel official, was struck by a form of black magic known as *bebaian*. When mantra were said over her and she was administered with holy water and the *wibuti* ash from a Sai Baba service, the afflicting spirit cried out in pain and begged them to stop. The spirit clung to her for most of the night as these ministrations continued, but finally fled when a photo of Baba was placed on her body. Since then she has become a devotee. Another commoner women, a thirty-three year old seamstress, suffered heart illness for a long time and, though examined and treated by several doctors, remained so ill that she was sure she was dying. A close friend who was a devotee encouraged her to attend the *bhajan* sessions and to meditate on Baba. Slowly her illness subsided and she stopped taking medicine. She is totally convinced that it was Baba who cured her.

For devotees the miraculous becomes part of everyday life, because the mundane and transcendant worlds are connected by Baba's permanent presence in both. What before were events and happenings of little significance now become signs of Baba's continuous involvement in devotees' lives. As Baba assumes greater prominence in their everyday existence, devotees claim that their activities are shaped by a higher purpose and meaning. Many devotees are successful in academic and business life, but the miraculous does not necessarily contradict their modern scientific and economic rationalism. Baba's constant love and protection give strength of purpose and inculcate habits of discipline, hard work and dedication, so that worldly success *and* miracles become the by-products and rewards of devotion. In other words, as Kent (2000: 12) has pointed out, devotees 'are not required to choose between spirituality and worldliness'. Because Baba's love procures worldly success, the self-justifying values of the secularized and modern world now receive a higher form of validation. This is further reinforced by the movement's stress on charitable service to the community and its rejection of forms of individual world renunciation. Spiritual salvation and worldly success are both realized by selfless service to others and devotion to work and duty, in a way partly reminiscent of Calvinist Protestant doctrine (Weber 1985).

Some people join when they are distressed with social or psychological problems and are brought to health by Baba. One young man, who works for an insurance company, contemplated suicide several times when his girlfriend deserted him. Only when he attended the *bhajan* sessions did he recover. He has now been a devotee for over five years. This category also includes those whose lives were being wasted. Some young men described their recent past as a vicious circle of gambling, drinking, petty crime, parental conflict and unemployment. Now they see Baba as a constant, protective companion, who infuses their lives with new meaning by providing a fixed centre and a purpose beyond the mundane. Several devotees told me that Baba has helped them control strong feelings of fear, anger, desire and jealousy, and that overcoming these 'internal enemies' (*musuh dalam*, Ind.) has been a greater challenge to them than dealing with the malicious insults of outsiders who condemn the movement.

Motives for adherence, then, frequently devolve on specific personal circumstances. Having said that, however, it is also true that a very important set of reasons for joining concerns religious convictions and disapproval of and opposition to the structures of *adat* religion. Devotees repeatedly accuse *adat* religion of being embedded in an oppressive caste order which emphasizes impersonal rituals, expensive offerings and domination by priests, which have thus made it exclusive, secretive and inaccessible. Devotees regularly complained that the responses to their queries about the point of ritual and religious practices were very unsatisfactory. What is the purpose (*makna*, Ind.) of offerings? Why do we do this ritual? What is the meaning of the priest's actions? Why do we sacrifice animals? The standard answer to such questions from parents, priests and others is '*mula kéto*', ('that's just how it is'). Such questions are increasingly asked by Balinese. Now requiring reasons for 'traditional' activities, many are no longer content with a customary evasiveness, interpreted either as ignorance or secretiveness.

Devotees find that lay leaders are often both able and willing to provide satisfactory explanations. An attractive aspect of the movement is the educational classes.[10] Religious knowledge and religious truth, they are told, should be widely distributed, rather than retained as esoteric secrets. 'There is no truth without understanding' is a common refrain of devotees. New members found it startling that 'teachers want you to learn and understand. They explain things in easy language, and repeat things and let you ask questions'. Such knowledge is meant to inform ordinary life and is not merely for the select few; it is neither arcane nor bound to status or gender. This religious knowledge is, however, not taught in a vacuum, but as a response to the doctrines and practices of other forms of Hinduism, a point elaborated in the following section.

It is not so much the content of this religious knowledge which is important as the attitude to it. What I think really matters is that the movement democratizes this knowledge. Many ordinary devotees may not, in practice, be very knowledgeable (although some can provide convincing explanations for *adat* ceremonies), but they know that this knowledge is readily available to them. Moreover, it is not the more esoteric knowledge, the kind that academic devotees have written books about, that interests ordinary members. Rather, it is Baba's simple maxims of selfless love, charity to others and community service which devotees quote with sincerity and eagerness. And, once again, it is the emotional feelings generated by devotion to Baba that make these significant.[11] Perhaps another reason why these social messages of gentleness, kindness and tolerance towards others stand out for devotees is that, while they may be 'basically common coin in the Hindu world' (Babb: 1986: 171), they are absent from Balinese religious traditions. *Adat* religion is dominated by ritual action, calculated reciprocity and an absence of sermonizing, while *agama Hindu* is pervaded by abstract and esoteric theology, which has little impact on the everyday lives of Balinese.

[10] The teaching is carried out by the movement's lay leaders, some of whom are lecturers at universities in Bali. They use material that either they or others have brought back from visits to Puttaparthi. Some have written books about Sai Baba (for example, Jendra 1996), and many have read quite widely in the Indian religious texts, which have been translated into Indonesian and English.
[11] If the religious classes provide a more systematic description and explanation of Baba's ideas and how these relate to Balinese ritual practices, the talks at services convey much more straightforward social messages. These are usually encapsulated in maxims such as 'love all, serve all'; 'help ever, hurt never'; 'duty without love is deplorable, duty with love is desirable'; 'the secret of success is to have the right priorities'; 'multiple desires distort priorities'; 'speak the truth and follow darma'; etc. These are sometimes presented in English and followed by extended explanations and examples in Indonesian. Other favourite topics include the need for discipline, 'optimal use of time', introspection and the importance of vegetarianism.

The practical benefits of being a member should not be forgotten. Life in a completely new kind of community and in a new social circle has many advantages. The community may act as a surrogate family for those who are alienated from their families of birth. Friendships are made with categories of Balinese one would not usually encounter in the ordinary course of events, and these friends can be invited to family rituals, giving them a prestige they would not otherwise have. The Sai Baba community also sometimes acts as a kind of job market. I know several working-class members who have been given regular work by wealthier devotees.

The critique of Balinese Hinduism

If adherence to *agama Hindu* provides an ethnic identity for urban and well-educated Balinese, there are none the less many in this amorphous category who are discontented with both *adat* ritual traditions and official Balinese Hinduism. A central dilemma for them is that securing essential religious truth has become problematic (because there are now different forms of Hinduism, each arguing that their teachings are divinely inspired). Consequently members of new religious movements picture themselves as being on a spiritual journey in quest of religious enlightenment.[12] But if they join Sai Baba a new religious conviction can lead to a new identity.

Devotees frequently say that they learn little from their questions about the fundamental meanings behind *adat* ceremonies. Low-caste temple priests (*pemangku*) are denounced as ignorant, their knowledge being confined to the proper conduct of rites. High-caste Brahmana priests are criticized for confining religious knowledge to themselves, both to exploit the masses, by selling supposedly indispensable ritual services, and as a form of social control, most Balinese fearing to break off relations with their high priests, who may curse them. Consequently, ritual is often described as automatic (*otomatis*, Ind.), mechanical and as having lost sight of its true spiritual aims.

Devotees widely acknowledge that the religious truths of the *weda* exist in the more sacred and magically potent palm-leaf texts owned by priests and others, since these are supposed to be based on original Indian scriptures. However, priests are accused of cynically justifying their unwillingness to divulge these mysteries by claiming that an undisciplined distribution of the contents of sacred texts to the ritually unprepared is dangerous. In *adat* forms of Hinduism, then, religious truth may be present, but it is unobtainable for the masses.

Followers of devotional Hinduism also condemn competitive ritual display, gambling, cock-fighting and the slaughtering and eating of animals, all of which are central to local *adat* tradition. In engendering sensual bodily desires and the acquisition of material goods for their own sake, such practices impede the cultivation of spirituality and lead instead to a dissipated life.

If parents, priests and others cannot provide enlightenment, what about school classes in religion? After all, these are based on the tenets of *agama Hindu*, purportedly derived from sacred Indian texts. However, devotees disparage this religious education. Teachers' accounts of Hindu theology are said to be divorced from

---

[12] While many Sai Baba followers have never been members of other new movements, I met several Balinese who had transferred their allegiance to Sai Baba on leaving Hare Krishna or other *aliran kepercayaan*. Typically they accounted for the switch by arguing that the latter suffered from the same problems as *adat* religion; the movements they had joined were authoritarian, secretive, exploitative, costly and egocentric and could not provide satisfactory solutions to their dilemmas.

everyday experience and unrelated to village ritual activities. Teachers are also denounced as hypocrites: after pontificating about the ills of gambling and drinking, they go to a cock-fight or a card game on their way home.

Sai Baba's relative egalitarianism also presents a criticism of Bali's hierarchical social order. Modern Hinduism's monotheism, as it exists in Bali, implies that all Balinese have the same relationship to God. This is profoundly different from *adat* practice, in which members of ranked descent groups worship their own deified ancestors, and the worship of those from an inferior group leads to being demoted in caste to the level of the latter. Sai Baba therefore provides a refuge for those who take the unity and transcendence of God seriously. Although devotees are separated from Baba by an immense gulf, amongst themselves they are formally equal and no intermediary or priest is allowed to intervene. Distinctions of caste within the movement are therefore irrelevant, both doctrinally and organizationally. This critique of hierarchy is reinforced by the movement's stress on individual spiritual development and the high values placed on hard work, the dissemination of knowledge and service to the community, all of which engender a rejection of ascriptive privilege and an endorsement of merit and achievement. Unsurprisingly, many devotees emphasize the *warna* theory of social structure, rather than the *kasta* theory (see Chapter 4), by arguing that it is how people behave which is important, not what status they have been born into.[13]

The main critique of Balinese Hinduism is that it has strayed from the path of true religion. Eternal religious truth, based on original revelations by Hindu sages, is to be found in Balinese palm-leaf texts. In the past it was available to all and was explicit, but over the course of time it has become overlain with the dross of ritual and buried beneath the venal and vested interests of priests and rulers working to bolster their privileges in the caste system. What passes for Balinese *adat* religion is a deviation from and a degradation of what it once was. A Brahmana female friend, a supporter but not an active devotee of Sai Baba, accused *adat* of constraining and shackling people with its emphasis on caste, privilege, offerings and male domination, and thought that unless a solution was soon found religious strife was inevitable.

No doubt many Balinese join Sai Baba because of opposition to the structures of hierarchy or the unsatisfactory nature of highly ritualized *adat* religion. However, a degree of caution is needed because these reasons may in part be an artefact of obtaining data only from existing devotees. Several members told me they began to think more clearly about the deficiencies of traditional forms of religion only after they had joined. It is therefore possible that their rationalized perspective is an *effect* of membership rather than a cause. Once socialized into the movement, their past may be reconceptualized as a spiritual quest in search of enlightenment or in terms of corrupt high priests, when in reality it was a function of personal troubles, a prior mystical experience of Baba, curiosity or a chance encounter.

---

[13] Unfortunately, I have very little information on how devotees interact with non-members in their home villages, and thus to what extent this egalitarian orientation is lived out in the context of the norms of hierarchical social relations. Although I visited the homes of several families of devotees, for various reasons these were all rather unusual. Members frequently told me that they used high Balinese to people of 'superior' titles only if these were worthy of respect in some other way, for example, because they led virtuous lives, worked hard, were generous and kind, etc. In informal moments during Sai Baba meetings, Indonesian was used as often as Balinese. More refined Balinese (*alus*), when it was used, tended to be directed to lay leaders, whether commoners or not, as a sign of their greater spirituality, rather than because they claimed a high ritual status.

Sai Baba incorporates Balinese Hinduism

Most members describe the critique of *adat* religion and *agama Hindu* as constructive rather than destructive. The aim is to improve and repair (*memperbaiki*, Ind.) these traditions, rather than exclude and destroy them. The point is to recover and promote a genuine religion that is said to have been submerged under layers of secrecy and falsehood. Devotees acknowledge that *agama Hindu* supposedly has the similar aim of restoring an authentic tradition, but they claim that this is impossible while it depends on the caste system and high priesthood, the two institutions deemed most responsible for perverting it. By showing how *adat* and *agama Hindu* have deviated from the path of true knowledge, the movement claims to supply an essential corrective which brings Hinduism back into line with its original source.

Sai Baba's principal message is that all religions are one and all forms of god are one. There is only one religion, the religion of love; only one caste, that of humanity; only one language, that of the heart (Klass 1991: 103). Baba once claimed that he was an incarnation of Jesus (Sandweiss 1975: 176); in Trinidad the movement occasionally uses Christian and Muslim devotional songs (Klass 1991: 131); in those few centres in Malaysia dominated by Chinese devotees, *bhajan* are sung in Chinese (Lee 1982: 135); and in one centre in Kuala Lumpur the symbols of eleven major religions hang on the wall above the altar (Kent 1999: 40). The movement thus preaches a universal and fundamentalist message aimed not simply at a return to a purer and truer form of Hinduism but rather at providing a foundation for all religions.[14] Consequently, Baba recommends devotees to maintain adherence to their respective religions because these need to be brought back into the fold of true religion.[15]

While this is essentially a religious argument, it also has an organizational impact. If Sai Baba insisted on conversion and an exclusive allegiance, the movement would almost certainly have been banned in Indonesia. No doubt devotees maintain their membership for many reasons, but surely one of them is that they are not obliged to cease their allegiance to *adat* religion.

The attempt to incorporate Balinese Hinduism is effected in several ways. In educational classes, in the sermons at meetings and during informal discussions, the numerous calendric ceremonies celebrated by the Balinese are given their 'true' (*benar*, Ind.) explanations, so that when members perform them in their own homes they understand the import of what they are doing. Consequently, devotees repudiate accusations that they undermine Balinese Hinduism, by arguing that they become more energetic, sincere and knowledgeable practitioners of their village religion.

[14] Sai Baba ideology promulgates the themes of 'unity in diversity' and 'all religions are one', but this religious tolerance is based on a 'doctrine of a hierarchy of religious truths wherein different religions are thought to have received partial revelations of a spiritual reality that is fully manifest only in Hinduism' (Lorenzen 1995: 8). This ambiguity between the equality of all religions and the subordination of other religions to Hinduism is not very important in Bali, because religious conflict and competition is confined within Hinduism. Elsewhere, as in Malaysia for example, where ethnicity, religious affiliation and power are very closely associated, such ambiguity is simultaneously both useful and dangerous (Lee 1982; Kent 1999, 2000).
[15] The permission to continue in other faiths leads to the accusation that Sai Baba exists by an eclectic mixing of elements drawn from these faiths. This is said to create confusion and disturbance among the religious community within which the movement develops. A good example of how Sai Baba can exist alongside other religions and accommodate itself to them is the way it interprets the Balinese practice of visiting a spirit medium. While some devotees condemn this, many say that it does not pose a problem because the spirit speaking through the medium is none other than Baba. If the medium cannot provide a revelation or if the revelation turns out to be inappropriate, this is because Baba has chosen a different channel through which to communicate. This may be a dream, a personal interview, a miracle or some other way.

This orientation to members' original religious allegiances means that, while the movement itself eschews ritual (though no doubt the *bhajan* singing could be glossed as a form of ritual) and even sees it as a hindrance to spiritual advancement (Kent 1999: 34), it nevertheless makes space for the ritual practices of *adat* religion. In no sense does Sai Baba attempt to dissuade devotees from performing their customary ceremonies in their own homes and villages. What it tries to do is redirect devotees' thoughts away from the ritual activity itself and towards the rational, spiritual and ethical foundations of those activities, which only the movement can supply.

Another tactic concerns vegetarianism. While this is not an iron rule, members are expected to change their own practices and, in this way, influence the wider population. Among devotees there are differences of opinion concerning the killing of animals. For some it is simply wrong because they are God's creatures. Moreover, killing animals for food or enjoyment (in cock-fights, for example) brings bad karma. I have also been told that meat eaters gradually take on the characteristics of the animals they consume, so that those who eat too much chicken speak nonsense, while those who consume too much pork become fat and lazy. One man told me that in the distant past the Balinese only ate rice and vegetables and all was peace and harmony; now, however, everyone eats meat and consequently people gamble, get drunk and fight all the time. For others, however, killing animals to make offerings is acceptable because the soul of the dead animal accrues merit and improves its karma.

On this particular issue of animal sacrifice, Sai Baba lay leaders are in agreement with the Parisada, in that both argue that the sacrifice of animals is based on a misconception which wrongly privileges the outward symbol over the inner meaning. One aspect of many rituals is to draw attention to the fact that human beings share with animals certain socially disjunctive characteristics (gluttony, self-ishness, etc.), which need to be suppressed. This can just as easily and more properly be accomplished using animal shapes made of rice, rather than the actual killing of animals.[16]

This ambivalent and tolerant perspective towards the use of animals for food and

---

[16] The idea that it is the removal or suppression of the bestial characteristics inherent in human beings which motivates the use of animals in rituals and that therefore this can be accomplished using symbols of animals instead of real ones is not a view which most Balinese would readily accept. In *adat* religion, animals are not just symbols; rather, they are offerings. Purificatory rites, known as *caru*, for example, require animals to be slaughtered because the malevolent spirits which are the focus of such rites demand blood, flesh and alcohol if they are to be placated and transformed into more benign entities. It would serve no purpose to offer them animal-shaped rice cakes. Most offerings contain meat, and the kind of meat used is determined by the spirit or deity to which it is offered.

Purified ancestors require the purer meat of ducks and chickens, while demons crave dog, goat and beef. There are some offerings, such as the massive *pula gembal*, which symbolize the 'world and all its contents' (*guminé tekén isinné*) and thus also require components constructed out of the body parts of animals.

An orthodox response to this, and one which some of the more erudite, literate and intellectual Balinese also propound, is that the demons and malevolent spirits (*buta kala*) are themselves just symbols of the more unpleasant aspects of human behaviour and personality. However, in general, this is not an inter-pretation shared by the majority of ordinary Balinese, who conceive of these spirits as completely real.

Moreover, the slaughtering of pigs and other animals is, for many, the centre-piece of large-scale cere-monies, which thus brings together groups of Balinese who co-operate in the work. Without this, the reciprocal labour obligations which are so crucial to the creation and maintenance of communal soli-darity in Balinese life would be severely impaired. In addition, of course, costly sacrifices are the backbone of substantial relations with the ancestors and any diminution of this through the substitution of animals for cheaper and lesser symbols would be supernaturally dangerous.

The arguments of Sai Baba and officials of *agama Hindu* consequently fail to acknowledge many of the most important aspects of the sacrificial use of animals in Balinese customary practice.

ritual purposes enables devotees, not without problems (see below), to continue practising their *adat* obligations alongside non-members. This almost certainly makes
devotees of Baba appear less fanatical and therefore more acceptable to their co-
villagers than the members of Hare Krishna, for whom vegetarianism is an iron rule.

These examples highlight the general orientation of devotees towards other forms
of Hinduism. Most members agreed that Sai Baba conflicts with *adat*, but the blame
for error is rarely placed on ordinary villagers who participate in condemned practices, since it is not their fault that they have been led astray. In a typical Balinese
metaphor, they are likened to chicks who have lost their mother hen and hence do
not know what is 'food' and what is 'rubbish'. Devotees therefore seek to teach,
persuade and provide a good example, and so change *adat* in a tolerant and gradual
way without resorting to confrontation. But there is a tension here. While devotees
are expected to try and change the bad habits of others, they are also sometimes
warned to avoid those who gamble and drink lest they are influenced by these
seductive pastimes. Instead devotees are urged to seek out spiritually advanced
members so that they can improve their own development.

Another way in which Sai Baba worship exists alongside and includes other forms
of Hinduism is that joining it is like adding one more temple to a family's religious
obligations. Balinese are members of several temple congregations, and so adherence
to Sai Baba need not be seen as abandoning other religious duties. Clearly it is a
different form of worship, but in no sense does it necessitate giving up other obligations. Moreover, although Sai Baba membership takes up time, it is not arduous.
There is no compulsion to attend meetings, there are no offerings to make and
expenses are small. It is also refreshingly different and ties one into a completely new
social circle.

Opposition to Sai Baba

Many criticisms of Sai Baba are similar to those made generally about indigenous
new religious movements, because opponents classify it as an *aliran kepercayaan* and
thus as inferior and a threat to *agama Hindu*. For example, Parisada officials, priests
and others note an increasing enthusiasm for religion among all sections of the
Balinese, but are concerned that if they are not provided with sound instruction and
direction they will fall into deviant movements. If this enthusiasm is not channelled
properly, people will become absorbed (*larut*, Ind.) by the search for 'inner potency'
(*sakti*), which should be prevented because it is 'very irrational' (*sangat irasional*, Ind.)
(*Bali Post*, 23 July 1997). The Governor of Bangli, in central Bali, is reported to have
told priests and religious officials to be more active in providing instruction and
correct interpretations of official religion so that ordinary people are not 'ensnared'
(*terjerat*, Ind.) by movements which 'deviate' and 'lead astray' (*menyesatkan*, Ind.)
(*Bali Post*, 25 April 1994). The accusation of deviation from true religion is therefore
used by all sides.

Such criticisms are expressed in another way. In an interview with a high-caste
priest, he argued that the Hindus of India are far ahead of Balinese Hindus in religious
development and in their knowledge of the *weda*, while the Balinese are 'not mentally
ready' (*tidak siap mental*, Ind.) to fully comprehend these teachings. Therefore great
care must be taken over the religious instruction people receive and who provides it.
Officially only priests and the learned experts of the Parisada should teach, while religious education given by others, such as Sai Baba, is suspect and dangerous.

Similarly, he said that Balinese are not yet 'resolute' (*mantap*, Ind.) in their religion; when they are confronted with conflicting teachings, they waver and become 'confused' (*bingung*, Ind.) and hence deviations (*penyimpangan*, Ind.) emerge.

More active official and authorized guidance is also seen as necessary to keep ordinary Balinese within the fold of *agama Hindu*, since otherwise they might join deviant movements which pursue *sakti* as a way of coping with stress, frustrated aspirations and the harsh economic facts of life. To prevent desertion and keep people on the 'true path' to religious certainty, the institutions of Balinese Hinduism must develop people's religious understanding, with both words and deeds (Supartha 1994: 102–3).

It is important to recognize both the differences and similarities between *adat* traditions of religion and *agama Hindu*. The statement, made by officials of *agama Hindu*, that the search for 'power' (*sakti*) is 'irrational' (see above) marks a major move away from *adat* traditions, for which this has been a central idea (Geertz 1995b).[17] But there is also a striking structural continuity as well. Traditional Balinese religious practices were directed from the top by rulers and high-caste priests, with the priests' power and authority based on long immersion in sacred texts and on rituals of purification. Underneath this, however, there have always existed more direct and illicit methods (dangerous rituals, spirit possession, gifts from god) for low castes to acquire independent sources of power with which to resist those who dominated them (Connor 1982). What is emerging now are new but nevertheless similar methods of obtaining power quickly and directly by joining movements in search of *sakti*. From the perspective of powerful state institutions which define orthodox religious teachings, elites again denounce such new methods as illegitimate and deviant. The insistence on a religious and theological orthodoxy stemming from the centre and its concern over a too-easily obtained and dangerous 'power' acquired by those from below clearly parallel the power structure of 'traditional' Bali. Thus the control of religion becomes a political weapon for maintaining authority and order.

Despite their claim that they are only interested in spiritual development, members of Sai Baba are often accused of surreptitiously trying to increase their stock of 'potency' (*sakti*). This is because vegetarianism, various abstentions, silent and private meditation and the recitation of mantra are easily interpreted by opponents as traditional forms of asceticism designed to augment *sakti*. One devotee told me he had a hard time convincing his friends that he was not trying to learn 'black magic'. In fact, devotees condemn the pursuit of *sakti* because it emphasizes self-interest and separates one from God, and thus merely brings the illusion of happiness. Raising one's spirituality, in contrast, draws one closer to God and thus brings real happiness.

Balinese village religion is communal and depends both on families and on the relationships between families. Religious ceremonies and communal activities require a solidary kin group, the different members of which have a range of obligations to each other and to other households and larger associations in the village. If a single adult reneges on these obligations, the ramifications can be far-reaching, and recalcitrant individuals are put under a great deal of social pressure to reform their behaviour. Because Sai Baba is individualistic, devotees are often accused by their relatives or co-villagers of sowing dissension in their families, since it is said that they

[17] It is interesting to note the frequent use of the concept of *rohani* (spiritual) in the many books published by the Parisada, and the way in which *agama* is defined in terms of spirituality (for example, Punyatmadja 1976b: 9). As already noted, there is no equivalent in Balinese of this Arabic-derived Indonesian term.

can no longer participate fully in household and village ritual activities and thus become a threat to family and village harmony. Practices of vegetarianism and the refusal to slaughter animals mean that their participation in communal ritual activities is problematic, and devotees are stereotyped as dogmatically critical of cock-fighting, which is the great Balinese male pastime. Devotees have repeatedly told me that their refusal to eat meat has caused long-term battles with close kin, who worry about their sanity or that they will leave *adat* religion, an outcome which invariably means social death. Younger members are frequently scolded by their parents and ordered to give up membership. Usually, however, as household members gradually find that the devotee continues to take part in all their ceremonies, they begin to soften their attitude, sometimes even to the extent that some of the devotee's kin also become members. Devotees are also said to force their wives and children to become members against their will, and indeed some men admitted that they have used heavy-handed tactics to get their wives to attend services. On the other hand, those female devotees I know appear to be very enthusiastic.

While members mostly argue that an aim of Sai Baba is to 'repair' Balinese Hinduism, its adversaries often argue that it is out to 'destroy' (*menghapus*, Ind.) it. That it is vegetarian, egalitarian, anti-ritual, and so forth, and that its 'god' is an obscure man from India are often taken to signify that it is fundamentally opposed to Balinese Hinduism, that the two cannot coexist and that it must therefore be resisted. As a result, it is branded as deviant, subversive and insidious.

Identity & the global world

The creation of *agama Hindu* has enabled Balinese to differentiate themselves from Muslims and Christians by defining their ethnic identity in terms of Hinduism. However, as discussed in the previous chapter, the process of ethnic identity formation has been complicated by the fact that Hinduism is no longer exclusive to Bali, and because competing varieties of Hinduism produce competing forms of identity.

For many long-time devotees, and especially those who have visited India and seen Baba, the attachment to Him becomes so strong that it encourages the formation of an identity which is removed from concerns that are peculiarly Balinese. The rejection of some *adat* practices on the basis of a universal message marks out devotees as increasingly committed to a global world. For example, in the talks at services, members make frequent reference to terms such as 'universal', the 'world' and 'global', and hardly mention 'Bali'.

This new identity is about the individual in the world or, more precisely, the individual in his or her specific relationship to the universal God. It is an identity based on the essential self deep within one. Experienced and dedicated devotees frequently speak about improving and developing themselves, monitoring and reforming their behaviour and policing their thoughts. Such a preoccupation with one's thoughts, desires and feelings implies an internalization of religion, in which the devotee's 'emotions, attitudes and conscience become increasingly pivotal in validating behaviour in a manner which recalls Protestant values' (Kent 2000: 12). This represents a considerable transformation of the Balinese self as it has been analysed by Geertz. In *adat* religion, communal harmony is a matter of the performance of divinely sanctioned relations with kin, other Balinese, ancestors and spirits, conceptualized as interdependent parts of a structured whole. In this it is the public, outer persona that is important, not an individual's particular personality or biography (Geertz 1973b). Failure to carry out obligations results in supernatural sanctions, pollution or ostracism by the community, and issues of sin and conscience are absent. According to Hardacre, writing about Japanese new religious movements, such a system sees the self as '*under*' the control of external powers. Devotion to Baba, however, begins to change all this. The relations which now matter are those within the self, within one's own mind and body, and those between oneself and Baba. In this transformed situation, the self is '*in*' control (Hardacre 1986: 15, her emphasis). Concretely this change appears to manifest itself in various ways: in how devotees speak about their attempts to control and overcome the 'internal enemies' of anger, jealousy and pride; in private meditation and prayer; in cleansing the mind and body through vegetarianism and abstentions from drugs and illicit sex; and so forth.

Over time this nascent identity progressively takes on a specific shape. It is moulded by the changes in lifestyle that members undergo, and gradually filled with content through participation in charitable events, educational classes, singing *bhajan*, listening to members' talks and even visiting Baba's ashram in India. With its focus on the divine person of Baba, this identity expands its horizon outwards as members come to realize that they share an essential commonality with fellow devotees from India, Europe, Africa and elsewhere. For many, of course, this identity remains partial and elusive, because they never leave Bali, but they do begin to experience it vicariously.

I suggest that this new identity gradually replaces or submerges the 'delusory' (Balinese) self which used to be socially presented to others (cf. Babb 1986: 191). Meditation, prayer, devotion and singing are the activities which help the devotee to discover, strengthen and develop the once hidden inner self. By modifying some of the ritual and communal connections with one's fellow Balinese through a quest for personal realization, members procure the conditions for establishing new spiritual relationships with others from very different cultural backgrounds, with Baba acting as the fixed centre drawing them all into a community of equals. Though devotees maintain their involvement in *adat* ritual practices, they have a changed orientation to them and a different understanding of what they are doing. For example, devotees have told me that during temple ceremonies they do not pray to Balinese gods, but to Baba. This separation from other villagers is reinforced by their vegetarianism, their abstention from cock-fighting and their regular prayer and meditation. Consciousness of these differences renders attachments to local identities (village, status, class, etc.) less meaningful and they begin to dissolve into the wider and more encompassing identity that grows from devotion to Baba. As Baba becomes the centre of their lives and as they become conscious that they belong to a worldwide 'imagined community' (Anderson 1983), being 'Balinese' – seeing oneself as 'Balinese' – assumes less significance. The creation of a transnational identity is therefore effected through a conversion of the essential inner self into a public outer self. It is as though the devotee is turned inside out, and indeed many claim they have been radically changed by Baba.

Conclusion

The importance of Sai Baba, as part of a broad front of Hindu reform ideas in Bali, appears to lie in how it articulates and defines patterns of social conflict. For nearly a century various Balinese institutions (high priesthood, hierarchy, elaborate and expensive ritual, etc.) have been the object of criticism by the Dutch colonial regime, state religious agencies and, mostly commoner, Balinese reformers. One especially significant response to this has been the creation of *agama Hindu*. However, this new religion has not been an unqualified success.

Initially emerging from debates between commoners and elites in the early part of the century, it subsequently developed into an orthodoxy shaped and controlled principally by state institutions such as the Parisada. Attempts to educate the Balinese population into this religion, through the school curriculum, standardization of religious practice, directives on how to stage important ceremonies and calendric festivals and the publication of books detailing its doctrines, have generated some unexpected responses.

Agama Hindu's rejection of the notion of *sakti*, an idea central to village and court traditions, has coincided with the emergence of religious movements (*aliran keper-cayaan*), which many ordinary Balinese have joined and in which the pursuit of *sakti* is a main, if not explicitly advertised, aim. In addition, because the tenets of *agama Hindu* are esoteric and unfamiliar, many Balinese have difficulty in applying them to customary activities and hence they remain tangential to everyday life.

Equally significant is the rise of devotional movements, such as Sai Baba. Members of these movements endorse *agama Hindu*'s substitution of spirituality for inner potency, its opposition to excessive ritual and the ritual use of animal flesh and its attempts generally to reinterpret the meaning and purpose of ritual activity along ethical lines. Despite this, *agama Hindu* is considered very unsatisfactory. Its theology and its high God are impersonal and abstract, its spirituality lacks substance and a focus, and its strictly controlled orthodoxy is inimical to religious liberty and pluralism. Moreover, the continuing support given by the Parisada (because it is still dominated by high priests and high castes) to the structures of hierarchy, however modified, has alienated many commoner Balinese. Joining Sai Baba provides the unique combination of a personal and loving relationship with a living God, together with a relatively egalitarian theology and social organization, which help maintain the struggle against the inequalities embedded in Balinese institutions.

However the matter cannot be left there because interpreting devotion to Baba as a reflection of how religious ideologies articulate forms of political conflict is too mechanical. I have noted that a rationalized perspective may be an effect of membership rather than a cause, that many people join because of problems related to purely personal circumstances, that the challenges faced by members are often more to do with overcoming strong and debilitating emotions than with opposition to the hierarchical structures of Balinese society, and because there is a simple desire to be good Hindus and better people and to enhance the general good of society by establishing a higher moral code. As a result, Sai Baba cannot be seen just as a religious vehicle for pursuing political ends; for many devotees, it is more a matter of adopting particular religious convictions which enhance their own lives.[18]

[18] A note on the relationship between Sai Baba and modernity in Bali is in order. In one sense, the movement expounds a fundamentalist doctrine, in that it tries to reach back to the essential teachings of God, but it is also avowedly modern. The talks given at meetings are provided not only by Balinese but by foreign visitors (including westerners) passing through, and the language used is modern Indonesian and sometimes English. Bali is a location of mass tourism, and tourism has become emblematic of 'modernity', 'development' and 'progress' (explicit goals of the Indonesian state). Balinese who travel to India are themselves tourists, who see the sights, take cameras and experience the wonders of a new culture. When they return and give a talk about their experiences, there is as much emphasis on the journey as on seeing

Baba, partly because the complex arrangements of buying tickets and getting visas are facilitated by the miraculous intervention of Baba (cf. Gombrich and Obeyesekere 1988: 54–5). The journey is also a pilgrimage. Like the Sai Baba movement in general, this is anti-ritual because offerings are not required to attach oneself to the source of religious knowledge; one can go there and experience it directly. The journey is thus a kind of alternative modernity, which combines tourism with a spiritual quest. Even if the talks given at meetings appear to be divided into a section on all aspects of the journey and a section on the religious experience, in fact these tell a single story.

Sai Baba is represented as the rediscovery of an ancient religious tradition which focuses on the fundamentals of religious faith and belief by stripping away the allegedly superfluous accretions of customary religious practices, which are said to have concealed this tradition. But it is also seen as a modern form of worship, tailored to the demands of a fast-paced society and more in tune with new ideologies of individualism, democracy and personal achievement.

9

Hare Krishna in Bali
mad for God

Introduction

The International Society for the Study of Krishna Consciousness, or ISKCON as it is known by devotees in the west and in the academic literature that has examined it, was established in Bali in the late 1970s.[1] However, because it was considered subversive and thought to harbour communist sympathies and because the police received complaints about its activities, the Parisada recommended to the Ministry of Religion that it was not in the general interests of the Balinese. As a result, it was banned in 1984 and remains an illegal organization to this day.

The movement was originally located in the area of Denpasar, known as Renon, at a time when this area was largely undeveloped. As Renon became the site of many government buildings, including the governor's office, the Hare Krishnas left. They moved twice more, until a devotee donated a plot of land in a largely empty area of the countryside on the coast, just north of the tourist resort of Sanur, where they have now built an ashram and a temple. This is the only centre that exists in Bali. One of the reasons the organization has remained in existence despite the ban is that it has always accepted that it must keep a distance, socially and physically, from centres of population. In its present position, the temple cannot even be seen from the unmetalled road which runs within fifty metres of it, and there are only two or three houses nearby.

In most respects the Hare Krishna movement constitutes a more radical departure from *adat* religion and *agama Hindu* than does Sai Baba. Vegetarianism is not an option but a strict rule; long-term membership entails initiation, which includes shaving the head, donning the *dhoti* (or *sari* for women) and taking a new name; and there is a much stronger opposition to certain aspects of *adat* ritual practice. Consequently, joining the movement entails a more decisive break with other forms of Balinese Hinduism, with some of the institutions of mainstream Balinese society and with past lifestyles. It is, however, very easy to leave the movement and re-enter more orthodox forms of Balinese Hinduism. While I do not know anyone who has left

---

[1] Probably because the rapid development of ISKCON in the United States and parts of Europe during the period of the counter-culture movement in the 1960s and 1970s gained it an unenviable reputation for the way it supposedly preyed on the weak and maladjusted, the academic literature on the Hare Krishnas is quite extensive. However, since much of this literature deals with ISKCON's reception in the west and concerns a context very different from that of the Hare Krishnas in Bali, I have not found much of it particularly relevant to my purposes. The material I have found useful is: Rochford (1985) and Bromley and Shinn (1989) who have written about ISKCON in the United States, and Burr (1984) and Knott (1986), who have described ISKCON in England. I provided some information on the emergence of the Hare Krishnas in America in Chapter 7.

Plate 9.1   Married woman devotee of Hare Krishna welcoming other members as they arrive at the Hare Krishna ashram situated on the outskirts of Denpasar. She has replaced her typical Balinese clothes for a more Indian style of dress

Plate 9.2 Portrait of A.C. Bhaktivedanta Swami Prabhupada, the founder of the Hare Krishna movement, in the worship hall at the Hare Krishna ashram

Sai Baba to join Hare Krishna, several ex-members of the latter have subsequently joined the former. They all told me that they quit the Hare Krishnas because it was too *keras* (Ind.), that is, too harsh and difficult.

Sai Baba members in general hold derogatory views of the Hare Krishnas. They are typified as quick to anger and as intolerant, and to have overblown 'egos' (their word). Considering themselves to have a monopoly on the truth, they harangue members if they do not follow the rules. It is possible that these and other disparaging comments made by members of Sai Baba about the Hare Krishnas are a displacement of similar stereotypes held by others concerning the activities and values of Sai Baba devotees. In relation to spiritual development, Sai Baba members claim that moving from Hare Krishna to the former is an advance (*maju*, Ind.), whilst the reverse is considered a retreat (*mundur*, Ind.).

My purpose in this chapter is to explain why the membership of Hare Krishna is very small and consists disproportionately of young men who are poor, unemployed and detached from many of the institutions of mainstream Balinese society. In brief, while ISKCON preaches a doctrine of spiritual development based on a devotional philosophy not dissimilar to Sai Baba, it does so in the context of a much stricter regimen of prohibitions, which makes its orientation to more orthodox forms of Balinese Hinduism considerably more radical and oppositional. This regimen requires members to undergo a quite dramatic change in their physical appearance and lifestyle as they are initiated into the movement.

An important consequence of such a change is the forced adoption of an exclusive identity, which, because the Hare Krishna organization is illegal and known to be despised by other Balinese, cannot be proclaimed in a positive way (except of course within the membership) but must remain hidden most of the time. It is true that the Hare Krishnas in Bali associate themselves with a worldwide religious tradition and, in this sense, like Sai Baba devotees, see themselves as participating in an imagined community. However, for several reasons which clearly distinguish the Hare Krishnas from the latter, this participation provides no practical opportunities at all to link members with the global network of ISKCON branches. There is no obvious centre in India to which they can make a pilgrimage; ISKCON members have virtually no resources to travel abroad; the founder of the movement, Prabhupada, is now dead; and members from other countries rarely, if ever, visit the centre in Bali. Consequently, the Hare Krishna movement on the island is not only isolated from the rest of Balinese society, but it is also cut off from Krishna devotees in the outside world.

The Hare Krishnas do not have any ethic of social service to the community, because they see involvement with the outside world as an obstacle to spiritual advancement. Anyway, charity work of the kind Sai Baba members perform would be very difficult, because Balinese society shuns the Hare Krishnas. Moreover, ISKCON is not focused on a living human being conceived of as God and who can perform miracles and be seen and touched, but has to rely instead on the more abstract entity of Krishna. Being illegal, it has to keep out of sight, but its partial invisibility only serves to heighten outsiders' suspicions of what its members are doing. In short, whereas Sai Baba has a broad appeal and builds bridges to the wider Balinese society, the Hare Krishna movement in Bali is extremely restricted.

The membership of Hare Krishna

The total membership of ISKCON in Bali, I was told, is probably about 1,000 people, from a total population of some 3 million (in Britain it is 9,000 at most (Knott 1986: 14)). However, the number who regularly attended the Sunday meetings at the temple rarely reached seventy-five. Regulars claimed that many more would come on a more frequent basis if they could afford the high costs of travel to cover the long distances which separate them from the ashram. On the other hand, it was admitted that many are probably lapsed members. Maintaining a commitment to the practices and values of the Hare Krishnas in their home villages, whilst surrounded by hostile non-believers and without the support of like-minded companions, was acknowledged to be very difficult. None the less, on Krishna's birthday in August, the temple is crowded, with perhaps 300–400 devotees in attendance.

I cannot be confident about the profile of the entire membership because I never met most of them. However, the profile of the core members who attend on most Sundays appears to be similar to that of ISKCON in the west (Burr 1984: 21), in that predominantly they are young, poor and male; the great majority in Bali are also commoners rather than high-caste. Many of them have left home, and either live permanently in the ashram, in temporary lodgings, or in shacks in the peri-urban districts of rapidly expanding Denpasar. A very small number of devotees have professional jobs and several are members of the gentry, and in these cases it is usually the entire family that has joined.[2] A majority of devotees are below the age of twenty-five when they become members. Since the movement has been in existence for at least fifteen years, the fact that most of the core members are still young suggests that turnover is rapid and that people remain members for relatively short periods.

I was told that the membership included some single, unmarried women, but I never encountered any. Many young men leave their home villages on finishing school if they cannot find work there, or experience difficult relationships with their parents and siblings, and they gravitate to the towns and tourist centres in search of jobs. Some young women also follow this course of action, but usually only if their reputations can be protected by finding them suitable accommodation, either with relatives or with their employers. Given the scandal and shame that would ensue for her family, it is almost inconceivable that a young, unattached woman would join an illegal, male-dominated and isolated organization such as the Hare Krishnas.

The small membership is, of course, partly a result of the ban imposed on the movement, which entails that ISKCON must keep a very low profile and upset as few people as possible. In the west, Hare Krishnas used to dance and sing in the streets with shaven heads and in full saffron dress, sell literature to passers-by and attempt to recruit people in public spaces, but in Bali such activities are illegal and their performance would quickly come to the notice of the police. Some members told me that they wished they could go out amongst the public so that they could spread

[2] Several of these families live in new suburbs of Denpasar, which appear at the moment to lack many of the institutions of village communal life. Since the new residents of these areas come from different areas of Bali, these new developments have not grown organically. There is no paddy land and so no *subak* associations which regulate water use. *Banjar*, if they have been formed at all, are very weak, and communal temples are almost non-existent. Families who have moved into these areas worship in their houseyard temples or return to the temples of their villages of origin. As there is less pressure to conform to *adat* religion, households are more at liberty to act independently of others, and as a result it is somewhat easier to belong to 'deviant' movements, such as Hare Krishna.

word of Krishna's love. However, those who have continuing relations with the wider community, through regular work or membership in *banjar* and other village associations, prefer not to publicize their involvement in a banned organization, and instead hide their identity by growing their hair and wearing ordinary clothing. About the only members who shave their heads and wear the *shikha* pony-tail are those who live in the ashram.[3] In more recent times, ISKCON members in the United States have taken to disguising their identity by wearing ordinary dress and wigs when they are out selling literature, asking for donations and attempting to recruit new members (Rochford, 1985: 179).

ISKCON's illegal status has created severe limitations on its sphere of operations and it is therefore cut off from the rest of Balinese society in a way that Sai Baba is not. As a result, recruitment to the movement is almost wholly through private introductions and the personal social networks of existing members. Moreover, because the movement has very few financial resources, the accommodation at the ashram remains very limited and most members are forced to live amongst non-believers. This makes for a difficult life and leads to a high drop-out rate and transfer to other movements.

The Hare Krishna movement has great problems reproducing itself, because its practices are more extreme than those of Sai Baba. Sai Baba's considerably more moderate theology enables its members to maintain close links with *adat* religion and *agama Hindu* and to keep up a dialogue with these, even if this is at times highly critical. Its social service ethic and the lack of an identifying uniform also encourage a much more tolerant attitude in the wider public. Sai Baba thus provides a haven for those Balinese who are unhappy with various aspects of *adat* religion but who wish to minimize the effect that membership in a suspect organization might have on their generally stable and respectable lives.

Doctrine & practice in ISKCON

ISKCON members have a rather similar orientation to its doctrine and theology to that of Sai Baba members to theirs. The former movement has a much more elaborate theology than the latter, but the only person who ever tried spontaneously to convey some of this to me was a middle-aged woman who teaches religious education in a primary school. Every other conversation I had with members about what it was that attracted them to join and what maintained their commitment always revolved around the impact that devotion to Krishna had personally made on their individual lives. It was not any abstruse philosophy which they talked about

---

[3] Balinese almost never shave their heads after childhood, and so Balinese perceive the practice of shaving the head amongst the Hare Krishnas to be quite extraordinary. In Bali, as elsewhere in the world, hair carries a heavy symbolic load, but it has ambiguous qualities. A child's head is first shaved during the ritual (*ngotonin*) conducted on its third birthday. On this occasion, the hair is said to be 'hot' (*panes*) and is supposed to be deposited in a pat of cow dung, which makes it 'cool' (*tis*). I have heard it said that the hair 'carries the gods' (*mundut déwa*) but, so to speak, only their negative qualities, and so cutting the hair is a kind of purificatory act. When adult, however, the hair is said to be 'cool' and has curative properties. When children wound themselves, a woman is likely to rub and press the wound with her hair after spitting on it. Ideally, the hair should only be cut on auspicious days, husbands should not cut their hair when their wives are pregnant, men should not cut their hair when the rice is ripening in the fields, and women and priests should never cut their hair at all (though today many women break this injunction and keep their hair short). For a Krishna devotee to appear in public with a shaven head is thus an act of dramatic separation, and one which is probably quite incomprehensible to most ordinary Balinese.

but real changes in their daily existence and in their emotional outlook. Devotees said they changed from being unhappy, angry and confused to being confident, healthy and calm (cf. Gelberg 1989: 147).

The first thing that most members mention is the protection which Krishna affords anyone who truly believes in Him. Krishna has power and authority (*berkuasa*, Ind.) over everything; He is the best and truest friend; and He is in everyone's heart and mind. The only way to gain truth and reach everlasting peace and contentment is to expand one's spiritual consciousness (*kesadaran*, Ind.) of Krishna so that He dominates one's thoughts. The route to bliss is always to think of Him and only Him, and the way to accomplish this is to adopt the strict regime that ISKCON lays down.

Broadly speaking, the regime consists of four elements: vegetarianism, chanting the Hare Krishna mantra, a daily routine of devotional rituals and adoption of the dhoti and shaven head. In Bali, while the first two are supremely important, the latter two are accorded much less significance. The reason for this is that vegetarianism and chanting the mantra can be maintained when absent from the temple, while the other two are geared to living in the ashram. Since only a few people are permanently resident in the ashram, the rituals and characteristic dress, which are a major aspect of daily life in ISKCON temples in the west, play only a small role in Bali.

The vast majority of Balinese are meat-eaters. There is no word in either Balinese or Indonesian to translate 'vegetarian' and consequently the English word is used. Even Brahmana eat meat, though most confine themselves to consumption of duck, chicken and pork, which are considered far less polluting than goat and beef, which are 'hot' (*panes*). The strict vegetarianism of the Hare Krishnas, which extends to a ban on eating eggs, therefore stands in stark contrast to typical Balinese practices and is one of the main reasons the movement is seen as unacceptable and deviant by ordinary Balinese.

In addition to meat and eggs, there is a ban on alcohol, drugs (including cigarettes), coffee, garlic and onions and on all forms of sexual relations other than for the procreation of children within marriage (Gelberg 1989: 143). Several reasons underpin the requirement for vegetarianism. All living creatures have souls, which can be improved to live in higher life forms, and so they should not be killed to provide enjoyment; and meat poisons the body, causing illness. But the principal reason for these prohibitions is that obeying them enables Krishna to be approached more easily and securely.

A distinction is drawn between the permanence of the soul and the transience of the body, but between the two there is a dynamic tension and struggle. The soul cannot exist on its own but requires the body to be its temporary container and vehicle. Since the body is a sensual object, it draws great pleasures from its functioning in the material world and therefore becomes extremely demanding. All meat, alcohol and spicy foods, though apparently enjoyable, eventually cause pain and illness, confuse the mind and increase feelings of sexual desire. The worldly pleasures that the tyranny of the body creates, however, are illusory and must be overcome if the soul is to develop spiritually. The problem is that, although Krishna exists in everyone, He occupies only a tiny place in one's soul and consequently life is dominated by bodily desires. The main aim of Hare Krishna practices is to subordinate the body to the soul through right action and devotion to Krishna, which thus enables Krishna's place in the soul to expand until the individual soul becomes one with Krishna. This is a monistic philosophy, in the sense that God and the soul are ultimately indivisible.

There appears, however, to be a doctrinal difference between ISKCON branches elsewhere in the world and the Hare Krishnas in Bali in regard to how members conceive of their bodies. In the British movement the point of vegetarianism and other prohibitions is to 'defeat' the body. A central concept is articulated in the idea: 'I am not my body, I am spirit-soul' (Burr 1984: 140). In their practice, members pursue this idea to its logical conclusion. Devotees reject their bodies as corrupt and project on to their bodies all the ills which they see as characteristic of the outside society. They have to live in their bodies and so, as they enter the temple with their bodies, they also bring 'society' into the temple. The body therefore becomes the site of the struggle they have with the materialism of the outside world, their bodies being a constant reminder of the perils of that world. Hare Krishnas therefore abuse their bodies and treat them badly: 'they deprive them of sleep, take cold baths, sleep on hard floors, put up with little heating in winter, accept a poor diet, and repress their sexual urges. Often devotees are very tired and not infrequently ill' (ibid.: 176–7).

I never noticed this aggression towards the body in Bali, and no member ever spoke to me in these terms. Those I got to know quite well seemed remarkably healthy and ate a good diet of rice, vegetables and plenty of fruit. When we were eating together, members often ate a lot and with enjoyment. As is normal during communal meals in Bali, members urged each other to take second helpings before they did so themselves. Members never prostrated their bodies in front of other members as they do elsewhere, did not seem to despise their bodies and did not mistreat them. Even those who lived in the ashram had beds to sleep on, and every time I visited I was immediately given several types of fruit to eat. The impression I gained was that they were not so much bent on defeating their bodies or denying an identification with them; rather, they cared for their bodies by closely monitoring what they consumed. I was frequently warned that alcohol, cigarettes and meat polluted the body, making it unfit for the soul. In that sense, they seemed more concerned to 'purify' their bodies than to defeat them. Members spoke of trying to keep their bodies 'clean' (*bersih*, Ind.), both by obeying prohibitions and by frequent bathing, the latter being a normal Balinese activity anyway. At one level, as with Hare Krishnas in Britain, Balinese devotees argued that the body is a hindrance to spiritual development, but at another level they made a distinction between bodies well cared for and kept uncontaminated and bodies fouled by the ingestion of prohibited substances.

I suspect this difference is due to the fact that the Hare Krishnas in Bali are isolated from the mainstream movement of ISKCON and do not have experts to teach them orthodox doctrine, and therefore they interpret the prohibitions using Balinese ideas. Unavoidably left to draw on their own conceptual resources, they derive their ideas about the relationship between the body and the soul from those widely extant in Balinese culture. In this the substantial body is the material envelope which contains the invisible spirit of the ancestor which descends from heaven and reincarnates into the body at birth. During life, the body often becomes polluted (*sebel, leteh*) and purificatory rituals are a central element of all rites of transition. At death, the polluting body is removed through the rituals of cremation, allowing the vital essence to join the purified ancestors. These ideas do not posit the body as an obstacle to the inner self; rather, the body is viewed positively as the necessary means by which life can exist on earth. Despite becoming devotees of Krishna, their ideas about the body and its relationship to the self remain very recognizably Balinese.

The vegetarianism and other prohibitions are, so to speak, the negative side of the attempt to subdue the body and distance oneself from the debilitating world of sensual pleasure. The positive side is the chanting of the Hare Krishna mantra:

Hare Krishna, Hare Krishna, Krishna Krishna, Hare Hare;
Hare Rama, Hare Rama, Rama Rama, Hare Hare.

The rule is that the mantra must be chanted a minimum of 1728 times each day. To facilitate this, each devotee is given a string consisting of 108 beads, called a *japa*, which is kept in a bag (*kantong japa*) slung over the shoulder. Each bead represents a single chant, and so to complete the requisite number of chants the devotee must go round the string sixteen times.

When not otherwise engaged, devotees return to their chanting, with their right hand inside the bag counting off the beads. As soon as they stop talking, they begin chanting. The mantra should be chanted out loud, so that animals and insects can hear it and derive merit. Such repetitive chanting is not a feature of any form of Balinese religion, and devotees acknowledged that both this and the vegetarianism made joining the movement problematic, and probably led to many abandoning it at an early stage. However, the Hare Krishnas do not insist on all the prohibitions being observed or a full complement of chants during the period in which potential recruits are deciding whether to commit themselves totally (cf. Shinn 1989: 129). It is only once a new member has been in the movement for some time and has become gradually accustomed to the regimes that the prohibitions must be fully adhered to.

Once this stage has been reached devotees completely reject the idea that chanting is a burden. The point of it is to direct one's thoughts to Krishna and thereby obliterate everything else. After a few minutes, the chanting begins to drown out competing thoughts in one's mind and, according to some, the problem is not how to continue but how to stop. The rhythmic tones of the chant induce a sense of peace and calm, which releases stress and makes it easier to focus on Krishna. As the chant fills one's head, it becomes impossible to think of anything else, and feelings of anger, envy and despondency are washed away. Several members told me that, unless they chant for a considerable period of time in the morning, they usually have a miserable day.[4]

An important difference between the Hare Krishna mantra and those used by Balinese priests, *balian* and other practitioners of magic (which are not chanted in a repetitive manner) is that the former is not and should not be secret. It should be disseminated as widely as possible, so that everyone may benefit from it, and it should be chanted out loud because listeners gain from hearing it. Because anyone can chant it, the mantra is democratic, egalitarian and universal (Knott 1986: 25).

A side-effect of the chanting is that it provides a structure to the day. A frequent theme of devotees' conversations with me was how their previous life was dominated by boredom and unproductive activity. Chanting begins on waking up in the morning. This is followed by a shower, more chanting and breakfast. If a member does not have regular work to go to, empty periods of the day can be filled with further chanting, alongside some study, meditation and prayer. No doubt, this is rather idealized, but the point is that their days now conform to this ideal much more closely than was the case in the past.

---

[4] According to Gelberg (1989: 152), the mantra literally is Krishna, 'and thus to invoke Krishna's holy names is to directly invoke Krishna Himself'. Krishna is the object of the Vedas and so His name contains all their knowledge, and so to chant is to become enlightened. Chanting eventually brings liberation and ecstatic love for Krishna. Although no Balinese devotee explicitly expounded this belief, it certainly corresponds with what they do say about the mantra.

Reasons for joining Hare Krishna

Most members were introduced to Hare Krishna by friends, who either gave them some literature to read or brought them to the ashram to see what went on. Several I spoke to had been members of *aliran kepercayaan*, such as Bambu Kuning, but had not profited from the experience and had left. Clearly some of these found Hare Krishna no more enticing and so moved on. Those who remained say they found the community friendly, sympathetic and welcoming. The fact that there are no dues to pay makes membership much easier.

Devotees provided reasons for joining which were remarkably similar to those given by Sai Baba devotees. They frequently remarked that they were unsatisfied with the lack of knowledge and understanding which villagers displayed about their ritual obligations. Parents, teachers and priests were regularly accused of being incapable of providing answers to the questions they had begun asking themselves about their religious activities. The hypocritical behaviour of schoolteachers and their inability to provide interesting and informative lessons on religious issues were subjected to a criticism every bit as strong as that I received from devotees of Sai Baba.

Hare Krishna members, like devotees of Sai Baba, also represent themselves as engaged on a spiritual quest. However, members' accounts of why they joined also regularly mentioned how their previous lives were made unhappy through some combination of unemployment, parental conflict, depression over a lost girlfriend, boredom and poverty. But these were rarely presented as the specific reasons for joining. In other words, while some young men possibly did embark on a spiritual journey galvanized by motives to discover deeper religious truths, it is just as likely that, having found themselves in a new community which performed many of the functions of a surrogate family and which provided some sense of meaning and purpose, they began to view their passage to a new life within the context of the religious doctrines they gradually acquired and the practices they adopted, and reinvented this as the spiritual quest of an enquiring mind, a series of chance encounters restructured into a destiny.[5]

Opposition to *adat* religion

In the west, ISKCON is extremely hierarchical and has structured its members' religious, administrative and other roles within a 'caste framework' (Burr 1984: 115–16). However, unlike in India, where caste status is inherited, in ISKCON it is conceived as achieved, so that members can improve their status as they move up from menial labouring jobs around the temple to managerial and priestly functions.

ISKCON in Bali is both similar and different. The dominant view is that because the world now exists in the fourth and most depraved era, the *kali yug*, the caste system is

---

[5] It is nevertheless worth pointing out that, in conversions to ISKCON in the United States, 'a strong common denominator was a quest for meaning that was finally satisfied in the specific teaching and stories' about Krishna (Shinn 1989: 132). However, there is a considerable problem with such explanations, since they are almost always derived from accounts of the process given several years after the event. It is likely that such accounts are reframed through a focus on the end result, which, having become very important to the individual life, supplies a new meaning and structure to what may have been a much more chaotic and directionless process.

in a hopeless mess. What people actually do bears little relation to the functions that the system ideally provides for the different ranks. In reality, today, all are *Sudra* and only Krishna can make real Brahmana. Consequently, while the Hare Krishnas do not have an ideological objection to the hierarchy, they interpret it not as *kasta* but as *warna* (see Chapter 4), an interpretation which is thus based on merit and (spiritual) achievement rather than on birth and ascription. In its views about hierarchy, then, ISKCON in Bali has a similar orientation to its counterparts in the west, and to the Sai Baba movement.

In practice, however, since there are very few members of the gentry in the organization, anti-caste feelings are frequently aired, especially in relation to high priests, and members are not given caste rankings as they are in branches of ISKCON elsewhere. High Balinese is rarely used and, as with Sai Baba, the use of Indonesian is prominent. As a result, ISKCON's 'political' stance is somewhat more egalitarian than that of Sai Baba, which goes part of the way to explaining the Parisada's antipathy to it. It is not surprising, therefore, that members blame priests and others in powerful positions for the organization's illegal status.

The causes of most of the problems which the Hare Krishnas claim *adat* religion suffers from are laid at the door of the priests. Their strict control of the dissemination of sacred religious literature condemns the general population to ignorance. Ordinary Balinese are wary of seeking permission to read the texts for fear of inciting the priests' anger. Devotees even assert that the priests themselves do not like to read these texts because the teachings contained in them conflict with their private material interests (*kepentingan pribadi*, Ind.). Consequently, Balinese only know how to perform their rituals and do not understand the religious truths on which they are founded. Cast adrift in this way, they have succumbed to the pleasures of the body, which is why they spend so much time gambling, drinking and eating meat. According to one devotee, all Balinese are mad (*gila*, Ind.), but while 'most are mad for cars, wealth, prestige and sex, we are mad for God'. Balinese are always angry and jealous of others' successes, and are thus engaged in an endless but fruitless competition with others.

Hare Krishna devotees, like those of Sai Baba, argue that fundamental religious truths are contained in *adat* religion, but they are locked away in certain palm-leaf texts, which most people cannot read, and the institutional structures of Balinese society make it almost impossible to release them.[6] In the distant past when, it is claimed, Bali was theologically much closer to India, these truths were widely known. But as contact was lost Bali began to diverge and the truths became hidden and subverted by the priests. One of the reasons for this is that the truths of Krishna must come down a direct line of teachers from Krishna, because this is the only guarantee of authenticity. As Bali went its own way, the teachings became confused and fragmented (*pecah*, Ind.). They became 'like a coconut which is thrown to the ground and smashes into many pieces', as one devotee explained. Ideally, the teachings must be handed down from hand to hand so that they remain intact.

Because *adat* religion and *agama Hindu* are said to be ultimately founded on the *weda*, even if this is not realized by their adherents, and even if the links between the rituals and the underlying theological truths have been lost or subverted, much that

---

[6] I am here referring to the more 'sacred' texts, written in a combination of Sanskrit and Kawi, which are used by high priests, the reading of which can cause madness unless one is ritually prepared. Many other palm-leaf texts (treatises on medicine, traditional buildings, chronicles, poems, such as the Ramayana, and so forth) have been published in accessible forms. It is the former, which still remain out of reach to most Balinese, which are the ones supposedly containing religious truth.

their adherents do is said to be in tune with Hare Krishna practice. In the company of their families and village communities, the members of Hare Krishna therefore perform many of the calendric rituals of other forms of Balinese Hinduism, but they do so with the added understanding of what they are all about.

The Hare Krishnas claim that in *adat* religion there is a gap between the performance of rituals and adherents' comprehension of why they must be conducted. This gap is filled with false ideas about 'tradition' (*tradisi*, Ind.) and an excessive concern with getting the offerings right. Galungan, for example, is a much loved pan-Bali festival when all the Balinese gods descend to earth. The focal act of the ceremony, apart from prayer in houseyard temples, is the communal slaughtering of pigs and, for some, the vast consumption of the delicacy known as *lawar* (cooked vegetables mixed with spices and raw pig's blood). The Hare Krishnas interpret Galungan as a ceremony about the defeat of evil, and therefore cannot countenance the killing of pigs, which is just another evil act. Consequently, they substitute jackfruits and coconuts, which they cut up and divide.

Two other issues which members often remark on are the extravagant offerings that accompany all Balinese rituals, and the diversity of village customs and ritual practices, which, in Balinese, is referred to as *desa kala patra*. Balinese ceremonies require many expensive offerings and are therefore criticized because the costs bear heavily on poorer people. This is made even worse because the real reasons for using them have been lost; consequently, offerings have become symbols for material interests rather than vehicles for religious truth. Moreover, since most offerings contain meat from sacrificed animals, they are an affront to God.

The Hare Krishnas also condemn the characteristic diversity of village religious practices, villages defining themselves against their neighbours by often deliberate attempts to do things in different ways. This is said to generate confusion, because emphasis is given to superficial differences, rather than to underlying similarities. For the Hare Krishnas, such customs are therefore 'local' (*setempat*, Ind.) and variable, whereas truth must be invariable and eternal.

The high priests, *pedanda*, are said to be the worst culprits, because they are supposed to be conversant with religious truth but are invariably ignorant. They have followers, called *sisya*, which means 'pupil', but, instead of teaching them, they confine themselves to lists of necessary offerings, the making of holy water and advice on propitious days on which to carry out important activities. In fact, Hare Krishnas note, *pedanda* often use the term *panjak* ('subjects'), rather than *sisya*, to refer to their followers, who, because they have to pay for the services they receive, are avariciously exploited. Much of the information which a priest provides is said to be freely available in the calendars and almanacs, which are now published annually and sold all over Bali. Several members of both Sai Baba and Hare Krishna felt sure that some priests obtained their information from these new calendars, but passed it off as exclusive. But *sisya* dare not leave their priests, for reasons I have already discussed. As one member concluded: 'People like me join Hare Krishna because here we can read the *Bhagavadgita* and other books. We teach each other and we begin to understand the purpose behind the ceremonies; we fill the gap with understanding.'

As with Sai Baba devotees, such considerations lead Hare Krishnas to claim that it is *their* religion (*agama*) which is developed (*berkembang*, Ind.), whilst *adat* is not, and so the ban is unjust and only remains in place because ISKCON threatens the vested interests of the rich and powerful. The latter are accused of valuing their wealth and possessions more than their souls. However, in a way which marks them off from Sai Baba, Hare Krishna is much more a religion of the poor. In one sense, their membership is a protest against the way in which they say Balinese religion acts more and more against the interests of the poor, making it extremely difficult for them to participate fully. It shames them when they fail to compete successfully, and thus increases the likelihood that they will leave and look for something better.

Spirituality, not potency

Devotees of Hare Krishna are as unequivocal as those of Sai Baba in their emphasis on the importance of spirituality (*kerohanian*). Some members told me they had abandoned *aliran kepercayaan*, such as Bambu Kuning, because the stress on the development of inner power (*sakti*), as a way to success and wealth in this world, was not what they were looking for.

Be that as it may, Krishna devotees face the same taunts from other Balinese that Sai Baba members do, only with greater force. The strict vegetarianism, taboos on alcohol and illicit sex, the shaving of heads, the chanting of the mantra, meditation, and so forth, encourage outsiders to think that these are ascetic practices specifically designed to accumulate *sakti*. When he joined three years previously, one young devotee told me he was repeatedly accused by some of his village friends of being involved with an organization that was illegal, 'evil' (*jahat*, Ind.) and a front for learning 'black magic'. But, if some villagers tormented him, others apparently feared him. Because the purpose of those who join other *aliran kepercayaan* is the cultivation of *sakti*, they assumed this must also be his intention. Unwilling to acknowledge this, he was accused of trying to increase his *sakti* in an underhand way. His parents thought he was mad and told him he would become ill. They insisted on his participation in houseyard and village ceremonies. He does, in fact, outwardly conform, but when he prays he thinks of Krishna and not the ancestors and deities of *adat* religion. He refuses to eat meat, saying that it pollutes his body. Eating meat, he once told me, is like an elephant washing; as soon as it has finished, it rolls around in the dirt.

Ironically, the claims of others that devotees of Hare Krishna seek to increase their *sakti* is a reason members frequently give to explain why the police leave them alone. Several members told me that, despite the ban, it is rare for the police to arrest a member. Partly this is because members play down their association and conduct their religious practices in an isolated spot. However, even when they are called into the police station to be interviewed about the movement's activities, members claim that the police merely 'talk a lot, ask for the mantra to be written down, and sometimes demand a bribe'. Devotees interpret this weak response as a result of the police believing that the Hare Krishnas command great *sakti*, and thus as being too frightened to impose more severe penalties. To confirm this, some members gave me examples of the dire fates (illness, accidents, bankruptcy, etc.) befalling those who complained about the movement to the police. This is not because 'we' have power, one hastened to add, but because 'Krishna protects us'.

The main distinction made by Hare Krishnas between spirituality and potency is that the former is already inside one's heart and its further development requires detachment from the material world, whereas the latter has to be drawn into oneself from external sources, such as spirits, and its development therefore increases attachment to the material world:

So yes, [those who have *sakti*] can become strong, and in a fight maybe they can take on four people and win. But what is the point? They simply want to be stronger than others, compete with them and beat them. It's like a mother and her child. When the child cries she gives it something to play with. Then the child stops crying and is happy, but it has forgotten its mother. So Bambu Kuning and [other similar organizations] are just like children. They are so concerned with boosting their own strength and their ego that they neglect the much more important thing, which is your spirituality. We want to develop what is already inside us. We don't want to fight or compete. This life is real, but it is transient [*sementara*, Ind.] and so trivial. What is important is our soul [*atma*] and what happens to it. Our way is surer. We are all Krishna's creations [*ciptaan*, Ind.], and so He protects us, especially if we act properly and devote our life to Him. When you follow Krishna you can extinguish your anger [*merendamkan kemarahan*, Ind.]. Bambu Kuning increases your anger because you become so egotistical. We try to smother our ego by devotion to Krishna.

(Krishna devotee)

Whereas attraction to Sai Baba is founded partly on his miracle working, Krishna devotees rarely mention miracles. However, devotion to Krishna releases His protection, which often takes miraculous form. Almost every member I spoke to gave me examples of this protection. One told me of how a dog bit his leg but instead of fighting back he remained still and the dog let go. When he looked at his leg there was no wound. Another described how he disturbed a bees' nest and, though he was stung many times, he felt no pain. Yet another recounted how he once lifted a pole from which was slung a large gong and too late realized a poisonous green tree-snake was wrapped around it. It struck at his face but, as he was wearing eyeglasses, the snake missed him. All these escapes were attributed to Krishna's constant protection.

Conclusion

Alongside the Hare Krishna and Sai Baba movements, there are at least fifteen *aliran kepercayaan* registered with the Department of Education and Culture, and several others which remain unauthorized. The emergence of these movements has created concern among the authorities and prompted them to speak of a 'spiritual crisis'. They admonish priests, schoolteachers, village leaders and other officials to provide better examples and role models, so that the masses will not be led astray by 'false' religious teachings. They warn that the new religious zeal sweeping the country and especially the younger generation is potentially dangerous if it is not properly directed and supervised by the priests and the Parisada. While the total number of people who join or in some sense sympathize with these new religious movements only amounts to a small fraction of Bali's population, the relatively sudden appearance of such a diverse range of movements suggests that they have tapped sources of widespread discontent within Balinese society.

This discontent is religious, political and cultural. Until about 1980 there was little outlet for those who were dissatisfied with or disadvantaged by the political and religious institutions of Balinese society, other than by mounting reformist critiques of hierarchy and the rituals which enact it. The appearance of new religious movements, however, has begun to reorientate Balinese towards new ways of managing and thinking about their lives in respect of these issues. While some movements reinterpret old ideas of *sakti* in novel ways, others have abandoned such ideas altogether in favour of completely new concepts, such as 'spirituality'. Sai Baba and Hare Krishna, in particular, represent forms of religion which emphasize universalism, individual development and the relative equality of worshippers. By sharply differentiating themselves from both the hierarchical, ritualistic and communal *adat* religion and the impersonal and esoteric religion of *agama Hindu*, they have also created new forms of identity more in tune with a modern and global world.

Although the doctrinal differences between Sai Baba and Hare Krishna are not very important, these lead to very significant differences in how the two movements are organized. Sai Baba is inclusive, builds bridges to the wider society and has friends in high places who protect and promote it and, while it is critical of *adat* and *agama Hindu*, it also stresses forms of cultural continuity with these. In contrast, the public badges of identity (hairstyle, special clothes, chanting the mantra, and so forth) mark out Hare Krishna as considerably more radical and exclusive, a separation made the more definite and explicit by the legal ban imposed upon it.

While the new universalist identity which some members of Sai Baba are in the process of constructing is problematic, in that it partly subverts other identities based on more local allegiances to village, caste and specifically Balinese forms of religion, it also complements these. Because of the concessions Sai Baba makes to the surrounding social and religious environment, and the way it seeks to both incorporate, and negotiate with, that environment, devotees can and do see themselves as having a stake in two traditions they are striving to bring into harmony. This is made the more possible now that the movement is seen as more acceptable and less threatening than in the recent past.

Members of Hare Krishna are in a quite different position. Almost every aspect about the movement defines it in starkly oppositional terms to other forms of Balinese religion. They have no economic, political or cultural resources to assist them in propagating their identity. Instead, their identity as devotees of Hare Krishna must be kept secret and hidden, and consequently it cannot complement a 'Balinese' identity in the way that adherents would like it to, or in the way that Sai Baba is beginning to achieve. As it stands, images of themselves as devotees of Krishna must be kept within the strictly defined limits of the ashram and the home. While Sai Baba is likely to to prosper and even expand, it is difficult to see how the Hare Krishna movement can overcome its isolation from the rest of Balinese society.

10
Conclusion

In this book I have tried to convey some of the complexity and dynamism of religious change and innovation in Bali since the beginning of the twentieth century, and to give an account of how such change has shaped and been shaped by political and social conflict. In concluding, I want to make some brief comments on two issues. One of these is the relationship between religion and politics, and the other concerns the emergence of new and distinct forms of religious experience.

On the basis that Christianity and Islam set the standard for what should count as religion, Dutch colonial officers, Javanese Muslim religious scholars and others scorned and belittled Balinese ritual practice, spirit worship and the absence of a high god, in what amounted to a charge that the Balinese hardly had a religion at all. An inability to counter these accusations encouraged Balinese to question their own activities and beliefs and then gradually to transform them.

Bali's Hindu heritage made it more or less inevitable that religious change would involve the Hinduization of Balinese religion, but it was largely the nineteenth-century neo-Hindu revival in India which supplied the basic framework for change. Balinese intellectuals, some of whom were educated in Indian universities, campaigned for the simplification and standardization of ritual, an emphasis on ethics, intention and action over mechanical ritual performance, the democratization of religious knowledge over priestly secrecy and control, the primacy of God over indiscriminate spirit worship, and the detachment of religion from the hierarchical social order.

What one might call a 'Protestant' form of Hinduism thus began to emerge in Bali in the course of the first half of the twentieth century. In 1958 this was eventually accepted as an official religion, sponsored and supported by the Indonesian state and provided with an agency, the Parisada Hindu Darma Indonesia, to run the affairs of the Hindu community. Named *agama Hindu*, this scriptural and bureaucratized religion became the ruling religious orthodoxy in Bali. Numerous books have since been published to propagate these new teachings, and the new doctrines also form a compulsory part of the school curriculum.

Once religious innovation had begun, it became impossible to contain and, sensitized to the variety of traditions practised in India, interested Balinese have since imported other, devotional, forms of Hinduism. The significance of these movements lies in their radical critique of both 'traditional' forms of religious expression based on the caste order and the esoteric and impersonal doctrines of *agama Hindu*. Sai Baba and Hare Krishna emphasize the spiritual development of the individual, a direct and deeply emotional relationship to a personalized God, the religious equality of believers and an antipathy to ritual and priestly mediation. The introduction of these imported forms in the early 1980s coincided with the rapid emergence of numerous, indigenous, new religious movements, known as *aliran kepercayaan*, which, by reworking traditional notions of personal power at the same time as adopting some of the doctrines of *agama Hindu*, exist in an uneasy tension with official religion.

The tremendous religious complexity that now characterizes contemporary Bali has been described by religious officials as a 'spiritual crisis'. The new-found enthusiasm for religion which commentators acknowledge is occurring amongst all groups of Balinese has been generally welcomed, but it has also elicited great anxiety concerning the deviant and dangerous forms into which such enthusiasm might be channelled unless correct instruction is given by those in authority. But it is partly these attempts to create and enforce a religious orthodoxy that have helped to foster conditions in which new religious movements arise and flourish. Consequently, religious diversity can be seen as both cause and effect of political conflict.

However, any discussion of the relationship between politics and religion in a society where these alien categories have only recently been adopted is bound to raise some difficult issues. For example, in the 1920s, when Balinese commoners and elites debated the nature of their religious practices and beliefs and the connection of these to the hierarchy, the question may be asked if this was politics masquerading as religion or religion masquerading as politics. In fact, of course, it was both, for the separation could hardly be made at that time: an argument about religion was equally an argument about political organization, and vice versa. This debate was conducted in the Indonesian language, in which there were, at least the rudiments of a religious and political vocabulary, which the participants could work with to sort out and explicate their positions in a way that helped to establish the distinction. Clearly Indonesian was also chosen because the discussions were addressed as much to an outside audience as to Balinese. But it is doubtful if the arguments could have been expressed with any great clarity had Balinese been used, for the distinction does not exist in this language.

This question remains just as elusive if we consider the situation in the 1980s. During the New Order period, almost all explicit political activity was forbidden, so it is relatively easy to argue that religious innovation and change were aimed at achieving political goals and that religion was therefore politics in disguise. I have, in fact, claimed that Balinese had to turn to a cultural politics of religion in order for commoners and others to sustain their challenge to the hierarchical caste order. I want to maintain that this was indeed the case, even if it was not the whole story. Many Balinese saw that various forms of social and economic inequality were underpinned by religious institutions and practices, and therefore initiated reforms of cremation rituals, sought to undermine the dominance of the high priests, and organized themselves in island-wide descent groups to challenge gentry hegemony. But any such phrasing of the issue has the unhappy and unintentional implication that, for the Balinese, religious change is somehow less important than political and societal reform, that it constitutes just a method of attaining more purely political ambitions. Using a language in which the division between the political and the religious runs very deep and which, in addition, tends strongly to valorize the centrality of politics over the marginality of religion makes it very difficult to bring into view the intrinsic significance of the religious ends of social change in a society where the distinction between politics and religion has, until recently, made little sense. In other words, a predisposition to think in terms of the political uses of religion, as opposed to the religious uses of politics, runs the risk of understating the centrality of religion and of misconstruing religious objectives for political ones. However, in relation to Muslims in Indonesia, Hefner (1997: 112) has queried this tendency of western scholars to see 'religion as no more than an instrument for achieving political-economic ends', and has instead advanced the view that many Muslims 'see the state and politics not as ends in themselves, but as means for the creation of a greater good, the realization of Islamic ideals in society'.

What struck me most forcibly, in the end, about the Sai Baba and Hare Krishna movements was the stress on values, personal development and salvation and the establishment in society of a higher moral code. To some extent, this entailed criticism of the political framework of religious orthodoxy, the state's political intolerance of religious pluralism and the continuing existence of social hierarchy, but one of the main motivations for many devotees was a more satisfying religious life. Generally speaking, the lay leaders of Sai Baba, most of them commoners, have academic and public-sector careers, which they have put in jeopardy by their continuing membership in the movement. As I mentioned in an earlier chapter, in its early years, several of these men were repeatedly harassed by the police and questioned about the movement's beliefs and practices and their role in it. Even today, when the Sai Baba movement appears considerably more secure than it did ten years ago, when it was widely branded as subversive, they are still very concerned about the state's surveillance of its activities. Several other prominent commoner members have important posts in the Parisada Hindu Darma Indonesia, and they have used these influential positions to argue quietly, but persistently, that Sai Baba is a force for good in Balinese society and that the state has nothing to fear from it. In this sense, those devotees who are able to are using existing political channels and opportunities to further a religious cause.

Similarly, ordinary members of Sai Baba (and Hare Krishna) are just as likely to justify their membership of this movement in terms of very personal reasons to do with their commitment to and love of Baba, their experiences of loss, illness, depression and anxiety, their desire for a better, healthier and more satisfying religious life, and their place in the local and global world. This does not preclude them from also voicing opposition to the structures of domination in Balinese society, which some do frequently and passionately, but it would be reductionist in the extreme to collapse the more personal and religious motivations for membership into the political ones. Anyway, I have argued that the latter tend to be expressed more explicitly subsequent to joining, which suggests that, for some devotees at least, they are less central than the former, and that devotees progressively learn to perceive their membership partly in these terms.

As with similar movements dedicated to charismatic god-persons in India, membership of Sai Baba in Bali also revolves around the problems of living in rapidly changing and modernizing urban environments. But treating what devotees say about their personal and family problems and their orientation to traditional forms of village religion as little more than the symptoms and manifestations of large-scale forces of economic rationality and modernity runs the risk of simplifying and impoverishing what is actually a more complicated situation, and of denigrating their keenly felt religious experiences. My point is that a considerable proportion of devotees do not necessarily feel a strong sense of detachment and alienation from *adat* traditions and hence perceive their membership in the movement more as a supplement (rather than as a substitute) to *adat*, as something they have come to for a very specific reason and from which they derive a particular benefit. This holds good for those for whom Baba has been instrumental in curing them of an illness, in much the same way that a Balinese may become tied to a traditional healer or to the god of a temple if either of these has helped the supplicant over a difficult problem. It also holds good for many women, for whom membership of Sai Baba is largely a function of their husbands' membership, even if the former come later to have their own reasons. At one point, I asked a dozen or so ordinary devotees what they would do if they had to choose between Sai Baba and *adat* religion, and the replies were split about two to one in favour of the latter, indicating that despite felt deficiencies in *adat* religion it retains devotees' primary allegiance. After all, leaving Sai Baba has few if any social consequences, whereas leaving *adat* amounts to social death.

I think that one of the more significant aspects of membership of these new movements is that devotees come to discover a new and very distinct kind of religious experience which is not available to them in other forms of religion in Bali. I have explained that traditional forms of religion in Bali are rather impersonal and mechanically ritualized, that temple deities are anonymous and distant and that worship, mediated by priests, does not fully engage the emotions. After ceremonies, Balinese may say they feel refreshed, purified and good, but it rarely goes beyond that. In contrast, after several visits to the Sai Baba centre, some devotees are overcome with uncontrollable emotion and find themselves crying. Devotees 'love' (*sayang, cinta*, Ind.) Baba, they 'long' and 'yearn' (*rindu*, Ind.) to see or touch Him, they dream of Him, and Baba becomes the pivot around which their lives revolve. Balinese never speak in such emotional ways in relation to their temple gods and ancestors. Singing *bhajan* brings some to a high pitch of emotional arousal, while for others it helps to drown out unpleasant feelings. Meditation calms and cleanses and helps to defeat the internal enemies of anger, jealousy and despair; vegetarianism and other abstentions improve the body and the mind. As a result, Baba comes to dwell within the devotee, guiding, protecting and soothing. These are some of the intense bodily experiences that cement the relation between devotee and Baba.

In my view, it is this emotional-cum-religious experience which is at the core of what makes devotion to Baba meaningful for most members. While the form and organization of religious expression (absence of priests, collective singing, sermonizing, equal status of believers, absence of *adat* dress, etc.) may well have political overtones, in the sense that they pose a challenge to the domination of priests and the inequalities of the caste hierarchy, what seems to matter most is the personal religious experience that each individual goes through and which is largely absent from more traditional forms of Balinese religion.

What is also striking is the creative manner in which Sai Baba combines the collective with the individual so that each builds on and benefits from the other. *Adat* religion is almost entirely a collective enterprise. It is true that individual Balinese may make personal vows and take on personal ritual commitments for particular reasons, but these are far less important than the collective household, temple and community rituals which comprise the greatest part of *adat* religion. These rituals are, of course, what make Balinese religion what it is and sustain Balinese in strong and cohesive communities. It is not so much religious experience that matters but the way ritual action and the reciprocal obligations this entails bind people together, at the same time as tying them to their gods and ancestors and to their village lands. This is a tradition which largely discounts the vagaries of an inner religious life and personal religious convictions and beliefs in favour of a more concrete communal harmony, forged through collective ritual practice. It does not really matter what anyone thinks, feels or believes, so long as everyone fulfils the ritual and other obligations. Friends have told me privately that, even if they do not believe in life after death or are sceptical of the ability of the dead to intervene in the lives of the living or think that witches do not exist, they dare not say so too publicly for fear that they will be ostracized and isolated. Individuals cannot simply cease performing rituals dedicated to their ancestors, on the basis that it is a waste of time and money, because this would effectively sever the all-important relationships to their co-villagers. Similarly, the problems which devotees of Sai Baba experience in their home villages almost always concern how they behave, rather than what they believe.

But Sai Baba makes space for such inner religious experience and, indeed, gives this priority. At this level, the movement appears to be a collection of individuals whose cohesiveness is founded on a commonality of belief in Baba and on the fact that each person forms his or her dyadic relationship to Baba. In this respect, the movement is highly individualistic, each devotee being encouraged to strive for personal spiritual development. This is paralleled by its organizational form. There are no obligations to the movement, no dues to be paid, no sanctions for non-atten- dance and no rules to break, and devotees can terminate their membership at any time without incurring penalties. At any service, it is a matter of personal decision whether to attend or not. Consequently, it is the figure of Baba that holds the members together, since there are no institutional relationships amongst the devotees. The movement does not in any sense constitute a corporate group.

And yet the devotees present at any particular service clearly do function as a collectivity. New members, who appear at very regular intervals, learn how to behave and, in all likelihood, what to experience by observing and talking to others. They have probably begun to learn something of what Sai Baba is about even before their first meeting, having read a book about Baba or been told of his miracles by existing members. Emotional arousal is given shape and meaning through discussion with other devotees, by attending educational classes and by listening to the sermons, and is thus converted into a distinct religious experience. Although some devotees have told me that they sing *bhajan* silently to themselves whilst at work or at home, the emotional force of singing devotional hymns is dependent on a highly structured and collective performance. Devotees are advised that, if they have problems, they should discuss them with other devotees rather than outsiders, who may lure them into temptation. In these and other respects, individual spiritual development and inner religious experience are achieved and interpreted partly on the basis of collective action.

To some extent, this kind of religious experience is becoming universalized within Bali, since *agama Hindu* is also gradually trying to substitute spirituality for power and belief for ritual. *Agama Hindu*'s emphasis on ethical intention, meaning and doctrine over ritual action requires Balinese priests to play a rather different role. High priests, whether from Brahmana or other groups, have to take exami- nations to demonstrate that they are conversant with the new doctrines. Rather than simply performing a ritual, they are now being encouraged to provide reli- gious instruction and to give sermons at temple ceremonies. Ordinary Hindus are increasingly taking to private prayer and meditation in their own houseyard temples, apparently in an effort to create a closer and more intense contact with God on an individual basis.

However, the degree to which this will prove successful in the short term is very difficult to gauge, though I think that in the long term these changes are irre- versible. There are, of course, many reasons for this, but I shall mention the three which are the most important. The first is simply that so much of what lies at the heart of Balinese social and cultural life depends on ritual action. Even leaving aside the status implications of ritual performance, which, as a consequence of new wealth being channelled into it, actually appears to be growing rather than declining, the significance of ritual lies in the fact that it underpins basic cultural understandings of the nature of human–supernatural relationships. Invisible deities, ancestors and spirits are main actors on the Balinese stage, and their interventions constitute many of the most important events in the lives of all Balinese Hindus. Eliciting their help and avoiding their sanctions are what engender health and prosperity, and the only way these can be accomplished is by frequent and substantial material offerings (of meat, fruit, dance, music, etc.). The notion that these offerings can be replaced merely by good intentions, prayer and devotion is not one which most Balinese are yet willing to entertain. Few Balinese go through life without finding out at first hand that laxity in the performance of ritual leads to very unhappy outcomes. Constant ritual performance might be a burden, but it is a very necessary one. Sai Baba has been successful partly because its intention is only to reform the less palatable practices of *adat* ritual and to supply underlying meanings for the rest of it.

The second reason concerns the relationship between culture, tourism and the state. The Indonesian state now encourages cultural diversity, both as a building block of national identity and as an obvious tourist attraction. Bali's economic growth and its place as Indonesia's jewel in the tourist crown would be severely threatened if its colourful ceremonies and rituals were to become diluted, and so Balinese have a pronounced economic incentive to preserve them.

Finally, just as it is likely to prove very difficult to replace ritual, it is also probable that ideas about power (*sakti*) will not easily be supplanted by notions of spirituality (*kerohanian*), because the former were and remain central to explanations of political organization and political action. In contemporary Bali, many people claim that others get ahead because they tap into sources of supernatural power, are wary of offending others because of the ever-present possibility of sorcery, and interpret the practices and abstentions of devotees of Sai Baba in terms of a pursuit of *sakti*. That said, it would none the less seem that new ideas concerning spirituality are gaining ground quickly. After all, these ideas inform most or all of the new religions of Bali, including *agama Hindu*, devotional movements and the numerous *aliran kepercayaan*, since even the last claim that their teachings are in ideological conformity with the new doctrines. But, as I have argued, this is rather misleading, since many of the *aliran*, in their activities, continue to endorse traditional notions of power, if in modified and more accessible forms. It may well be that the labelling of practices to do with *sakti* as irrational and the attempt to substitute new ideas of spirituality by official religious agencies, are in fact among the main reasons accounting for the rapid emergence of *aliran* in recent decades. It is also relatively clear that even movements such as Sai Baba face problems when it comes to encouraging Balinese to think in terms of spirituality and to relinquish ideas of power, as the following vignette demonstrates.

On several occasions I was able to visit the homes of devotees and by and large found that the services they conducted there were very similar to those at the centre. However, I did meet one young man (I will call him Balik) whose activities at home seemed to be as much about *sakti* as about *kerohanian*. At centre meetings he appeared very orthodox, if perhaps more fanatical than many others. He frequently asked me to join him at home because he wanted to show me the power of Baba and introduce me to his 'pupils' (*murid*, Ind.). I found this very intriguing because

Plate 10.1 Balik, a young member of the Sai Baba movement, conducting a ceremony at the shrine of Baba in his own home

having pupils implies one is a 'teacher' (*guru*), but the movement explicitly states that Baba is the only *guru* and that no one else can act in this capacity. This actually constitutes a major problem for the movement, because no arrangements have been made for how it should continue when Baba eventually dies.

I spent a day at Balik's shack in the fields on the outskirts of Denpasar, where he lives with his infirm mother. On that occasion, three of his five pupils were present. Two of these were young women, both commoners like Balik himself, while the other was a man with a *déwa* title.

On the one hand, Balik preached to us very conventional messages about how improving one's spirituality enabled one to discriminate between truth and falsehood, how the 'caste' system was wrong because it is action that matters, not birth, and how the Sai Baba movement was not in conflict with *agama* but only with those *adat* practices that have degraded religion. On the other, the service he performed included some very unorthodox activities. For a start, Balik dressed like a temple priest and intoned prayers calling down all the Balinese gods, during which time he made the requisite hand movements (*mudra*) common to priestly activity, though whether these were accurate I have no idea. We were then instructed to meditate for five minutes, after which we sang several devotional hymns. At several points during the singing, Balik shook violently for several seconds as though he was possessed, something I have never seen at centre meetings. When we finished the final hymn, he stood up to face us and, one by one, his three pupils performed an act of obeisance (*sujud*, Ind.) by kneeling in front of him and pressing their foreheads to his feet. This is an act of extreme subordination which the movement only countenances between a devotee and Baba Himself. I asked Déwa if he was not shy to do this, and he replied that in this context Balik's status was irrelevant and that 'what matters is that he is my *guru* and so I can kiss his feet'.

This completed, Balik asked us what we had experienced during the singing and the meditation. Each of his pupils answered in turn with a series of dream-like images. Eka, his most experienced pupil, said she saw herself seated on top of the clouds and below her the world was spinning. She saw Arjuna and Krishna bathed in intense white light talking to each other. Then Baba appeared hovering above them and the three seemed to coalesce. The scene then changed and she saw a shaded pool, where different animals came to drink and, as they did so, they changed into people. Several times during her recollections, Balik told us that what she was saying indicated that we were becoming united and that distinctions of wealth and caste were irrelevant. The second girl, Juni, gave a remarkably similar account, talking of Arjuna and Krishna, of clouds and pools and animals. Déwa, who had never attended a meeting at the centre and was only a very recent addition to Balik's circle, had virtually nothing to say, merely recounting that he felt good, peaceful and calm.

After the service, Balik instructed the two girls to concentrate and 'travel' to England to 'see' my home, my family and what my life was like there. When they were none too successful, he placed a hand on my head and his other on the head of one of the girls so that my thoughts could pass to her through him. This and similar activities continued for some time, Balik again experiencing several episodes of apparent possession.

Clearly, to some extent, Balik has tried to set himself up as a *guru* and therefore as a source of power independent of Baba and the movement, and, despite him talking in terms of spirituality, he was acting more like someone concerned to demonstrate his *sakti*. In one context he appears to be an orthodox and committed devotee of

Baba, whilst in another he seems to be adapting his new religious resources to rather traditional ambitions.

This tension between spirituality and supernatural power, as also those between ritual and belief, hierarchy and equality, and the collective and the individual, is at the heart of the dynamics of religious change in modern Bali. How these tensions will be resolved will have to remain the subject of future research.

References

Acciaioli, G. 1985. 'Culture as art: from practice to spectacle in Indonesia'. *Canberra Anthropology*, 8, 148–72.

—— 1997. 'What's in a name? Appropriating idioms in the south Sulawesi rice intensification program'. In J. Schiller & B. Martin-Schiller (eds), *Imagining Indonesia: Cultural Politics and Political Culture*. Athens, Ohio: Ohio University Centre for International Studies.

Ackerman, S.E. & Lee, R.L.M. 1990. *Heaven in Tansition: Non-Muslim Religious Innovation and Ethnic Identity in Malaysia*. Kuala Lumpur: Forum.

Adams, K.M. 1997. 'Touting "primadonnas": tourism, ethnicity and national integration in Sulawesi, Indonesia'. In M. Picard & R. E. Wood (eds), *Tourism, Ethnicity and the State in Asian and Pacific Societies*. Honolulu: University of Hawaii Press.

Adas, M. 1981. 'From avoidance to confrontation: peasant resistance in precolonial and colonial Southeast Asia'. *Comparative Studies in Society and History*, 23, 217–47.

Agung, I.A.A.G. 1988. *Bali pada Abad XIX*. Yogyakarta: Gajah Mada Press.

Anandakusuma, S.R. 1974. *Ceritera tentang Orang Bali dan Pura Besakih*. Klungkung, Bali: Pusat Satya Dharma Indonesia.

Anderson, B.R.O'G. 1972a. 'The idea of power in Javanese culture'. In C. Holt (ed.), *Culture and Politics in Indonesia*. Ithaca: Cornell University Press.

—— 1972b. *Java in a Time of Revolution*. Ithaca: Cornell University Press.

—— 1977. 'Religion and politics in Indonesia since independence'. In B. Anderson, M. Nakamura & M. Slamet (eds), *Religion and Social Ethos in Indonesia*. Clayton, Australia: Centre of Southeast Asian Studies, Monash University.

—— 1983. *Imagined Communities: Reflections on the Origin and Spread of Nationalism*. London: Verso.

—— 1990a. 'The languages of Indonesian politics'. In his *Language and Power: Exploring Political Cultures in Indonesia*. Ithaca: Cornell University Press.

—— 1990b. Sembah-Sumpah: the politics of language and Javanese culture. In his *Language and Power: Exploring Political Cultures in Indonesia*. Ithaca: Cornell University Press.

—— 1990c. *Language and Power: Exploring Political Cultures in Indonesia*. Ithaca: Cornell University Press.

Appadurai, A. 1990. 'Topographies of the self: praise and emotion in Hindu India'. In C. Lutz & L. Abu-Lughod (eds), *Language and the Politics of Emotion*. Cambridge: Cambridge University Press.

Aspinall, E., Feith, H. & van Klinken, G. (eds). 1999. *The Last Days of President Suharto*. Clayton, Australia: Monash Asia Institute.

Atkinson, J.M. 1987. 'Religions in dialogue: the construction of an Indonesian minority religion'. In R.S. Kipp & S. Rodgers (eds), *Indonesian Religions in Transition*. Tucson: University of Arizona Press.

—— 1989. *The Art and Politics of Wana Shamanship*. Berkeley: University of California Press.

Babb, L. 1986. *Redemptive Encounters: Three Modern Styles in the Hindu Tradition*. Berkeley: University of California Press.

Bagus, I.G.N. n.d. 'A short note on the modern Hindu movements in Balinese society'. Denpasar: Jurusan Antropologi Budaya, Universitas Udayana.

—— 1969. *Pertantangan Kasta dalam Bentuk Baru pada Masjarakat Bali*. Denpasar: Universitas Udayana.

—— 1975. 'Surya kanta: a kewangsan movement of the jaba caste in Bali'. *Masyarakat Indonesia*, 2, 153–62.

Bailey, F. 1957. *Caste and the Economic Frontier*. Manchester: Manchester University Press.

Bakhtin, M.M. 1968. *Rabelais and his World*. Cambridge: MIT Press.

Bakker, F.L. 1993. *The Struggle of the Hindu Balinese Intellectuals: Developments in Modern Hindu Thinking in Independent Indonesia*. Amsterdam: VU University Press.

Barber, C.C. 1979. *Dictionary of Balinese–English*, 2 vols. Aberdeen: Aberdeen University Library, Occasional Publications No. 2.

Barth, F. 1993. *Balinese Worlds*. Chicago: Chicago University Press.

Bateson, G. 1970. 'An old temple and a new myth'. In J. Belo (ed.), *Traditional Balinese Culture*. New York: Columbia University Press.

Beatty, A. 1999. *Varieties of Javanese Religion: an Anthropological Account*. Cambridge: Cambridge University Press.

Belo, J. 1953. *Bali: Temple Festival*. Seattle: University of Washington Press.

Bendesa, I.K.G. & Sukarsa, I.M. 1980. 'An economic survey of Bali'. *Bulletin of Indonesian Economic Studies*, 16, 31–53.

Blackwood, E. 1995. 'Senior women, model mothers, and dutiful daughters: managing gender contradictions in a Minangkabau village'. In A. Ong & M. Peletz (eds), *Bewitching Women, Pious Men: Gender and Body Politics in Southeast Asia*. Berkeley: University of California Press.

Bloch, M. 1982. 'Death, women and power'. In M. Bloch & J. Parry (eds), *Death and the Regeneration of Life*. Cambridge: Cambridge University Press.

Boland, B.J. 1982. *The Struggle of Islam in Modern Indonesia*. The Hague: Martinus Nijhoff.

Boon, J. 1977. *The Anthropological Romance of Bali, 1597–1972*. Cambridge: Cambridge University Press.

—— 1990. 'Balinese twins times two: gender, birth order and "household" in Indonesia/Indo-Europe'. In J.M. Atkinson & S. Errington (eds), *Power and Difference: Gender in Island Southeast Asia*. Stanford: Stanford University Press.

Bosch, F.D.K. 1961. *Selected Studies in Indonesian Archaeology*. The Hague: Martinus Nijhoff.

Bourchier, D. 1997. 'Totalitarianism and the "national personality": recent controversy about the philosophical basis of the Indonesian state'. In J. Schiller & B. Martin-Schiller (eds), *Imagining Indonesia: Cultural Politics and Political Culture.* Athens, Ohio: Ohio University Centre for International Studies.

Bourdieu, P. 1977. *Outline of a Theory of Practice.* Cambridge: Cambridge University Press.

Bowen, J. 1986. 'On the political construction of tradition: gotong-royong in Indonesia'. *Journal of Asian Studies,* 45, 545–61.

Breman, J. 1983. *Control of Land and Labour in Colonial Java.* Dordrecht: Foris Publications.

Brenner, S.A. 1998. *The Domestication of Desire: Women, Wealth and Modernity in Java.* Princeton: Princeton University Press.

Bresnan, J. 1993. *Managing Indonesia: the Modern Political Economy.* New York: Columbia University Press.

Bromley, D. & Shinn, L. (eds). 1989. *Krishna Consciousness in the West.* London & Toronto: Associated University Press.

Budiman, A. (ed.). 1990. *State and Civil Society in Indonesia.* Monash University: Centre of Southeast Asian Studies.

Budiman, A., Hatley, B. & Kingsbury, D. (eds). 1999. *Reformasi: Crisis and Change in Indonesia.* Clayton, Australia: Monash Asia Institute.

Burghart, R. 1978. 'Hierarchical models of the Hindu social system'. *Man,* 13, 519–36.

Burr, A. 1984. *I Am Not My Body: a Study of the International Hare Krishna Sect.* New Delhi: Vikas Publishing House.

Clifford, J. 1986. 'Introduction: partial truths'. In J. Clifford & G.E. Marcus (eds), *Writing Culture: the Poetics and Politics of Ethnography.* Berkeley: University of California Press.

Cole, W.S. 1983. 'Balinese food-related behaviour: a study of the effects of ecological, social and cultural processes on rates of change'. Unpublished PhD dissertation, Washington University.

Connor, L. 1979. 'Corpse abuse and trance in Bali: the cultural mediation of aggression'. *Mankind,* 12, 104–18.

—— 1982. 'In darkness and light: a study of peasant intellectuals in Bali'. Unpublished PhD thesis, University of Sydney.

—— 1995. 'The action of the body on society: washing a corpse in Bali'. *JRAI,* 1, 537–60.

—— 1996. 'Contestation and transformation of Balinese ritual: the case of ngaben ngirit'. In A. Vickers (ed.), *Being Modern in Bali: Image and Change.* New Haven: Yale University Southeast Asia Studies.

Covarrubias, M. 1937. *Island of Bali.* London: Cassell.

Creese, H. 1995. 'In search of Majapahit: defining Balinese identities'. Paper delivered at the Bali in the Late Twentieth Century conference, Sydney University, 3–7 July.

Cribb, R. (ed.). 1990. *The Indonesian Killings, 1965–1966: Studies from Java and Bali.* Monash University: Centre for Southeast Asian Studies.

Crouch, H. 1988 [1978]. *The Army and Politics in Indonesia*. Ithaca: Cornell University Press.

Cunningham, C.E. 1965. 'Order and change in an Atoni diarchy'. *South Western Journal of Anthropology*, 21, 359–82.

Daroesman, R. 1973. 'An economic survey of Bali'. *Bulletin of Indonesian Economic Studies*, 9, 28–61.

Deadwyler, W. 1989. 'Patterns in ISKCON's historical self-perception'. In D. Bromley & L. Shinn (eds), *Krishna Consciousness in the West*. London & Toronto: Associated University Press.

de Heusch, L. 1997. 'The symbolic mechanism of sacred kingship: rediscovering Frazer'. *JRAI*, 3, 213–32.

de Kat Angelino, P. 1920. 'De robans en parekans op Bali'. *Kol. Tijdschr.*, 10, 590–608.

Derrett, J.D.M. 1976. 'Rajadharma'. *Journal of Asian Studies*, 35, 597–609.

Dirks, N.B. 1987. *The Hollow Crown: Ethnohistory of an Indian Kingdom*. Cambridge: Cambridge University Press.

—— 1989. 'The original caste: power, history and hierarchy in South Asia'. *Contributions to Indian Sociology, (n.s.)* 23, 59–77.

Dumont, L. 1962. 'The conception of kingship in ancient India'. *Contributions to Indian Sociology*, 6, 48–87.

—— 1980. Homo hierarchicus: *the Caste System and its Implications*. Chicago: Chicago University Press.

Eiseman, F.B. 1990. *Bali: Sekala and Niskala*, vol. 2. Berkeley: Periplus Editions.

Emmerson, D.K. 1978. 'The bureaucracy in political context: weakness in strength'. In K.D. Jackson and L.W. Pye (eds), *Political Power and Communications in Indonesia*. Berkeley: University of California Press.

—— (ed). 1999. *Indonesia beyond Suharto: Polity, Economy, Society, Transition*. London: M.E. Sharpe.

Errington, J. 1998. *Shifting Languages: Interaction and Identity in Javanese Indonesia*. Cambridge: Cambridge University Press.

Errington, S. 1989. *Meaning and Power in a Southeast Asian Realm*. Princeton: Princeton University Press.

—— 1990. 'Recasting sex, gender and power: a theoretical and regional overview'. In J.M. Atkinson & S. Errington (eds), *Power and Difference: Gender in Island Southeast Asia*. Stanford: Stanford University Press.

Evans-Pritchard, E. 1962. 'The divine kingship of the Shilluk of the Nilotic Sudan'. In his *Essays in Social Anthropology*. London: Faber and Faber.

Fegan, B. 1986. 'Tenants' non-violent resistance to landowner claims in a central Luzon village'. *Journal of Peasant Studies*, 13, 87–106.

Feith, H. 1962. *The Decline of Constitutional Democracy in Indonesia*. Ithaca: Cornell University Press.

—— 1963. 'Indonesia's political symbols and their wielders'. *World Politics*, 16, 79–97.

Forge, A. 1980. 'Balinese religion and Indonesian identity'. In J. Fox (ed.), *Indonesia: the Making of a Culture*. Canberra: Australian National University.

Foulcher, K. 1990. 'The construction of an Indonesian national culture: patterns of hegemony and resistance'. In A. Budiman (ed.), *State and Society in Indonesia*. Monash University: Centre of Southeast Asian Studies.

Friederich, R. 1959 [1849]. *The Civilisation and Culture of Bali*. Calcutta: Susil Gupta.

Fuller, C.J. 1984. *Servants of the Goddess: the Priests of a South Indian Temple*. Cambridge: Cambridge University Press.

—— 1992. *The Camphor Flame: Popular Hinduism and Society in India*. Princeton: Princeton University Press.

Gal, S. 1995. 'Language and the "arts of resistance"'. *Cultural Anthropology*, 10, 407–24.

Galey, J.C. 1989. 'Reconsidering kingship in India: an ethnological perspective'. *History and Anthropology*, 4, 123–87.

Geertz, C. 1959. 'Form and variation in Balinese village structure'. *American Anthropologist*, 61, 991–1012.

—— 1960. *The Religion of Java*. Chicago: Chicago University Press.

—— 1963a. *Agricultural Involution: the Processes of Ecological Change in Indonesia*. Berkeley: University of California Press.

—— 1963b. *Peddlers and Princes: Social Development and Economic Change in Two Indonesian Towns*. Chicago: Chicago University Press.

—— 1967. 'Tihingan: a Balinese village'. In Koentjaraningrat (ed.), *Villages in Indonesia*. Ithaca: Cornell University Press.

—— 1973a. '"Internal conversion" in contemporary Bali'. In his *The Interpretation of Cultures*. London: Hutchinson.

—— 1973b. 'Person, time and conduct in Bali'. In his *The Interpretation of Cultures*. London: Hutchinson.

—— 1980. *Negara, the Theatre State in Nineteenth-century Bali*. Princeton: Princeton University Press.

—— 1983. *Local Knowledge*. New York: Basic Books.

—— & Geertz, H. 1975. *Kinship in Bali*. Chicago: Chicago University Press.

Geertz, H. 1995a. *Images of Power: Balinese Paintings Made for Gregory Bateson and Margaret Mead*. Honolulu: University of Hawaii Press.

—— 1995b. 'Sorcery and social change in Bali: the sakti conjecture'. Paper delivered at the Bali in the Late Twentieth Century conference, Sydney University, 3–7 July.

Gelberg, S. 1989. 'Exploring an alternative reality: spiritual life in ISKCON'. In D. Bromley & L. Shinn (eds), *Krishna Consciousness in the West*. London & Toronto: Associated University Press.

Gellner, D.N. 1983. 'Review of C.Geertz, *Negara, the Theatre State in Nineteenth-century Bali*'. *South Asia Research*, 3, 135–40.

Gombrich, R. & Obeyesekere, G. 1988. *Buddhism Transformed: Religious Change in Sri Lanka*. Princeton: Princeton University Press.

Gonda, J. 1952. *Sanskrit in Indonesia*. Nagpur: International Academy of Indian Culture.

Goris, R. 1960. 'The temple system'. In J.L. Swellengrebel (ed.), *Bali: Studies in Life, Thought and Ritual*. The Hague: W. van Hoeve.

Grader, C.J. 1937a. 'Tweedeeling in het oud-Balische dorp'. *Mededelingen van de Kirtya Liefrinck-van der Tuuk*, 5, 45–71.

—— 1937b. 'Madenan (desa-monographie)'. *Mededelingen van de Kirtya Liefrinck-van der Tuuk*, 5, 73–122.

—— 1960. 'The state temples of Mengwi'. In J.L. Swellengrebel (ed.), *Bali: Studies in Life, Thought and Ritual*. The Hague: W. van Hoeve.

Gregory, C. 1982. *Gifts and Commodities*. London: Academic Press.

Guermonprez, J.-F. 1985. 'Rois divins et rois guerriers: images de la royauté à Bali'. *L'Homme*, 95, 39–70.

—— 1987. *Les Pandé de Bali: la Formation d'une Caste et la Valeur d'un Titre*. Paris: Eçole Française d'Extrême-Orient.

—— 1989. 'Dual sovereignty in nineteenth-century Bali'. *History and Anthropology*, 4, 189–207.

—— 1990. 'On the elusive Balinese village: hierarchy and values versus political models'. *RIMA*, 24, 55–89.

Hall, D.G.E. 1981. *A History of South-East Asia*. London: Macmillan

Hanan, D. 1993. 'Nji Ronggeng: another paradigm for erotic spectacle in the cinema'. In V.M. Hooker (ed.), *Culture and Society in New Order Indonesia*. Kuala Lumpur: Oxford University Press.

Hanna, W.A. 1976. *Bali Profile: People, Events, Circumstances, 1001–1976*. New York: American Universities Field Staff.

Hardacre, H. 1986. *Kurozumikyo and the New Religions of Japan*. Princeton: Princeton University Press.

Hatley, B. 1997. 'Nation, "tradition", and constructions of the feminine in modern Indonesian literature'. In J. Schiller & B. Martin-Schiller (eds), *Imagining Indonesia: Cultural Politics and Political Culture*. Athens, Ohio: Ohio University Centre for International Studies.

Hefner, R. 1985. *Hindu Javanese: Tengger Tradition and Islam*. Princeton: Princeton University Press.

—— 1997. 'Islamization and Democratization in Indonesia'. In R. Hefner & P. Horvatich (eds), *Islam in an Era of Nation-states*. Honolulu: University of Hawaii Press.

Hertz, R. 1960. *Death and the Right Hand*. London: Cohen and West.

Hill, H. 1994a. The economy. In H. Hill (ed.), *Indonesia's New Order: the Dynamics of Socio-Economic Transformation*. St Leonards: Allen and Unwin.

—— (ed.). 1994b. *Indonesia's New Order: the Dynamics of Socio-Economic Transformation*. St Leonards: Allen and Unwin.

Hinzler, H. 1976. 'The Balinese Babad'. In S. Kartodirdjo (ed.), *Profiles of Malay Culture: Historiography, Religion and Politics*. Jakarta: Ministry of Education and Culture.

—— 1986. 'The Usana Bali as a source of history'. In T. Abdullah (ed.), *Papers of the Fourth Indonesian-Dutch History Conference: Literature and History*, vol. 2. Yogyakarta: Gajah Mada University Press.

Hirsch, E. 1990. 'From bones to betel nuts: processes of ritual transformation and the development of "national culture" in Papua New Guinea'. *Man*, 25, 18–34.

Hobart, A. 1987. *Dancing Shadows of Bali: Theatre and Myth*. London: KPI.

Hobart, A., Ramseyer, U. & Leemann, A. 1996. *The Peoples of Bali*. Oxford: Blackwell.

Hobart, M. 1975. 'Orators and patrons: two types of political leader in Bali'. In M. Bloch (ed.), *Political Language and Oratory in Traditional Society*. London: Academic Press.

—— 1978. 'The path of the soul'. In G.B. Milner (ed.), *Natural Symbols in South-east Asia*. London: School of Oriental and African Studies.

Hobsbawm, E. & Ranger, T. (eds). 1983. *The Invention of Tradition*. Cambridge: Cambridge University Press.

Hocart, A.M. 1950. *Caste: a Comparative Study*. London: Methuen.

Hollan, D. 1988. 'Pockets full of mistakes: the personal consequences of religious change in a Toraja village'. *Oceania*, 58, 275–89.

Holt, C. 1970. '"Bandit island", a short exploration trip to Nusa Penida'. In J. Belo (ed), *Traditional Balinese Culture*. New York: Columbia University Press.

Hooker, V.M. (ed.). 1993. *Culture and Society in New Order Indonesia*. Kuala Lumpur: Oxford University Press.

Hooykaas, C. 1977. *A Balinese Temple Festival*. The Hague: Martinus Nijhoff.

Hopkins, T. 1989. 'The social and religious background for transmission of Gaudiya Vaisnavism to the West'. In D. Bromley & L. Shinn (eds), *Krishna Consciousness in the West*. London & Toronto: Associated University Press.

Howe, L. 1980. 'Pujung, an investigation into the foundations of Balinese culture'. Unpublished PhD thesis, Edinburgh University.

—— 1983. 'An introduction to the study of traditional Balinese architecture'. *Archipel*, 25, 137–58

—— 1984. 'Gods, people, spirits and witches'. *Bijd. Taal-, Land-, Volk*, 140, 193–222.

—— 1987. 'Caste in Bali and India: levels of comparison'. In L. Holy (ed.), *Comparative Anthropology*. Oxford: Basil Blackwell.

—— 1989a. 'Peace and violence in Bali: culture and social organization'. In S. Howell & R. Willis (eds), *Societies at Peace: Anthropological Perspectives*. London: Routledge.

—— 1989b. 'Hierarchy and equality: variation in Balinese social organisation'. *Bijd. Taal-, Land-, Volk.*, 145, 47–71.

—— 1990. *Being Unemployed in Northern Ireland: an Ethnographic Study*. Cambridge: Cambridge University Press.

—— 1991. 'Rice, ideology and the legitimation of hierarchy in Bali'. *Man*, 26, 445–67.

—— 1994. 'Ideology, domination and unemployment'. *Sociological Review*, 42, 315–40.

—— 1998. 'Scrounger, worker, beggarman, cheat: the dynamics of unemployment and the politics of resistance in Belfast'. *JRAI*, 4, 531–50.

—— 2000. 'Risk, ritual and performance'. *JRAI*, 6, 63–79.

Hughes, J. 1968. *The End of Sukarno: a Coup that Misfired, a Purge that Ran Wild*. London: Angus and Robertson.

Hull, T.H. & Jones, G.W. 1994. 'Demographic perspectives'. In H. Hill (ed.), *Indonesia's New Order: the Dynamics of Socio-economic Transformation*. St Leonards: Allen and Unwin.

Humphrey, C. 1994. 'Remembering an "enemy": the Bogd Khann in twentieth-century Mongolia'. In R.S. Watson (ed.), *Memory, History and Opposition under State Socialism*. Santa Fe: School of American Research Press.

Hunter, T. 1988. 'Balinese language: historical background and contemporary state'. Unpublished PhD thesis, University of Michigan, Ann Arbor.

Hutajulu, R. 1995. 'Tourism's impact on Toba Batak ceremony'. *Bijd. Taal-, Land-, Volk*, 151, 639–56.

Jayasuriya, S. & Nehen, I.K. 1989. 'Bali: economic growth and tourism'. In H. Hill (ed.), *Unity and Diversity: Regional Economic Development in Indonesia since 1970*. Singapore: Oxford University Press.

Jendra, I.W. 1996. *Variasi Bahasa Kedudukan dan Peran Bhagawan Sri Sathya Sai Baba dalam Agama Hindu*. Surabaya: Paramita.

Kahin, G.M. 1952. *Nationalism and Revolution in Indonesia*. Ithaca: Cornell University Press.

Kahn, J. 1993. *Constituting the Minangkabau: Peasants, Culture and Modernity in Colonial Indonesia*. Oxford: Berg.

Kartodirdjo, S. 1984. *Modern Indonesia: Tradition and Transformation*. Yogyakarta: Gajah Mada University Press.

Kasturi, N. 1975. *Sathyam, Shivam, Sundaram*, part 2. New Delhi: Bhagavan Sri Sathya Sai Seva Samithi.

Keeler, W. 1983. 'Shame and stage fright in Java'. *Ethos*, 11, 152–65.

—— 1987. *Javanese Shadow Plays, Javanese Selves*. Princeton: Princeton University Press.

—— 1990. 'Speaking of gender in Java'. In J.M. Atkinson & S. Errington (eds), *Power and Difference: Gender in Island Southeast Asia*. Stanford: Stanford University Press.

Keesing, R. & Tonkinson, R. (eds). 1982. 'Reinventing traditional culture: the politics of kastom in island Melanesia'. *Mankind* (special issue), 13, 4.

Kent, A. 1999. 'Unity in diversity: portraying the visions of the Sathya Sai Baba movement of Malaysia'. *Crossroads*, 13, 29–51.

—— 2000. 'Creating divine unity: Chinese recruitment in the Sathya Sai Baba movement of Malaysia'. *Journal of Contemporary Religion*, 15, 5–27.

Kersten, J. 1984. *Bahasa Bali*. Ende, Flores: Nusa Indah.

Kipp, R. 1993. *Dissociated Identities: Ethnicity, Religion and Class in an Indonesian Society*. Ann Arbor: University of Michigan Press.

Klass, M. 1991. *Singing with Sai Baba: the Politics of Revitalization in Trinidad*. Boulder: Westview.

Knott, K. 1986. *My Sweet Lord: the Hare Krishna Movement*. Wellingborough: Aquarian.

Korn, V.E. 1932. *Het adatrecht van Bali*. s'Gravenhage: G. Naeff.

—— 1933. *De dorpsrepubliek Tnganan Pagringsingan*. Santpoort.

Kulick, D. 1996. 'Causing a commotion: public scandal as resistance among Brazilian transgendered prostitutes'. *Anthropology Today*, 12 (6), 3–7.

Kung, L. 1978. *Factory Women in Taiwan*. Columbia: Columbia University Press.

Lansing, J.S. 1983a. *The Three Worlds of Bali*. New York: Praeger.

—— 1983b. 'The "Indianization" of Bali'. *Journal of South East Asian Studies*, 14, 409–21.

—— 1991. *Priests and Programmers: Technologies of Power in the Engineered Landscape of Bali*. Princeton: Princeton University Press.

Lee, R.L.M. 1982. 'Sai Baba, salvation and syncretism: religious change in a Hindu movement in urban Malaysia'. *Contributions to Indian Sociology (NS)*, 16, 125–40.

Legge, J.D. 1972. *Sukarno, a Political Biography*. Harmondsworth: Penguin Books.

Leigh, B. 1991. 'Making the Indonesian state: the role of school texts'. *RIMA*, 25, 17–43.

Lekkerkerker, C. 1926. 'De kastenmaatschappij in Britisch-Indie en op Bali'. *Mensch en Maatschappij*, 2, 175–213, 300–34.

Lev, D.S. 1966. *The Transition to Guided Democracy: Indonesian Politics, 1957–1959*. Ithaca: Cornell Modern Indonesia Project.

Liefrinck, F.A. 1927. *Bali en Lombok: Geschriften*. Amsterdam.

Linnekin, J. & Poyer, L. (eds). 1990. *Cultural Identity and Ethnicity in the Pacific*. Honolulu: University of Hawaii Press.

Lorenzen, D. (ed.). 1995. *Bhakti Religion in North India: Community Identity and Political Action*. Albany: State University of New York Press.

Lynch, O. 1969. *The Politics of Untouchability: Social Mobility and Social Change in a City in India*. London: Columbia University Press.

Lyon, M.L. 1980. 'The Hindu revival in Java: politics and religious identity'. In J. Fox (ed.), *Indonesia: the Making of a Culture*. Canberra: Australian National University.

MacRae, G. 1998. 'Ritual networks in south Bali: geographical form and historical process'. *RIMA*, 32, 110–44.

—— 1999. 'Acting global, thinking local in a Balinese tourist town.' In R. Rubenstein and L. Connor (eds), *Staying Local in the Global Village: Bali in the Twentieth Century*. Honolulu: University of Hawaii Press.

Mayer, A. 1985. 'The king's two thrones'. *Man*, 20, 205–21.

Meillassoux, C. 1973. 'Are there castes in India?' *Economy and Society*, 2, 89–111.

Mencher, J. 1974. 'The caste system upside down'. *Current Anthropology*, 15, 463–93.

Moertono, S. 1968. *State and Statecraft in Old Java: a Study of the Later Mataram Period*. Ithaca: Cornell Modern Indonesia Project.

Morfit, M. 1986. 'Pancasila orthodoxy'. In C. MacAndrews (ed.), *Central Government and Local Development in Indonesia*. Singapore: Oxford University Press.

Mortimer, R. 1974. *Indonesian Communism under Sukarno: Ideology and Politics, 1959–1965*. Ithaca: Cornell University Press.

Mrazek, R. 1994. *Sjahrir: Politics and Exile in Indonesia*. Cornell University: Southeast Asia Program.

Nakatani, A. 1995. 'Contested time: women's work and marriage in Bali'. Unpublished PhD thesis, Oxford University.

Needham, R. 1967. 'Percussion and transition'. *Man*, 2, 606–14.

Ong, A. 1987. *Spirits of Resistance and Capitalist Discipline: Factory Women in Malaysia*. Albany: SUNY Press.

Ortner, S. 1984. 'Theory in anthropology since the sixties'. *Comparative Studies in Society and History*, 26, 126–66.

—— 1989. *High Religion: a Cultural and Political History of Sherpa Buddhism*. Princeton: Princeton University Press.

—— 1995. 'Resistance and the problem of ethnographic refusal'. *Comparative Studies in Society and History*, 37, 173–93.

Parker, L. 1992a. 'The creation of Indonesian citizens in Balinese primary schools'. *RIMA*, 26, 42–70.

—— 1992b. 'The quality of schooling in a Balinese village'. *Indonesia*, 54, 95–116.

Parry, J. 1979. *Caste and Kinship in Kangra*. London: Routledge and Kegan Paul.

—— 1980. 'Ghosts, greed and sin: the occupational identity of the Benares funeral priests'. *Man*, 15, 88–111.

Pemberton, J. 1994. *On the Subject of 'Java'*. Ithaca: Cornell University Press.

Pendit, N.S. 1954. *Bali Berjuang*. Jakarta: Gunung Agung.

Persoon, G. 1998. 'Isolated groups or indigenous peoples: Indonesia and the international discourse'. *Bijd. Taal-, Land-, Volk*, 154, 281–304.

Picard, M. 1990a. '"Cultural tourism" in Bali: cultural performances as tourist attraction'. *Indonesia*, 49, 37–74.

—— 1990b. 'Kebalian orang Bali: tourism and the uses of "Balinese culture" in New Order Indonesia'. *RIMA*, 24, 1–37.

—— 1995. 'Adat, budaya, agama: the discourse of kebalian between national integration and tourism promotion'. Paper delivered at the Bali in the Late Twentieth Century conference, Sydney University, 3–7 July.

—— 1996. *Bali: Cultural Tourism and Touristic Culture*. Singapore: Archipelago Press.

—— 1997. 'Cultural tourism, nation-building and regional culture: the making of a Balinese identity'. In M. Picard & R.E. Wood (eds), *Tourism, Ethnicity and the State in Asian and Pacific Societies*. Honolulu: University of Hawaii Press.

—— 1999. 'The discourse of Kebalian: transcultural constructions of Balinese identity'. In R. Rubinstein & L. Connor (eds), *Staying Local in the Global Village: Bali in the Twentieth Century*. Honolulu: University of Hawaii Press.

Pigeaud, Th. 1960–63. *Java in the 14th century*, 5 vols. The Hague: Martinus Nijhoff.

Pitana, I.G. 1997. 'In search of difference: origin groups, status and identity in contemporary Bali'. Unpublished PhD thesis, Australian National University.

—— 1999. 'Status struggles and the priesthood in contemporary Bali'. In R. Rubinstein & L. Connor (eds), *Staying Local in the Global Village: Bali in the Twentieth Century*. Honolulu: University of Hawaii Press.

Poffenberger, M. 1983. 'Changing dryland agriculture in eastern Bali'. *Human Ecology*, 11, 123–44.

Poffenberger, M. & Zurbuchen, M. 1980. 'The economics of village Bali: three perspectives'. *Economic Development and Cultural Change*, 29, 91–133.

Punyatmadja, I.B.O. 1976a. *Cilakrama*. Denpasar: Parisada Hindu Dharma Pusat.

—— 1976b. *Pancha Cradha*. Denpasar: Parisada Hindu Dharma Pusat.

Quigley, D. 1993. *The Interpretation of Caste*. Oxford: Clarendon Press.

Raffles, T.S. 1817. *The History of Java*, 2 vols. London: Black, Parbury and Allen.

Raheja, G.G. 1988a. *The Poison in the Gift*. Chicago: Chicago University Press.

—— 1988b. 'India: caste, kingship and dominance reconsidered'. *Annual Review of Anthropology*, 17, 497–522.

—— 1989. 'Centrality, mutuality and hierarchy: shifting aspects of inter-caste relationships in north India'. *Contributions to Indian Sociology*, 23, 79–101.

Ramstedt, M. 1995. 'Preliminary reflections on an ambiguous relationship: agama Hindu Bali vis-a-vis Hindu Dharma Indonesia'. Paper delivered at the Bali in the Late Twentieth Century conference, Sydney University, 3–7 July.

—— 2001. 'Indonesianisation, globalisation and Islamisation; parameters of the Hindu discourse in contemporary Indonesia'. *International Journal of Hindu Studies*, 5.

Rassers, W.H. 1922. *De Panji roman*. Antwerp.

Reeve, D. 1985. *Golkar of Indonesia: an Alternative to the Party System*. Singapore: Oxford University Press.

Reuter, T. 1999. 'People of the mountains, people of the sea: negotiating the local and the foreign in Bali'. In R. Rubinstein & L. Connor (eds), *Staying Local in the Global Village: Bali in the Twentieth Century*. Honolulu: University of Hawaii Press.

Ricklefs, M. 1974. *Jogjakarta under Sultan Mangkubumi, 1749–1792*. London: Oxford University Press.

—— 1981. *A History of Modern Indonesia*. London: Macmillan.

Robinson, G. 1992. 'The economic foundations of political conflict in Bali, 1950–1965'. *Indonesia*, 54, 59–93.

—— 1995. *The Dark Side of Paradise: Political Violence in Bali*. Ithaca: Cornell University Press.

Robison, R. 1986. *Indonesia: the Rise of Capital*. Sydney: Allen and Unwin.

Rochford, E.R. 1985. *Hare Krishna in America*. New Jersey: Rutgers University Press.

Rose, M. 1987. *Indonesia Free: a Biography of Mohammed Hatta*. Cornell University: Southeast Asia Program.

Rubinstein, R. 1987. 'Beyond the realm of the senses: the Balinese ritual of kekawin composition'. Unpublished PhD thesis, Sydney University.

—— 1991. 'The brahmana according to their babad'. In H. Geertz (ed.), *State and Society in Bali*. Leiden: KITLV Press.

—— 1995. 'Brahmana networks: cohesion and division in the 1990s'. Paper delivered at the Bali in the Late Twentieth Century conference, Sydney University, 3–7 July.

—— 1996. 'Allegiance and alliance: the Banjar war of 1868'. In A.Vickers (ed.), *Being Modern in Bali: Image and Change*. New Haven: Yale University Southeast Asia Studies.

Ruddick, A. 1986. 'Charmed lives: illness, healing power and gender in a Balinese village'. Unpublished PhD thesis, Brown University.

Sandweiss, H.S. 1975. *Sai Baba: the Holy Man ... and the Psychiatrist*. New Delhi: M. Gulab Singh & Sons.

Santri, R. 1993. *Kasta dalam Hindu: Kesalahpahaman Berabad-Abad*. Denpasar: Yayasan Dharma Naradha.

Schefold, R. 1998. 'The domestication of culture: nation-building and ethnic diversity in Indonesia'. *Bijd. Taal-, Land-, Volk*, 154, 259–80.

Schiller, A. 1997. *Small Sacrifices: Religious Change and Cultural Identity among the Ngaju of Indonesia*. Oxford: Oxford University Press.

Schiller, J. & Martin-Schiller, B. (eds). 1997. *Imagining Indonesia: Cultural Politics and Political Culture*. Athens, Ohio: Ohio University Centre for International Studies.

Schrieke, B. 1957. *Ruler and Realm in Early Java*. The Hague: W. van Hoeve.

Schulte Nordholt, H. 1986. *Bali: Colonial Conceptions and Political Change, 1700–1940*. Erasmus University: Comparative Asian Studies Programme.

—— 1988. 'Een Balische dynastie: hierarchie en conflict in de negara Mengwi 1700–1940'. Unpublished PhD thesis, Free University of Amsterdam.

—— 1991a. 'Temple and authority in south Bali, 1900–1980'. In H. Geertz (ed.), *State and Society in Bali*, Leiden: KITLV Press.

—— 1991b. *State, Village and Ritual in Bali*. VU Amsterdam: University Press

—— 1992. 'Origin, descent and destruction: text and context in Balinese representations of the past'. *Indonesia*, 54, 27–58.

—— 1993. 'Leadership and the limits of political control. A Balinese "response" to Clifford Geertz'. *Social Anthropology*, 1, 291–307.

—— 1996. *The Spell of Power: a History of Balinese Politics, 1650–1940*. Leiden: KITLV Press.

Schwarz, A. 1994. *A Nation in Waiting: Indonesia in the 1990s*. St Leonards: Allen and Unwin.

Scott, J. 1985. *Weapons of the Weak*. New Haven: Yale University Press.

—— 1990. *Domination and the Arts of Resistance*. New Haven: Yale University Press.

Sellato, B. 1995. 'Culture, history, politics and the emergence of provincial identities in Kalimantan'. In M. Charas (ed.), *Beyond the State: Essays in Spatial Structuralism in Insular Southeast Asia*. Paris, CNRS: Lasima.

Sen, K. 1993. 'Repression and resistance: interpretations of the feminine in New Order cinema'. In V.M. Hooker (ed.), *Culture and Society in New Order Indonesia*. Kuala Lumpur: Oxford University Press.

—— 1998. 'Indonesian women at work: reframing the subject'. In K. Sen & M. Stivens (eds), *Gender and Power in Affluent Asia*. London: Routledge.

Seneviratne, H.L. 1987. 'Kingship and polity in Buddhism and Hinduism'. *Contributions to Indian Sociology*, 21, 147–55.

Shinn, L. 1989. 'The search for meaning in conversions to ISKCON'. In D. Bromley & L. Shinn (eds), *Krishna Consciousness in the West*. London & Toronto: Associated University Press.

Shiraishi, S. 1997. *Young Heroes: The Indonesian Family in Politics.* Cornell University: Southeast Asia Program.

Siegel, J. 1986. *Solo in the New Order: Language and Hierarchy in an Indonesian City.* Princeton: Princeton University Press.

Siegel, L. 1991. *Net of Magic: Wonders and Deceptions in India.* Chicago: Chicago University Press.

Soedjatmoko, Ali, M., Resnik, G.J. and Kahim, G.McT. (eds). 1965. *An Introduction to Indonesian Historiography.* Ithaca: Cornell University Press.

Stivens, M. (ed.). 1991. *Why Gender Matters in Southeast Asia Politics.* Clayton, Victoria: Centre of Southeast Asian Studies, Monash University, Monash Papers on Southeast Asian, No. 23.

Stoler, A. 1985. *Capitalism and Confrontation in Sumatra's Plantation Belt, 1870–1979.* New Haven: Yale University Press.

Strathern, A.J. 1969. 'Finance and production: two strategies in New Guinea Highlands exchange systems'. *Oceania,* 40, 42–67.

Stuart-Fox, D. 1987. 'Pura Besakih: a study of Balinese religion and society'. Unpublished PhD dissertation, Australian National University.

—— 1991. 'Pura Besakih: temple–state relations from precolonial to modern times'. In H. Geertz (ed.), *State and Society in Bali.* Leiden: KITLV Press.

Suasta, P. & Connor, L. 1999. 'Democratic mobilization and political authoritarianism: tourism developments in Bali'. In R. Rubinstein & L. Connor (eds), *Staying Local in the Global Village: Bali in the Twentieth Century.* Honolulu: University of Hawaii Press.

Sueta, I.M. 1993. *Babad Ksatrya Taman Bali.* Denpasar: PT. Upada Sastra.

Sukarno, 1965. *Sukarno, an Autobiography (as Told to Cindy Adams).* Hong Kong: Gunung Agung.

Supartha, W. (ed.). 1994. *Memahami Aliran Kepercayaan.* Denpasar: PT Bali Post.

Supomo, S. 1979. 'The image of Majapahit in later Javanese writing'. In A. Reid & D. Marr (eds), *Perceptions of the Past in Southeast Asia.* Singapore: Heinemann.

Suryadinata, L. 1989. *Military Ascendancy and Political Culture.* Athens, Ohio: Ohio University Centre for International Studies.

Sutton, M. 1991. 'Social sciences and ordinary understanding: coming to terms with tourism in Bali'. Unpublished PhD thesis, Stanford University.

Sutton, R. 1995. 'Performing arts and cultural politics in south Sulawesi'. *Bijd. Taal-, Land-, Volk,* 151, 672–99.

Swallow, D.A. 1982. 'Ashes and power: myth, rite and miracle in an Indian godman's cult'. *Modern Asian Studies,* 16, 123–58.

Swellengrebel, J.L. 1947. *Een Vorstenwijding op Bali.* Leiden: Mededeelingen van het Rijksmuseum voor Volkenkunde.

—— 1960. 'Introduction'. In J.L. Swellengrebel (ed.), *Bali: Studies in Life, Thought and Ritual.* The Hague: W. van Hoeve.

Tambiah, S.J. 1976. *World Conqueror and World Renouncer.* Cambridge: Cambridge University Press.

—— 1985a. 'A reformulation of Geertz's conception of the theatre state'. In his *Culture, Thought and Action: an Anthropological Perspective*. Cambridge, MA: Harvard University Press.

—— 1985b. 'The galactic polity in Southeast Asia'. In his *Culture, Thought and Action: an Anthropological Perspective*. Cambridge, MA: Harvard University Press.

Taylor, P.M. 1994. 'The *nusantara* concept of culture: local traditions and national identity as expressed in Indonesia's museums'. In P.M. Taylor (ed.), *Fragile Traditions: Indonesian Art in Jeopardy*. Honolulu: University of Hawaii Press.

Tisna, I.G.P. 1935. *Ni Rawit, Tjeti Pendjoeal Orang*. Jakarta: Balai Pustaka.

Titib, I.M. 1994. *Ketuhanan dalam Weda*. Denpasar: PT Pustaka Manikgeni.

Trautmann, T. 1981. *Dravidian kinship*. Cambridge: Cambridge University Press

Tsing, A.L. 1987. 'A rhetoric of centres in a religion of the periphery'. In R.S. Kipp & S. Rodgers (eds), *Indonesian Religions in Transition*. Tucson: University of Arizona Press.

—— 1990. 'Gender and performance in Meratus dispute settlement'. In J.M. Atkinson & S. Errington (eds), *Power and Difference: Gender in Island Southeast Asia*. Stanford: Stanford University Press.

—— 1993. *In the Realm of the Diamond Queen*. Princeton: Princeton University Press.

Upadeca, 1968. *Upadeca: Tentang Ajaran-Ajaran Agama Hindu*. Denpasar: Parisada Hindu Dharma.

van der Kraan, A. 1983. 'Bali: slavery and slave trade'. In A. Reid (ed.), *Slavery, Bondage and Dependency in Southeast Asia*. St Lucia: University of Queensland Press.

van der Veer, P. 1994. *Religious Nationalism: Hindus and Muslims in India*. Berkeley: University of California Press.

van Leur, J.C. 1955. *Indonesian Trade and Society*. The Hague: W. van Hoeve.

Vickers, A. 1980. 'Gusti Madé Deblog: artistic manifestations of change in Bali'. *RIMA*, 14, 1–47.

—— 1987. 'Hinduism and Islam in Indonesia: Bali and the Pasisir'. *Indonesia*, 44, 31–58.

—— 1989. *Bali, a Paradise Created*. Berkeley: Periplus.

—— 1991. 'Ritual written: the song of the Ligya, or the killing of the rhinoceros'. In H. Geertz (ed.), *State and Society in Bali*. Leiden: KITLV Press.

—— 1996. 'Modernity and being *moderen*: an introduction'. In A. Vickers (ed.), *Being Modern in Bali: Image and Change*. New Haven: Yale University Southeast Asia Studies.

Volkman, T.A. 1984. 'Great performances: Toraja cultural identity in the 1970s'. *American Ethnologist*, 11, 152–69.

—— 1985. *Feasts of Honour: Ritual and Change in the Toraja Highlands*. Urbana: University of Illinois Press.

—— 1990. 'Visions and revisions: Toraja culture and the tourist gaze'. *American Ethnologist*, 17, 91–110.

Warna, I.W. 1978. *Kamus Bali-Indonesia*. Denpasar: Dinas Pengajaran Propinsi Daerah Tingkat I Bali.

Warren, C. 1989. 'Balinese political culture and the rhetoric of national development'. In P. Alexander & J. Alexander (eds), *Creating Indonesian Cultures*. Sydney: Oceania Publications.

—— 1990. 'Rhetoric and resistance: popular political culture in Bali'. *Anthropological Forum*, 6, 191–205.

—— 1993. *Adat and Dinas: Balinese Communities in the Indonesian State*. Kuala Lumpur: Oxford University Press.

—— 1998. 'Tanah Lot: the cultural and environmental politics of resort development in Bali'. In P. Hirsch & C. Warren (eds), *The Politics of Environment in Southeast Asia: Resources and Resistance*. London: Routledge.

Weber, M. 1985. *The Protestant Ethic and the Spirit of Capitalism*. London: Unwin.

Wenban, G. 1993. 'Golkar's election victory: neither smooth nor fair'. *Inside Indonesia*, 37, 12–14.

White, C. 1986. 'Everyday resistance, socialist revolution and rural development: the Vietnamese case'. *Journal of Peasant Studies*, 13, 49–63.

White, C.S.J. 1972. 'The Sai Baba movement: approaches to the study of Indian saints.' *Journal of Asian Studies*, 31, 863–78.

Wiana, I.K. 1992. *Sembahyang Menurut Hindu*. Denpasar, Bali: Yayasan Dharma Naradha.

—— 1995. *Yajna dan Bhakti dari Sudut Pandang Hindu*. Denpasar: P.T. Pustaka Manikgeni.

Wiener, M. n.d. 'Kings or committees: changing ritual hegemonies in Bali'. Unpublished manuscript.

—— 1995. *Visible and Invisible Realms: Power, Magic and Colonial Conquest in Bali*. Chicago: Chicago University Press.

Wolf, D.L. 1992. *Factory Daughters: Gender, Household Dynamics and Rural Industrialization in Java*. Berkeley: University of California Press.

Worsley, P.J. 1972. *Babad Buléléng*. The Hague: Martinus Nijhoff.

—— 1979. 'Preliminary remarks on the concept of kingship in the Babad Buléléng'. In A. Reid & L. Castles (eds), *Pre-colonial State Systems in Southeast Asia*. Kuala Lumpur: Royal Asiatic Society.

Yampolsky, P. 1995. 'Forces of change in the regional performing arts in Indonesia'. *Bijd. Taal-, Land-, Volk*, 151, 700–25.

Zurbuchen, M. 1987. *The Language of Balinese Shadow Theatre*. Princeton: Princeton University Press.

Index